Reforming the Welfare State

A National Bureau
of Economic Research
Conference Report

Reforming the Welfare State
Recovery and Beyond in
Sweden

Edited by **Richard B. Freeman, Birgitta Swedenborg,
and Robert Topel**

The University of Chicago Press

Chicago and London

RICHARD B. FREEMAN is the Herbert Ascherman Professor of
Economics at Harvard University and a research associate at the
National Bureau of Economic Research. BIRGITTA SWEDENBORG is
an economist and former vice president and research director of the
Center for Business and Policy Studies (SNS) in Stockholm, Sweden.
ROBERT TOPEL is the Isidore Brown and Gladys J. Brown Professor
in Urban and Labor Economics at the Booth Graduate School of
Business, University of Chicago, and a research associate of the
National Bureau of Economic Research.

The University of Chicago Press, Chicago 60637
The University of Chicago Press, Ltd., London
© 2010 by the National Bureau of Economic Research
All rights reserved. Published 2010
Printed in the United States of America

19 18 17 16 15 14 13 12 11 10   1 2 3 4 5
ISBN-13: 978-0-226-26192-8 (cloth)
ISBN-10: 0-226-26192-1 (cloth)

Library of Congress Cataloging-in-Publication Data

Reforming the welfare state : recovery and beyond in Sweden / edited
    by Richard B. Freeman, Birgitta Swedenborg, and Robert Topel.
        p. cm.
    Includes bibliographical references and index.
    ISBN-13: 978-0-226-26192-8 (alk. paper)
    ISBN-10: 0-226-26192-1 (alk. paper)
    1. Sweden—Economic policy. 2. Sweden—Economic
conditions—1945– 3. Manpower policy—Sweden. 4. Labor
market—Sweden. 5. Welfare state—Sweden. I. Freeman, Richard B.
(Richard Barry), 1943– II. Swedenborg, Birgitta, 1941– III. Topel,
Robert H.
HC375.R422 2010
330.9485—dc22

                                                    2009024336

♾ The paper used in this publication meets the minimum requirements
of the American National Standard for Information Sciences—
Permanence of Paper for Printed Library Materials, ANSI Z39.48-1992.

Relation of the Directors to the
Work and Publications of the
National Bureau of Economic Research

1. The object of the NBER is to ascertain and present to the economics profession, and to the public more generally, important economic facts and their interpretation in a scientific manner without policy recommendations. The Board of Directors is charged with the responsibility of ensuring that the work of the NBER is carried on in strict conformity with this object.

2. The President shall establish an internal review process to ensure that book manuscripts proposed for publication DO NOT contain policy recommendations. This shall apply both to the proceedings of conferences and to manuscripts by a single author or by one or more co-authors but shall not apply to authors of comments at NBER conferences who are not NBER affiliates.

3. No book manuscript reporting research shall be published by the NBER until the President has sent to each member of the Board a notice that a manuscript is recommended for publication and that in the President's opinion it is suitable for publication in accordance with the above principles of the NBER. Such notification will include a table of contents and an abstract or summary of the manuscript's content, a list of contributors if applicable, and a response form for use by Directors who desire a copy of the manuscript for review. Each manuscript shall contain a summary drawing attention to the nature and treatment of the problem studied and the main conclusions reached.

4. No volume shall be published until forty-five days have elapsed from the above notification of intention to publish it. During this period a copy shall be sent to any Director requesting it, and if any Director objects to publication on the grounds that the manuscript contains policy recommendations, the objection will be presented to the author(s) or editor(s). In case of dispute, all members of the Board shall be notified, and the President shall appoint an ad hoc committee of the Board to decide the matter; thirty days additional shall be granted for this purpose.

5. The President shall present annually to the Board a report describing the internal manuscript review process, any objections made by Directors before publication or by anyone after publication, any disputes about such matters, and how they were handled.

6. Publications of the NBER issued for informational purposes concerning the work of the Bureau, or issued to inform the public of the activities at the Bureau, including but not limited to the NBER Digest and Reporter, shall be consistent with the object stated in paragraph 1. They shall contain a specific disclaimer noting that they have not passed through the review procedures required in this resolution. The Executive Committee of the Board is charged with the review of all such publications from time to time.

7. NBER working papers and manuscripts distributed on the Bureau's web site are not deemed to be publications for the purpose of this resolution, but they shall be consistent with the object stated in paragraph 1. Working papers shall contain a specific disclaimer noting that they have not passed through the review procedures required in this resolution. The NBER's web site shall contain a similar disclaimer. The President shall establish an internal review process to ensure that the working papers and the web site do not contain policy recommendations, and shall report annually to the Board on this process and any concerns raised in connection with it.

8. Unless otherwise determined by the Board or exempted by the terms of paragraphs 6 and 7, a copy of this resolution shall be printed in each NBER publication as described in paragraph 2 above.

Contents

Acknowledgments   xi

Introduction   1
Richard B. Freeman, Birgitta Swedenborg,
and Robert Topel

1.   **Searching for Optimal Inequality/Incentives**   25
     Anders Björklund and Richard B. Freeman

2.   **Policies Affecting Work Patterns and Labor**
     Income for Women   57
     Ann-Sofie Kolm and Edward P. Lazear

3.   **Wage Determination and Employment in**
     Sweden Since the Early 1990s: Wage Formation
     in a New Setting   83
     Peter Fredriksson and Robert Topel

4.   **Labor Supply, Tax Base, and Public Policy**
     in Sweden   127
     Thomas Aronsson and James R. Walker

5.   **Did Active Labor Market Policies Help Sweden**
     Rebound from the Depression of the Early 1990s?   159
     Anders Forslund and Alan Krueger

6.   **How Sweden's Unemployment Became More**
     Like Europe's   189
     Lars Ljungqvist and Thomas J. Sargent

7.   **Economic Performance and Market Work Activity
        in Sweden after the Crisis of the Early 1990s**   225
        Steven J. Davis and Magnus Henrekson

8.   **Competition, Regulation, and the Role of Local
        Government Policies in Swedish Markets**   253
        Stefan Fölster and Sam Peltzman

9.   **What Have Changes to the Global Markets for
        Goods and Services Done to the Viability of the
        Swedish Welfare State?**   285
        Edward E. Leamer

        Contributors   327
        Author Index   329
        Subject Index   333

This volume is dedicated to our late friend
and colleague Sherwin Rosen, who contributed
greatly to our original study and whose insights
on the Swedish recovery from crisis we sadly miss.

Acknowledgments

The contributions in this volume are the result of a research project on the Swedish welfare state organized jointly by the Center for Business and Policy Studies (SNS) in Sweden and the National Bureau of Economic Research (NBER) in the United States. Most contributions are authored jointly by an American and a Swedish economist associated with the NBER and SNS, respectively.

The SNS is a private, nonpartisan, nonprofit organization with the aim of promoting research on economic and social issues of importance to public decision making and of making it readily available to a broad audience. As an organization, SNS does not take a stand on policy matters.

The research for this volume has been made possible by financial support, first and foremost from the Jan Wallander and Tom Hedelius Foundation and the Tore Browald Foundation. Support has also been received from the Sven and Dagmar Salén Foundation and the Bank of Sweden Tercentenary Foundation.

Introduction

Richard B. Freeman, Birgitta Swedenborg, and
Robert Topel

The Swedish economic model is perhaps the most ambitious and publicized effort by a capitalist market economy to develop a large and active welfare state. For a long time, many viewed the Swedish model as a more humane and successful form of capitalism and thus as a model for other countries to emulate. This view was shaken when Sweden fell into severe economic crisis in the early 1990s.

Between 1990 and 1993, open unemployment rose from 1.4 percent to 9 percent of the labor force. An additional 5 percent of the labor force participated in labor market programs so that 14 percent of the labor force was jobless. The employment rate fell by 12 percentage points from its pre-crisis peak. The economic decline brought government spending above 70 percent of national income, raised the budget deficit to 12 percent of gross domestic product (GDP), and forced the government to reduce public-sector employment. Between 1990 and 1994, the ratio of debt to GDP doubled. Even before the crisis, however, Sweden's economic performance was not exemplary. Slow productivity growth had eroded Sweden's position in real per capita income relative to other Organization for Economic Cooperation and Development (OECD) countries; private-sector employment had not

Richard B. Freeman is the Herbert Ascherman Professor of Economics at Harvard University and a research associate of the National Bureau of Economic Research. Birgitta Swedenborg is an economist and former vice president and research director of the Center for Business and Policy Studies (SNS) in Stockholm, Sweden. Robert Topel is the Isidore Brown and Gladys J. Brown Professor in Urban and Labor Economics at the Booth Graduate School of Business, University of Chicago, and a research associate of the National Bureau of Economic Research.

grown since the 1960s; and recurring current account deficits led to currency devaluations. The Swedish model was no longer anyone's envy.

In response to the crisis, Sweden undertook substantial and in some cases painful policy reforms to correct problems. These reforms presumably helped the economy recover more quickly from the economic decline than it otherwise would have, while still preserving the low levels of poverty and modest levels of income inequality that characterized the Swedish model. But even over a decade of recovery left some problems unresolved—particularly in the labor market, where employment did not recover to precrisis levels.

This volume is about Sweden's recovery from crisis and the role that the country's welfare state institutions and policy reforms played in that recovery. Many of the reforms reflect distinctly Swedish problems connected to its large welfare state. But Sweden's experience has broader lessons for other countries. It is especially relevant as the United States and the rest of the world struggle with the financial and economic crisis that began with the 2007/2008 U.S. financial meltdown. The immediate causes for Sweden's early 1990s crisis are similar to those that set off America's late 2008 crisis: the deregulation of financial markets and excessive credit expansion fueled a real estate bubble that burst, causing a contraction of economic activity that spread from the banking sector to the economy as a whole. Prior to the crises, moreover, both the United States and Sweden faced persistent deficits in the balance of trade and in the government budget. In both cases, the ensuing economic contraction drew comparisons with the 1930s and induced huge injections of liquidity into the financial system to avoid the collapse of banking and credit.

That Sweden recovered more rapidly than most analysts expected offers an optimistic note about the possibility for recovery from the large economic downturn with which the United States and the rest of the world are struggling as this volume goes to press. Sweden and the United States differ greatly in various ways, from the size of the economy to the importance of the welfare state. The similarity in their economic crises highlights the universality of economic problems and suggests that differences in institutions notwithstanding, the United States and other countries may learn something from Sweden's response to its earlier crisis. Indeed, some commentators have drawn attention to the way Sweden successfully dealt with its financial meltdown[1] and present Sweden as a model for the United States and other countries to follow. What interests them now is Sweden's ability to pragmatically deal with problems borne of policy blunders and unforeseen events—not its welfare state.

---

1. See, for example, Carter Dougherty, "Stopping a Financial Crisis, the Swedish Way," *New York Times,* September 23, 2008, and Holger Schmieding, "A Lesson from Stockholm," *Newsweek,* October 13, 2008. See also *The Economist,* "Stockholm Syndrome," November 29, 2008, to December 5, 2008.

NBER-SNS Analyses of the Swedish Economic Model

This book is the second National Bureau of Economic Research (NBER) study of the Swedish economy. The first study began in 1993, when the Center for Business and Policy Studies (SNS) and the NBER convened a team of American and Swedish economists to study the problems of the Swedish economy. The hope was that the combination of outside specialists, unencumbered by Swedish political discourse and sensibilities, and of Swedish economists, knowledgeable about Sweden's data and institutions, could clarify issues and sharpen debate at a time of crisis in Sweden. As Sweden is an exemplar of the large welfare state, its experiences could also illuminate the economics of this variant of capitalism more broadly. Welfare state and institutional interventions are so large in Sweden that if these policies have substantial economic consequences, they should show up in Sweden.

Much of what the American outsiders saw in Sweden puzzled them. They found it remarkable that Sweden had *eliminated* poverty through interventions in markets without running into serious economic problems before the crisis. They wondered how wage-bargaining institutions could compress the distribution of pay without creating widespread unemployment among the least skilled. If lower-skilled Swedes were paid more than they would earn in an unconstrained market, why did employers continue to hire them? They wondered also at the market work ethic of Swedes in the face of a huge tax-induced wedge between productivity and disposable income that produced a ratio of posttax spendable income to pretax earnings in Sweden that was less than half the comparable U.S. ratio. Why did the average Swede invest in schooling and work as much as they did (albeit less than Americans), with limited pecuniary rewards? Was the early 1990s crisis the death knell of the welfare state, or was it a transient downturn that sensible policy reforms would cure?

The main conclusions of this first study were presented at a conference in Stockholm in 1995 and published in the NBER volume *The Welfare State in Transition* in 1997 (Freeman, Topel, and Swedenborg 1997). The take-home message was that Sweden's recovery required economic reforms to strengthen the role of the market in various domains. We argued that Sweden's success in eliminating poverty and reducing inequality gave it economic space to make such reforms without undoing the welfare state successes that Assar Lindbeck had called a "major achievement of modern civilization."[2] Given the crisis of the early to mid-1990s, failure to make reforms indeed seemed to pose the greatest threat to the welfare state.

The analyses in *The Welfare State in Transition* suggested that the Swedish welfare state was an interrelated system, whose parts fit together and

2. Lindbeck (1993, 97).

reinforced each other in sometimes surprising ways. Researchers analyzing different aspects of the Swedish economy stressed different linkages, but the picture that emerged was of an economic system with a logic that differed from that of the market-driven United States. Welfare state and wage policies that limited poverty and inequality generated other policies designed to offset the likely adverse economic effects of the first set of policies. For example, wage compression was associated with near-constant private-sector employment, which meant that full employment required expansion of jobs in the public sector. This required high taxes, but it also required the production of government services that people would support politically. In turn, high taxes made it easier for high-skill workers to accept wage compression. The taxes and compressed wage structure also raised the incentive for short working hours with long vacations, leading to work sharing of sorts. Finally, these incentives and responses fed back onto the industrial structure, regulatory policies, and wage and price determination.

Our analysis questioned the long-term viability and value of some of these policies due to the loss of economic efficiency at the tax and benefit/program levels the country had chosen. It highlighted the possible fragility of such a system when faced with economic problems and the need for changes in policies to sustain the system. We noted that some programs seemed relatively ineffective in accomplishing their goals. The active labor market programs, which some analysts viewed as underpinning Sweden's traditional full employment, in particular, did not appear to produce the benefits that justified their large costs, and public works displaced private investment and production. Other spending programs, such as subsidized day care, caused huge distortions in private decision making. Regulations hindered competition and productivity growth. High marginal taxes and compressed wages distorted choices on the allocation of effort and hours among activities and reduced investment in human capital from what it might otherwise have been. Generous social insurance benefits caused *moral hazard* and overuse of unemployment and sickness insurance. All of these distortions hindered economic growth.

Some critics viewed *The Welfare State in Transition* as slanted toward an Anglo-American, market-driven form of capitalism. It is true that the difference between the U.S. and Sweden's welfare state affected how the American economists saw issues, but our research was not a case of dueling paradigms. The Americans were impressed by Sweden's success in eliminating poverty, especially given the failure of the U.S. War on Poverty. And the studies were undertaken with Swedish colleagues, some of whom viewed the U.S. economic model skeptically. In any case, we were not alone in worrying that Sweden faced large economic costs because of engineered outcomes that often diverged far from market fundamentals. Even before the crisis, Swedish policymakers had begun to reform the tax code and product market regulations, and firms and unions had moved toward more decentralized wage setting. The crisis accelerated reform efforts, forcing the government to reduce public-sector jobs and to cut the replacement rate for unemployment insurance, among other changes. The 1993 Lindbeck Report (Lindbeck et al. 1994) criticized many aspects of the Swedish economy and suggested 113 specific reforms to restore the country's economic health.

How would Sweden deal with the crisis? The magnitude of the early 1990s Swedish economic decline led many economists and policymakers to fear that recovery would be long and arduous. Japan had experienced a decade of economic stagnation. Germany became mired in high joblessness and low growth as it struggled to join East Germany with West Germany. It was a decade after the Thatcher reforms before British economic performance picked up noticeably. And East European transition countries suffered years of economic decline before market capitalism began to improve outcomes compared to their communist past.

In 2005, we decided to do a follow-up analysis of the Swedish welfare state to assess its recovery from crisis, engaging most of the same analysts as in the original study. The result is the current volume, *Reforming the Welfare State: Recovery and Beyond in Sweden.* The main message here is that Sweden had a relatively robust and successful recovery in which the welfare state maintained low levels of poverty, even as market reforms led to modestly higher inequality. But the evidence also shows that the recovery did not bring Sweden back to the precrisis levels of employment, which previous policies may have made artificially high.

How robust was the recovery? It was stronger and faster than almost anyone expected. Between 1995 and 2004, productivity grew at 2.4 percent annually, well above the OECD average of 2.2 percent. Manufacturing productivity grew faster than in any other OECD country.[3] Overall economic growth was higher than in any comparable period since the 1960s, and private-sector employment expanded for the first time in decades. In part, the robust recovery reflects the fall of output far below productive capacity in the crisis. In part, it reflects higher growth through much of the developed world after 1993. Sweden's per capita output *relative* to other advanced countries remained below its precrisis level. But in contrast to the American experience, where gains from productivity growth largely went to the wealthiest, the Swedish recovery raised income throughout the income distribution, though more so for the higher paid than for the lower paid.

What policies contributed to the recovery? The first important policy change was that Sweden adopted flexible exchange rates and inflation targeting. This caused an immediate and substantial weakening of the currency, leading to a prolonged period of export-led growth. The growth of exports put the current account into surplus for over a decade. Other

3. See table 1.1 in the *OECD Economic Surveys: Sweden* report (2007).

critical policy changes included a contraction of the public sector, reduced generosity in social insurance systems, and the deregulation of many markets. The accompanying appendix provides a broad overview of important reforms and shows that the country adopted more market-oriented policies in many domains. In the government sector, Sweden sought to eliminate its budget deficit through expenditure cuts, tax hikes, and a slimmer public sector. These policies and the rapid economic growth in the recovery reduced government spending to 52 percent of GDP in 2006—higher than in most advanced countries, but significantly below the precrisis level—and reduced central government debt from nearly 80 percent of GDP in 1996 to about half that in 2006—bringing Sweden in line with other advanced economies and well within EU guidelines.[4]

Did the crisis and ensuing reforms undo Sweden's success in eliminating poverty and maintaining low levels of inequality? The interesting fact is that inequality and poverty did rise, but by remarkably little. The welfare state provided strong safety net support for those at the bottom of the income distribution so that poverty remained low. Inequality increased modestly (as it did in many countries), but Sweden remained among the lowest inequality countries in the world. Swedish income inequality remains far lower than in the United States and rose by less in the 1990s. The collective-bargaining system proved flexible to the needs of the economy in wage settlements, and the market-oriented reforms that raised inequality provided incentives that seem to have helped the recovery. Swedish workers and young people responded to the new market realities with sizable mobility and investments in education. Educational earnings differentials that were modestly higher than in the past (but far below those in the United States) made university education more economically attractive. Sweden moved to the top of global rankings in the number of university graduates and PhDs relative to the age-relevant population.

Were there economic problems that the recovery did not fully resolve? The recovery did not bring Sweden back to its historical position as an exemplar of high employment. As of 2006, the employment-population ratio was substantially below precrisis levels. Labor force participation stabilized at 77 percent of the working-age population, below the government's 80 percent target. In 2006, open unemployment was 5.4 percent (7.1 percent, according to the International Labor Organization [ILO] definition, a measure that Sweden has now adopted and that adds students looking for work). With 2.6 percent of the workforce on active labor market programs, however, the joblessness rate was 8 percent—far above what it had been before the crisis—and by the ILO definition, joblessness exceeded 9 percent. One

---

4. Government expenditures in percent of GDP went from 24 in 1950 to 30 in 1960, 43 in 1970, 60 in 1980, 58 in 1990, 54 in 2000, and 52 in 2006. This first reflected the rapid expansion of the welfare state and then showed the gradual retrenchment after the 1990s crisis (Statistics Sweden 2008).

reason for high joblessness was that the duration of jobless spells increased to resemble the long periods found in many EU countries.

What has Sweden done since the recovery? In 2006, Sweden elected a center-right government that undertook further policy changes along the lines begun by the Social Democratic government that led the country during the recovery. The new government reduced replacement rates in unemployment insurance (UI) and limited the duration of benefits; it also changed and reduced the extent of active labor market programs. To assure incomes and work opportunities for low-paid workers, the government introduced an earned income tax credit that was designed to draw them into employment while buttressing their living standards. It exempted individuals from payroll tax if they were unemployed, sick, or on early retirement for over a year, and it reduced taxes for firms. One of the contributors to this volume, Anders Forslund (2008), estimated that increasing work incentives may have lowered unemployment by 1.5 to 2 percentage points compared to what it otherwise would have been.[5]

Recovery and Beyond

The studies in this volume examine the way changes in the labor market, in tax and benefit policies, in local government policy, and in industrial structure and international trade affected Sweden's recovery. The analyses clarify the trade-offs between the egalitarian outcomes that Sweden seeks and economic efficiency. Welfare state interventions that lower inequality generally distort private decisions and create social costs. The costs rise with the square of the distortions,[6] so they can become very high in a large welfare state. This makes it important for Sweden to find and adopt the least costly ways to attain given distributional goals and to weigh carefully the costs and benefits of redistribution. Whether any given level of egalitarian outcomes exceeds the costs of interventions is a value judgment to be made by Swedes, in general, and by Swedish policymakers, in particular.

Our studies fit into the following three broad categories.

Income Equalization, Gender Equality, and Wage Compression

As noted, a hallmark of the Swedish welfare state is its far-reaching egalitarianism. This equality has been achieved through a combination of wage-setting institutions that narrow the dispersion of market wages, of government benefits that supplement the incomes of the lower-paid and non-working population and that often encourage work by linking the benefits to employment, and of taxes that reduce the incomes of the higher paid.

5. Forslund (2008).
6. This is the standard result in computing welfare triangles, in which taxes or other costs induce behavioral responses that extract additional costs beyond the direct cost of the intervention.

In chapter 1, Anders Björklund and Richard Freeman examine the extent to which the economic crisis and recovery affected the egalitarian goal of the welfare state. They show that while inequality increased in the 1990s, Sweden maintained its position as one of the most egalitarian economies in the world and continued its successful conquest of poverty. Rising inequality in Sweden took the form of faster income growth for higher-income families rather than of lower real income for poorer families. The welfare state buttressed the incomes of those at the bottom. The area in which inequality increased most dramatically was in the distribution of hours worked, due to a higher rate of nonemployment and lower labor force participation among low-wage individuals, reflecting Sweden's failure to recover its full employment status after the crisis. In their contribution to the first NBER volume, Björklund and Freeman highlighted the fact that Sweden's narrow income distribution reflected not only a compressed wage structure, welfare state tax, and spending policy, but also reflected narrow dispersion in hours worked, as most adults had jobs and worked comparable hours.

The increase in inequality raised incentives for some forms of productive behavior. Relative to others, earnings increased for persons with university degrees and in firms with greater value added. This presumably contributed to rising enrollment in higher education and to shifts in the workforce from lower- to higher-productivity sectors. The authors cite evidence that within Sweden, areas with higher inequality had greater growth over the period. Surprisingly, given that returns to higher education remained lower in Sweden than in most other advanced countries, Swedish young persons invested heavily in higher education, particularly at the doctorate level. Sweden produced five times as many doctorate scientists and engineers per capita as the United States. The increased supply of relatively low-cost (due to wage compression) scientific workers helped Sweden move to the forefront of OECD countries in research and development relative to GDP and placed it second to the United States in the OECD measure of investment in the knowledge economy.

Did the increased inequality affect Swedish preferences for egalitarian outcomes? Survey evidence suggests that attitudes hardened against inequality, which may have influenced some reversals of policy when the crisis was over. There was no decrease in reported well-being or life satisfaction, despite continued high joblessness, implying that the unemployed adapted their attitudes to the new state of the job market. Even with high levels of equality, Swedes still wanted greater equality.

Gender equality is another egalitarian goal to which Sweden is committed, and economic policy has sought to improve the economic status of women. In the 1997 NBER study, Sherwin Rosen noted that all employment growth from the 1960s to the 1990s occurred in the public sector, and virtually all of it occurred among women. He argued that subsidies to day care to encourage female employment were motivated as a second-best policy in a high-tax society, but the Swedish level of subsidies was excessive and created large efficiency losses. In chapter 2 of this volume, Ann-Sofie Kolm and Edward Lazear ask how two cornerstones of Swedish family policy—paid parental leave and subsidies to day care—and two additional policies that the country recently enacted—subsidies to other household goods and earned income tax credit—affect the incentive to work of married and divorced women with children. They note that paid parental leave encourages labor force participation of mothers but prolongs the periods that mothers stay home with their children, which may reduce future income. Reserving a month of paid parental leave for fathers induces women to return to work sooner. Subsidizing day care encourages market work and improves the future economic situation of mothers, including single mothers. Because of this, single mothers are more likely to be self-sufficient than to be dependent on the state. This reduces Rosen's estimated social cost of the program. In-work benefits aimed at low-income women with children can increase labor force participation, at the cost of negative incentive effects at the incomes where the tax credit is phased out. On net, Kolm and Lazear conclude that the programs strengthen the economic independence of women. They create a high excess burden by being financed through higher taxes, but because the benefits go disproportionately to women, while the costs are borne disproportionately by men, the policies aid women.

Despite their institutional differences, both Sweden and the United States are among the world's leaders in female market work. Female labor force participation is somewhat higher in Sweden than in the United States, but annual work hours among women aged 16 to 54 years in Sweden are 12 percent lower than in the United States—988 annual hours in Sweden versus 1,118 in the United States. However, women with children are more likely to be in the workforce in Sweden than in the United States, plausibly because of the subsidization policies.

High rates of unionization and collective bargaining are central to the Swedish model. The analysis in our earlier volume stressed the importance of collective bargaining in compressing wages and expressed concern that solidarity wage policy that raised the pay of the less skilled would eventually increase their unemployment. This appears to have happened to some extent. In chapter 3, Peter Fredriksson and Robert Topel note that since the crisis, wage formation has become more decentralized. Centralized bargaining continues to set minimum wages in different sectors, but firms and unions bargain above the minimum and decide on specifics in local bargaining. The decentralization contributed to rising wage dispersion, as wage outcomes were more likely to reflect market valuations for particular skills. The ratio of 90th percentile to 10th percentile of gross earnings of full-time workers in Sweden increased substantially from 1992 to 2003. In 1992, the wage of an individual at the 90th percentile of the wage distribution was about 73 percent higher than that of a worker at the 10th percentile. By 2003, the

90th-percentile wage was over double the 10th-percentile wage. Even with this increase, however, the 90/10 wage ratio in Sweden was far below that in the United States in 2003.

Some of the 1990s increase in wage dispersion in Sweden presumably reflects catching up with market forces, but the catch-up does not seem complete, given the changing economic environment. Joblessness remains high. The immigrant population from non-OECD countries, who are disproportionately in lower-skill groups, is much larger than in the past and now makes up roughly the same proportion of the working-age population as in the United States. Also, global competition in traded goods and services with low-wage countries has become more intense. The educational premium remains low, and like other dimensions of compressed wage differences, it may impede human capital investment, which is key to economic growth and long-run welfare. Assuming that an additional year of schooling raises skill proportionately as much in Sweden as in other advanced economies, we would expect to find similar financial *returns* to schooling in Sweden as elsewhere. In fact, the Swedish returns are much lower, reflecting the compression of differentials due to wage-setting institutions. The low return to education in the late 1960s through the 1980s kept enrollment in higher education below what it otherwise would have been, but enrollments rose as the differentials widened and would likely rise even more with higher returns. Egalitarian wage policies also may have reduced Sweden's stock of highly skilled workers by encouraging the most skilled Swedes to emigrate. Immigrants from egalitarian Nordic countries are especially concentrated at the top of the U.S. wage distribution.

Employment outcomes are worse for low-skilled persons and non-OECD immigrants than for other workers. In 2003, the employment gap between non-OECD immigrants and the Swedish-born population was 23 percentage points. The small market for private services in Sweden may help explain this. If Sweden had the U.S. mix of industries, the greater scale of retail trade, hotels, and restaurants would have raised employment for the low skilled by about 6 percent. However, in the 1990s, the minimum wage increased in hotels and restaurants, which disproportionately employ the less skilled, presumably contributing to the low share of these sectors in the economy.

Impacts of Compressed Incentives

How have labor supply decisions responded to the taxes and benefits of the welfare state and to the changes in those taxes and benefits during the recovery? Economists emphasize that incentives matter in decisions, but the key issue is how much they matter. Measured by number of contracted hours of work, the evidence in all countries is that men do not alter hours worked much to changes in incentives, while women alter hours moderately. In Sweden, estimated elasticities of hours worked to net wages are on the order of 0.05 to 0.12. Distortions in choices other than simple hours, such as educational and occupational choice and entrepreneurial activity, are more difficult to measure.

In chapter 4, Thomas Aronsson and James Walker survey studies on labor supply from crisis through recovery. They note that the welfare state creates strong incentives to be in the labor force by making many benefits conditional on labor force participation, but it also creates strong incentives not to work many hours, which helps explain why Swedes work relatively few hours. Much of the labor supply adjustment in Sweden, however, takes place in dimensions other than contracted hours of work. One such adjustment is through sickness absence. Swedes, like people in other developed countries, have steadily gotten healthier since the 1960s. The physical burden of the typical job has declined, and life spans have increased with advances in medical care and public health. Yet, Swedes are more prone to take sickness leave than in the past, and Sweden has proportionately more persons on sickness leave than any other country. Why? The natural explanation is the generous social insurance system and associated moral hazard to make use of the system, even when one is not truly sick. Empirical studies show that sickness absence in Sweden varies when qualifying periods and replacement rates change. There is substantially more absence when it is less costly to call in sick. Another area of adjustment is in the length of working life, which in part depends on pension policies. Sweden's 1999 pension reform converted a defined benefit system to a notional defined contribution system, quasi-funded and more actuarial. The reform increased the long-term viability of the pension system and improved incentives to save and work. Here, Sweden is ahead of the United States—where the private pension system has been in crisis and where there is no national consensus on how to deal with Social Security—and the United Kingdom, where pension system reforms created a funding crisis.

Empirical evidence on the elasticity of taxable income with respect to the marginal tax rate suggests higher labor supply responses in other dimensions than in hours worked. Taxable income captures not only the effects of taxes and a compressed wage distribution on hours of work but also their effects on effort, career choice, and grey economy activity. Swedish studies find an elasticity of taxable income in response to tax rates comparable to U.S. estimates—around 0.4. Holmlund and Söderström (2008) report that as a result of responses to high taxes, lowering top marginal rates would have little effect on tax revenues. Another Swedish study explains the greater market work in the United States than in Sweden by differences in taxes.

A cornerstone of the Swedish model is reliance on active labor market policy (ALMP) to deal with labor market problems. One controversial finding in our earlier volume was that labor market programs did little to move workers to employment and were not worth the substantial resources that the country devoted to them. In chapter 5 in this volume, Anders Forslund and Alan Krueger report that ALMP did little to help Sweden recover from the unemployment crisis of the early 1990s. During the 1990s, unemployment increased more rapidly and fell more slowly than one would expect from historical experience. Both the inflow to unemployment and the duration of unemployment increased. Duration peaked in 1995 at twenty-five weeks unemployment, but when treating breaks in unemployment due to participation in ALMP as part of joblessness, jobless durations increased steadily during the 1990s, reaching 110 weeks (over two years) by 2000. Over 14 percent of the unemployed in 1999 and over 7 percent in 2005 were registered as unemployed for more than three years. The ALMP contributed to long jobless durations by allowing participants to remain eligible for continued unemployment benefits.

If ALMP training produced better matches between workers and jobs or if it improved skills, the benefits from the programs might exceed the cost of inducing longer periods of joblessness. Evaluation studies of the effectiveness of particular programs, however, indicate that training programs in the 1990s had little or no impact on labor market success. Perhaps the rapid growth of the programs in the crisis and the fact that participation qualified people for unemployment insurance reduced their effectiveness as training. The only programs that led to a new job more quickly than simple job search were those that most resembled regular jobs. But the more the program resembles regular jobs, the more likely it is that the program displaces private-sector jobs that produce the same or similar services. Estimates of this displacement effect are well over 50 percent. It is noteworthy that time-use data shows that unemployed Swedes spend considerably less time (one-tenth the time) on job search than do unemployed American workers. A plausible reason is the more generous unemployment compensation in Sweden.

In 2000, Sweden changed its ALMP policies. It broke the link between program participation and UI so that participation in ALMPs would no longer qualify an individual for new periods of UI. It introduced the activity guarantee, which requires full-time presence of the participants—time that participants can use for job search or for other program participation, such as job training, at the normal UI rate. This is designed to rule out participants who are using UI to finance leisure or to supplement black market income.

A major concern in our earlier study was that the crisis would produce the long spells of unemployment and high inequality in job holding found in many large EU countries. That is what happened. In chapter 6, Lars Ljungqvist and Thomas Sargent argue that the reason is that the unemployment benefit system has not adjusted to new forms of economic turbulence. Building on their contribution to our 1997 volume, they identify institutional features that might explain differences in equilibrium unemployment between a welfare state like Sweden's and a more laissez-faire economy like that in the United States.

The problem in attributing the greater unemployment in Sweden and much of Europe to generous welfare state benefits is that the countries with large welfare states and more generous unemployment benefits had lower unemployment than the United States from the 1950s through the 1970s and had higher unemployment thereafter. The question is, why would welfare state policies contribute to unemployment in the latter period and not in the former? The authors observe that the change in relative unemployment rates was not due to an increased inflow of persons to unemployment but rather to increased unemployment duration. In Europe, duration increased so that the long-term unemployed came to make up about half of total unemployment, while in the United States, the durations of unemployment spells did not change much. They argue that the change is due to the *interaction* of welfare state benefits with changing economic shocks. In the 1950s through the 1970s, employment protection and generous UI lowered frictional unemployment in Europe. In the 1980s to 2000s, by contrast, they hypothesize that technological change and globalization meant that the skills of unemployed workers became obsolete more quickly, which meant that the long duration of UI eligibility in Europe came to prolong the duration of joblessness. The reason is that unemployment insurance is paid relative to the past wage, so if skills decline, thereby reducing earnings on a new job, workers have a greater incentive to stay on benefits.

Ljungqvist and Sargent also develop a new indicator of joblessness in Sweden that treats the growth of the number of persons on long-term sickness leave and early retirement as a disguised part of unemployment. They take the percentage of individuals who were on long-term sickness leave or early retirement in 1974 and 1963 respectively as estimates of the size of those populations in the absence of the later shocks that induced overuse of the benefit systems, and they treat the increased percentages of persons on those programs over time as disguised unemployment. Adding this form of joblessness to measured unemployment produces an adjusted jobless rate for Sweden in 2005 of nearly 16 percent of the labor force.

Industrial Structure, Public Sector, and International Trade

Steven Davis and Magnus Henrekson in chapter 7 argue that Sweden is missing less-skilled jobs that compete with household or black market work. These jobs are found in the private-service sector, which is exceptionally small in Sweden. They attribute the missing jobs to tax policies and wage-setting practices that distort the industrial structure of employment.

Tax policy distorts the industrial structure by creating a tax wedge between what the buyer of services must earn before tax to purchase the service and what the seller of a service receives net of tax. The bigger the wedge, the smaller the share of workers in the formal service sector will be. In Sweden, this wedge is twice as big as in the United States. The authors estimate that a Swedish buyer of a service must earn 2.5 to 3.5 times more than the seller of the service to make it fruitful to buy services rather than to do it themselves. High payroll, income taxes, and consumption taxes make it economically sensible for many persons to engage in household and black market production rather than to buy services in the market, even though the market is more productive in delivering those services. The compression of the wage distribution makes it more expensive for the more skilled to hire the less skilled to undertake various jobs, while lowering the opportunity cost of the more skilled to do the work. The result is an inefficient allocation of time and effort. They also suggest that within the service sector, employment protection may make it difficult for small firms to form and expand, particularly in competition with the public sector in social service production.

Consistent with this, time-use surveys reveal that Swedes devote more time to household work than do Americans, who are more likely to rely on markets. Many Swedes also work in the underground economy. Statistics Sweden now makes an upward adjustment to Swedish GDP accounts to capture black market activities. The largest adjustments are in auto repairs, restaurants, taxi services, and hair dressing. The National Tax Board estimates black market activity at 4 to 5 percent of GDP. Davis and Henrekson conclude that because manufacturing is unlikely to be an engine of job growth, Sweden will need to consider policies to encourage the development of private-service jobs. Finally, they note that cross-country evidence indicates that high taxes reduce the employment and output shares of tax-sensitive industries, such as retail trade, hotels, and restaurants.

In their contribution to the first NBER-SNS study, Stefan Fölster and Sam Peltzman found that Sweden's high prices and weak productivity growth were partly attributable to lax competition policy and anticompetitive regulations. These policies made it difficult for new firms to enter some markets, effectively protecting less-efficient producers. The country's change in policies in these areas has opened up regulated markets to competition and has contributed to an increased import penetration, from 29 to 48 percent, which presumably helped to raise productivity and to keep prices lower than they otherwise would have been. But because the public sector is so important in Sweden, Fölster and Peltzman in chapter 8 in this volume shift their focus to how local public-sector policy affects the local economy—particularly the private sector.

Local governments in Sweden account for approximately one quarter of GDP and of total employment, which is about twice the corresponding U.S. figures. They dominate most publicly financed social services, such as health care, education, child care, and elderly care, as well as many technical services. Some privatization has occurred, with the private providers' share of publicly financed services reaching 20 percent in Stockholm and 9 percent in the country as a whole in the mid-2000s.

Using panel data for 290 municipalities and various indicators of public policy, including local tax rates and an index of perceived business friendliness from a survey of business, Fölster and Peltzman find that municipalities that have low tax rates or that are perceived as friendly to business have higher incomes. Reading the relation between tax rates and income as going from tax rates to income, they estimate that a 1-point increase in local tax rates, corresponding to a 3 percent tax hike, is associated with 2.4 percent lower income. The implicit elasticity suggests that most of the revenue increase from the tax hike is eroded by a reduction in the tax base. Causation could run the other way, however, as low-income municipalities must have higher taxes to fund mandated public services. But Sweden's intramunicipality equalization system largely equalizes the tax base and different spending needs due to demographic differences to enable local governments to provide mandated services uniformly. This makes it unlikely that the main causal effect runs from low incomes to high taxes. Moreover, taxes at the beginning of the period are associated with lower growth—a striking finding that aroused considerable interest and controversy at our conference.

At the opposite end of the economic spectrum is the global economy. In our earlier volume, Edward Leamer and Per Lundborg warned that increased competition from low-wage countries such as China and the ex-Soviet bloc would reduce the country's success in the international economy. Unless Sweden could maintain a more skill-intensive product mix in its exports—moving away from the comparative advantage of these new entrants—it would find itself in head-on competition with low-wage countries in labor-intensive products.

In chapter 9, Leamer presents correlations between the product mix of different countries' exports in 1987 and 1999 that reveal dramatic changes in the competition between high-income and low-income countries. In 1987, the correlation between the export product mix of high-income countries and low-income countries in the U.S. and EU markets was low, because capital-rich countries specialized in capital-intensive products, while labor-rich countries specialized in labor-intensive products. By 1999, this had changed. Product mixes in all countries had become more similar. The correlation between the product mixes of China and Sweden in exports to the European Union rose to over 0.50, implying some direct competition between high-wage Sweden and low-wage China. China also became a more serious competitor with Sweden in the U.S. market. The reason is that China has increased its presence in Sweden's most important export sectors: machinery and electrical machinery. Still, because there are great differences in technology and products within industries, within-industry specialization should allow Sweden to avoid much direct competition with low-wage Chinese firms for some time. Leamer concludes that the key issue is to invest in human and physical capital in order to avoid direct competition with low-wage countries. Yet, that may not be enough. He speculates that the Internet and the personal computer may be altering the labor market's compensation for talent, creating "a Hollywood kind of inequality" that cannot easily be compensated by increased education. Talent has become the scarce resource and must be rewarded more to work more hours. Such wage inequality creates a problem for an egalitarian welfare state.

The Welfare State in (Continuous) Transition

The old saying, "If it ain't broke, don't fix it"—I never bought into that. I think you try to get things working the best you can and don't wait until the whole thing is falling apart and then figure out there's a problem. A lot of times you see the problems before they actually occur if you look carefully.
—Bill Belichick, U.S. football coach, at a press conference on December 22, 2005

The first NBER-SNS project analyzed the Swedish economy when it was "broke," and it was unclear if the economy could make a strong or rapid recovery. Recovery required tough reforms and more reliance on market forces, we argued. Sweden rose to this challenge in many ways.

In the decade following the crisis, Sweden adopted a flexible exchange rate and a more disciplined monetary policy; lowered government employment and the government share of national income and eliminated a huge budget deficit; lowered unemployment insurance modestly; and began to reform its sickness pay insurance—all of which arguably helped the economic recovery by reducing distortions in economic incentives. The country also deregulated markets, reformed taxes, privatized the delivery of some social services, and strengthened the pension system in economically sensible ways. The reforms were accompanied by a moderate rise in income inequality, but the vast majority of Swedes benefited from the changes, with disposable incomes improving throughout the income distribution. Real disposable income increased for the first time in decades.

The economy is no longer broken, but it still faces important challenges. In an interconnected welfare state, problems can compound to endanger fiscal stability and the sustainability of prosperity, as the early 1990s experience made clear. Because the welfare costs of social interventions rise with the square of the magnitude of the intervention, it is critical that countries with large welfare states run programs efficiently and squeeze programs that do not deliver the desired gains in equity. Currently, public benefit schemes, including unemployment, sickness insurance, and early retirement, support 20 percent of working-age individuals. This requires sizable budgetary expenses and taxes that reduce the rewards to working relative to benefit levels. Wage compression and large tax wedges contribute to the weakness in the job market by creating incentives for nonmarket and black market work relative to employment in small private-service firms in the regular market economy.

Given the evidence that active labor market programs do not work well in Sweden and that the sickness insurance system encourages more sickness leave than elsewhere, these would seem to be areas where further reforms could improve efficiency without harming equity. The evidence also shows that Sweden's high taxes, which create a large wedge between an individual's productivity and ability to consume, cause disincentives and distortions and could be lowered at little or no cost to egalitarian goals. In light of economic developments worldwide that favor skilled labor, there is a potential long-term danger that over time, Sweden's wage distribution will deviate more and more from market realities, which raise the cost of egalitarianism.

On the basis of its post-1994 recovery, the Swedish economy seems capable of bending to changing market forces without sacrificing its extraordinary success in eliminating poverty, but that presumably will require continual policy innovation. The large fraction of national output devoted to public consumption that benefits all citizens, regardless of their personal incomes, and its strong social safety net give Sweden, more than many other countries, the space to experiment with policies that produce more efficiency without sacrificing egalitarian goals.[7] With a population that seems to respond substantially to modest changes in incentives, perhaps because given changes carry more weight in a relatively egalitarian society than in a society with a highly unequal distribution of earnings, even modest changes might produce substantial gains in efficiency.

Conclusion

We began this introduction by noting that the Swedish welfare state was arguably the most ambitious effort by a capitalist market economy to reduce inequality and eliminate poverty. The 1990s crisis and the slow economic growth that preceded it highlighted the Swedish model's deficiencies and fragility. During our first study, there was fear that the Swedish model was no longer viable. If the precrisis assessment of the Swedish model was overly optimistic, the crisis-period assessment was overly pessimistic. Sweden's recovery shows that it is possible to run a reasonably successful market economy while still devoting considerable resources to a welfare state that maintains economic equality and to surmount an economic crisis. This is probably easier to do in smaller economies than in larger ones and in more homogeneous countries than in more heterogeneous ones, so Sweden's experiences are not easily transferable to the United States or other

---

7. In its 2007 Sweden report, the OECD (79) shows that neither eliminating the top state income tax bracket nor reducing the state income tax by 5 percent would alter Sweden's position as the country with the second-most equal income distribution (after Denmark) among OECD countries. Eliminating the state income tax completely, thereby making the income tax scale flat (lowering top marginal rates from 55 to 30 percent), would move Sweden from number two to number four in the ranking of countries, according to income equalization.

large economies. It is also easier to do so in a society where the vast bulk of the citizenry is committed to egalitarian goals, as in Sweden, rather than in societies where the polity is divided over the weight to place on equity compared to efficiency. Faced with crisis, Sweden modified policies and reduced some benefits that had substantial efficiency costs. It became more market reliant and open to competition and to individual choice, giving a stronger economic base for maintaining the welfare state. Sweden's market-oriented reforms arguably had a first-order impact on efficiency but only a second-order impact on equity, buttressing the welfare state while improving the general economic welfare of Swedes.

We recognize that our reading of the evidence contrasts with the views of some other analysts of Sweden's welfare state, who are less inclined toward market reforms and who are fearful that moves to the market invariably endanger the welfare state. Walter Korpi, a long-time scholar and defender of the welfare state, argues that economists put too much emphasis on the adverse effects of high taxes (and presumably, wage compression) on incentives and economic efficiency:

> If citizens find that they get significant benefits in return for their taxes, their take-home pay is no longer the only basis for work incentives. . . . If tax payments are seen as providing individual benefits and the free-rider problem can be overcome, the effects of tax wedges will tend to decrease. (Korpi and Palme 1998, 682)

To be sure, citizens with the attitudes described by Korpi are likely to respond less to taxation than others, which will decrease the distortionary effects of taxes, benefits, and compressed wages. But it is hard to see why individuals should have these attitudes—the taxes they pay are not tied to the benefits they receive, so why would the benefits induce a willingness to work? The conditioning phrase, "If . . . the free rider problem can be overcome," merely sweeps the problem under the rug. Experiments with prisoner's dilemma and public-goods games show that some people behave as free riders, while others are more likely to play cooperatively. More directly, the problem is apparent in the Swedish data we have been discussing—it is simply implausible, for example, that the extraordinarily high rates of sickness absence in Sweden reflect anything other than free riding on a system that provides benefits for not working.

The critical question is whether responses to tax wedges/wage compression are large enough in the aggregate to affect market outcomes. One approach to this question has been to compare the growth performance of countries with different degrees of market intervention or sizes of governments or to compare Sweden's performance with that of other developed economies (Korpi 2005; Agell, Ohlsson, and Skogman Thoursie 2006; Håkansson and Lindbeck 2005; Fölster and Henrekson 2001). However, specifying aggregate growth equations is a risky operation that has not yielded clear conclusions.

The analyses in this volume take a different approach, empirically examining the impacts of Swedish institutions at a more micro level. They direct attention to several areas in which responses to tax wedges/wage compression do seem to affect market outcomes: hours worked in the market compared to hours worked in household production or grey market activities; the abnormally small private-service sector; the expansion of university training as the education differential rose; the abnormally large amount of time spent in sickness leave; and the increased duration of unemployment spells associated with the long duration of benefits and time on active labor market programs that do not improve skills much, if at all. The issue of the magnitude of the effects of tax wedges is one of positive social science, not one of normative analysis. Whether the estimated costs in efficiency are large or small relative to the gains in equity from any intervention is a normative issue that the body politic decides through democratic processes. The typical American is much less committed to egalitarian ideals than is the typical Swede, is more trusting of markets, and is more sensitive to the costs of government programs, which leads the United States to rely more on markets than does Sweden. But the basic economics in assessing the effects of programs in attaining their goals and the efficiency costs thereof is the same. Decisions about how to deal with the costs and trade-offs between economic performance and equity that we and other economists point out will be made within the context of the social institutions and goals desired by Swedes. It is, after all, the *Swedish* model.

We have been impressed that in dealing with the crisis and other economic problems that have beset the Swedish model, public- and private-sector decision makers have been creative in finding economically sensible solutions to problems—in some cases, with greater success than the United States, such as in pension reform. Our research suggests that such adjustments are a necessary part of a welfare state operating in a market economy. Welfare state policies cannot remain static but must continuously evolve to meet changing economic realities. New market conditions driven by technology, trade, and international migration impinge on what policy and institutions can achieve. The welfare state should be a learning state that adjusts policies to changes in their costs and in their success in attaining egalitarian ideals. The reforms that Sweden has undertaken since the crisis show, political differences among parties notwithstanding, that Sweden is a pragmatic reformer, willing and able to undertake reforms when necessary, while continuing to preserve the essence of its welfare state.

Facing and dealing with the trade-offs between equity and performance requires considerable political and social will. Countries that admire Sweden's distributional outcomes presumably would need similar capacity to respond to costs and crisis. From one perspective, a welfare state requires greater social and political perspicuity about economics, particularly by policymakers, than an economy driven more by the invisible hand of markets.

The latter has problems of its own, as the current meltdown in U.S. financial markets has demonstrated. Nevertheless, the welfare state remains a work in progress that must balance the benefits of more egalitarian outcomes against the social costs of market inefficiencies caused by those very benefits. Perhaps the most important lesson for other countries from the Swedish experience is that it isn't easy to be Sweden.

Appendix

Important Policy Changes, 1985 to 2008 (Year it became effective in parentheses)

The years of enactment show that important market-oriented reforms were decided by Social Democratic and center-right governments alike. Sweden had a center-right government from 1991 to 1994 and again from September 2006—five of the twenty-three years covered in this box. The broad outline of reforms has had broad political support and has meant that welfare state arrangements have remained largely intact, but government expenditures have been reined in and the economy has become more competitive.

Macro policy reforms:

Financial market deregulation (1985)
Restrictions on international portfolio investment lifted (1989)
Flexible exchange rate cum inflation targeting (1992)
EU membership (1994)
Electoral periods at national and local levels lengthened from three to four
     years (1994)
New budget process for central government (1997)
Independent central bank (1999)
Surplus target for consolidated public budgets (central and local govern-
     ments, public pension system; 2000), currently set at 1 percent of GDP

The deregulation of financial markets contributed to the credit expansion in the late 1980s and subsequently to the serious crisis in the early 1990s. Later macro policy reforms helped the economy stabilize by maintaining a low rate of inflation and by reducing public expenditures and the deficit. The new budget process, with expenditure ceilings for central government expenditures set for three years at a time, meant that total expenditures could no longer be arrived at by adding together individual expenditures from the bottom up. The lengthening of electoral periods was intended to lengthen the decision horizon of policymakers. European Union membership was finally more of a political than an economic change. It did not drastically alter Sweden's relationships with the EU market, because access in most areas had been granted under the previous European Economic Space (EES) agreement, but it made Sweden a more integrated part of the political union.

Tax and funding reforms:

Tax reform (1991)
Pension reform (1999)
Gift and inheritance tax abolishèd (2005)
Wealth tax abolished (2007)
Earned income tax credit (2007)
Tax relief on household services (2007)

The 1990/1991 tax reform, which broadened the base and reduced top marginal rates, reduced the many distortions caused by the old tax system. The pension reform was forward-looking and transformed the pay-as-you-go system to a quasi-funded and more actuarial system, which is more resilient to demographic and economic changes. The earned income tax credits are significant in size and help to make work more profitable than living off of social benefits for low earners. Tax relief for household services is intended to offset the tax wedge, which discourages the purchase of such services outside the grey/black economy and the growth of a small private-service sector.

The abolition of the gift and inheritance tax was intended to facilitate small, owner-run firms to pass to the next generation. The abolition of the wealth tax was motivated by the fact that it was no longer paid by the really wealthy, that most other EU countries had done away with it, and that it may encourage those who had moved their funds abroad to bring them back to Sweden.

Competition policy and deregulation of traditional monopolies:

Taxi (1989)
Railways (1989)
Aviation (1992)
Telecommunications (1993)
Telephone and postal services (1993)
New competition law (1993)
Electricity (1996)

The deregulation of network industries and other traditional monopolies allowed new entry and increased competition in these industries, and as a result, it contributed to increased productivity. The new competition law recognized that the government could play a role in ensuring a competitive economy.

Public-sector reforms:

Private provision of local government-financed services (after 1990)
Voucher system for primary and secondary schools (1991)

The services continue to be tax financed. The school voucher system allows private schools (including for-profit schools) to compete freely with the public school system.

Replacement rates in social insurance:

Sickness insurance lowered (1993 to 1998), then restored (1998)
Unemployment insurance lowered (Capping has eroded replacement rates for above-median wages since 1992; from 2007, it was also lowered below the cap, from 80 to 70 percent after forty weeks and from 70 to 65 percent after sixty weeks.)

Terms and replacement rates in social insurance have changed frequently, back and forth. When benefit conditions have been tightened, sickness rates and unemployment have gone down. Replacement rates in UI for above-median earners have fallen substantially.

Active labor market program reforms:

Participation no longer qualifies for UI (2000)
Programs scaled down (2007)

The ALMP has undergone a substantial change, which, at least in normal times, means that there will be considerably fewer participants in the reformed programs.

References

Agell, J., H. Ohlsson, and P. Skogman Thoursie. 2006. Growth effects of government expenditure and taxation in rich countries: A comment. *European Economic Review* 50 (1): 211–8.

Fölster, S., and M. Henrekson. 2001. Growth effects of government expenditure and taxation in rich countries. *European Economic Review* 45 (8): 1501–20.

Forslund, A. 2008. *Den svenska jämviktsarbetslösheten—en översikt.* IFAU Rapport no. 2008:17. Uppsala, Sweden: Institute for Labor Market Policy Evaluation.

Freeman, R. B., R. Topel, and B. Swedenborg, eds. 1997. *The welfare state in transition: Reforming the Swedish model.* Chicago: University of Chicago Press.

Håkansson, C., and A. Lindbeck. 2005. Korpi vilseleder igen [Is Sweden lagging behind? Korpi misleads again]. *Ekonomisk Debatt* 33 (1): 58–65.

Holmlund, B., and M. Söderström. 2008. Estimating dynamic income responses to tax reforms: Swedish evidence. IFAU Working Paper no. 28. Uppsala, Sweden: Institute for Labor Market Policy Evaluation.

Korpi, W. 2005. Does the welfare state harm economic growth? Sweden as a strategic test case. In *Social policy and economic development in the Nordic countries,* ed. O. Kangas and J. Palme, 186–210. Hampshire, England: Palgrave MacMillan.

Korpi, W., and J. Palme. 1998. The paradox of redistribution and strategies of equality: welfare state institutions, inequality, and poverty in Western countries. *American Sociological Review* 63 (5): 661–87.

Lindbeck, A. (1993). *The welfare state: The selected essays of Assar Lindbeck.* Cheltenham, UK: Edward Elgar Publishing.

Lindbeck, A., P. Molander, T. Persson, A. Sandmo, B. Swedenborg, and N. Thygesen. 1994. *Turning Sweden around.* Cambridge, MA: MIT Press.

Organization for Economic Cooperation and Development (OECD). 2007. *OECD economic surveys: Sweden,* vol. 2007, no. 4. Paris: OECD.

Statistics Sweden (SCB). 2008. *Public finances in Sweden.* Stockholm: SCB.

1

Searching for Optimal Inequality/Incentives

Anders Björklund and Richard B. Freeman

Economic inequality is Janus-faced. Inequality creates incentives for people to move from lower-rewarding activities to higher-rewarding activities, which raises output and should reduce the difference in rewards. Inequality also produces differences in living standards that can lead some into poverty and social exclusion. In public debate, persons on the right stress the effect of inequality on incentives and work effort, while persons on the left stress the effect of inequality on living standards for those with low incomes. Both are important.

Since the 1960s, Sweden has been a world leader in reducing inequality and poverty. In the labor market, institutional wage determination compressed hourly earnings for persons with similar measured skills and limited differentials across skill groups (Björklund and Freeman 1997), while dispersion of literacy and numeracy skills in Sweden was also low compared to the United States (Devroye and Freeman 2002). Family background played a smaller role in labor market success than in the United States (Solon 2002; Björklund and Jäntti 1997; Björklund et al. 2002). Inequality was lower in Sweden than in the United States in long-run/permanent earnings and income, as well as in the transitory component (Aaberge et al. 2002).[1] Generous welfare benefits and high tax rates extended egalitarianism beyond the working population so that the disposable income in the bottom decile of

Anders Björklund is a professor of economics at the Swedish Institute for Social Research (SOFI) at Stockholm University. Richard Freeman is the Herbert Ascherman Professor of Economics at Harvard University and a research associate at the National Bureau of Economic Research. Anders Björklund acknowledges financial support from the Swedish Council for Working Life and Social Research.

1. Sweden was not the only country with a highly egalitarian distribution of income. Other Scandinavian countries and Belgium also had low inequality in labor market earnings and in total income, and Japan has low inequality in total income.

the income distribution was closer to the median than in most other countries.[2] As a result, a poor child in Sweden had a higher income than a poor child in the United States, despite the United States having higher per capita gross domestic product (GDP). These facts led Social Democrats in Sweden and elsewhere to see the country as establishing an attractive welfare state alternative to more market-driven capitalist economies.

The huge recession that hit Sweden from 1991 to 1994 challenged the viability of the Swedish model. Rates of unemployment rose from below 2 percent to over 9 percent,[3] and the proportion of the workforce on labor market programs reached 5.5 percent in 1994. The employment-to-population rate fell from 83.1 in 1990 to 70.7 in 1997,[4] in large part because Sweden reduced public-sector employment to deal with a crisis in public finances. The rise in unemployment, job loss, and fiscal problems were a wake-up call that the economy was not as healthy as touted. Many analysts believed that Sweden had strayed too far from market solutions for the long-term success of the welfare state and called for market reforms that invariably increased inequalities.

From the mid-1990s through the mid-2000s, the Swedish economy recovered smartly from recession. Real GDP per capita in purchasing power parity terms increased rapidly from 1993/1994 to 2006, though Sweden still ranked lower in GDP per capita among those countries than it had in the 1980s. Productivity increased more in Sweden than in most other advanced Organization for Economic Cooperation and Development (OECD) countries, including the United States, and was accompanied by growth in real wages (Fredriksson and Topel, chapter 3 in this volume). The current account in the balance of trade became positive. The country moved to the top rung in what the OECD has termed investment in knowledge—research and development spending, investment in higher education, and investment in information technology. The World Economic Forum *Global Competitiveness Report* (2008) placed Sweden fourth out of 131 countries in competitiveness in 2007/2008.

But job growth lagged the recovery overall.[5] Between 1994 and 2000, private-sector employment expanded by 300,000, while public-sector

2. In 1991, the disposable income of adults aged twenty to sixty-four in the bottom decile of the income distribution was 60 percent of the median. Among children aged zero to seventeen, the ratio of disposable income of those in the bottom decile was 67 percent of median income. Among adults, the ratio of disposable income in the top decile to income in the bottom decile was 2.67, while among children, the ratio of income in the top decile to income in the bottom decile was 2.23 (Björklund and Freeman 1997).

3. Unemployment rates vary, depending on whether they have been adjusted for international comparability. The National Institute of Economic Research (Sweden) gives quarterly open unemployment rates that reach 9.4 percent in the fourth quarter of 1993 and in the first quarter of 1997. The OECD gives standardized unemployment rates of 1.7 percent in 1990 that rise to 9.6 percent in 1996 and 9.9 percent in 1997.

4. Available at: http://ocde.p4.siteinternet.com/publications/doifiles/302005041P1T050.xls.

5. OECD (2005); this occurred as well in the United States, Korea, and other countries.

employment stagnated. After exceeding the rate of unemployment in the European Union at the peak of the recession, Sweden's unemployment rate fell to 4 percent in 2001 and 2002. The proportion of the workforce on labor market programs (which is not counted as part of unemployment) also fell, bottoming out at 2.1 percent in 2003, but even so, the jobless rate, including labor market programs, remained high. As of 2005, the employment-population rate in the country was several points below the prerecession 1991 level.[6]

What happened to Sweden's egalitarian outcomes during the crisis and recovery? Did the crisis lead Swedes to view inequality and life and job satisfaction differently than in the past? Did the incentives from increased inequality contribute to the recovery and competitiveness? Why has Sweden done so well in investing in knowledge and competitiveness, despite lower inequality and pecuniary incentives than most other advanced economies?

This chapter examines these questions. Section 1.1 shows that inequality in earnings and income increased moderately through the early 2000s, while inequality in hours worked increased substantially, making it the most important form of inequality in the society. But the rise in inequality notwithstanding, Sweden remained a leading egalitarian economy in the world. Section 1.2 shows that Swedes are aware of the inequity and incentive sides of inequality and that their tolerance for inequality, while less than that of Americans, is similar to that of persons in most other advanced economies. It also shows that satisfaction with living conditions has been relatively stable, while satisfaction with wages has become modestly lower. Section 1.3 argues that the increased earnings inequality was productivity enhancing but that factors other than pecuniary rewards in the labor market underlie Sweden's large investment in university training and success in knowledge-intensive activity.

1.1 Earnings, Hours Worked, and Income Inequality

To determine how the distribution of earnings changed in the 1990s to the early 2000s period of recession and recovery, we examined employer reports on earnings from Statistics Sweden and individual reports on earnings from the Level of Living (LNU) Survey. Figure 1.1 displays the ratios of the earnings of employees in the 90th percentile of the before-tax monthly earnings distribution to the earnings of employees in the 10th percentile (90/10 ratio) and the comparable ratios of earnings for persons at the 90th percentile relative to median earnings (90/10) and of earnings at the median to earnings at the 10th percentile (50/10). All of the earnings are adjusted

6. U.S. Department of Labor, Bureau of Labor Statistics, Office of Productivity and Technology; see table 5 of *Comparative Real Gross Domestic Product per Capita and per Employed Person, Fifteen Countries, 1960–2005,* June 16, 2006; available at: http://www.bls.gov/fls.

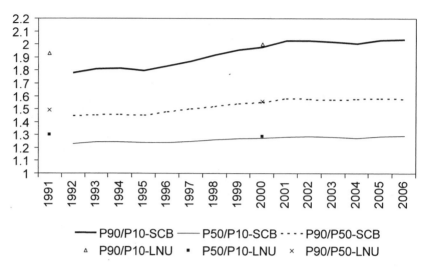

Fig. 1.1   Hourly earnings inequality: 1992 to 2006 (according to Statistics Sweden) and 1991 and 2000 (according to the Level of Living Survey)

Source: Statistics Sweden (SCB) and own computations from the Level of Living Survey (LNU). The former is based on full-time equivalent monthly earnings reports from employers. The latter is based on home interviews with individuals. Each of the data sources has advantages and disadvantages.

to a full-time equivalent basis from employer records for 1990 to 2006. The data show that the 90/10 ratio went from 1.8 in 1995 to 2.0 in 2003, with the rise roughly divided equally between an increase in the 90/50 ratio and an increase in the 50/10 ratio. These increases in inequality are substantive in low-inequality Sweden. The figure also gives percentile income ratios from the 1991 and 2000 LNU. The LNU data shows a smaller rise in inequality. The LNU had a higher level of inequality than the employer-based data in 1991 and a similar rate in 2000.

Björklund and Freeman (1997) found that Sweden's relatively egalitarian distribution of annual earnings was due as much to a narrow distribution of hours worked as to the more publicized narrow distribution of hourly earnings. To see how hours worked changed over the 1990s, we tabulated the distribution of working hours from the 1991 and 2000 LNU surveys, which give annual hours for 1990 and 1999, respectively. The hours measure includes hours paid for but spent on vacation time and hours employed when the worker is on short-term absences due to sickness or to caring for a sick child.

Table 1.1 gives the mean hours worked, the coefficient of variation in hours worked, and the distribution of hours worked for individuals aged nineteen to sixty-four. It shows a substantial increase in inequality of hours worked, with the coefficient of variation in hours worked rising from 0.52 to 0.63. The increase is almost entirely due to an increase in the proportion of

Table 1.1   **The distribution of working hours: 1990 and 1999**

	Individuals							
	All, 19–65 years		19–24 years		25–54 years		55–65 years	
	1990	1999	1990	1999	1990	1999	1990	1999
Mean	1,650	1,510	1,170	770	1,825	1,690	1,340	1,350
Coefficient of variation	.51	.63	.72	1.07	.41	.51	.69	.74
Proportions								
0 hours	.099	.179	.114	.309	.059	.122	.249	.287
1–1,000 hours	.100	.102	.329	.336	.070	.074	.058	.049
1,001–1,500 hours	.113	.080	.151	.121	.092	.069	.164	.089
1,501–2,000 hours	.155	.158	.110	.087	.172	.179	.119	.130
2,001–2,500 hours	.449	.407	.273	.129	.508	.468	.355	.377
2,501+ hours	.080	.075	.021	.016	.098	.088	.055	.066
N	4,423	4,458	622	559	3,054	3,005	747	894

Source: Own computations from the Level of Living (LNU) surveys.

persons working zero hours and thus who are long-term unemployed. Disaggregating hours for the age groups nineteen to twenty-four, twenty-five to fifty-four, and fifty-five to sixty-four shows that the largest increase is among nineteen- to twenty-four-year-olds, which reflects both the unemployment of those out of school and the increased proportion of young persons in school without any accompanying time worked. The growth of inequality in hours is smallest for older people, possibly due to the incentives the reformed pension system gives to persons to keep working through age sixty-seven.[7] The social problem with high inequality in hours worked is not that high-wage workers put in many hours (which arguably exaggerates inequality in well-being due to the notion that leisure is a normal good) but that low-wage workers work fewer hours and/or are unemployed.

Rising inequality in monthly earnings and hours worked increased the dispersion of annual disposable income among families during the recession and into the ensuing recovery. Panel A of figure 1.2 displays the Gini coefficient measure of inequality measured by Statistic Sweden's pre-1991 tax reform income definition (labeled old) and by its post-1991 tax reform definition (labeled new). The Gini from both definitions in the overlap period shows that the more inclusive definition increased inequality so that an accurate reading of trends requires that we compute them separately. The Gini under the new definition increased from 0.23 to a peak of 0.31 in 2000 and then fell to 0.28/0.29 through 2005. Panel B of the figure, which measures inequality by income ratios for different deciles, tells a similar story. The income at the 90th percentile relative to that at the 10th percentile

7. We obtained similar results with hours worked per adult household member.

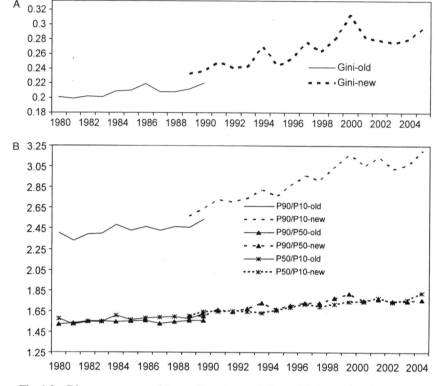

Fig. 1.2   **Diverse measures of inequality of annual disposable income, 1980 to 2005:**
A, **Gini coefficients;** *B,* **Ratios of disposable income by deciles: P90/P10, P90/P50,**
and P50/P10 ratios; *C,* **Real disposable income at the median (P50), 10th (P10), and**
90th (P90) percentile of the distribution: 1980 to 2005 in 2006 prices

Note: Old is based on the more narrow income concept used before the 1991 tax reform. The
individual is the unit of analysis, and the household is the unit of income. Income includes
capital gains, which were particularly high in 1994 and 2000 due to changes in tax rules. Statistics Sweden's equivalence scales are applied.

Source: Statistics Sweden and special tabulations by Kjell Jansson for the authors.

went from 2.55 in 1991 to 3.20 in 2005. The lines for the ratio of income for
the 90th percentile to the median and for the median to the 10th percentile show, as with ratios of earnings in figure 1.1, that the rise in the 90/10
ratio is roughly divided equally between rises in the 90/50 ratio and the
50/10 ratio.

The rise in inequality, however, was not associated with losses of income
for lower-income families. Panel C of figure 1.2 shows the real disposable
income of persons in different percentiles in the 1980s and in the period of
rising inequality. The real disposable household incomes at the 10th percentile fell from 1989 to 1997 but then recovered to be about 10 percent higher
than in 1991. The increased inequality took the form of greater growth of
incomes for higher-income families, shown by the sharp upward trend in the

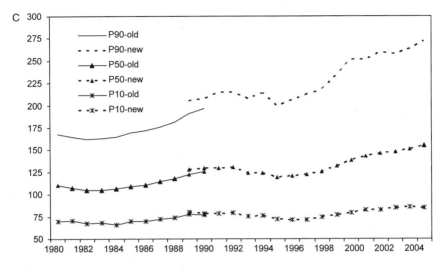

Fig. 1.2   (cont.)

earning of persons in the 90th percentile from 1995 through 2005—a gain of about 37 percent—rather than in declines of incomes for lower-income families.

To what extent did Sweden's welfare state maintain incomes of households at the bottom of the distribution during the recession? Table 1.2 uses data specially tabulated for our study by Statistics Sweden on the percentage of household disposable income that is accruing to persons in different deciles from earnings, capital returns, pensions, and various government programs. If welfare state programs provided a stable safety net, we would expect that the share of incomes from programs such as sickness and parental leave, unemployment insurance (UI), and labor market programs, as well as universal tax-free benefits and means-tested tax-free benefits, would rise sharply between 1991 and 1995 and would fall thereafter for persons in the low-income deciles but not for those in higher-income deciles. The table shows such a pattern. In 1991, the sum of the share of income in the three program areas in the bottom part of the table is 30.1 percent for the bottom decile, 26.7 percent for the next-lowest decile, and 24.2 percent for the third-lowest decile. In 1995, the sum of the shares of income for these groups are 49.8 percent, 41.5 percent, and 32.2 percent, respectively—increases of 23.1 points, 25.8 points, and 6.9 points. By contrast, the share of income from these programs barely changes for persons from the fourth decile to the top decile. In the recovery, although the shares of income from these programs falls for the lower-income deciles, they remain higher than in the past for persons in the bottom and second-bottom deciles.

The data in table 1.2 also show jumpiness in capital incomes at the bottom of the distribution and in the share of pension incomes. The fall in the share of capital incomes indicates that many persons were in the lowest

Table 1.2   Percentage of household disposable income net of taxes by different source, by decile groups: 1991, 1995, 2001, and 2005

Decile group	Earnings for employees and self-employed				Capital				Pensions			
	1991	1995	2001	2005	1991	1995	2001	2005	1991	1995	2001	2005
1	21.3	33.8	33.7	27.1	5.0	−9.0	−19.2	−1.7	43.6	25.4	40.4	29.6
2	18.0	24.1	21.8	24.2	4.6	2.4	1.1	1.5	50.6	32.2	43.2	43.3
3	32.4	30.5	26.8	26.7	4.4	2.0	0.9	1.5	39.0	35.3	44.2	47.1
4	43.8	38.0	39.8	38.8	4.6	2.7	2.1	1.5	31.1	32.5	37.0	40.4
5	53.6	50.0	56.1	53.6	5.5	3.3	2.4	1.9	23.7	27.8	25.5	29.8
6	62.4	57.7	63.1	64.0	5.3	4.0	2.6	2.4	18.9	23.8	21.8	22.8
7	65.6	61.3	70.0	69.5	5.9	4.1	2.6	2.5	16.8	23.3	16.9	19.8
8	70.7	67.1	73.4	75.1	5.8	4.5	3.5	3.0	14.4	20.0	14.7	15.8
9	72.2	69.3	78.7	77.3	7.1	5.4	3.7	4.0	13.3	18.7	12.0	14.2
10	65.5	67.2	63.8	57.6	19.7	14.8	22.8	29.2	10.1	15.1	10.4	11.4
All	57.7	56.1	60.2	58.1	8.5	5.5	6.7	8.8	20.7	22.9	20.5	22.1

	Sickness, parental leave, UI, and labor market program benefits				Universal tax-free benefits				Means-tested tax-free benefits			
	1991	1995	2001	2005	1991	1995	2001	2005	1991	1995	2001	2005
1	9.1	16.7	11.8	11.7	9.8	16.0	18.2	19.8	11.2	17.1	15.2	13.5
2	7.5	16.2	10.0	9.4	6.4	10.3	10.8	10.2	12.8	15.0	13.1	11.4
3	9.2	13.4	9.9	8.2	7.1	6.9	7.7	5.9	7.9	11.9	10.4	10.6
4	10.5	12.6	10.6	11.2	6.3	6.1	6.4	5.5	3.6	8.2	4.1	2.7
5	10.6	10.7	10.0	8.8	4.9	4.7	4.8	4.7	1.6	3.5	1.1	1.1
6	8.5	8.8	8.2	6.7	3.9	4.0	3.6	3.7	1.0	1.8	0.7	0.4
7	7.9	7.4	7.3	5.2	3.1	2.7	3.0	2.5	0.6	1.3	0.2	0.5
8	7.0	5.8	6.1	4.2	1.8	1.9	1.9	1.8	0.3	0.7	0.3	0.2
9	5.8	5.1	4.1	3.4	1.3	1.4	1.3	1.1	0.2	0.1	0.2	0
10	3.8	2.2	2.4	1.3	0.7	0.6	0.5	0.5	0.1	0.1	0.2	0
All	7.2	7.8	6.4	5.3	3.4	3.9	3.7	3.5	2.5	3.8	2.5	2.3

Source: Statistics Sweden and special tabulations done by Kjell Jansson for the authors.
Note: Relevant taxes are subtracted for taxable income sources.

decile because of capital losses, while the changing share of pension incomes implies that pensions kept older persons from falling in the distribution in the recession.

1.1.1   Long-Run Inequality versus Transitory Inequality

So far, we have looked at cross-sectional inequality in incomes. Such measures can be misleading indicators of changes in permanent incomes, because they are affected by transitory factors.[8] To see whether the picture of Swedish inequality before, during, and after the crisis, shown in figures

8. A common hypothesis is that compared to European social welfare states, the United States has greater income mobility over the career so that comparisons of income inequality based on cross-sectional incomes exaggerate U.S.-European differences. Research through the early 1990s has shown that the United States is not much different than Germany (Burkhauser and Poupore 1997) or than the Nordic countries (Aaberge et al. 2002) in this respect.

1.1 and 1.2, changes markedly if we take account of income mobility, we use Swedish register data that follow individuals' earnings over time. We look at inequality based on annual earnings and five-year averages for four cohorts of Swedish men from 1981 to 2005, based on a 35 percent sample of the whole Swedish-born population of men, including the zero observations for those who did not have any earnings from work.[9]

Figure 1.3 reports results from this analysis for cohorts of men born in 1950, 1955, 1960, and 1965. For each cohort, we report measures of earnings inequality from age thirty-one onward. We start at age thirty-one to avoid the large increase and volatility in earnings that usually take place during the process of labor market entrance. The figure shows first that the older cohorts had lower inequality at each age level than did the younger cohorts. For example, the 1950 cohort aged thirty-one to thirty-five years in 1981 to 1985 had a coefficient of variation around 0.40 to 0.45, compared to a coefficient of variation around 0.6 for the 1965 cohort at the same age. The same pattern of greater inequality at the same age is found for successively younger cohorts. Second, the figure shows rising earnings inequality by age for a specific cohort. This pattern—which presumably reflects differential investments in on-the-job training—is so strong that it is hard to discern a clear rise in inequality during the crisis period from 1991 to 1995. Third, the measures of inequality that cover five-year earnings show sufficiently large increases in inequality to rule out increased short-run earnings volatility as an important factor behind rising inequality in the Swedish labor market.

Finally, figure 1.4 gives a measure of earnings mobility, based on annual and long-run inequality—the so-called Shorrocks measure.[10] It shows some differences between the cohorts, but the magnitude of mobility is too low to challenge the conclusion of rising longer-run measures of inequality given in the cross-sections of annual inequality in figures 1.1 and 1.2. Thus, our analysis supports Gustavsson's (2007) finding that the increased inequality is largely due to changes in the long-run component of earnings rather than in transitory earnings.

1.1.2   International Perspective

Income inequality rose in many countries during the 1990s through the mid-2000s. How did Sweden's rise of inequality compare to the changes in other advanced countries?

Table 1.3 gives our best estimate of the change in inequality among countries and of Sweden's rank in terms of the magnitude of the change. Panel A records the ratios of earnings at the 90th percentile to earnings at the

---

9. The income concept is called "arbetsinkomst" and includes income from short-term sickness and parental leave but not UI benefits or labor market training stipends.

10. The measure is defined as one minus the ratio of long-run inequality and weighted annual inequality and takes on values between zero and one for a standard class of inequality measures. See Shorrocks (1978).

a) Men born 1950

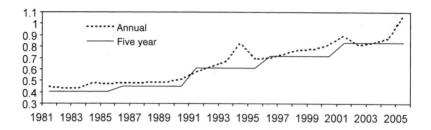

b) Men born 1955

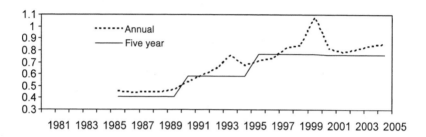

c) Men born 1960

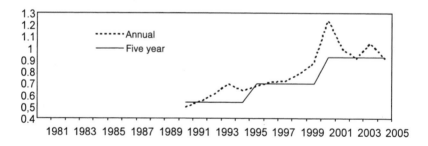

d) Men born 1965

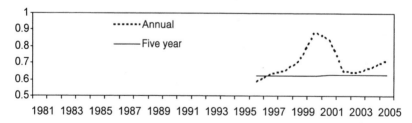

Fig. 1.3   Coefficient of variation of annual earnings and of five-year average earnings, 1981 to 2005, four cohorts of men: *A,* Men born 1950; *B,* Men born 1955; *C,* Men born 1960; *D,* Men born 1965

Source: Swedish register data.

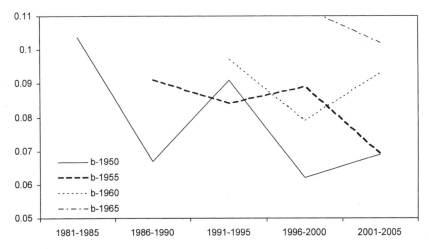

Fig. 1.4 Earnings mobility for cohorts of men born in 1950, 1955, 1960, and 1965
Source: Swedish register data.

10th percentile in 1990, or in two cases, an earlier period, and in 2003, or the latest period for which data was available from the OECD earnings database of full-time dependent employees, and it gives the percentage-point changes in earnings ratios. It ranks the countries by increasing inequality, and Sweden fits in the middle of the distribution: it had the sixth-largest increase in earnings ratios among the thirteen countries. Panel B records comparable earnings ratios and Gini coefficients from the Luxembourg Income Study (LIS), with the countries listed in order of increasing inequality in the earnings ratio in that data set. There are some striking inconsistencies between the OECD and LIS rankings: the OECD, for example, shows Finland with declining inequality, while the LIS shows it with rising inequality, and while the OECD has Danish inequality falling, the LIS shows it rising. Some of this difference may be due to differences in years covered, in treatment of part-time workers, and so on. For the purposes of this study, however, the LIS data place Sweden in a similar position as the OECD data. In terms of increases in the 90/10 earnings ratio, Sweden is tied for eighth out of nineteenth countries. In terms of increases in the Gini coefficients, Sweden is tied for third with the United States and Spain. Thus, Sweden's increase in inequality put it reasonably high in the ranking of countries by the magnitude of increased inequality.[11]

Even so, however, inequality was sufficiently low in Sweden so that the country remained one of the lowest inequality countries in the world. In table 1.3, Sweden has the lowest 90/10 ratio of earnings in the OECD data

11. Our data tell a different story than that of Smeeding (2002), who puts Sweden in the lower third or so of countries by increased inequality in the 1990s.

Table 1.3   **Level and changes in 90/10 ratios of earnings from 1990s to early 2000s in OECD and level and changes in 90/10 ratios of earnings and Gini coefficients in Luxembourg Income Study: late 1980s/early 1990s through 2000**

A. *OECD earnings database of full-time employees*

Countries in order of increasing inequality in OECD	90/10 ratio early year	90/10 ratio last year	Change
New Zealand, 1990–2003	2.34[a]	2.90	0.56[a]
Switzerland, 1990–2003	2.71	3.22	0.51
United States, 1990–2003	4.34	4.67	0.33
Denmark, 1990–2003	2.16	2.63	0.47
The Netherlands, 1985/1989–1955/1999	2.55	2.85	0.30
Sweden, 1990–2003	**2.01**	**2.30**	**0.29**
Germany, 1990–2002	2.76	3.04	0.28
Australia, 1990–2003	2.81	3.07	0.26
Italy, 1985/1989–1955/1999	2.29	2.40	0.11
United Kingdom, 1990–2003	3.41	3.50	0.09
Finland, 1990–2002	2.49	2.45	−0.04
France, 1990–2002	3.26	3.13	−0.13
Japan, 1990–2003	3.16	2.94	−0.22

B. *Luxembourg Income Study data: 1987 to 2000*

Countries and years covered in order of increasing inequality in LIS earnings ratio	90/10 earnings ratios			Gini coefficients		
	First year	Last year	Change	First year	Last year	Change
Spain, 1990–2000	3.96	4.69	0.73	.303	.336	.033
Belgium, 1988–2000	2.77	3.30	0.53	.232	.279	.047
Finland, 1987–2004	2.59	3.04	0.45	.209	.252	.043
Germany, 1989–2000	2.99	3.37	0.38	.257	.275	.018
Canada, 1987–2000	3.89	4.19	0.30	.283	.311	.028
Austria, 1987–2000	2.85	3.15	0.30	.227	.257	.030
Luxembourg, 1991–2000	2.97	3.25	0.28	.239	.260	.021
Sweden, 1987–2000	**2.71**	**2.96**	**0.25**	**.218**	**.252**	**.034**
Ireland, 1987–2000	4.23	4.48	0.25	.328	.313	−.015
Australia, 1989–2003	4.19	4.24	0.05	.304	.312	.008
Norway, 1991–2000	2.76	2.80	0.04	.223	.251	.028
United States, 1991–2004	5.65	5.68	0.03	.338	.372	.034
France, 1989–2000	3.46	3.45	−0.01	.287	.278	−.009
Italy, 1987–2000	4.49	4.47	−0.02	.332	.333	.001
United Kingdom, 1991–1999	4.67	4.57	−0.10	.336	.343	.007
The Netherlands, 1987–1999	2.94	2.78	−0.16	.256	.231	−.025
Switzerland, 1991–2002	3.62	3.37	−0.25	.307	.274	−.023
Denmark, 1987–2004	3.23	2.78	−0.45	.254	.228	−.026

Source: Panel A is tabulated from the OECD *Society at a Glance* (2006). Trends in earnings dispersions of full-time workers in the twenty OECD members and the changes from 1985/1989 to 1995/1999 for the Netherlands and Italy are from table 3.2 in the *OECD Employment Outlook* (2004). Panel B is tabulated from the Luxembourg Income Study, available at: http://www.lisproject.org/key-figures/key-figures .htm.

Table 1.3   (continued)

[a]New Zealand data is estimated as follows: OECD figures for all workers cover 1997 to 2003 and show an increase in the ratio from 2.56 to 2.90—a rise of 0.34 points. Separate data for men and women show an increase of 0.38 points in the 90/10 ratio for men from 1990 to 1997 and show an increase of 0.06 points in the 90/10 ratio for women. The data also show increases for men from 1990 to 2000 of 0.97 points and for women of 0.22 points. As a crude approximation, we take the average change in the ratios from 1990 to 1997 for the two genders and add 0.22 points to get the 0.56 points. This is of the same magnitude as the average change for the two genders from 1990 to 2003 of 0.60 points.

in 2003 and has the third-lowest 90/10 ratio of earnings in the LIS data set. It is tied for fifth with Finland in its Gini coefficient in the 2000 LIS data. Table 1.4 records additional measures of inequality circa 2000 from other sources: OECD earnings data published in the *Employment Outlook* (2004); ratios of 90/10 levels of disposable income from the LIS, earnings ratios from a study by Martins and Pereira (2004), Gini coefficients from the United Nations (UN) *Human Development Report* (2005), and other LIS measures. In all of these statistics, Sweden remains among the lowest inequality countries in the advanced world. Sweden ranges from second to fourth in having lower-income inequality. It has the second or third lowest 90/10 earnings ratio, behind Norway and Denmark in column (1), behind Norway in column (2), and behind Germany in column (3). It has the third-lowest Gini in column (4) and the fourth-lowest Gini in column (5). It is third in the fraction of persons whose disposable incomes place them below 50 percent of the median income in columns (6) and (7).

To see the extent to which the narrow wage dispersion affects incentives to invest in skill in Sweden relative to other advanced countries, we examined OECD data on the relative earnings for workers with tertiary education for twenty-two countries. In 2004, earnings for those with tertiary education relative to average earnings was 1.28 in Sweden, compared to 1.72 in the United States. This placed Sweden third lowest in relative earnings for university graduates among the countries. For "tertiary-type A and advanced research programmes," the relative income ratio was 1.39 in Sweden, compared to 1.81 in the United States.[12] Other OECD data confirm this picture. Estimating log earnings equations for twenty-one OECD countries for 2001, Boarini and Strauss (2007, table 1) report a coefficient for tertiary education relative to secondary education for men of 0.26 in Sweden (second lowest in the countries covered) and of 0.21 for women (the lowest), compared to 0.65 for men and 0.64 for women in the United States, which was the highest among the countries covered.

In short, despite the rise in inequality during the period of crisis and recovery, Sweden remained one of the lowest inequality countries in the world,

12. See table B-12.1, "Relative earnings of the population with income from employment," in the *OECD Science, Technology and Industry Scoreboard* (2007b).

Table 1.4 **Measures of earnings and income inequality in Sweden and other advanced economies and percent of persons in relative poverty: around 2000 (Sweden rank in parentheses)**

	90/10 ratios			Gini coefficients		Fraction in relative poverty	
	Earnings (OECD)	Disposable income (LIS)	Earnings (M and P)	Disposable income (UN HDR)	Disposable income (LIS)	All (LIS)	Kids (LIS)
Norway	1.96	2.80	2.21	25.8	25.1	0.064	0.034
Denmark	2.16[a]	3.15	2.39	24.7	—	—	—
Sweden	**2.23 (#3)**	**2.96 (#2)**	**2.08 (#2)**	**25.0 (#3)**	**25.2 (#4)**	**0.065 (#3)**	**0.042 (#3)**
Belgium	2.28[a]	3.31	—	25.0	27.7	0.080	0.067
Finland	2.36	2.90	2.53	26.9	24.7	0.054	0.028
Italy	2.40	4.48	2.67	36.0	33.3	0.127	0.166
Switzerland	2.69	3.34	2.53	33.1	28.0	0.077	0.089
Holland	2.85	2.98	2.83	30.9	24.8	0.073	0.098
Germany	2.87	3.29	1.45	28.3	26.4	0.083	0.090
Spain	—	4.78	—	—	34.0	—	—
Australia	2.94	—	—	35.2	—	—	—
Japan	2.99	—	—	24.9	—	—	—
France	3.07	—	—	32.7	—	—	—
United Kingdom	3.45	4.59	3.33	36.0	34.5	—	—
Austria	3.56[a]	3.37	2.28	30.0	26.6	0.077	0.078
Canada	3.65	3.95	—	33.1	30.2	0.114	0.149
Portugal	3.76[b]	—	4.58	38.5	—	—	—
Ireland	3.97	4.56	4.74	35.9	32.3	0.165	0.172
United States	4.59	5.45	3.45	40.8	36.8	0.170	0.219

Source: The OECD (2004, table 3.2), the Luxembourg Income Study (LIS), and the United Nations Development Program *Human Development Report* (UN HDR: 2005). Data for Spain and Greece are from Martins and Pereira (M and P; 2004, table 1).

[a]Data for Austria, Belgium, and Denmark are from 1995 to 1999.

[b]Data for Portugal are from 1990 to 1994.

with an exceptionally low wage gap between university and high school graduates. Inequality rose greatly in hours of work and employment, but the high social safety net partially offset the effects of this on family incomes.

1.2   Attitudes Toward Inequality/Incentives

How do Swedes view the incentive and inequity components of inequality described in our introduction? Are Swedes more or less sensitive to those components when compared to Americans and citizens in other countries, and if so, why?

Table 1.5 records the responses of persons to questions relating to inequality[13] from the 1999 International Social Science Program (ISSP) *Social Inequality III* survey.[14] By way of summary, the agree-disagree lines give the differences between the percentages that agree or that strongly agree with a statement and the percentages that disagree or that strongly disagree with it. The upper four panels give the responses to statements about the incentive component of inequality: whether people get rewarded for effort, whether differences in income are necessary for national prosperity, whether people get rewarded for skill, and whether study requires additional pay as an incentive. The data show that proportionately fewer Swedes believe in the incentive effects of inequality than do Americans. For instance, fewer Swedes than Americans agree or agree strongly that "people get rewarded for effort" and that people get "rewarded for skill," and more Swedes than Americans disagree strongly with the idea that differences in income are necessary for prosperity. But Swedish responses are similar to those for other advanced countries. The odd country is the United States, not Sweden.

The next three panels summarize responses to questions about the inequity component of inequality: whether inequality benefits the rich, whether differences in income are too large, and whether one must be corrupt to get to the top. In all of these cases, Swedes show more concern about the inequitable aspects of income inequality than do Americans, but again, the attitude of Swedes is not peculiar. Indeed, proportionately fewer Swedes than persons in the composite of other countries agree that inequality exists because it benefits the rich, that the income differences in their country are too large, and that you have to be corrupt to get on top. But Swedes are closer to others in their views than they are to those of Americans.

Where Swedes and the citizens of the other countries differ most from

13. These economies are Australia, Austria, Canada, Denmark, France, Germany (West), Great Britain, Japan, New Zealand, Northern Ireland, Norway, and Spain.

14. The ISSP is a cross-national collaboration on surveys covering topics important for social science research, which has the virtue that it asks the same questions of persons in different countries, facilitating cross-country analyses. In addition to the United States and Sweden, our analysis covers Australia, Austria, Canada, Denmark, France, Germany (West), Great Britain, Japan, New Zealand, Northern Ireland, Norway, and Spain as a group.

Table 1.5   **Attitudes of Swedes, Americans, and persons in other advanced countries toward the incentive and inequity components of inequality: 1999**

	People get rewarded for effort			Differences in income necessary for prosperity		
	Sweden	United States	Others	Sweden	United States	Others
Strongly agree	3	11	5	3	4	4
Agree	31	50	35	17	20	16
Neither	36	22	25	29	27	22
Disagree	20	9	25	31	31	35
Strongly disagree	5	2	7	15	8	17
Don't know	6	6	3	5	9	6
Agree-Disagree	**9**	**50**	**8**	**−26**	**−15**	**−32**

	People get rewarded for skill			Study requires additional pay		
	Sweden	United States	Others	Sweden	United States	Others
Strongly agree	3	15	6	19	21	27
Agree	35	55	43	50	37	44
Neither	37	16	23	16	13	11
Disagree	15	7	20	11	18	12
Strongly disagree	4	1	5	2	4	4
Don't know	6	6	3	3	7	3
Agree-Disagree	**19**	**62**	**24**	**56**	**36**	**55**

	Inequality benefits rich			Differences in income too large			Must be corrupt to get on top		
	Sweden	United States	Others	Sweden	United States	Others	Sweden	United States	Others
Strongly agree	16	12	24	29	23	36	4	4	8
Agree	42	32	44	41	38	41	14	12	20
Neither	21	24	14	18	20	12	29	22	20
Disagree	13	16	11	8	9	7	24	35	30
Strongly disagree	3	4	3	2	3	1	16	21	18
Don't know	8	11	4	1	7	3	13	6	5
Agree-Disagree	**42**	**24**	**54**	**60**	**49**	**69**	**−22**	**−40**	**−20**

	Government must reduce differences			Rich should pay more taxes		
	Sweden	United States	Others	Sweden	United States	Others
Strongly agree	23	10	25	16	20	25
Agree	35	22	35	59	39	50
Neither	22	24	16	22	30	19
Disagree	12	23	14	1	1	1
Strongly disagree	6	14	6	0	1	1
Don't know	3	7	5	2	8	4
Agree-Disagree	**40**	**−5**	**40**	**74**	**57**	**73**

Source: Tabulated from the 1999 ISSP *Social Inequality III* survey.

Americans is in their belief that government should intervene to reduce income differences. The two panels at the bottom of table 1.5 show a huge difference between Swedes and Americans in the belief that government must reduce income differences and that rich people should pay more taxes. Again, the attitudes of Swedes more closely resemble those of citizens in the other advanced countries than those of Americans.[15]

What might cause the wide differences in attitudes between Swedes and persons in most other advanced economies from those in the United States? There is growing evidence that attitudes toward fairness in economic trans-actions are hard-wired into human beings, with people favoring egalitarian splits of incomes in some circumstances, such as the ultimatum game, but it is hard to imagine some genetic basis for differences in attitudes toward inequal-ity. One appealing hypothesis is that the attitudes to some extent reflect eco-nomic reality: in the United States, the wide dispersion in earnings and high returns to skill should lead more people to believe that people are rewarded for effort and skill (because they are) than in Sweden and other countries, where the narrower distribution of earnings and lower returns to skill in fact means that people are rewarded less for skill and effort. The differences in attitudes also might be greatly influenced by social rhetoric—the U.S. story of the land of opportunity versus the Swedish story of egalitarianism.

1.2.1   Changes in Attitudes

Did Swedish views about inequality change in the 1990s, as inequal-ity rose? To the extent that attitudes toward inequality respond to exist-ing inequality, we would expect persons to become more tolerant toward inequality as it increases in society ("it is the way the world is"). On the other side, increases in inequality in a society where people are committed to more egalitarian outcomes might generate more negative attitudes toward increased inequality and a desire for government policies to reduce income differences more than in the past.

As a first step to seeing how attitudes in fact change, we contrast the responses of Swedes to the 1999 ISSP survey to their responses to the same questions in Stefan Svallfors's (1992) survey of Swedish attitudes toward inequality that, which became part of the 1992 ISSP *Social Inequality II* survey. Table 1.6 gives the results of this comparison.[16] Focusing on the difference between the proportion that agrees or agrees strongly and the proportion that disagrees or disagrees strongly with the statements, the data

---

15. As U.S. income inequality has risen, however, the Syracuse University Maxwell Poll (2007) has reported increased belief that income inequality is a serious problem and that government should do more to try to reduce it; available at: http://www.maxwell.syr.edu/campbell/programs/maxwellpoll.htm.

16. This table reports statistics for those who gave explicit answers, eliminating "don't know" responses. This causes a modest difference in the 1999 percentages from those in table 1.5. The way we treat "don't know" answers does not affect the findings in either case.

Table 1.6   Changes in attitudes to inequality in Sweden: 1991 to 1999

	Income differences too large		Income differences needed for prosperity		Inequality benefits rich	
	1991	1999	1991	1999	1991	1999
Strongly agree	24	28	5	3	21	17
Agree	35	42	25	17	32	44
Neither	22	18	31	29	25	22
Disagree	14	8	30	31	17	14
Strongly disagree	5	2	9	15	5	3
Agree-Disagree	**40**	**60**	**-9**	**-26**	**31**	**44**

	Rich should pay more taxes		Government should reduce income differences		People study to earn money	
	1991	1999	1991	1999	1991	1999
Strongly agree	14	16	17	24	25	20
Agree	62	60	36	36	47	52
Neither	23	22	18	22	14	16
Disagree	1	1	19	13	12	11
Strongly disagree	0	0	10	6	2	2
Agree-Disagree	**75**	**75**	**24**	**31**	**48**	**49**

Source: Tabulated from the ISSP (1992; 1999); the 1992 ISSP is based on Svallfors (1991).

tell a clear story. Over the 1990s, proportionately more Swedes became concerned with the adverse effects of inequality than with the incentive effects of inequality. The difference in the proportion who view income differences as too large rises from 40 points to 60 points, and the difference in the proportions who believe inequality benefits the rich rises from 31 points to 44 points, while the difference between those who think income differentials are needed for prosperity and those who do not falls from –9 points to –26 points. The proportions that agree and disagree that the rich should pay more taxes and the proportions that believe and do not believe that people study to earn money remain essentially constant, but the proportion that believes government should reduce income differences increases. In short, the rise in inequality reduced the proportion of Swedes attuned to the efficiency aspects of inequality and increased the proportion who favored policies to reduce inequality on these questions.

The 1991 and 2000 LNU surveys asked a different question on attitudes toward inequality: what people thought about "the idea of going in for a society where income differentials are small." On the basis of the ISSP results, we would expect that the proportion favoring a lower income differential society would rise, but the LNU data show a slight movement in the opposite direction. The fraction that thought that going for a small income differential society was very good fell modestly from 1991 to 2000, while the fraction who thought this was quite good and the fraction who thought it quite bad rose modestly.[17] The different pattern in the LNU than in the ISSP suggests that the precise wording of questions may cause different patterns of response across the surveys and thus makes us cautious about drawing any firm conclusions.

The ISSP surveys contain another set of questions that cast light on how attitudes toward inequality in Sweden have changed over time relative to attitudes in other countries during the 1990s rise of inequality. The ISSP asks respondents the pay they believe workers make in different occupations: "What do you think people in these jobs *actually earn*?" Respondents are also asked what they believe people should make: "How much do you think people in these jobs *ought to earn*?" These questions were asked for nine occupations in 1987 and for eleven occupations in 1992 and 1999.[18] Responses about the earnings people actually earn provide one way of assessing whether perceptions of income differences reflect actual differences among countries and over time.[19]

To analyze these data, we calculated *for each individual* the standard deviation of the ln (natural logarithm) earnings that they said people *earned* across occupations and the standard deviation of the ln earnings they said people *should earn* across occupations. The standard deviation of the ln earnings summarizes their responses into a single statistic that measures dispersion. Figure 1.5 displays the country averages of the standard deviations of the ln of actual earnings and of "should" earnings. Almost all of the data points fall below the 45 degree line. This indicates that regardless of the perceived level of dispersion of wages, respondents favor lower dispersion. A linear regression of the average standard deviation of the ln earnings that

17. Here are the tabulations:

The idea of going in for a society where income differentials is small

	2000	1991	Change
Very good	20	26	06
Quite good	32	29	03
Neither good nor bad	17	17	00
Quite bad	20	18	02
Very bad	07	07	00

18. The occupations are from the following list: bricklayer, doctor in general practice, bank clerk, shop owner, chairman of a large company, skilled worker in a factory, farm laborer, secretary, city bus driver, unskilled worker in a factory, and cabinet minister.

19. Asking respondents to report on earnings in specific occupations before asking them what they think people should make arguably grounds responses in reality more than do questions about inequality in general.

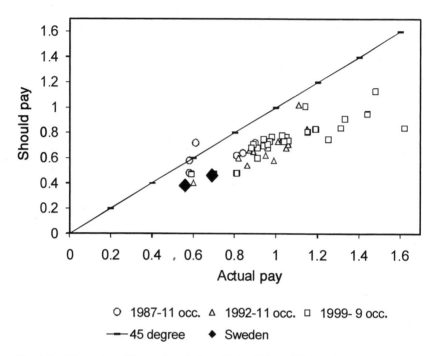

O 1987-11 occ. △ 1992-11 occ. □ 1999- 9 occ.

━━ 45 degree ◆ Sweden

Fig. 1.5   Dispersion of ln earnings believed "should be paid" in different occupations and the dispersion of ln perceived actual earnings, by country: 1987, 1992, and 1999

Source: Tabulated from the International Social Science Program (ISSP) surveys for 1987, 1992, and 1999. Sweden data are from Svallfors (1992) and the 1999 ISSP survey.

Note: The regression line:

$$\text{SD(LnShld)} = 0.11 + 0.61 \text{ SD(LnActual)} + \text{YDs} + 0.15 \text{ ComD } N = 52,$$
$$\quad\quad\quad (0.06) \quad\quad\quad\quad\quad\quad\quad\quad\quad\quad (0.07)$$

where LnShld is the natural log of the earnings that respondents believe should be paid in an occupation, LnActual is the natural log of the earnings that respondents believe is paid in an occupation, YDs are two year dummies, and ComD is a dummy for countries that were Communist in 1987—East Germany, Hungary, and Poland. The standard deviations (SD) are averages of standard deviations reported by all respondents from the country.

respondents believe should be paid on the average standard deviation of the ln earnings they believe people are actually paid fits the data reasonably well, with a slope of 0.61. This positive slope implies that as the perceived actual dispersion is larger, the dispersion people believe is appropriate rises, but at lower than a one-for-one rate.[20]

The data points for Sweden (denoted with the large diamond) fit the regression line. Persons in Sweden perceive (correctly) that the country has

20. Further analyses that treat individuals rather than country averages as observations yield similar results for the 1999 ISSP; they show no noticeable difference in the regression coefficients of the standard deviation of the ln pay that respondents say people should receive in an occupation on the standard deviation of the ln earnings that respondents believe people actually receive between Sweden, the United States, and other countries as a group.

a lower difference in earnings among occupations than persons in most other countries perceive in their countries. But low dispersion of perceived earnings notwithstanding, Swedes seem to want to narrow occupational pay differences even more. The 1999 observation for Sweden lies above the 1991 observation. (Sweden was not part of the 1987 ISSP *Social Inequality I* survey.) The higher dispersion for perceived actual pay fits with the reality of rising inequality in earnings shown in figure 1.1. The higher dispersion in the earnings that respondents think should be paid in the various occupations, however, is inconsistent with the responses about income inequality given in table 1.6, as it implies that as inequality rose, so too did tolerance of inequality. The way in which we measure the desire to reduce inequality evidently produces different patterns of response across the surveys.[21]

1.2.2   Satisfaction with Personal Outcomes

An alternative way to assess how increased inequality has impacted Swedish citizens is to relate their self-reported satisfaction with their living conditions, jobs, and wages or income before and after the economic recovery. People's feelings toward their personal situation may differ from attitudes toward what is happening in the economy as a whole. Ms. A might be doing personally well but may be troubled by inequality or unemployment in the country, while Mr. B might be having personal economic difficulties but may be satisfied with economic conditions broadly.

Table 1.7 tabulates the responses to five questions on the 1991 and 2000 LNU surveys relating to the satisfaction of individuals with their own circumstances. The responses to questions about the individuals' personal situations or changes in situation or life satisfaction do not vary much over time. Responses relating to job satisfaction and satisfaction with wages show declines in well-being and increased dispersion in these forms of personal well-being. There is a 10 percentage-point drop in the proportion very satisfied with their job and a large shift in the distribution of responses on wage satisfaction from very/rather satisfied to very/rather dissatisfied. To see whether the reduction in job and wage satisfaction are related to objective factors, we regressed them on the log of hourly wages and reported working conditions in 1991 and 2000, conditional on family conditions, age, gender, and education. The results, summarized in table 1.8, show that wages are strongly related to wage satisfaction, while measures of working conditions are closely linked to job satisfaction. The large coefficients on the log of hourly wages, combined with the rising standard deviation in the hourly wages, could help explain the increased dispersion in the responses

---

21. In calculations for the 1999 ISSP, we have found that persons who are more concerned about the adverse effects of inequality and less concerned about the incentive effects in the questions report smaller dispersions of earnings that they think should be paid across occupations. Thus, there is no inconsistency in attitudes among persons within the survey. The problem is in the trend across surveys over time.

Table 1.7   Satisfaction with living conditions, job, and wages: Nineteen- to sixty-five-year-olds

	Overall life		Job		Wages	
Satisfaction	1991	1999	1991	1999	1991	1999
Very good/satisfied	41	43	43	33	10	9
Rather good/satisfied	53	51	45	50	45	38
Neither good/satisfied nor bad/dissatisfied	4	4	9	11	22	22
Rather bad/dissatisfied	2	2	2	5	17	21
Bad/very dissatisfied	1	1	1	2	7	10
Good/satisfied-Bad/dissatisfied	**91**	**91**	**85**	**76**	**31**	**16**

Change in your situation	1991	1999	Daily life source of personal satisfaction	1991	1999
Improved	52	56	Yes, most often	58	57
More/less same	35	31	Yes, sometimes	35	36
Deteriorated	13	13	No	7	7
Improved-Deteriorated	**39**	**43**	**Yes-No**	**86**	**86**

Source: Tabulated from the Level of Living (LNU) surveys based on the following questions: (a) "We have now been through a lot of questions about your living conditions in different areas. How do you yourself view your own conditions? By and large, do you think that your situation is very good, rather good, rather bad, or very bad?" (b) "If you look back over the last ten years, do you think that your living conditions during this time have deteriorated, improved, or remained more or less the same?" (c) "Do you usually feel that your daily life is a source of personal satisfaction?" (d) "On the whole, how satisfied are you with your present job?" and (e) "How satisfied are you with your present wages (income from work)?" The questions were asked to those employed "last week"—that is, either employed or self-employed during the week preceding the interview. The sample sizes ranged from 3,473 to 4,527, depending on the year and question.

to the question about satisfaction with wages. The changes in the fraction of persons reporting different objective working conditions, however, are too small to explain much of the change in that variable on the basis of the estimated coefficients. Exploiting the longitudinal component of the LNU, we also examined changes in wage satisfaction and job satisfaction between 1991 and 2000 and obtained comparable results: a large coefficient on ln wages in the wage satisfaction equation, which implies that increases in the standard deviation of ln wages contributed to the increased dispersion in wage satisfaction.[22]

Because unemployment is a major depressing factor on happiness, the surprise in table 1.7 is the stability in life satisfaction, despite higher and longer unemployment between the two surveys.[23] We probe this finding fur-

22. The coefficient in the wage satisfaction equation on change in log wages was 1.681 (0.125). Changes in job conditions had modest coefficients on the work conditions variables.

23. The proportion of persons who were unemployed went from 7.0 percent in the 2000 LNU to 3.7 percent in the 1991 LNU, and the duration of unemployment went from 0.46 of a year to 1.61 years.

Table 1.8   Regression coefficients (standard errors) for the effect of working conditions, log wage, and demographic variables on job and wage satisfaction: Nineteen- to sixty-five-years of age

Variable	Sample mean (standard deviation)		Job satisfaction		Wage satisfaction	
	1991	2000	1991	2000	1991	2000
Job satisfaction	4.248	4.040				
	(0.804)	(.873)				
Wage satisfaction	3.317	3.092				
	(1.074)	(1.160)				
Log hourly wage	**4.344**	**4.700**	**.110**	**.132**	**1.243**	**1.460**
	(.290)	**(.310)**	**(.056)**	**(.059)**	**(.076)**	**(.076)**
Years of education	11.6	12.7	−.011	−.021	−.037	−.039
	(3.14)	(3.14)	(.005)	(.006)	(.007)	(.007)
Influence over job tasks	.466	.490	.141	.240	.075	.026
			(.028)	(.031)	(.038)	(.041)
Learn new things at the job	.485	.472	.281	.237	.016	.056
			(.028)	(.032)	(.038)	(.041)
Heavy lifting	.169	.154	−.024	−.105	−.171	−.166
			(.038)	(.045)	(.052)	(.059)
Sweaty at job	.227	.229	−.069	−.040	.028	−.160
			(.034)	(.040)	(.047)	(.052)
Mentally demanding	.493	.518	−.163	−.247	−.171	−.366
			(.027)	(.031)	(.038)	(.040)
Monotonous job	.182	.190	−.509	−.471	−.068	−.122
			(.038)	(.042)	(.052)	(.055)
Repetitive movements	.411	.461	−.040	−.026	−.040	.050
			(.030)	(.033)	(.041)	(.042)
Age	39.8	41.2	.0031	.0008	−.0012	−.0121
			(.0014)	(.0016)	(.0019)	(.0020)
Male	.500	.509	−.120	−.041	−.148	.086
			(.029)	(.033)	(.040)	(.043)
Married/cohabiting	.719	.723	.061	.021	−.065	−.046
			(.041)	(.044)	(.056)	(.057)
Divorced	.058	.058	.020	−.000	−.236	−.086
			(.068)	(.077)	(.093)	(.100)
Widowed	.010	.015	.174	.132	−.059	.054
			(.141)	(.134)	(.195)	(.174)
Any kids	.686	.690	−.025	−.023	−.167	−.102
			(.038)	(.041)	(.052)	(.053)
N	3,265	2,963	3,264	2,961	3,264	2,961
Adjusted R^2			.1520	.1302	.0941	.1778

Source: Tabulated from Level of Living surveys.

ther through multivariate regressions that link the level and duration of unemployment to how people assess their life situation/living conditions and their life satisfaction in 1991 and 2000, conditional on a variety of covariates. Table 1.9 summarizes the regression findings in terms of the coefficients on unemployment measured as a 0/1 variable and the coefficients on dummy variables for the duration of unemployment. Being unemployed has a sizeable adverse impact on both the persons' assessment of their life situation/living conditions and on their life satisfaction. There is no clear generalization to reach. Comparing the coefficients on unemployment in regressions (1) and (2), we see that unemployment had a larger impact in reducing the person's assessment of their living conditions in 2000 than in 1991. By contrast, in the life satisfaction regressions in columns (3) and (4), the impact of unemployment is lower in the 2000 survey than in the 1991 survey, which implies that the impact of unemployment on life satisfaction lessened.

The increase in the duration of unemployment suggests that comparisons of the unemployed in the two periods may be confounded by changes in the group that is unemployed. Regressions (5) through (8) give regression coefficients for the effect of being in the specified level of duration on the life situation/living conditions and life satisfaction measures. The impact of the duration of unemployment variables on life situation varies across the groups. There is a large drop in effect of unemployment on the person's own conditions for every group but those with less than 0.3 year of unemployment, with a particularly large drop for those with two years or more of unemployment. The impact of the duration of unemployment variables on life satisfaction are smaller in 2000 than in 1991, implying a substantial drop in unhappiness with unemployment at all durations. The data seem to suggest that people adjusted to unemployment between 1991 and 2000 so that with the higher rates, they were less impacted in their living conditions and in their life satisfaction, despite the longer durations of joblessness.

1.3 Inequality and Sweden's Position in Competitiveness

Sweden's recovery from the early 1990s recession was sufficiently strong so that by 2007/2008, it ranked number four in the World Economic Forum ranking of countries in global competitiveness. It was number two in the OECD ranking of countries by investment in knowledge.

Did the increased inequality help the recovery and improve the country's high position in competitiveness?

1.3.1 Inequality and Recovery

There are three criteria for assessing whether an increase in inequality is likely to be incentive increasing and thus a potential contributor to economic recovery.

Table 1.9   **Regression coefficients (standard errors) for estimates of the effect of unemployment and duration of unemployment on life situation/living conditions and life satisfaction: Nineteen to sixty-five-years of age**

| Measure of unemployment | Proportion in group | | Coefficients (standard errors) on unemployment measure | | | |
| | | | Life situation/living conditions | | Life satisfaction | |
	1991	2000	1991	2000	1991	2000
Regressions with unemployment status			(1)	(2)	(3)	(4)
Dummy for unemployment	.037	.070	−.249 (.053)	−.293 (.039)	−.212 (.049)	−.126 (.038)
Adjusted R^2			.0579	.0604	.0408	.0321
Regressions with dummy variables for duration of unemployment			(5)	(6)	(7)	(8)
< 0.3 year	.02298	.0264	−.099 (.066)	−.232 (.065)	−.150 (.062)	−.099 (.062)
0.3–0.6 year	.0067	.0117	−.439 (.122)	−.266 (.091)	−.224 (.114)	−.076 (.087)
0.6–1.0 year	.0022	.0064	−.620 (.206)	−.416 (.124)	−.243 (.193)	−.004 (.119)
1.0–2.0 years	.0038	.0079	−.297 (164)	−.159 (.109)	−.385 (.153)	−.141 (.104)
> 2 years	.0013	.0174	−1.086 (.267)	−.409 (.075)	−.664 (.250)	−.234 (.072)
Adjusted R^2			.0615	.0608	.0411	.0321

Source: Each regression included dummy variables for whether the worker was full-time or part-time, self-employed, a helper in the family, retired, a houseworker, or other, and for age, and sex. The life situation/living conditions outcome is based on the question, "We have now been through a lot of questions about your living conditions in different areas. How do you yourself view your own conditions? By and large, do you think that your situation is very good, rather good, rather bad, or very bad?" The life satisfaction question is, "Do you usually feel that your daily life is a source of personal satisfaction?"

First, the increase should affect observable incentives, such as returns to skill or wage differentials among firms or industries that signal workers to shift to the sectors with increased pay. If the increase shows up solely in higher returns to unmeasured factors (residuals), it is difficult for anyone to know what to do. Examining changes in mean earnings across groups by education, occupation, or industry shows that at least some of the increased inequality in Sweden in the 1990s was associated with changes among persons with observable characteristics. Studies of earnings patterns (Gustavsson 2006; Fredriksson and Topel, chapter 3 in this volume) find that the payoff to schooling increased over the 1990s, which created an incentive for additional school attendance that appears to underlie the observed increase in enrollment in higher education in the period (Fredriksson and Topel, chapter 3 in this volume).[24] Examining data by plant, Nordström Skans, Edin, and Holmlund (2009) found that a trend rise in between-plant wage inequality accounts for the entire increase in wage dispersion, which presumably would motivate workers to move from the lower-wage to the higher-wage plants.

Second, the increase should induce economic behavior that reduces the inequality. For instance, a rise in inequality to education should produce an increased investment in skills, and an increase in inequality among sectors or firms should induce workers to move where pay has increased. Nordström Skans, Edin, and Holmlund (2009) report modest positive correlations between entry rates and wage changes and the standard deviation of wages within plants, which suggest that the increases in wages across and within plants may have induced workers to shift toward workplaces with rising earnings relative to others.

Third, the increase should be associated with improved national economic outcomes. Lindquist (2005) and Nahum (2005) suggest that the moderate increases in skill differentials and inequality have helped raise economic growth and efficiency in Sweden. Lindquist related the increased income inequality between high- and low-skilled workers in Sweden to changes in relative demand due to the presence of capital-skill complementarity in production. Nahum finds that inequality within Swedish counties has a positive relation with the ensuing growth of the county's economy. While these studies must make bold assumptions for their estimates, their different data and methodologies suggest that at least some of the rise in inequality helped economic recovery.

On the other hand, it is difficult to see how increased inequality in hours worked can create incentive. Some of this increase is associated with sickness absenteeism. While workers who are not employed or who work relatively few hours may be doing productive work in the household, it is difficult to imagine that this compensates for the absence of market work. It also makes little sense for persons on sickness absence who are doing household work to be paid the benefits of someone who is truly incapacitated. Reductions of the inequality in hours worked would more likely enhance output.

1.3.2   Sweden in the Knowledge Economy

The doubling of the global labor force, due to China, India, and the ex-Soviet bloc joining the world economy, pressured advanced countries to invest heavily in higher education and research and development and in

---

24. Our estimated earnings equations from the 1991 and 2000 LNU surveys also found that the earnings of university graduates increased relative to that of less-educated workers. We also found that the relative earnings of experienced workers fell, which increased equality, but it is unclear if this is a reduction in skill prices or in institutionally determined seniority.

high-tech industries. A priori, some analysts might expect that Sweden's low inequality and modest gross wage premium to tertiary education would provide insufficient incentive for investments in schooling, so the country would lag behind in the supply of highly educated persons compared to economies with higher premium, and this would keep the country from the front ranks of the research and development (R and D) and technology frontier. To be sure, the relatively low cost of highly skilled Swedish workers would increase firms' demand for these workers, but the firms would face a supply constraint and would fall behind countries such as the United States, where the premium to university training is much higher. Nothing could be further from the truth.

Panel A of table 1.10 shows that Sweden is in the top rank of countries in investment in knowledge. It is number one in the world in R and D spending over GDP, number one in software investment over GDP, and number seven in higher education spending over GDP. Summing the three measures, the OECD's investment in knowledge indicator places Sweden in the second spot, only behind the United States.

The data on educational attainment in panel B suggest that the OECD measure of higher education spending understates Sweden's success in university education, particularly in science and engineering (S and E). Sweden is fourth in the world (after Japan, Korea, and Canada) in degrees granted per twenty-five- to thirty-four-year-olds. Sweden is second among OECD countries (behind Korea) in the share of degrees awarded in science and engineering. Its S and E share of degrees is more than twice the U.S. share. At the doctorate level, Sweden is number one in PhDs and in science and engineering PhDs granted per young person. If the United States had the Swedish rate of S and E PhDs per young person, it would be producing over 100,000 doctoral graduates in those disciplines.

What motivates so many young Swedes to invest in higher education? Even after the 1990s to mid-2000s increase in earnings inequality, pay differences between highly educated workers and less-educated workers were lower in Sweden than in the United States and most other countries, at both the tertiary and advanced research program levels. The increased earnings differential between university graduates and high school graduates in the 1990s and the high unemployment during and after the recession contributed to the *growth* of university enrollments in Sweden (Fredriksson and Topel, chapter 3 in this volume) but cannot account for the concentration on science and engineering or the extraordinary proportion of persons obtaining PhDs in science and engineering.

One factor that helps compensate for the lower labor market differentials is the low cost of attending universities. Students are eligible for grants and loans, with repayments that are income contingent, to help them through the student years. Indeed, for graduate studies, the norm is that the students are eligible to a wage at the level-of-living wage. But OECD estimates of internal rates of return to tertiary education (Boarini and Strauss 2007,

Table 1.10   Sweden compared to the United States, the Organization for Economic
                    Cooperation and Development Countries, and the European Union in
                    knowledge economy: 2004

A. *OECD investment in knowledge*

	R and D/GDP (rank of 18)	Software (rank of 18)	Higher education (rank of 18)	Investment in knowledge (rank of 18)
Sweden	3.98 (1)	1.54 (1)	0.93 (7)	6.44 (2)
United States	2.74 (4)	1.46 (2)	2.36 (1)	6.56 (1)
OECD	2.41	1.08	1.42	5.10
EU	2.02	0.80	0.79	3.62

B. *Young persons in higher education*

	Bachelor's/ 25–34 years old (rank of 30)	S and E share of Bachelor's (rank of 30)	PhDs/age (rank of 34)	S and E PhDs/ age (rank of 31)
Sweden	42.3 (4)	31.7 (2)	3.1 (1)	1.6 (1)
United States	39.1 (7)	14.7	1.3 (11)	0.3 (22)
OECD	31.0	21.2	1.3	0.5
EU19	—	23.4	1.4	0.6

C. *Scientific output*

	Scientific articles per capita (rank of 38)	Relative prominence of cited articles (rank of 39)	Patents/millions (rank of 32)
Sweden	1,143 (2)	0.86 (5)	72.3 (5)
United States	726 (31)	1.03 (2)	55.1 (8)
OECD	441	—	43.9
EU19	573	0.74	32.4[a]

Source: Panel A: OECD (2007b), figure A1.1, "Investment in knowledge as percent of GDP 2004." Panel B: OECD (2007a, 180), "Tertiary attainment for age group 25–34"; figure B1.2, "S&E degrees as a percentage of total new degrees"; and figure B1.1, "Graduate rates at the doctorate level." Panel C: OECD (2007b), figure D.5.1, "Scientific articles per million population 2003"; figure D1.4, "Triadic patent families per million population"; and figure D5.2, "Relative importance of scientific literature."

Note: "R and D" = research and development; "S and E" = science and engineering. Figure A2.1, "R&D intensity," compares R and D over GDP in thirty-three countries; Sweden ranks number one, while the United States ranks number seven. In this compilation, the Swedish R and D/GDP ratio is nearly twice that for the European Union and 70 percent higher than the OECD average.

[a]EU25.

figure 11) show that while this improves Sweden's ranking in returns and lowers the return to the United States, it still leaves Sweden in the bottom third of countries by rate of return. There are no readily available estimates of the return to graduate training across countries to see how Sweden fits on that margin.

Panel C in table 1.10 records measures of the output of Sweden's investment in scientific and engineering activity and research and development. In terms of research output, Sweden ranks second (after Switzerland) in terms of scientific articles published per capita. Citation indices per article place Sweden fourth in the world in the prominence of its published research. Finally, Sweden has a high number of patents measured per million inhabitants. When the share of Swedish companies with innovative activity is compared internationally, Swedish companies are above the average of EU countries.

Much of Sweden's investment in R and D is due to activities of the Swedish multinational firms, such as Ericsson, which conduct much of their research and development in the country, while locating the bulk of production outside the country. This would appear to be an economic response to the country's large supply of undergraduate and graduate degree recipients, particularly in science and engineering, and their relatively low cost, but it still leaves open the question of how the country has overcome the low pecuniary returns in order to induce so many young persons to obtain advanced research and other degrees.

Finally, it is Sweden's exemplary position in these and other measures of technological prowess, innovation, higher education and training, and business sophistication that underlie its position as the fourth-top country in the World Economic Forum *Global Competitiveness Report* (2008). By contrast, the competitiveness report gives Sweden lower marks for its high taxes and such labor market factors as flexibility of wage determination and hiring and firing practices. To some extent, however, these desirable and less-desirable aspects of the welfare state are intertwined: high taxes fund investments in higher education and research and development, which buttress innovativeness.

1.4   Conclusion

This chapter has examined the pattern of change and correlates of Sweden's national effort to produce egalitarian labor market outcomes and the interplay between the level and change in inequality and attitudes toward inequality. It has found the following:

1. Earnings and income inequality increased after the early 1990s recession, with smaller increases in income for persons at the bottom of the income distribution than for those higher in the distribution. Government safety net programs buttressed disposable income for those with low incomes during the 1990s recession.

2. Despite the increase in inequality, Sweden remained one of the most egalitarian economies in the world. The rise in inequality raised earnings for identifiable groups and seems to have contributed to economic recovery.

3. The low level of inequality and labor market returns to skill notwithstanding, Sweden moved to the top of the league tables in knowledge-intensive activities. Five times as many Swedes obtained PhDs in science and engineering as Americans relative to the population, and Sweden was the world leader in R and D over GDP. These achievements highlight the ability of Sweden to overcome some of the incentive problems of a welfare state.

4. With respect to attitudes, Swedes are more attuned to the inequity face of inequality than to the incentive face of inequality than are Americans. But Swedish attitudes are closer to those of persons in most other countries. It is the American attitudes that are divergent.

5. Proportionately more Swedes expressed concern over the inequity of inequality after the rise in inequality in the 1990s than in the past, but there are sufficient differences in changes among measures of attitudes to rule out any firm conclusions about how the recession and recovery affected how people feel toward inequality.

6. Swedes expressed greater dissatisfaction with wages and conditions at work during the 1990s, but the rise in unemployment did not reduce overall subjective well-being, seemingly because individuals adapted to higher levels of unemployment.

Perhaps the most intriguing question that emerges from our analysis is how Sweden managed to reach the top of world tables in the proportion of young persons gaining PhDs and bachelor's degrees and in competitiveness, with only a moderate increase in earnings inequality and low return to tertiary education. Could it be that limited pecuniary incentives motivate Swedes to distinguish themselves in other productive ways? Or, could it be that in a highly egalitarian society, seemingly small changes in inequality can motivate people more than they might in an economy with a wider dispersion of overall earnings? Whichever the reason, Sweden did well in the inequality front in its recovery from the early 1990s economic disaster.

References

Aaberge, R., A. Björklund, M. Jäntti, M. Palme, P. J. Pedersen, N. Smith, and T. Wennemo. 2002. Income inequality and income mobility in the Scandinavian countries compared to the United States. *Review of Income and Wealth* 48 (4): 443–69.

Björklund, A., T. Eriksson, M. Jäntti, O. Raaum, and E. Österbacka. 2002. Brother correlations in earnings in Denmark, Finland, Norway, and Sweden compared to the United States. *Journal of Population Economics* 15: 757–72.

Björklund, A., and R. Freeman. 1997. Generating equality and eliminating poverty: The Swedish way. In *The welfare state in transition: Reforming the Swedish model,* ed. R. B. Freeman, R. Topel, and B. Swedenborg, 33–78. Chicago: University of Chicago Press.

Björklund, A., and M. Jäntti. 1997. Intergenerational income mobility in Sweden compared to the United States. *American Economic Review* 87 (5): 1009–18.

Boarini, R., and H. Strauss. 2007. The private internal rates of return to tertiary education. OECD Working Paper no. 591. Paris: Organization for Economic Cooperation and Development.

Burkhauser, R., and J. G. Poupore. 1997. A cross-national comparison of permanent inequality in the United States and Germany. *Review of Economics and Statistics* 79 (1): 10–17.

Devroye, D., and R. Freeman. 2002. Does inequality in skills explain inequality of earnings across advanced countries? CEP Discussion Paper no. 0552. London: Center for Economic Performance, November.

Gustavsson, M. 2006. The evolution of the Swedish wage structure: New evidence for 1992–2001. *Applied Economics Letters* 13 (5): 279–86.

———. 2007. The 1990s rise in Swedish earnings inequality: Persistent or transitory? *Applied Economics* 39 (1): 25–30.

International Social Science Program (ISSP). 1987. *Social Inequality.* Available at: http://www.issp.org/.

———. 1992. *Social Inequality II.* Available at: http://www.issp.org/.

———. 1999. *Social Inequality III.* Available at: http://www.issp.org/.

Lindquist, M. J. 2005. Capital-skill complementarity and inequality in Sweden. *Scandinavian Journal of Economics* 107 (4): 711–35.

Luxembourg Income Study (LIS). Available at: http://www.lisproject.org/keyfigures.htm.

Martins, P., and P. T. Pereira. 2004. Does education reduce wage inequality? Quantile regression evidence from 16 countries. *Labour Economics* 11 (3): 355–71.

Maxwell School, Campbell Public Affairs Institute, Syracuse University. 2007. *The Maxwell Poll: Civic engagement and inequality.* Available at: http://www.maxwell.syr.edu/campbell/programs/maxwellpoll.htm.

Nahum, R.-A. (2005). Income inequality and growth: A panel study of Swedish counties 1960–2000. Working Paper no. 2005:8. Uppsala University, Department of Economics. Available at: http://ideas.repec.org/p/hhs/uunewp/2005_008.html.

Nordström Skans, O., P.-A. Edin, and B. Holmlund. 2009. Wage dispersion between and within plants: Sweden 1985–2000. In *The structure of wages: An international comparison,* ed. E. Lazear and K. Shaw, chap. 7. Chicago: University of Chicago Press.

Organization for Economic Cooperation and Development (OECD). 2004. *OECD employment outlook 2004.* Paris: OECD.

———. 2005. *Economic survey of Sweden 2005.* Paris: OECD.

———. 2006. *Society at a glance: OECD social indicators.* Paris: OECD.

———. 2007a. *OECD factbook 2007: Economic, environmental and social statistics.* Paris: OECD.

———. 2007b. *OECD science, technology and industry scoreboard 2007: Innovation and performance in the global economy.* Paris: OECD.

Shorrocks, A. 1978. Income inequality and income mobility. *Journal of Economic Theory* 19 (2): 376–93.

Smeeding, T. 2002. Globalization, inequality and the rich countries of the G-20: Evidence from the Luxembourg Income Study (LIS). LIS Working Paper no. 320. Luxembourg: Luxembourg Income Study, July.

Solon, G. 2002. Cross-country differences in intergenerational earnings mobility. *Journal of Economic Perspectives* 16 (3): 59–66.

Svallfors, S. 1992. Attitudes to inequality 1991: A Swedish survey. SND manuscript no. 0297. Göteborg: Swedish National Data Service, November.
United Nations Development Program. 2005. *Human development report 2005.* Available at: http://hdr.undp.org/en/reports/global/hdr2005/.
World Economic Forum. 2008. *Global competitiveness report 2007–2008.* Available at: http://www.weforum.org/en/initiatives/gcp/Global%20Competitiveness%20 Report/index.htm.

Policies Affecting Work Patterns and Labor Income for Women

Ann-Sofie Kolm and Edward P. Lazear

2.1 Introduction

Taxes on labor income reduce the incentive for women to work. Child care subsidies, on the other hand, increase the incentive for women with children to work. Given the taxes on labor income, it may improve welfare to introduce subsidies or tax relief on substitutes for mothers' time in the household. However, ten years ago, Sherwin Rosen argued that the child care subsidies in Sweden were inefficiently high from a welfare perspective (Rosen 1997). He noted that the subsidy, in addition to encouraging labor supply, also distorts the consumption choice between child care services and other types of goods. By making the relative cost of child care services cheaper, the subsidy stimulates a socially excessive consumption of child care, at the expense of other types of goods. Finding the most efficient child care subsidy is a matter of balancing the distortion on the consumption mix with the tax-induced labor supply distortion (see Rosen 1997; Sorensen 1997; and Kleven 2004).

Ann-Sofie Kolm is an associate professor of economics at Stockholm University. Edward P. Lazear is the Morris Arnold Cox Senior Fellow at the Hoover Institution, the Jack Steele Parker Professor of Human Resources Management and Economics at the Graduate School of Business, Stanford University, and a research associate of the National Bureau of Economic Research.

Our work follows on that initiated by Sherwin Rosen. Sherwin was a truly insightful economist, who thought about economic issues deeply. His instincts were superb, and he had the ability to see the essence of the problem. His early work on Swedish family programs laid the groundwork for our thinking. We are indebted to him for inducing us to work on what is a very important issue, and we miss his continued guidance. In addition, we want to thank Birgitta Swedenborg, Richard Freeman, Annette Bergemann, Rickard Eriksson, Anders Forslund, Bertil Holmlund, Alan Krueger, Mats Persson, Nina Smith, Marianne Sundström, Bob Topel, and the seminar participants at the National Bureau of Economic Research/Center for Business and Policy Studies meetings in Boston and Stockholm.

In this chapter, we analyze the effects of child care subsidies and other policies on female labor supply decisions in a life-cycle context that has not been fully considered in the previous literature. Our starting point is that a woman's labor market decision today may affect her standard of living later in life. Consider, for example, a married woman who chooses to devote all of her time to family and children, eschewing market work in the expectation that she will remain with her husband for her entire life. If her marriage dissolves, she will be without the skills necessary to earn a decent living in the labor market. Specializing in household production was the wrong decision. Even if women took into account the possibility of being single later in life, which would lead them to do some market work as insurance against the family breakup, those investing little in work skills who experienced marital breakup would end up poor and then may require social support. Knowing that social assistance will cushion the blow to women who find themselves without their husband's income, moreover, women will likely choose to work too little in the market from a social perspective. The implication is that previous analyses have understated the value of policies such as child care that are designed to encourage women to work.

We consider child care subsidies and three other policies that impact women's labor supply: paid parental leave, in-work benefits, and tax relief on substitutes for household goods and services. Child care subsidies and paid parental leave have long been studied as cornerstones of the Swedish welfare state, while the last two policies are relatively new, with little attention to their impact on women with children. Our measures of labor supply are labor force participation, work time, and time in parental leave, based on data from the labor force surveys. We develop a new model to examine the impact of the policies on the work outcomes, and we then link the model to observed behavior. We conclude by showing that policy instruments beyond child care subsidies could stimulate the labor supply of women with children as effectively as child care subsidies would, without inducing the overconsumption of child care services that troubled Rosen.

2.2   Labor Supply of Women and Women with Children

To begin, table 2.1 summarizes the employment patterns for women and men in Sweden, and by way of comparison, in the United States. In the developed world, Sweden's family policies are among the most generous, and the average tax rate and benefits when not working are among the highest, while the U.S. family policies, taxes, and benefits are among the lowest, giving us a sharp contrast.

The table shows that labor force participation among women is higher in Sweden than in the United States but that American women are more

Table 2.1   **Employment patterns for men and women in Sweden and the United States, ages sixteen to fifty-four: 2005**

	Work hours/ population	Work hours/ present workers	Present workers/ employed	Employed/ labor force	Labor force/ population
Women (Sweden)	19.0	33.3	0.81	0.94	0.78
Women (United States)	21.5	33.1	0.95	0.95	0.72
Men (Sweden)	26.1	39.3	0.87	0.93	0.82
Men (United States)	29.6	38.3	0.97	0.95	0.84

Source: The labor force surveys, Arbetskraftsundersökningar (AKU) for Sweden, and the Current Population Survey (CPS) for the United States. The AKU went through some changes in 2005; see: www.scb.se.

Note: The measures of average actual weekly work hours of those who are present at the workplace (column [2]) is based on the age group sixteen to sixty-four for Sweden and the United States. The work hours/present workers for the United States is based on March 2005 and not the yearly number.

likely to be at work at any given time. Multiplying the first column in table 2.1 by the total number of weeks per year, we calculate the annual average work hours in the two societies. The average annual work hours of women aged sixteen to fifty-four in Sweden is 988, compared to 1,118 in the United States. For women and men aged sixteen to fifty-four, average annual hours are 1,173 in Sweden and 1,329 in the United States. These numbers are comparable with what is reported in other studies (see Freeman and Schettkat 2005).

From the mid-1960s until the early 1990s recession, female labor force participation in Sweden increased dramatically. Since then, female participation has been stable, with only cyclical variations. In contrast, male labor force participation trended down modestly before the recession but has been stable, except for cyclical changes since the beginning of the 1990s. Women's labor force participation at 80 percent is almost as high as that of men at 85 percent.

Women with children have high rates of labor force participation in Sweden, although the rate is slightly lower for mothers with small children (figure 2.1). However, some of this difference may reflect different measurement protocols. Swedish statistics count women who are on paid parental leave from a job as employed. Because parental leave is popular in Sweden, with an average time on paid parental leave of ten months, and because fathers take a modest share of the family's paid parental leave (20 percent in 2006, up from 10 percent in 2000), this biases female participation upward relative to that in the United States. For a better comparison, we need to redefine women on parental leave as being out of the labor force in Sweden. As that is not possible in the aggregate labor force survey data, we treat all women who have children below one year of age as being on parental leave and out of the labor force. This is crude but realistic, as more than 80 percent of mothers who have a child younger

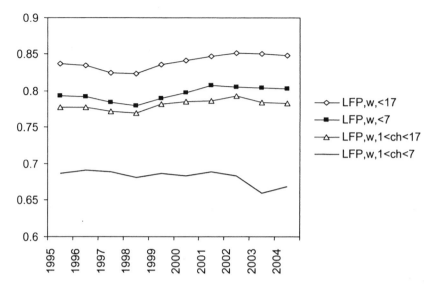

Fig. 2.1   Labor force participation rate (labor force/population; LFP) for women with children (children less than seventeen years old) and for women with small children (children less than seven years old)

Source: The labor force surveys (AKU), Statistics Sweden.

Note: The two lower graphs account for women with children below one year who are on parental leave and defined as out of the labor force.

than one year old are not present at the workplace during the week of measurement.[1] Figure 2.1 reveals that this correction substantially reduces participation rates.

Parental leave is one reason to be absent from work, but there are also other reasons, such as vacation, sick leave, sick children, and so forth. Figure 2.2 shows the employment rate and the rate of presence at the workplace for women with children. Counting only women who were present at the workplace sometime during the week of measurement, the rate falls to around 50 percent for mothers with small children.

Finally, table 2.2 shows that even if we assume that all women in Sweden who have a child younger than one year of age are on parental leave and are counted as being out of the labor force, women with children have higher labor force participation in Sweden than in the United States. There is a real behavioral difference in the differing participation of women with children in the United States and Sweden.

1. Moreover, we know that mothers take an average of about ten months of paid parental leave (Ekberg, Eriksson, and Friebel 2005). Additionally, we know that mothers tend to lengthen their maternity leave by using the low flat rate paid parental leave (Westerlund, Lindbald, and Larsson 2005).

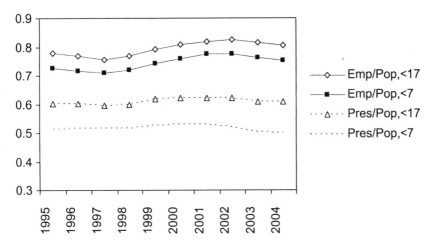

Fig. 2.2   Swedish female employment and presence at the workplace relative to population by category
Source: The labor force surveys (AKU), Statistics Sweden.

Table 2.2   **Labor force participation as percent in labor force of women and men (ages sixteen to sixty-four) by age of youngest child in household in Sweden and the United States: March 2005**

	With child age < 17	With child age < 7	All	With child age < 17 and > 1	With child age < 7 and > 1
Women (Sweden)	84	81	74	78	67
Women (United States)	71	63	69	—	—
Men (Sweden)	93	94	78	—	—
Men (United States)	94	96	81	—	—

Source: The labor force surveys, the CPS (United States), and AKU (Sweden).

Note: The first two columns show the labor force participation rate (labor force/population) for women and men with children (children less than seventeen years old for Sweden and less than eighteen years old for the United States) and for women and men with small children (children less than seven years old in Sweden and less than six years old in the United States). The fourth and fifth columns assume that women with children below one year of age are on parental leave and are defined as out of the labor force. Dashed cells = not applicable.

2.2.1   Working Time

Women are less likely to work full-time than men, and women with children, especially those with small children, are less likely to work full-time than those without children (see figure 2.3). Comparing Sweden and the United States, table 2.3 indicates that women with children work less than women without children in both countries, while table 2.4 shows a similar pattern in hours worked per week. To see whether the lower work time of

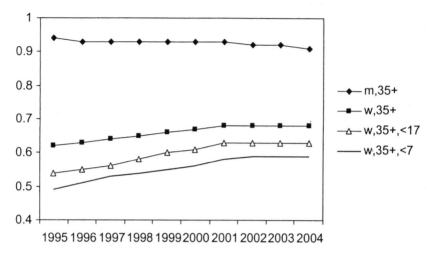

Fig. 2.3   **The share working more than thirty-five hours a week for men, women, women with children less than seventeen years old, and women with children less than seven years old**
Source: The labor force surveys (AKU), Statistics Sweden.

Table 2.3   **Percentage of persons working part-time in total employment by category: 2004**

	Women				Men		
	No children	One child	Two or more children	Total	No children	With children	Total
Sweden	14.6	16.7	22.2	17.9	5.2	3.4	4.3
United States	10.1	15.8	23.6	14.6	3.5	1.8	2.7

Source: Women at Work: An Economic Perspective (Boeri, Del Boca, and Pissarides 2005).

women with children is due to mothers reducing their working time, it is necessary to use microdata. Kennerberg (2007) does this, comparing the working time of women before and after they have a child to their childless counterparts. Prior to childbirth, 90 percent of women worked in a full-time job, just as women without children did. After the birth of the first child, about 10 percent of mothers reduced their work time when returning to work after their parental leave, whereas women who did not have a child increased their work time slightly over the same period.

While women are more likely to work part-time after having children, the reverse is true for men. This suggests that there is some substitutability of males for female work time and/or that men with children feel more compelled to earn instead of taking leisure. Selection into marriage could also be an explanation, as men who are likely to be part-timers may not get married

Table 2.4   Female and male actual average weekly work hours among those who worked in Sweden and the United States, ages sixteen to sixty-four: March 2005

	Actual work hours
Sweden	
Women	31.2
Women with child age < 7	28.7
Men	36.5
Men with child age < 7	36.5
United States	
Women	33.1
Women with child age < 6	30.6
Men	38.3
Men with child age < 6	41.5

Source: The labor force surveys, AKU (Sweden), and the CPS (United States).
Note: The numbers are average hours worked in preceding week for the U.S. sample. In Sweden, they are the actual hours worked among those who worked.

to the same extent as others. We do not know of any longitudinal study that differentiates these effects for men.

2.2.2   Work Incentives and Single Women with Children

The work behavior of single women with children is also important in female labor supply and in the level of poverty. Families with a single female parent and no male parent are disproportionately represented in poverty. In countries where female labor force participation is high, the share of poor among single mothers is also relatively low.[2] What are the incentives to work for single women with children? How responsive is this group to incentives?

An important measure of work incentives is the replacement rate when not working. In most countries, this replacement rate is higher at lower-income levels, where single mothers are overrepresented. For Sweden, Flood, Pylkkänen, and Wahlberg (2007) calculate the average replacement rate for single mothers on social assistance in 1999 to be 91 percent for a half-time job and 79 percent for a full-time job. Andrén (2003) and Flood, Pylkkänen, and Wahlberg (2007) have estimated structural static models of labor supply for single mothers that suggest that Swedish single mothers do respond positively to increased returns to work. Moreover, the labor supply elasticities are significantly larger for single mothers than for other groups. Flood, Hansen, and Wahlberg (2004) estimate a structural static model of household labor supply to capture labor supply among two-parent families in Sweden. We summarize in table 2.5 the estimated elasticities.

2. See Nyberg (2005) and Datta Gupta, Smith, and Verner (2006).

Table 2.5   The labor supply elasticity of single mothers, women, and men in Sweden

	Single mothers	Women	Men
Labor supply elasticity	0.62–0.77[a]	0.1[b]	0.05[b]

[a]Flood, Pylkkänen, and Wahlberg (2007) and Andrén (2003).
[b]Flood, Hansen, and Wahlberg (2004).

2.2.3 Fertility

In the 1950s through the 1970s, countries with high fertility had low rates of labor participation for women, but in the 1980s through the 1990s, this pattern reversed itself. Sweden and the United States, in particular, combined high rates of female participation with high fertility for an advanced country (figure 2.4). During the crisis years in the beginning of the 1990s, the fertility rate in Sweden dipped, but the rate is still high and has begun to catch up to its old levels. Figure 2.4 records the total fertility rate for Sweden and the United States. Because Sweden's large welfare state requires tax revenues from a working population, combining work and fertility may be more important for Sweden's success than for that of the United States.

2.3 Policies that Affect Participation of Women with Children

We consider next the four welfare state policies that are most relevant to the participation of women with children.

2.3.1 The Paid Parental Leave System

Since 1955, employed Swedish women have had the right to paid maternal leave by way of the social insurance system. Table 2.6 provides a description of the parental leave scheme since 1995. In 1974, Sweden became the first country to replace the maternity leave system with a parental leave system, where the same rules for fathers and mothers applied. Parental leave initially covered six months of payment, but it was gradually extended over the years to cover fifteen months by the year 1990. In 1993, parents shared 360 days, with a compensation corresponding to 90 percent of gross earning up to a ceiling and another ninety days at the guaranteed flat rate of sixty Swedish kronor (SEK) per day.

The Swedish parental leave system is unique in terms of generosity and flexibility. Government expenditures on paid parental leave is about 17 billion SEK, or about 0.7 percent of gross domestic product (GDP). Parents have the legal right to take parental leave for up to eighteen months without the risk of losing their jobs. Parents can use their days of paid parental leave in a flexible way until the child becomes 8 years old. In addition, parents have the legal right to reduce their working time to 75 percent of a normal work week at the workplace until the child turns 8 years old. In 1995, the

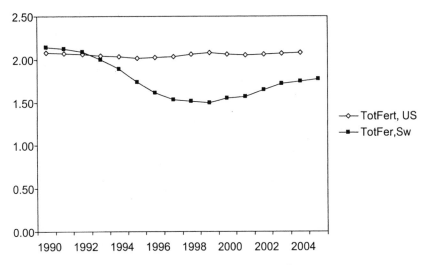

Fig. 2.4 Total fertility rates for Sweden and the United States

Table 2.6   The parental leave scheme

Year	Total days	Reserved/ parent	Duration	Replacement rate (%)	Ceiling (*PBA)	PBA
1995	450	30	360	80	7.5	35,700
1996	450	30	360	75	7.5	36,200
1997	450	30	360	75	7.5	36,300
1998	450	30	360	80	7.5	36,400
1999	450	30	360	80	7.5	36,400
2000	450	30	360	80	7.5	36,600
2001	450	30	360	80	7.5	36,900
2002	480	60	390	80	7.5	36,900
2003	480	60	390	80	7.5	38,600
2004	480	60	390	80	7.5	39,300
2005	480	60	390	80	7.5	39,400
2006[a]	480	60	390	80	10	39,700
2007	480	60	390	80	10	40,300
2008	480	60	390	80	10	41,000

Source: Bergemann and van den Berg (2006) and information from publications of the National Social Insurance Board. See: http://www.forsakringskassan.se/.

Note: The daily flat compensation for the ninety days has been 60 SEK from 1995 to 2005 and 180 SEK from July 1, 2006. The price base amount (PBA) is a yearly adjusted amount used, among other things, to ensure that various benefits do not decline in value because of an increase in the general price level (inflation).

[a]The ceiling was raised for children born after July 1, 2006.

government introduced the so-called daddy month, which required one month of the paid parental leave to be used by each parent. In practice, fathers could no longer transfer all their paid parental leave to the mother. Unless at least one month was used by the father, it could not be used by either parent. In 2002, a second father quota was implemented. The reform reserved two months for each parent. At the same time, the total time of entitlement to paid parental leave for the family increased by thirty days. In practice, this implied that an extra month available only for fathers was added to the existing paid parental leave scheme.

2.3.2   Child Care Subsidies

Publicly provided child care was introduced in the mid-1960s. The pressure on municipalities to provide day care became larger in the mid-1970s, and by 1983, publicly provided day care covered 52 percent of preschool children. By 2004, over 80 percent of preschool children were in public day care, and nearly 80 percent of children aged six to nine years were enrolled in after-school centers.

Gradually increasing fees for child care in the 1990s and differences in fees across municipalities led the government to impose a ceiling on fees, the maximum fee system, in 2002. The reform fixed the fees for child care at a certain percent of parental income and specified a maximum cost to the household.[3] The maximum fee system reduced differences in fees across municipalities and cut the child care fee for most families. The share of child care costs covered by private fees fell from around 20 percent to around 10 percent.

From 2001 to 2003, the program was expanded to allow the children of parents who were unemployed and on parental leave the right to attend preschool at least fifteen hours per week. Universal preschool for four- and five-year-olds was also introduced. Although preschool is not compulsory, the municipalities are obliged to provide places in preschool for the children of parents who wish it.

The average cost per child in preschool was almost 96,000 SEK in 2004. The total cost for preschool in 2004 was about 34 billion SEK, or about 1.3 percent of GDP.

2.3.3   In-Work Benefits

Following the lead of the United States and the United Kingdom, many industrialized countries have adopted some kind of in-work benefit[4]—a ben-

3. In 2005, the child care fee for a family with one child in day care was 3 percent of family income, with a maximum fee of 1,260 SEK per month. The fee for the second child was 2 percent of family income, with a maximum fee of 840 SEK per month. For the third child, the fee was 1 percent of family income, with a maximum fee of 420 SEK a month. There was no fee for the fourth child.
4. Belgium, Canada, Denmark, Finland, France, Ireland, the Netherlands, and New Zealand now have such systems.

efit or tax credit conditioned on labor income that aims to improve work incentives and reduce poverty. In January 2007, Sweden also introduced a system of in-work benefits in the form of a tax credit for the employed. The tax credit became more generous in January 2008 and January 2009. The tax credit, in combination with a general income tax allowance, implies that no tax needs to be paid on labor income up to yearly earnings of about 39,000 SEK. This can be compared to the median income, which is about 220,000 SEK per year. Then, about 25 percent of labor income earned on top of this limit is tax exempt, until a yearly income level of 116,000 is reached. For income above this limit, only about 6.5 percent of labor income is tax exempt. The maximum tax allowance is reached when the yearly labor income is about 300,000 SEK. The maximum tax credit amounts to about 18,000 SEK per year. The credit is not phased out, and it is more generous for workers above age sixty-five.

2.3.4   Tax Relief for Household Substitutes

A number of countries in Europe—Austria, Belgium, Denmark, Finland, and France—have introduced systems of subsidies or tax relief on the purchase of substitutes for household services. After a long debate, in July 2007, Sweden introduced the benefits of tax relief on household services, including house cleaning, laundry, ironing, gardening, and babysitting. As long as the service is carried out within the home, half of the labor costs of the substitute labor up to a ceiling is deductible from the income tax payments of the buyer.

2.4   A Model of Female Work Behavior

How have Sweden's family policies in the form of parental leave and child care subsidies affected women's labor supply and their economic situation? How might the more recent changes of in-work benefits and tax relief for household services affect these outcomes?

We examine these questions in the context of a small theoretical model of female decision making. This section gives a nontechnical presentation of the model and summarizes the main results. The appendix contains details.

The model is set in two periods. In the first period, women are married. In the second period, there is an exogenous probability that the marriage dissolves. At the beginning of the first period, the woman makes her career choice: allocating available time into market work and family work. As the allocation of time also has consequences for the future, she takes into account the possibility that the marriage may dissolve in period two when making her period-one time allocation decision. Viewing labor supply in the first period as an investment, we let the woman's labor supply in the first period also determine her supply in the second period. This assumption captures the fact that the decision to choose a weak labor market attachment early in life is likely to induce a lower income in the future.

Women derive utility from general goods consumption and from the consumption of a family good. The family good can be produced in the household by the use of own time, or it can be purchased in the market. These are perceived to be substitutes, although not necessarily at a one-to-one ratio. The payoff from investing time in the family is the utility the home-produced family good yields. The payoff from investing time in market work is market income net of taxes. We use the model to predict consequences of changing each of the four policies described in section 2.3 for the behavior or poverty of women with children.

2.4.1   Paid Parental Leave

Increased generosity in paid parental leave should reduce women's investment in a more market-oriented career. This is because there is a direct negative effect on market investment when the payments for family time increase. In addition, the increased taxation that funds the leave will have a negative effect on work incentives. We expect poverty among divorced women to increase, because women should invest more in a family-oriented career, and because the reform requires higher taxes.

The effect of the first daddy-month reform in 1995, which cut the leave time for mothers, depends on whether mothers choose to exhaust the paid parental leave periods. The reform is more likely to increase female labor supply if women exhaust their leave periods. The second daddy-month reform in 2002 added an extra month of parental leave, which, in practice, was only available for fathers. Counterintuitively, this tends to reduce women's investment in market-oriented careers. The reason is that an increase in the father's time at home increases the female spouse's consumption of the family good, which induces her to buy less care time on the market. In fact, she reduces her market purchases of the family good by more than the father's increased contribution. The reason for this is that the reform needs to be financed. An increase in the paid home time for fathers requires increased tax rates to finance the reform, which reduces the incentives to supply market work. Therefore, female market work is reduced, which implies that she works more in the household in response to the father's increased contribution of the family good. The marginal care of children is provided by market-supplied child care rather than by the mother, whose time is inframarginal. It is the father's time that substitutes for market purchases of child care—not for the mother's time. The reduction in market demand for child care, coupled with the tax effect, causes female market time to decline with the second reform. Poverty among divorced women increases, both because women invest more in family-oriented careers, and because the reform requires higher taxes.

2.4.2   Child Care Subsidies

Introducing a child care subsidy should increase women's time in the market and reduce poverty among divorced women, provided women finance a minor share of the government expenditures on the child care subsidy. The opposite holds when women must finance a major part of the subsidy. Furthermore, the ceiling on fees has a positive effect on labor supply. This is because the dampening effect on labor supply is removed when the fee no longer increases with income. Thus, women invest more in market-oriented careers in case the child care fee is uniform and fixed instead of income related. However, for low-income families, the negative effect of income-dependent fees remains. Moreover, such a reform increases the welfare gap between married and divorced women. This follows, as a ceiling reduces the fee for high-income earners relative to low-income earners.

2.4.3   In-Work Benefits

The model yields the following result: if women finance a minor share of the government expenditures on the in-work benefit, a steeper phase-in profile increases women's time in the market, reduces poverty among divorced mothers, and reduces the welfare gap between married and divorced women for women in the phase-in region. If women finance a major share of the in-work benefit, the effect is ambiguous. When women can transfer the burden of financing the in-work benefit to other citizens, the direct effect of the benefit dominates the tax effect, and women will invest more time in the market. The poverty among divorced women falls, both because women choose more market careers, and because the in-work benefit increases.

The more generous in-work benefit, which is only available to divorced women in the model, will reduce the dispersion in well-being between married and divorced women. This follows because the in-work benefit directly increases the income of divorced women, and because labor income increases as women invest more in market-oriented careers.

A steeper phase-out range has an ambiguous effect on market investments, poverty, and welfare dispersion for women in the phase-out region.

2.4.4   Household Substitutes

If the market for household substitutes is small, introducing a price subsidy on the purchased household goods will induce women to invest more in market careers and to consume more household goods; it will also reduce poverty among divorced women and reduce the welfare gap between married and divorced women.

A subsidy reduces the price of the market-produced household goods, increasing total consumption of household goods. As market-purchased goods become relatively cheaper, the amount of household goods bought from the market increases, at the expense of home-produced household goods. Thus, women will invest more in market-oriented careers, as they find it optimal to substitute household goods produced by own time for market-produced household goods. This is the distortion that Rosen focused on in the context of market-provided child care. But higher market investments also improve women's economic situations in case of divorce, thus reducing poverty among divorced women.

In addition, subsidizing market-provided household goods reduces the welfare difference between married and divorced women, even though one assumes that only married women buy the subsidized household service. The primary effect of subsidizing market-provided household goods is to induce women to invest more in labor market skills during the investment years. This has more value to women who eventually divorce than to married women. Married women work more after the investment period than they would in the absence of the subsidy, but most of that income merely replaces household production with market production. Although there is a small increase in welfare from using the cheaper technology to produce the same goods (and therefore to consume more total goods), most of the income nets little gain, because it merely allows technology substitution. Divorced women use the incremental income to purchase additional goods rather than to produce the same goods with a different technology. As a result, the gain to divorced women from the additional labor supply is first order, whereas the gain to married women is second order. This narrows the gap in welfare between married and divorced women.

At the same time, the tax increases needed to subsidize the household substitutes imply higher taxes on work. This in turn discourages women from investing in market-oriented careers. This effect, however, will be small when the market for household goods is small. Then, the cost of financing the subsidy and the required tax increase will be low, implying a modest adverse impact on women's investment in market work.

2.5   Linking the Model of Policy Effects to Work Patterns and Labor Income for Women

Having described the employment patterns of women (section 2.2) and having developed a theoretical model to determine how women's labor market outcomes can be linked to the four policies in focus (section 2.4), we now examine the relation between the patterns and the model.

2.5.1   Paid Parental Leave

The generous duration and levels of parental leave payments in our model are the most likely factors explaining the long time spent in maternity leave in Sweden. This view is supported by empirical evidence (Pylkkänen and Smith 2004), which shows that a higher compensation rate during parental leave prolongs the break from market work. Mothers in Sweden take an average of ten months off for paid maternity leave.

It is likely, moreover, that the right to paid parental leave, combined with the legal right to return to previous employment, explains some of the high participation rate among mothers in Sweden (even when all mothers with children below the age of one are counted as out of the labor force; see table 2.2). This is consistent with empirical research. Ruhm (1998), using data for nine European countries over the period from 1969 to 1993, found that the right to paid leave *raises* the percentage of women employed by between 3 and 4 percent. Only about one-quarter of this effect can be attributed to an increase in women who are registered as employed but are absent from work due to the parental leave program. Ruhm offers two explanations. First, women who would otherwise choose not to participate may search for a job in order to qualify for the paid parental leave scheme. (Because parental leave is disproportionately enjoyed by women but is paid for by men, the policy raises the value of work for women.) Second, the scheme may speed up the reentry to work. The reason is that some mothers who would have quit their jobs to take a long leave period now find it worthwhile to return to work sooner in order to remain in their old job. In the Swedish case, Ronsen and Sundström (2002) find that the right to paid parental leave, coupled with the legal right to return to their previous jobs, speeds up the return to employment for women. However, once these rights exist, prolonging the maternity leave period and extending the right to it may reduce labor supply, as it prolongs the time in parental leave. This suggests that a slightly less generous parental leave scheme—in terms of payment and duration—would increase female labor supply—in terms of a shorter maternity leave—without inducing women to drop out of the labor force.

The Swedish parental leave scheme provides parents with the legal right to reduce their work time to 75 percent of a full-time job (at their full-time hourly wage) until the child is eight years of age. This rule encourages less work hours but most likely contributes to higher labor force participation. Cross-country analyses have shown that there is a positive link between part-time job opportunities and female labor force participation (see Del Boca and Pasqua 2005). Thus, the legal right to reduce work time from full-time to part-time may have a positive effect on the participation decision but a potentially negative effect on the intensity decision.

Consistent with our theoretical analysis, the empirical evaluations of the daddy-quota reforms (Ekberg, Eriksson, and Friebel 2005; and Eriksson 2005) indicate that the first daddy-quota reform increased women's labor supply, whereas the second reform reduced it. See table 2.7 for a comparison of the use of parental leave days before and after each daddy-quota reform. This suggests that the second reform, which restricted the number of transferable months and extended the total family leave time, was not successful from a female labor supply perspective.

The parental leave system probably affects the wages of women relative to men. As parental leave is mainly used by mothers, the program may reduce human capital of women relative men, which may affect earnings differentials. Of course, this does not imply that the women are worse off with the program than without it.

Table 2.7   **Mean number of parental leave days for the first and second daddy-month reforms: the first seventeen months**

	1995 reform		2002 reform	
	Before	After	Before	After
Father	23	28	31	34
Mother	311	286	259	264

Source: Eriksson (2005). The total family parental leave days with an income-based payment in 1995 and 2002 are 360 and 390, respectively.

Note: Note that the number of parental leave days in this table is measured seventeen months after the birth. We know that fathers use their parental leave days to a larger extent when the child is older, which tends to underestimate the number of parental leave days the father is using, as well as his share of the total days (see Eriksson 2005).

Datta Gupta, Smith, and Verner (2006) discuss how a differentiated take-up rate of parental leave may induce a high personal penalty for fathers who take leave. They argue that mothers may be induced to select into relatively low-paid jobs in the public sector, where it is easy to combine a career with family and where the personal penalty of leave is especially low, whereas men sort into the private sector and become the family breadwinner. They also argue that the large employment opportunities in the public sector, which supply particularly generous and flexible parental leave schemes, may have induced gender-segmented labor markets in the Nordic countries (see also Albrecht, Edin, and Vroman 1999).

2.5.2   Child Care Subsidies

Studies of the effects on labor supply of child care policy find that high availability and subsidized fees tend to increase female labor supply. The size of the effects, however, is less clear (Jaumotte 2003). A study of the access and price of child care in Denmark found that availability had a positive effect on female labor supply, whereas higher fees had a negative effect (Simonsen 2005). Domeij and Klein (2008), in a calibrated dynamic life-cycle model for Germany, show that the labor supply of mothers with small children would be large if Germany expanded the availability of highly subsidized child care.

But Sweden appears to be an outlier in this respect. An evaluation of the Swedish child care fee reform of 2002 did not find that the reform significantly affected female work hours and participation (Lundin, Mörk, and Öckert 2007). A possible interpretation is that although child care subsidies have historically played an important role for female labor supply by reducing the costs of working, further increases in an already-high subsidy may have only marginal effects on mothers' labor supply. If true, this suggests that a reduction in the child care subsidy would not cause major dropout from the labor market.

2.5.3   In-Work Benefits

In-work benefits have only recently been implemented in Sweden, so we rely on theory and experiences in other countries to suggest the directions and size of effects.

The United States introduced the earned income tax credit (EITC) more than thirty years ago and has expanded it significantly since then. The EITC is now the largest cash transfer program at the federal level for low-income families. In 2003, about 20 million families received a total of $34 billion in benefits from it. The EITC is targeted toward low-income families with children. The largest group receiving the in-work benefit is single mothers.[5] It has a phase-in region, where the size of the tax credit is given as a proportion of earned income. Once the maximum EITC is reached, the credit is held fixed at its maximum level until the phase-out region starts. The tax credit is eventually phased out completely.[6]

Evaluations of the EITC in the United States draw quite a positive picture of the impact of the EITC on labor supply. Eissa and Liebman (1996) compared the labor supply responses of single women with children to the responses of single women with no children when the earned income tax credit expanded in 1986. They showed that between 1984 to 1986 and 1988 to 1990, single women with children increased their relative labor force participation by up to 2.8 percentage points. Meyer and Rosenbaum (2001) found that 63 percent of the increase in labor force participation of single families in the United States between 1984 and 1996 was due to the expansion of the EITC. The participation decision rather than the hour decision appears most influenced by the EITC.[7]

Will this type of policy have a similar effect in Sweden and in other less market-oriented economies as in the United States? Kolm (2008) provides a discussion of an earned income tax credit in a Swedish context. Simulation studies that take account of European institutional settings when estimating the effect of in-work benefits on labor market performance suggest that this will be the case. Although the Swedish tax credit is slightly different than the U.S. one and is not targeted specifically toward single mothers, the

5. See Eissa and Hoynes (2006).
6. For the year 2006 (tax year 2005), income must have been less than $35,263 ($37,263 married filing jointly) with two or more qualifying children; less than $31,030 ($33,030 married filing jointly) with one qualifying child; or less than $11,750 ($13,750 married filing jointly) with no qualifying children. The maximum credits are $4,400 with two or more qualifying children; $2,662 with one qualifying child; or $399 with no qualifying children. Available at: www.irs.gov/eitc.
7. The drawback with a tax credit of the EITC type is that the increased marginal tax rates in the phase-out region might create disincentives to work for those already in the labor market. The evaluations of the EITC seem to show that these effects exist but that the magnitude is small. The EITC also tends to reduce incentives to enter the labor market for secondary family earners. Eissa and Hoynes (2004) show evidence for such an effect, but again, the effect seems to be small.

empirical evidence of the labor supply elasticity of single mothers reviewed earlier suggests that they are likely to respond to improved work incentives in the desired direction.

2.5.4 Tax Relief on Household Substitutes

This policy is also so recent in Sweden that we have to rely on the experience of other countries. Our model exercise suggests that tax relief on household substitutes enables women to work more in the labor market, as they can substitute market-purchased household services for own household time. It improves welfare to introduce subsidies or a tax relief on household substitutes, child care being the most significant example. Sketchy evaluations of the systems in other countries show that the policies appear to increase employment. However, more careful empirical evaluations are needed in order to clarify the contributions of these policies.

It also may be important to have access to a market for household substitutes. Freeman and Schettkat (2005) propose this as an explanation for much of the EU-U.S. employment and hour differences that are observed. They argue that in the United States, there has been a more extensive shift of traditional household production—food preparation, child care, elderly care, house cleaning—to the market than in Europe. However, Sweden differs from the EU average in some important ways. When it comes to child care, the generous child care subsidies in Sweden have induced an extensive shift of child care from the household to the market sector. Freeman and Schettkat (2005) present numbers on the percentage of children under the age of three enrolled in formal day care. In Sweden, 48 percent use formal day care, whereas the number is 54 percent in the United States; the European average is 29 percent. But markets for other types of household services are either nonexistent or relatively small in Sweden. Swedes spend about 7.7 hours a week cooking at home, whereas U.S. citizens spend only about 4.1 hours a week cooking at home (see Freeman and Schettkat 2005).

Detailed time-use data for Sweden and the United States show that women spend more time cooking, cleaning, and so forth than women in the United States. Employed women in Sweden allocate thirteen hours a week on such tasks, compared to ten hours for women in the United States. The corresponding numbers for men are almost seven hours for Sweden and a bit over three hours for the United States. Employed women in the United States, however, do work more in the market and consume less leisure than Swedish women. The same pattern holds for men.

High taxes and relatively high wages at the lower end of the wage distribution make household substitutes expensive in Sweden. The child care subsidy is one notable exception that is pushing in the direction of increased labor supply, and the question is whether tax relief on household substitutes can further increase women's attachment to the labor market, as suggested by our model. It probably can.

2.6   Conclusion

This chapter has linked the distinctive features of the labor supply of Swedish women, particularly those with small children, to Swedish family policies—especially the paid parental leave system and the child care subsidies. Based on our theoretical framework, as well as on previous theoretical and empirical research, we conclude that the Swedish flexible parental leave system, with its generous legal rights to return to the previous employer and its heavily subsidized day care, helps explain the high labor force participation rate among women with children. However, the generosity of the paid parental leave system, in terms of payment and duration, also most likely explains why we observe such long career breaks for women following childbirths in Sweden. In addition, the two daddy-quota reforms that were carried out in 1995 and 2002, respectively, seem to have encouraged fathers to take longer parental leave but have not induced mothers to work more—at least not the 2002 reform.

Returning to Rosen's analysis of the Swedish child care subsidies from an efficiency viewpoint with which we began, a natural concluding question is, could child care subsidies be replaced by another policy instrument that can stimulate the labor supply of women with children, without distorting the consumption mix in favor of child care services? Our answer is yes.

The subsidized child care in Sweden, which is available only to employed parents, can be viewed as an in-work benefit.[8] As the mother is usually the primary caretaker and thus the last person to leave the household for a job, the child care subsidy can be expected to have a qualitatively similar positive effect on her labor force participation as would a tax credit on earned income.[9]

Child care subsidies affect labor force participation positively, as does an in-work benefit, but the child care subsidy is in kind. It distorts consumption in favor of child care, as Sherwin Rosen pointed out. An alternative that would avoid this distortion would be to transform the child care subsidy into a lump-sum transfer to families with small children, conditional on both parents working a significant number of work hours. Such a policy would provide the same incentives to work but would not distort the consumption mix.

Were the current child care subsidy, which is about 85,000 SEK per child and per year (slightly less than one-third of the median income), instead distributed as a check to eligible families, they could spend this transfer

8. Since the 2001 reform, unemployed workers have had limited access to child care (fifteen hours per week).

9. As our model analysis reveals, the incentives to choose work hours for those already working will be different if we compare the Swedish child care subsidy with an in-work benefit of the EITC type. This is a consequence of differences in how they are constructed in terms of income indexation of the benefit.

on market-purchased child care or solve their child care problems through flexible work times, relatives, or some other way, so they could instead use this transfer for consumption of other goods and services. While this is a policy worth considering, it is not without its own potential distortions. For example, publicly provided high-quality child care can be viewed as education, which has potentially positive externalities.

Appendix

A Model of Female Work Behavior: The Case of Paid Parental Leave

In this appendix, we build a basic model to study the effects on female career choices and incomes of the two daddy-month reforms. Available for download at: http://people.su.se/~akolm/, you will also find the formal analysis of the other policy reforms considered in this chapter.

The basic model is set in two periods. In the first period, women are married, whereas in the second period, there is an exogenous probability, $1 - p$, that the marriage will be dissolved. At the beginning of the first period, the woman makes her career choice. By allocating her available time into market work, L_M, and family work, L_H, she can decide how much of a market-oriented career and how much of a family-oriented career she wants to make. As the allocation of time also has consequences for the future, she allows for the future possibility that the marriage will dissolve when making her time allocation decision. The payoff from investing in market work is given by the net wage income, $wL_M - T(wL_M; .)$, where w is the wage, and $T(wL_M; .)$ is the tax payments. The tax schedule is $T(wL_M; .) = B(wL_M)^2 - A$, where A and B are parameters.

Women derive utility from material good consumption, C, and from the consumption of a family good, F, which we interpret here as care for children. The family good can be produced/consumed at home by the mother, F_H, or by the father, $\bar{F}$, or it can be purchased in the market, F_M, where these are perceived to be perfect substitutes; that is, $F = F_M + F_H + \bar{F}$. The mother produces the family good by use of own time, L_H, through the concave production function $F_H = L_H^\alpha$, $\alpha < 1$.[10] The payoff from investing time in the family is the utility the care time yields.

The financial aspect of the paid parental leave is allowed for by adding a proportional subsidy for each time unit allocated to family activity in the first period. The derived utility of the first period is $v(F) + wL_M -$

10. It does not matter for the results that $\bar{F}$ is introduced as linear in father's time, although the woman's time enters through a concave function. Moreover, it does not affect the results if we assume that $F_M = L_M - \bar{F}$; that is, if we assume that the demand for child care has to be equal to the time when no one is at home.

$B(wL_M)^2 + A - kF_M + S(L_H;.)$, where $v(F)$ captures the utility from care for children, and $wL_M - B(wL_M)^2 + A - kF_M + S(L_H;.)$ captures the utility from material good consumption. Material good consumption is simply given by the income net of taxes and the payment from paid parental leave, $S(L_H;.)$, subtracting the expenses for market-purchased child care, kF_M, where k is the price of market-purchased care for children. The payment from paid parental leave is given by $S(L_H;.) = sL_H$ if $L_H \le \overline{L}_H$, and $S(L_H;.) = s\overline{L}_H$ if $L_H > \overline{L}_H$. Thus, if staying home with children more hours than $\overline{L}_H$, then the ceiling of the paid parental leave is reached. The female spouse cannot then reap more paid parental leave by increasing her family time.

In the second period, the children are older (possibly grown-up), and the utility is simply given by the income net of taxes, which is used for material good consumption, $wL_M - B(wL_M)^2 + A$. Imposing the time constraint, $\overline{T} = L_M + L_H$, and ignoring discounting, the expected present value can be written:

$$EV = v[F_M + \overline{F} + (\overline{T} - L_M)^\alpha] + 2wL_M$$
$$- 2B(wL_M)^2 + 2A - kF_M + S(\overline{T} - L_M;.).$$

The female spouse chooses both the time allocation and how much of the family good she wants to purchase from the market in order to maximize the expected present value. For an interior solution, $L_M, L_H \in (0,\overline{T})$ and $F_M > 0$, the following first-order conditions determine the optimal choices:[11]

$$\frac{\partial EV}{\partial L_M} = -v'(F)\alpha(\overline{T} - L_M)^{\alpha-1} + 2w - 4Bw^2L_M - S'(\overline{T} - L_M;.) = 0$$

$$\frac{\partial EV}{\partial F_M} = v'(F) - k = 0,$$

where $S'(L_H;.) = s$ if $L_M > \overline{L}_M$, and $S'(L_H;.) = 0$ if $L_M \le \overline{L}_M$.

The objective function is continuous but has a kink point at $L_M = \overline{L}_M$ in the presence of the paid parental leave system. We have to consider both cases: when female spouses choose to exhaust their periods of paid parental leave, $L_M \le \overline{L}_M$, and when they do not use all of the periods of paid parental leave they are entitled to, $L_M > \overline{L}_M$.

The government budget constraint is fulfilled at all times by allowing for adjustments in the parameter B:

$$2[BL_M^2 - A] = \delta[S(\overline{T} - L_M;.) + s\overline{F}],$$

where $\delta \in [0,1]$ captures the share of the government expenditures that is financed by the female workers.

11. Note that this particular policy problem can be solved independent of the size of p; for the analysis of the other policies in this chapter, see http://people.su.se/~akolm/.

The Daddy Months

In 1995, the first daddy month was introduced. The reform implied that one month of the paid parental leave must be used by each parent. In practice, it meant that fathers could no longer transfer all their paid parental leave to the mother. Unless at least one month was used by the father, it could not be used by either of the parents. In 2002, the second daddy month was implemented. The reform reserved two months for each parent. At the same time, the total time of entitlement to paid parental leave for the family increased by thirty days. In essence, this implied that an extra month available only for fathers was added to the existing paid parental leave scheme.

We represent these two types of reforms by letting $\bar{F}$ increase. By increasing $\bar{F}$, we increase the father's family time. In a reform similar to the 2002 reform, this will have no impact on the mother's available time for paid leave, $\bar{L}_M$. The results are as follows:

PROPOSITION A1: *Increased paid family time of fathers, $\bar{F}$, will reduce or have no impact on women's investment in a market career and will increase poverty among divorced women.*

PROOF: All propositions follow from the differentiation of the first-order conditions and the government budget constraint. Poverty among divorced women, for simplicity, is measured by the disposable income of divorced women. The welfare gap is measured by the utility difference of married and divorced women.

An increase in the father's time at home initially induces the mother to reduce the market-purchased care time by an equivalent amount. However, as the reform is financed by increased taxation, the mother finds it optimal to work less and instead spends more time at home (reducing her market purchase of care time even more). The reform thus induces mothers to stay home longer with their children in response to fathers increasing their parental leave time. Poverty among divorced women increases, both because they choose to invest less in a market career, and because the reform induces tax increases.

Also, if women bunch at the kink point (i.e., $L_M = \bar{L}_M$), the required tax increases will reduce the incentives to work. However, the budget effect may not be strong enough to counteract the bunching at the kink point.

When considering the 1995 reform, we have to allow for the fact that this reform implies that L_M falls by an equivalent amount, leaving the family's total time of paid parental leave periods intact. The results are as follows:

PROPOSITION A2: *Increased paid family time of fathers. $\bar{F}$, leaving the total time of paid parental leave intact, will (a) leave women's investment in market work and poverty among divorced women unaffected if women allocate more time to the family than the paid leave pays for; (b) reduce women's investment* *in market work and increase poverty among divorced women if women do not exhaust their periods of paid parental leave; or (c) increase women's investment in market work and reduce poverty among divorced women if women bunch at the kink point.*

In case women take more leave than the system pays for, there is no need to increase taxes in order to finance the reform. The reform is self-financed, as the lump-sum parental leave payments to women are reduced by the same amount as the cost of financing a longer paid parental leave for fathers. Therefore, the career choices and economic situation of divorced women are unaffected.

On the other hand, in case women do not exhaust their periods of paid parental leave, the reduction in $\overline{L}_M$ has no effect on women's investment in a market career. Thus, the analyses of the previous proposition hold.

In case the father's paid family time increases in a situation where women bunch at the kink point, female investment in a market-oriented career will increase. Women who choose exactly to exhaust their periods of paid parental leave face a reduction in the marginal cost of working when their available periods of paid leave are reduced. This follows because increased working time is no longer associated with a reduction in the benefits of paid parental leave. Thus, the incentive to invest in a more market-oriented career has improved, which also improves the economic situation of divorced women.

References

Albrecht, J., P.-A. Edin, and S. Vroman. 1999. Career interruptions and subsequent wages: A reexamination using Swedish data. *Journal of Human Resources* 34 (2): 294–311.

Andrén, T. 2003. The choice of paid childcare, welfare, and labor supply of single mothers. *Labour Economics* 10 (2): 133–47.

Bergemann, A., and G. J. van den Berg. 2006. From childbirth to paid work: A structural analysis of the effects of adult education on labor market outcomes of prime-aged mothers. Paper presented at the European Cooperation in Science and Technology (COST) A23 meeting. 19–20 October, Essen, Germany.

Boeri, T., D. Del Boca, and C. Pissarides, eds. 2005. *Women at work: An economic perspective.* Oxford: Oxford University Press.

Datta Gupta, N., N. Smith, and M. Verner. 2006. Child care and parental leave in the Nordic countries: A model to aspire to? IZA Discussion Paper no. 2014. Bonn, Germany: Institute for the Study of Labor, March.

Del Boca, D., and S. Pasqua. 2005. Labor supply and fertility in Europe and the US. In *Women at work: An economic perspective,* ed. T. Boeri, D. Del Boca, and C. Pissarides, 125–54. Oxford: Oxford University Press.

Domeij, D., and P. Klein. 2008. Should daycare be subsidized? Manuscript, February. Available at: http://www.eco.uc3m.es/temp/agenda/mothers080214.pdf.

Eissa, N., and H. Hoynes. 2004. Taxes and the labor market participation of married couples: The earned income tax credit. *Journal of Public Economics* 88 (9/10): 1931–58.

———. 2006. Behavioral responses to taxes: Lessons from the EITC and labor supply. In *Tax policy and the economy,* vol. 20, ed. J. M. Poterba, 73–110. Cambridge, MA: National Bureau of Economic Research.

Eissa, N., and J. Liebman. 1996. Labor supply response to the earned income tax credit. *Quarterly Journal of Economics* 111 (2): 605–37.

Ekberg, J., R. Eriksson, and G. Friebel. 2005. Parental leave: A policy evaluation of the Swedish "daddy-month" reform. IZA Discussion Paper no. 1617. Bonn, Germany: Institute for the Study of Labor, May.

Eriksson, R. 2005. Parental leave in Sweden: The effects of the second daddy month. SOFI Working Paper no. 9/2005. Stockholm University, Swedish Institute for Social Research, December.

Flood, L., J. Hansen, and R. Wahlberg. 2004. Household labor supply and welfare participation in Sweden. *Journal of Human Resources* 39 (4): 1008–32.

Flood, L., E. Pylkkänen, and R. Wahlberg. 2007. From welfare to work: Evaluating a proposed tax and benefit reform targeted at single mothers in Sweden. *Labour* 21 (3): 443–71.

Freeman, R., and R. Schettkat. 2005. Marketization of household production and the EU-US gap in work. *Economic Policy* 20 (41): 5–50.

Jaumotte, F. 2003. Female labour force participation: Past trends and main determinants in OECD countries. OECD Economics Department Working Paper no. 376. Paris: Organization for Economic Cooperation and Development.

Kennerberg, L. 2007. Hur förändras kvinnors och mäns arbetssituation när de får barn? IFAU Rapport no. 2007:9. Uppsala, Sweden: Institute for Labor Market Policy Evaluation.

Kleven, H. 2004. Optimum taxation and the allocation of time. *Journal of Public Economics* 88 (3/4): 545–57.

Kolm, A.-S. 2008. Comment on Bruce Meyer: The earned income tax credit—A Swedish perspective. *Swedish Economic Policy Review* 14 (2): 81–85.

Lundin, D., E. Mörk, and B. Öckert. 2007. Maxtaxan inom barnomsorgen— Påverkar den hur mycket föräldrar arbetar? IFAU Rapport no. 2007:2. Uppsala, Sweden: Institute for Labor Market Policy Evaluation.

Meyer, B., and D. Rosenbaum. 2001. Welfare, the earned income tax credit and the labor supply of single mothers. *Quarterly Journal of Economics* 116 (3): 1063–114.

Nyberg, A. 2005. Har den ekonomiska jämställdheten ökat sedan början av 1990– talet? Makt att forma samhället och sitt eget liv—jämställdhetspolitiken mot nya mål. SOU 2005:66 Forskarrapporter. Stockholm: Swedish Government Official Reports.

Pylkkänen, E., and N. Smith. 2004. The impact of family-friendly policies in Denmark and Sweden on Mothers' career interruptions due to childbirth. IZA Discussion Paper no. 1050. Bonn, Germany: Institute for the Study of Labor, March.

Ronsen, M., and M. Sundström. 2002. Family policy and after-birth employment among new mothers. *European Journal of Population* 18 (2): 121–52.

Rosen, S. 1997. Public employment, taxes, and the welfare state in Sweden. In *The welfare state in transition: Reforming the Swedish model,* ed. R. B. Freeman, H. Topel, and B. Swedenborg, 79–109. Chicago: University of Chicago Press.

Ruhm, C. 1998. The economic consequences of parental leave mandates: Lessons from Europe. *Quarterly Journal of Economics* 113 (1): 285–317.

Simonsen, M. 2005. Availability and price of high quality child care and female employment. Working Paper no. 2005–8. University of Aarhus, School of Economics and Management, May.

Sorensen, P. B. 1997. Public finance solutions to the European unemployment problem? *Economic Policy* 12 (25): 223–64.

Westerlund, L., J. Lindblad, and M. Larsson. 2005. *Föräldraledighet och arbetstid: hur mycket jobbar föräldrar som varit hemma med barn.* LO Rapport. Stockholm: Landsorganisationen i Sverige.

Wage Determination and Employment in Sweden Since the Early 1990s:
Wage Formation in a New Setting

Peter Fredriksson and Robert Topel

3.1 Introduction

Much of what is called the Swedish model has to do with Sweden's labor market institutions, which are far different than those of the United States. Simplifying only slightly, wage and employment outcomes in the United States are mainly the result of decentralized decisions by buyers and sellers of labor services. Less than 8 percent of American private-sector workers belong to labor unions, while government intervention and participation in the labor market is comparatively small.[1] Sweden represents the opposite extreme. In Sweden, over 80 percent of workers belong to labor unions. Thus, wages and working conditions for the vast majority of Swedes are the negotiated outcomes of collective-bargaining agreements, which have had some uniquely Swedish characteristics that we describe next. And the

Peter Fredriksson is Director-General of the Institute for Labor Market Policy Evaluation (IFAU) and a professor at the Department of Economics, Uppsala University. Robert Topel is the Isidore Brown and Gladys J. Brown Professor in Urban and Labor Economics at the Booth Graduate School of Business, University of Chicago, and a research associate of the National Bureau of Economic Research.

We acknowledge the helpful comments of Birgitta Swedenborg, the other members of the Center for Business and Policy Studies/National Bureau of Economic Research group, and conference participants—especially Nils Gottfries (our discussant) and Bertil Holmlund. We also thank Albin Kainelainen, Kjell Salvanes, Per Skedinger, and Roope Uusitalo for help with the data. We are responsible for the errors. Some of the work on this chapter was done while Fredriksson was at the Institute for International Economic Studies, Stockholm University.

1. Even at its peak during the 1950s, union coverage in the United States never exceeded 35 percent. Private-sector unionism has been in steady decline since. Union coverage has increased only in the public sector, where roughly 36 percent of workers now belong to unions. Government intervention in labor markets has increased over time, mainly as a result of workplace regulations and the erosion of the employment at will doctrine that has historically characterized much of U.S. employment relations. Public employment as a fraction of total employment remains low by international standards.

Swedish government is a major labor market actor. By 1990, the public sector accounted for one-third of all jobs in Sweden, compared to only 15 percent in the United States. The government also supports an extensive set of labor market policies and programs meant to maintain full employment while facilitating human capital formation and labor mobility. Last, Sweden's large public sector implies high taxes on labor incomes—Swedish taxes are typically over half of gross domestic product (GDP), nearly double the share in the United States.

These features of the Swedish labor market evolved over roughly four decades, from the 1940s to the 1970s. And by the mid-1970s, Swedes enjoyed one of the world's highest living standards, along with the most egalitarian income distribution of any advanced country. Poverty had been largely eliminated, and conventional measures of economic and labor market performance were enviable—the unemployment rate fluctuated around 2 percent, while average wage and productivity growth met or exceeded the average for developed countries.[2] In concert with other welfare state policies, it appeared to many that the Swedish model of labor markets was an effective mechanism for delivering long-run prosperity and employment opportunities. It seemed the equity-efficiency trade-off was not so important—at least in Sweden.

Doubts began to emerge in the late 1970s. Sweden's relative economic growth slowed, especially after 1975, while burgeoning welfare state institutions greatly increased the tax burden on the typical worker. The ratio of wage costs to disposable (after taxes) income per hour worked exceeded 4 to 1 in the 1980s—in fact, real disposable wages per hour worked did not grow at all from 1975 to 1993, in spite of rising pretax wages and productivity.[3] Nearly all employment growth after 1970 was due to the rapid expansion of public-sector jobs for women, which fueled rising female labor force participation. Private-sector employment stagnated. On the collective-bargaining front, large employers became progressively disillusioned with the redistributive and distortionary aspects of centralized bargaining, which had greatly compressed the wage distribution. The employers' confederation abandoned its support for centralized bargaining in the 1970s, and the system began to unravel in 1983, when large industrial employers negotiated separate agreements with their unions.[4]

Concerns with the Swedish model peaked with the economic crisis of the 1990s. Buffeted by a perfect storm of international recession, a banking crisis, and unsustainable public spending—which had risen above 70 percent of GDP—both private and public employment fell. The employment rate

2. See Lindbeck (2000) for a discussion.
3. On real wages and productivity, see Edin and Topel (1997, figure 4.5). On labor supply, see Burtless (1987) and Aronsson and Walker (1997).
4. We describe the evolution of centralized bargaining in greater detail next. The last central frame agreement was negotiated in 1987, though it seems to have had little effect. The Swedish Employers' Confederation (SAF) closed its collective-bargaining unit in 1990.

of working-age Swedes declined by over 12 percentage points between 1993 and 1997, a reduction in overall employment of about 500,000. Open unemployment—which excludes jobless individuals enrolled in public retraining and other programs—reached nearly 10 percent. The Swedish labor market was no longer anyone's envy. Both the present and the future of Swedish prosperity seemed at stake, along with faith in the Swedish model itself.

This chapter is a follow-on to the analysis of Edin and Topel (1997), which was written in the midst of the crisis. Edin and Topel analyzed the allocative effects of labor market institutions and policies in Sweden over a period of roughly thirty years and drew implications for the future performance of the Swedish labor market. Among their conclusions were the following:

1. *Centralized bargaining and wage compression.* Centralized bargaining had been an important contributor to wage compression, resulting in wage disparities that were smaller than what would have been generated by market forces or even by decentralized collective bargaining. This compression had lasting effects on the structure of the Swedish economy and labor market: low-wage sectors and low-wage employers were priced out of existence, while large industrial employers of skilled labor were subsidized. For a time, artificially high wages for less-skilled workers did not result in higher measured unemployment.

2. *Wage compression, taxes, and efficiency.* The artificial compression of wage differences distorted incentives on many margins, affecting decisions to work, to employ, and to invest in productive skills. These distortions were magnified by the large tax wedge generated by high income, payroll, and value-added taxes. For skilled workers, the combined effect of these taxes meant that take-home pay fell to only 21 percent of pretax wages, which were already artificially low. Of particular concern for long-run productivity, the private returns to investments in human capital—such as schooling—were unusually low. And low returns appeared to adversely affect human capital investment.

3. *Labor market policies and the public sector.* Much of Sweden's large public sector is devoted to the maintenance of full employment. Yet, active labor market policies (ALMP) had little impact on unemployment or on subsequent productivities of participants. Although the rapid expansion of public-sector jobs did not have much (direct) impact on the employment of men, the growth of the public sector helped raise and maintain the labor market fortunes of women—virtually all of the post-1970 increase in women's employment was due to the expansion of the public sector. Women's wages and labor force participation converged toward those of men, in part because the public sector would employ whatever labor supply was forthcoming at the chosen public-sector wage.

If egalitarian policies raised the wages of the least skilled and displaced substantial employment, why didn't those policies also generate widespread unemployment? Edin and Topel attributed part of the answer to the rapid growth of public-sector employment, though that explanation did not seem especially satisfying for men. To resolve this puzzle, Edin and Topel constructed a simple model that rationalized the major facts about precrisis labor markets in Sweden—including wage compression, migration, and restructuring—along with the ultimate demise of centralized bargaining in the 1980s.

In their analysis, centralized bargaining and associated egalitarian policies delivered short-run rents to skill-intensive sectors. Consistent with the goals of Swedish Trade Union Confederation (LO) economists who had advocated wage compression in the 1960s, skill- and capital-intensive sectors of the economy expanded, while low-wage jobs were priced out of existence. Inefficiencies caused by distorted wage setting mounted over time, however. Sweden's wage and income compression was swimming against the tide of technological changes that favored rising relative wages of skilled labor, so incentives to invest in skills were reduced at exactly the time that skilled labor became more valuable. The result was an ever-worsening skills shortage, which impeded human capital formation and economic growth. In the longer run, it became progressively more difficult for employers to hire skilled labor, precisely because skills were artificially cheap—which is what may have caused employers to ultimately reject centralized bargaining. For these and other reasons, Edin and Topel concluded that somewhat greater income inequality would have a first-order impact on economic efficiency and prosperity but only a minor impact on equity. In their view, a little more inequality would be a small price to pay for improvements in labor market performance.

We return to many of the same issues studied by Edin and Topel—but with the advantage of hindsight and the challenge of a greatly changed economic environment. We address two broad questions. First, how did Swedish policies and institutions adapt to the crisis? Second, were these adjustments and their effects consistent with the earlier analysis of Edin and Topel?

With regard to the first question, the central fact documented next is that economic forces, in general, and the crisis, in particular, have forced some relaxation of welfare state policies and constraints. The result is a move toward but not to decentralized market outcomes. The most prominent symptom is that wage inequality increased substantially. Most of this increase occurred at the top of the wage distribution so that skill differentials among the most skilled increased. Among the least skilled and least educated, wage disparities did not increase much at all—negotiated wage minima are still the rule in collective-bargaining contracts—which apparently caused employment to take up the slack. With declining demand for less-skilled labor and increased supply from a surge in low-skill immigration, relative employment rates of the least skilled fell sharply in the 1990s and did not recover.

Coincident with the rise in wage inequality, the importance of the public sector as a source of employment has diminished. In the 1980s, government jobs accounted for over 40 percent of all employment in Sweden, peaking at 43 percent in 1993. That fraction steadily declined thereafter, reaching about 35 percent in 2001. This evidently reduced overall labor demand; though private-sector employment increased as part of the recovery, the employment-to-population ratio is roughly 8 points lower today than it was in 1990.

Are these outcomes consistent with the analysis offered by Edin and Topel? At a broad level, we believe they are. Edin and Topel argued that welfare state institutions greatly affected the employment and productivity landscape in Sweden. Skill differentials in wages and incomes were artificially compressed, which benefited employers of skilled labor for a time, but which produced ever-increasing distortions, as (a) technical progress raised the demand for skilled labor, while (b) small returns to human capital investment discouraged Swedes from becoming skilled. Less-skilled workers benefited from the excess demand for skilled workers and from the growing public sector, so unemployment remained low. But market fundamentals eventually forced a retreat: the public sector shrank, taxes fell, and centralized bargaining gave way to more decentralized negotiations. The attendant rise in inequality was part of an overall move toward lower distortions, which improved efficiency, incentives, and economic performance.

The impact on egalitarian outcomes has been relatively minor, however. Even today, labor market outcomes in Sweden are the most egalitarian in the developed world, and unlike in the United States, postcrisis productivity increases have benefited both high- and low-wage workers. Given the modest increase in inequality that has occurred and its apparent benefits, Edin and Topel's original conclusion may still apply: a little more inequality might go a long way—especially because one can reasonably argue that the efficiency price of a set of egalitarian policies is even greater today than it was in 1990.

The chapter is organized as follows. By way of background, section 3.2 offers a brief account of the setting. For a variety of reasons, wages in Sweden are set in a very different environment today than twenty or thirty years ago. Section 3.3 documents the evolution of wage and employment differentials since the early 1990s. Section 3.4 addresses the link between wage policy and skill formation. In section 3.5, we turn to the other end of wage distribution and examine the link between the wage compression at the low end of wage distribution and the employment prospects of the less skilled. Section 3.6 concludes.

3.2   The (New) Setting

A stylized description of the Swedish labor market in the 1970s and early 1980s is as follows. More than 80 percent of Swedish workers were members of labor unions so that wages and working conditions were largely the result of collective bargaining. A key feature was that the negotiations were centralized—wages and working conditions were spelled out in central frame agreements negotiated between the Swedish Employers' Confederation (SAF) and the labor unions representing blue-collar (LO), white-collar (Swedish Confederation of Professional Employees, or TCO), and professional (Swedish Confederation of Professional Associations, or SACO) employees. Centralized bargaining was the key institutional feature that promoted egalitarian outcomes; for example, between 1970 and 1983, the log wage difference between blue-collar workers in the 90th and 10th percentiles of the wage distribution fell by over 40 percent (Hibbs 1990).

Centralized bargaining started to crumble in 1983 when Verstadsföreningen—which represented such large employers as ASEA Brown Boveri (ABB), Saab, and Volvo—negotiated outside the LO/SAF frame and reached a separate agreement with the largest industrial union, Metall. This began a trend toward more decentralized wage setting, though still firmly within a framework of collective bargaining. There subsequently have been further changes to wage formation. Yet, unionization rates remain high, and collective bargaining features as prominently today as it did prior to the demise of centralized bargaining in the 1980s.

In 1980, about 10 percent of the working-age (twenty to sixty-four) population was foreign-born. The majority of immigrants (almost 60 percent) came from other Nordic countries, which have similar cultures and institutions, and which are similarly developed (see Edin and Fredriksson 2000). About 15 percent of the Swedish working-age population had a university degree, while 48 percent of the population had compulsory education. Years of completed schooling for the average Swede were lower than for the average American worker but higher than the EU average (Wasmer et al. 2007).

In the beginning of the 1990s, Sweden experienced its most severe macroeconomic shock since the Great Depression. Around the same point in time, Sweden entered the European Union, successfully curbed inflation, reduced the government's share of national output, and started to deregulate many markets. The educational attainment of the Swedish population continued to increase, and immigration flows, mainly driven by less-skilled refugees from outside the Organization for Economic Cooperation and Development (OECD), reached postwar highs. This shift in the skill composition of immigrants has put further pressure on egalitarian wage policies: by 2003, non-OECD immigrants accounted for around 15 percent of low-wage workers, which is roughly similar to the concentration of immigrants among low-skilled workers in the United States.

It is fair to say that wages are set in a very different environment today than twenty or thirty years ago. Our purpose in what follows is to describe this environment in greater detail. We begin with the macroeconomic setting, followed by a description of changes in population and labor force demographics. Finally, we describe the changes in the institutional setup for wage formation.

3.2.1   Aggregate Developments Since the Early 1990s

Beginning in the early 1990s, Sweden experienced its most severe economic downturn since the 1930s. In just three years, (open) unemployment rose from 2 percent to almost 10 percent of the labor force.

The crisis of the early 1990s is readily visible in figure 3.1, which illustrates the evolution of the employment-to-population ratio among sixteen-to sixty-four-year-olds from 1976 to 2004. After rising steadily from the 1970s to 1990, the ratio dropped by more than 10 percentage points between 1990 and 1992 (from 83.1 percent in 1990 to 72.6 percent in 1992). Employment continued to decline until 1997—the overall peak-to-trough decline in the employment rate was about 12 percentage points—and since then has recovered only slightly. Even after fourteen years, by 2004, the overall employment rate remained more than 8 percentage points below its 1990 peak. This fact alone may suggest that the very high employment rates of the late 1980s were untenable.

The shock of the early 1990s hit the manufacturing sector first, leading to a decline in private-sector employment that began in 1990. Manufacturing employment fell by 240,000 jobs between 1989 and 1993—a decline of 26 percent. Figure 3.2 shows that the ratio of overall private-sector employment to the working-age population fell by about 7 percentage points between 1990 and 1993. More permanent cutbacks in the size of the public sector followed: the public employment-to-population ratio fell from 31 percent to 23 percent between 1990 and 1997—a decline of 26 percent—and did not subsequently rebound. Notice that the overall decline in the employment-to-population ratio—shown in figure 3.1—is mainly due to the contraction of the public sector. Private-sector employment as a share of the population returned to its precrisis level. The public share of total employment thus has ratcheted down, and with it has gone the impact of the welfare state on overall labor demand.[5] The Swedish private sector accounted for just more than half of total employment in the late 1980s and the early 1990s. By 2004, the private-sector share had increased to nearly two-thirds. In this respect, the developments of the 1990s are very different than in the preceding two decades, when the public share of total employment steadily increased, accounting for virtually all of net job creation between 1970 and 1990 (Edin and Topel 1997; Rosen 1997).

An important macroeconomic development is that Sweden successfully curbed inflation during the 1990s. From 1971 to 1990, annual inflation

---

5. Some of the decline in the public sector is due to the privatization of some public-sector activities. The decline in the share of public employment to total employment is certainly real, however. Even under the extreme assumption that the entire decline in the public sector is due to privatization, this would only account for half the increase in the private sector.

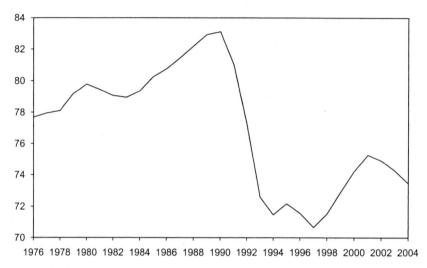

Fig. 3.1   Employment rate among sixteen- to sixty-four-year-olds, 1976 to 2004 (%)
Source: Labor force surveys.

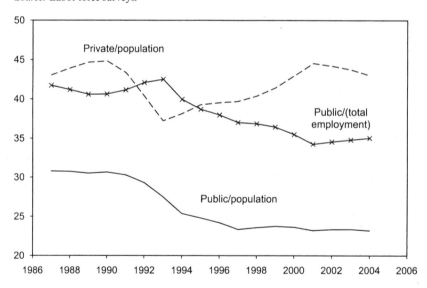

Fig. 3.2   Private- and public-sector employment, 1987 to 2004 (%)
Source: Labor force surveys.

averaged 8.5 percent. In 1990, the rate of change in the Consumer Price Index (CPI) reached 10.5 percent, its highest level since 1980/1981. It fell sharply during the crisis years and has averaged just 1.3 percent since 1994. As can be seen in figure 3.3, despite relatively solid employment growth between 1998 and 2001, since 1994, inflation has generally remained within the bands

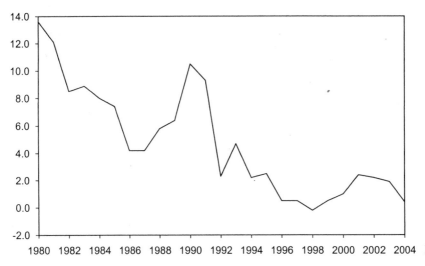

Fig. 3.3   Rate of inflation, 1980 to 2004 (%)
Source: Statistics Sweden.

stipulated by the central bank's inflationary target (2 ± 1 percent), with the only exceptions occurring when inflation was below 1 percent in 1996 to 2000 and in 2004 to 2005. This low-inflation regime was presumably achieved via a combination of a more restrictive monetary policy—implemented by an independent central bank—a rapid worsening of labor market conditions, and possibly of more wage coordination in national level negotiations.

Labor productivity grew faster during the 1990s than during the 1970s and 1980s. Between 1992 and 2003, labor productivity grew at an average annual rate of 2.5 percent (see figure 3.8). In part, this upturn of productivity growth reflects the cleansing effects of the recession, which forced the least productive plants to close and compelled the recovery from the depths of recession. Yet, the steady pace of productivity growth also indicates real improvements in economic performance and growth. Using (precrisis) 1991 as a base, real GDP per capita grew by 27.6 percent between 1991 and 2004, nearly identical to per capita income growth in the United States over this period (27.7 percent).[6] As we shall see, this growth was far more equally distributed in Sweden than in the United States, where productivity gains accrued almost exclusively to high-wage earners.

On top of these developments, Sweden's integration in world labor and product markets continues. Some would argue that this development favors a widening of wage differentials, as technical progress has favored more skilled labor, and globalization has increased the relative supply of goods produced by low-skilled foreign labor (see Leamer, chapter 9 in this volume).

6. *OECD Economic Surveys: Sweden* (2005).

These pressures likely are exacerbated by reduced barriers to international migration, because a generous welfare state may be more attractive to the less skilled, while talented Swedes may seek their fortunes abroad. We return to these points later.

3.2.2   Changes in Population Characteristics Since the Early 1990s

Wage dispersion and employment outcomes depend on the characteristics of the underlying population, for two reasons. First, by construction, wage dispersion will be greater when the skills of the working population are more heterogeneous. Second, changes in the shares of different skill categories affect relative wages for the usual factor-proportions reasons—absent the conditions for strict factor price equalization, a reduction in the share of less-skilled workers will raise their relative wage, and so on. On the first point, data from the International Adult Literacy Survey (IALS) indicate that countries with greater inequality of skills also have greater wage dispersion (e.g., Nickell and Layard 1999; and Leuven, Oosterbeek, and van Ophem 2004). On the second, changes in within-country factor proportions affect within-country relative wages, contrary to what one would expect in a simple factor price equalization model of wage determination (Topel 1997).

Compared to the United States, the Swedish population was relatively homogenous in the beginning of the 1990s. An indication of this is that the variance of measured skills in the IALS was substantially lower in Sweden than in the United States. But the heterogeneity of the Swedish population arguably has increased. The most obvious indication of this is that immigration surged dramatically, primarily during the first half of the 1990s. At a superficial level, the importance of immigrants in the Swedish labor force does not appear much different than in the United States. The share of immigrants in the Swedish population in 2003—see table 3.1—is similar to what one finds for the United States; as of 2003, 13.5 percent of the working-age population was foreign-born. Moreover, the increase since the early 1990s—almost 3 percentage points—is also comparable to the U.S. experience. But Sweden experienced an important and rapid shift in the source countries of new immigrants during the 1990s. In 1992, Nordic and non-OECD immigrants each accounted for 4.7 percent of the Swedish population. But by 2003, non-OECD immigrants accounted for 8.7 percent of the population, more than double the (declining) share of Nordic immigrants. Non-OECD immigrants now account for nearly two-thirds of the immigrant population, but they made up less than half a decade ago. As a share of immigrant *inflows,* these changes in the stock of immigrants imply a very large shift toward non-OECD immigrants. On average, the skills of these new immigrant groups are less apt to the Swedish labor market, which puts greater pressure on redistributive policies.

Continuing previous trends, educational attainment in the Swedish population increased substantially during the 1990s; see table 3.2. From 1992 to

Table 3.1　　　　　**Immigration**

	Immigrant share, population aged eighteen to sixty-four (%)			
Year	Total	Nordic	OECD	Non-OECD
1992	10.8	4.7	1.5	4.7
1997	12.3	4.0	1.3	6.9
2003	13.5	3.4	1.4	8.7

Source: Calculations based on Longitudinal INdividual DAta (LINDA); see Edin and Fredriksson (2000).

Table 3.2　　　　　**Educational attainment**

Year	Schooling ≤ 9 years	Schooling 9–12 years	Schooling > 12 years
	Population aged to eighteen to sixty-four (%)		
1992	27.5	49.9	22.6
1997	23.9	49.6	26.5
2003	19.2	49.2	31.6
	Population aged twenty-five to sixty-four (%)		
1992	28.4	46.7	24.9
1997	23.5	48.2	28.3
2003	17.9	48.5	33.7

Source: Calculations based on LINDA; see Edin and Fredriksson (2000).

2003, the share of the population with more than twelve years of schooling increased by 9 percentage points, as younger, more-educated cohorts replaced older, less-educated cohorts. At the other end of the schooling distribution, there is thus a mirror decline in the share of the population with compulsory schooling (or less).

These changes in the composition of the working-age population have implications for the effects of wage policies and labor market institutions. The decline in the share of less-educated labor relaxes market pressures for low wages among the least skilled so that redistributive wage policies may distort less, other things being the same.[7] In this context, the contraction of public-sector employment in the mid-1990s, which increased the importance of private-market outcomes, probably had less impact on inequality and employment than would have occurred in the 1970s or 1980s. Yet, the rising share of refugee immigrants in the Swedish population, together with technical progress that has favored skilled

7. If changes in the skill composition of the labor force have not kept pace with technical and other changes in the skill composition of demand, then the distortions caused by redistributive policies may have increased.

labor, is an opposite force that poses a challenge to Sweden's egalitarian goals.

3.2.3   Institutional Changes

Given the substantial changes in the environment, it perhaps would have been surprising if wage-setting institutions had not changed as well. In some important ways, the institutional setup is indeed different than during the preceding decades.[8] As we will describe next, there was both more coordination *and* more decentralization in wage setting. Yet, collective-bargaining agreements and unions appear to be as important in the Swedish labor market as they have been historically. Union density remained unchanged during the 1990s, and the prominence of collective agreement remains in place in labor legislation.[9]

The crisis years of the early 1990s saw an interlude, however. After centralized bargaining was largely abandoned in the 1980s, there was a temporary reversion of wage bargaining to a highly centralized level. A stabilization drive in 1990 resulted in a government-appointed commission that delivered a proposal for wage restraint during 1991 through 1993. The proposal was finally accepted after negotiations with over one hundred organizations. Wage inflation fell from over 10 percent per annum in the late 1980s to 4 percent in 1992 and to 2 to 3 percent in 1993 to 1994.

The years that followed involved a return to the largely decentralized wage bargaining at the industry level of the 1980s. But in 1997, a new regime emerged. The so-called industrial agreement (IA) was struck between unions and employers in the manufacturing sector. This agreement involves a set of procedural rules for labor negotiations, similar in many ways to the laws that govern collective bargaining in the United States. It stipulates, inter alia, timetables for negotiations and rules for conflict resolution, and it gives a prominent role for mediators to resolve disputes. The IA model has been followed by similar agreements in other sectors of the economy. By 2002, almost 60 percent of the labor force was covered by IA-type agreements (Elvander 2003).

While the IA model may have delivered incentives for wage restraint at the aggregate level, it is reasonable to think that it has had a minor influence on the wage structure. The agreement seems to have resulted in fewer instances of industrial action in comparison with 1993 to 1997. Nevertheless, it only establishes a set of procedural rules of the game. While there is a bargain struck at the national level, in general, the negotiated wage increases only come into operation should there be disagreement at the local level.

The wage structure probably is influenced more by another institutional change in wage formation—a substantial move toward the decentralization

---

8. This section builds on Holmlund (2003).
9. Union density stood at 80 percent in 1990 and 79 percent in 2000 (OECD 2004).

of wage negotiations. This started in the beginning of the 1990s, when some central agreements for white-collar workers in the private sector contained neither total wage increases nor minimum wage increases. It was entirely up the employer and the employee to determine the wage increase (see Lindgren 2005). The pace of decentralization has varied by sector and worker categories. Many central wage agreements specify a fall-back wage increase, in case there is disagreement at the local level, and a minimum guaranteed wage increase for each individual. In table 3.3, we outline the wage agreement modes that existed in the Swedish labor market in 2004. As the table illustrates, a wide variety of wage-setting practices exists in the Swedish labor market today.

In table 3.3, we have ordered the models with respect to the influence given to the local bargaining parties. So, model 1 has complete freedom for the local parties, while there is no local influence in model 7. Thus, rows (1) through (3) indicate that 36 percent (18 + 4 + 14) of employees are covered by agreements where local bargaining determines the local, employee-specific wage increase (in some cases subject to the restriction that individuals are guaranteed some minimal wage increase); another 47 percent are covered by agreements where the local parties determine the allocation of a given wage increase (the wage frame). An additional 10 percent have local bargaining with some influence on the distribution. Finally, 7 percent have their wages set by the central agreement. Interestingly, all of the agreements where there is no local influence over the size and allocation of wage increases can be

Table 3.3   **Wage agreement modes**

Model		Employees (%)		
	All	Private	Central government	Local public
1. Local bargain without restrictions	18	7	38	28
2. Local bargain with a fallback	4	8	0	0
3. Local bargain with a fallback plus a guaranteed wage increase	14	16	62	0
4. Local wage frame without a guaranteed wage increase	30	12	0	72
5. Local wage frame with guarantee or a fallback regulating the guarantee	17	28	0	0
6. General pay increase plus local wage frame	10	18	0	0
7. General pay increase	7	11	0	0

Source: National Mediation Office (2004).

Notes: A fallback means that the central agreement specifies a general wage increase that comes into operation should the local parties not agree. A guaranteed wage increase means that each individual is guaranteed a wage increase of a certain amount of Swedish krona (SEK). A local wage frame means that the local parties are given a total wage increase but can decide on the distribution of that increase over individuals.

found in the private sector, which now accounts for about two-thirds of employment. In fact, in the public sector, previously rigid wage schedules were abandoned in the mid-1990s. In theory, wages are determined locally in the entire public sector, and there is considerable leeway for employers to tailor wages so that they can recruit and retain employees.

Many central bargains are still binding when it comes to the lower tail of the wage distribution, however. Wage settlements for blue-collar workers involve centrally determined minimum wages, and some 40 percent of employees are covered by agreements that guarantee each individual a certain pay increase. In general, wage determination for white-collar workers is subject to fewer restrictions than for blue-collar workers (National Mediation Office 2004).

3.3   Changes in Wage and Employment Differentials

With the changes in the environment and institutions as a background, we now proceed to document the changes in the wage structure and employment that have occurred since the early 1990s, with particular emphasis on wage dispersion and employment differentials across skill groups.[10]

3.3.1   Changes in Wage Differentials

Figure 3.4 summarizes some basic facts about the evolution of the wage distribution since the early 1990s, based on individual data recorded in the Longitudinal INdividual DAta (LINDA) panel survey. The solid line shows the standard deviation of log wages; the dotted line graphs wage dispersion within industries, while the dashed line corresponds to the residual log wage distribution after controlling for experience, education, gender, immigrant status, and years since migration.[11]

The basic fact is that wage inequality increased. The raw standard deviation of log wages increased from 0.25 in 1992 to 0.30 in 2003. This increase occurred both within industries (the dotted line) and within worker categories (the dashed line). The fact that residual wage inequality is uniformly lower than overall but that it increased by the same amount indicates that virtually all of the increase in wage inequality was due to changes in the returns to unmeasured characteristics of workers.

Figure 3.5 examines wage differentials between individuals at various percentiles of the wage distribution. The solid line shows a steady increase in the

10. There of course are other relevant papers on this; see, for example, Gustavsson (2004), Le Grand, Szulkin, and Tåhlin (2001), and Nordström, Edin, and Homlund (2006).
11. The numbers presented in this section come from the wage data contained in LINDA; see Edin and Fredriksson (2000) for a description of these data. In the pre-1998 data, there is stratified sampling by firm size in the private sector. We correct for this by weighting, using the inverse of the sampling weights at the industry level. We describe this procedure—and other data issues—in the appendix.

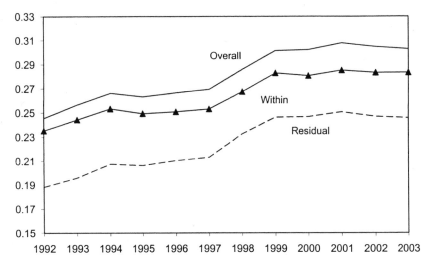

Fig. 3.4   Overall and residual standard deviation of log wages
Source: Calculations based on LINDA.

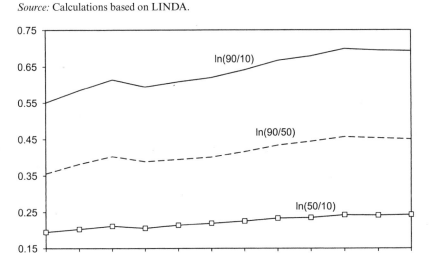

Fig. 3.5   Wage differentials at different points in the wage distribution, 1992 to 2003
Source: Calculations based on LINDA.

ratio of the wage at the 90th percentile of the overall wage distribution to the wage at the 10th percentile—the 90/10 ratio. This ratio increased by some 15 log points between 1992 and 2001. Put differently, in 1992, the wage of an individual at the 90th percentile of the wage distribution was about 73 percent higher than that of a worker at the 10th percentile (exp(0.55) = 1.73). By 2003, the 90th-percentile wage was over double the 10th-percentile wage ($\exp(0.70) = 2.01$). The dashed and dotted lines decompose the 90/10 wage differential into 90/50 and 50/10 components, respectively. The increasing spread of the wage distribution was pervasive, in the sense that both the 90/50 and 50/10 gaps widened. However, as in the United States, most of the increase occurred in the upper half of the wage distribution—the 90/50 ratio rose by about 10 log points from 1992 to 2001, accounting for two-thirds of the change in the 90/10 ratio. The widening of wage differentials appears to have stopped in 2001.

Despite the trends in figures 3.4 and 3.5, it is still the case that there is far less inequality of wages and incomes in Sweden than in the United States. In 2003, after roughly two decades of rising inequality in Sweden, the ratio of wages at the 90th and 10th percentiles stood at about 2.01. By comparison, the 90/10 wage ratio in the United States was about 5.5—over twice the Swedish ratio. In other words, by any measure, wage inequality in the United States dwarfs inequality in Sweden. This suggests that rising wage inequality in Sweden has some distance to go before it would be considered a meaningful threat to egalitarian ideals. Yet, the rise in inequality in Sweden is important—at least by Nordic standards.

We noted earlier that the trend toward decentralized bargaining has been more pronounced among white-collar workers than among blue-collar workers. In figure 3.6, we show that wage dispersion increased the most among white-collar workers. By 1992, the 90/50 differential among white-collar employees had regained its 1970 value, and it has remained above that level since. Compared to 1970, the only meaningful change in within-category relative wages occurred among low-wage white-collar workers, for whom

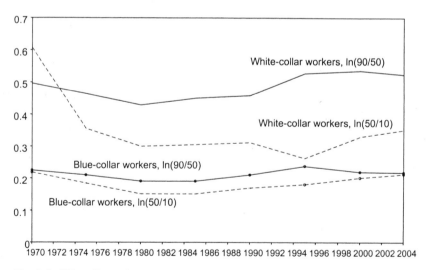

Fig. 3.6   Wage dispersion by worker category in the private sector, 1970 to 2004
Source: Private-sector wage data reported in Lindgren (2005).

inequality declined sharply between 1970 and 1980. Among blue-collar workers, inequality is uniformly lower, as skill heterogeneity itself is likely narrower for this group. Notice that increasing blue-collar wage differences since 1985—soon after the collapse of centralized bargaining in 1983—have brought within-group inequality full circle since 1970, continuing the trend noted by Hibbs (1990) and Edin and Topel (1997, figure 4.2). The data in figure 3.6 pertain to the private sector, but the analysis in Lundborg (2005) shows that these conclusions are also valid for the economy as a whole.

Rising wage inequality in Sweden is a much-dampened reflection of what has occurred elsewhere since about 1980, especially in the United States and United Kingdom (e.g., Katz and Autor 1999). Figure 3.7 shows the evolution of wage inequality in the United States since 1980; the 90/10 wage ratio increased by about 30 log points. In 1980, workers at the 90th percentile of the U.S. distribution earned roughly four times the wages of those at the 10th percentile. By 2000, that ratio had risen to 5.5. By comparison, even after a nearly twenty-year secular in wage inequality, the corresponding ratio in Sweden stood at 2.01, or roughly half the 1980 level of inequality in the United States.[12]

The U.S. workforce is far more heterogeneous than that of Sweden, so direct comparison of inequality measures is problematic—few would claim that Sweden would have U.S. wage outcomes if it adopted American labor market institutions, or conversely. Other Nordic countries provide an alternative benchmark, albeit with similar wage-setting institutions. Nordic countries share the feature of having very low wage inequality. In Finland, nothing seems to have happened to inequality during the 1990s. Using annual earnings of full-time employees as a wage measure, the log of the 90/10 wage ratio in Finland was 0.91 in 1990—comparable to Sweden but well below most other developed countries. By 2003, this ratio was virtually unchanged (0.89).[13] It is noteworthy that there have been no institutional changes in wage formation since 1990 in Finland; industry bargaining has prevailed throughout the time period.[14] Norway provides another Nordic benchmark. In 1990, the log of the 90/10 ratio among full-time working employees stood at 0.88. By 2002, the ratio stood at 0.90. And as in Finland, there have been no changes in the institutional setup of wage bargaining in Norway.[15]

Around 1990, the return to education was relatively low in Sweden—it averaged about 5 percent per additional year of education. This was somewhat

12. According to the OECD (2004), earnings dispersion around the turn of the century is low in Sweden compared with other OECD countries. (It is comparable to countries such as Finland, Italy, and Norway.) But the change in dispersion from the late 1980s to the early 2000s is greater than in the United Kingdom.

13. In 2003, the log of 90/10 earnings ratio (defined analogously) stood at 0.93 in Sweden.

14. Thanks to Roope Uusitalo for supplying this information.

15. We thank Kjell Salvanes for supplying this information.

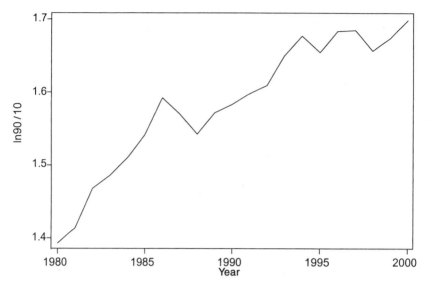

Fig. 3.7   Log of the 90/10 ratio in the United States, 1980 to 2000
Source: Calculations based on the Current Population Survey (CPS)

lower than in other developed countries and well below the estimated returns to schooling in the United States, where average Mincerian returns to an additional year of schooling had reached about 14 percent by 1990—nearly three times the Swedish return. Over the ensuing decade, the U.S. return stayed roughly constant, while returns in Sweden rose slightly. This is illustrated in table 3.4, which reports standardized wage differentials by observed characteristics at successive points in time. The estimates are obtained from wage regressions that were run separately for each year shown. Explanatory variables include schooling (sometimes splined), potential experience (dummies for each five-year interval), gender, immigrant status (separate dummies for Nordic, OECD, and non-OECD immigrants), and years since migration (dummies for each five-year interval).

Though most of the increase in wage dispersion occurs within groups defined by observable characteristics, there is some action in the returns to those characteristics, as well. The first row in the table shows that the return to education increased by 1.5 points (roughly 30 percent) over the 1990s. The returns to an additional year of schooling at the university level has been consistently higher than the return at lower levels, and it has increased more since the early 1990s. This, too, offers a contrast to the United States, where returns *per year* are roughly equal across schooling levels. This may be further evidence that Swedish wage-setting institutions have a relatively larger impact among the least skilled. As previously shown, wages are more compressed among less-skilled workers than among more-skilled ones.

Table 3.4   **Log wage differentials by observed characteristics**

	Year			
	1992	1996	2000	2003
Additional year of schooling (s)				
Average	0.049	0.052	0.061	0.064
s ≤ 12	0.030	0.031	0.038	0.038
s > 12	0.066	0.068	0.077	0.079
New entrants (relative to peak wage earners)	−0.242	−0.286	−0.270	−0.276
Women (relative to men)	−0.165	−0.182	−0.181	−0.167
Immigrants by region of origin (relative to native born)				
Nordic	−0.001	0.005	0.005	−0.002
OECD	−0.034	−0.023	−0.023	−0.019
Non-OECD	−0.050	−0.068	−0.085	−0.091

Note: New entrants row pertains to those with zero to five years of potential experience relative to those with thirty to thirty-five years of potential experience.

Table 3.4 also shows that there is a minor increase in the return to experience, as measured by the gap between new entrants and peak earners, and that the male-female wage gap has remained fairly constant. Wage differences among Nordic and OECD immigrants have remained small, presumably reflecting their similarity to native Swedes. The story is different for non-OECD immigrants, for whom relative wages fell by about 4 percentage points over the decade.

The upshot of the facts presented here is that skill premiums for observed measures of skill, as well as residual wage inequality, increased during the 1990s. But why? Given the institutional setting and evidence on driving forces in other countries, two explanations are plausible. The first is skill-biased technical change that has raised the relative productivity of those with greater skills. The second is the decentralization of wage bargaining, which may facilitate the impact of technical change. We think the evidence favors a combination of these forces, with greater weight on changes in the institutional features of wage formation. The reasons are twofold. First, nothing much has happened to wage dispersion in Norway and Finland; in these countries, there were no changes to the institutional setup of wage bargaining, and they arguably were exposed to the same forces of technical change as in Sweden. Second, we see the greatest increase in wage dispersion among white-collar workers in Sweden, and it is for this group of workers that the changes in the institutional features of wage formation have been most pronounced.[16] Yet, technology-driven changes in the value of skills

16. Moreover, direct observation on segments of the labor markets where there were distinct changes in the wage-setting institutions are consistent with the conclusion that change in the institutional setup is a major factor driving the increase in wage inequality (see Söderström 2006; and Granqvist and Regnér 2006).

may have played an important role in this. The evidence from the United States is that wage inequality and returns to education and experience grew rapidly during the 1980s, while these effects were greatly dampened in Sweden. The fact that inequality in Sweden increased during the 1990s can be interpreted as Swedish wage-setting institutions delaying the tide of rising inequality caused by the increased value of skills.

3.3.2   Employment Differentials

We now turn to the evolution of employment outcomes for different groups.[17] Table 3.5—which has the same structure as table 3.4—shows standardized differences in employment rates by observed characteristics.

The first two rows show employment differentials by education. For those with compulsory schooling or less, the contraction of the early 1990s caused a sharp and apparently permanent decline in relative employment opportunities. The fact that the university educated also lost ground relative to upper-secondary graduates is more surprising. But recall from section 3.2 that this period corresponded to a large increase in the relative supply of university-educated workers, which was likely a contributing factor.

The experience of non-OECD immigrants suggests a similar interpretation: their employment prospects have not recovered fully from the 1990s contraction, which was likely exacerbated by the large influx of refugee immigrants during the same time period. Perhaps contrary to expectations, the contraction of the public sector did not cause a decline in the relative employment rate of women. Instead, a secular pattern of increased female employment (relative to men) continued through the decade.[18]

3.3.3   Wages and Employment by Skill Group

In this section, we address the question of how wages and employment have evolved for different skill groups since the early 1990s. Our approach is similar to the approach of Juhn, Murphy, and Topel (1991), who tracked the evolution of wage and employment inequality in the United States. We develop a consistent set of wage-indexed skill categories by estimating a single-wage equation for 2003, conditioning it on observable characteristics. Given these skill prices for labor force participants, we predict wages for the entire population in each year from 1992 to 2003. We then rank individu-

17. The definition of employment is obtained by combining wage and earnings data; the basic strategy is explained in the appendix. The level of employment generated by this procedure is too low relative to the labor force surveys; however, the changes in employment correspond well to the labor force surveys. The reason for not using the labor force surveys at this stage is that we only observe foreign citizenship rather than immigrant status in these data. The possibility of standardization of the employment differentials of course is an additional virtue of using the microdata.

18. This is the one instance where our analysis produces something substantively different than the labor force surveys. This difference may have to do with our definition of employment or with the fact that we are reporting standardized employment differences.

Table 3.5   Employment differentials by observed characteristics (percentage points)

	Year			
	1992	1996	2000	2003
Education (relative to those with upper-secondary schooling)				
Compulsory schooling or less	−3.2	−8.0	−8.1	−9.5
More than upper-secondary school	8.4	6.5	3.8	3.8
New entrants (relative to peak wage earners)	−38.1	−43.5	−36.3	−39.9
Women (relative to men)	−7.0	−5.3	−5.0	−4.3
Immigrants by region of origin (relative to native born)				
Nordic	0.3	−2.2	−2.5	−2.3
OECD	−9.2	−9.4	−7.0	−9.2
Non-OECD	−9.6	−15.6	−13.4	−12.7

Note: New entrants row pertains to those with zero to five years of potential experience relative to those with thirty to thirty-five years of potential experience

als by skill (i.e., their predicted wage) and gauge the evolution of average wages and nonemployment within deciles of the predicted wage distribution over the entire period. This procedure will most likely place nonemployed individuals too high in the skills distribution—it overpredicts wages for non-workers, because it ignores the role of unobserved skills—but we proceed with those caveats in mind.

Figure 3.8 shows real wage growth for workers in different intervals of the overall wage distribution, along with growth in economy-wide labor productivity (output per hour). Real productivity grew by roughly 28 percent between 1992 and 2003, or at a compound (and stable) rate of about 2.3 percent annually. This increase in productivity drove real wage increases of similar overall magnitude, but the figure also demonstrates that associated wage gains were not distributed equally across skill groups. Importantly, this pattern of growing real wages stands in sharp contrast to the period from 1975 to 1995, when real wages did not grow at all (see Edin and Topel 1997). Wages for the most skilled individuals led the way, with an average annual growth of 2.7 percent, while workers from the lowest decile experienced wage increases at the lower but still substantial rate of 1.7 percent per annum. Inequality increased—wage growth is perfectly rank ordered across intervals of the (predicted) wage distribution—but the data clearly indicate that rising productivity in the 1990s served to raise all boats.

The fact that real wages have grown for all skill groups in Sweden during the 1990s is in sharp contrast to the skill distribution of wage and productivity gains in the United States, where many boats were not lifted, in spite of similar increases in measured labor productivity and compensation per hour. Figure 3.9 shows the growth in average productivity per hour across

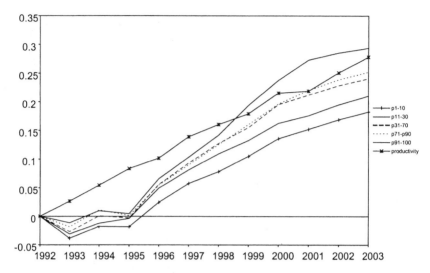

Fig. 3.8   Growth in average productivity and real wage growth by skill group (predicted wage percentile), 1992 to 2003 (1992 = 0)

Source: Calculations of real wage growth are based on LINDA. Productivity comes from Statistics Sweden and the National Institute of Economic Research

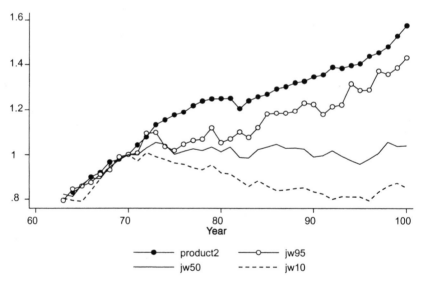

Fig. 3.9   Growth in average productivity (output/hour) and real wage growth by percentile, 1963 to 2000 (1970 = 1)

Sources: The CPS and the National Income and Product Accounts (NIPA).

Note: "product2" = productivity; "jw10" = 10th percentile; "jw50" = 50th percentile; and "jw95" = 95th percentile.

all workers in the United States (top line), along with wage growth for the 95th, 50th, and 10th percentiles of the wage distribution from 1963 to 2000. Unlike in Sweden, during the 1990s, only those at the top of the U.S. wage distribution experienced wage growth comparable to growth in aggregate real productivity. Individuals at or below the median of the U.S. wage distribution experienced negligible real wage growth during the 1990s. Some of this difference between productivity and wage growth reflects growth in nonwage compensation in the United States—employer-provided health insurance is the most obvious example—but most of the gap appears to be due to the growing inequality of productivities that favored wage earners at the highest reaches of the distribution.[19]

Figure 3.10 shows the evolution of nonemployment for the same skill categories used in figure 3.8. It is evident that the least skilled (p1 to p10) are more susceptible to economic contraction than individuals around the median in the skill distribution (p31 to p70). Nevertheless, the employment prospects for all other groups have improved since 1992. The decline in the employment prospects for the least skilled since 1992 relative to the change for the median is significant at conventional levels. (The difference in the changes has a t-ratio of –9.6.) Thus, the evolution of employment rates for the least skilled compounds the pattern of rising inequality shown in figure 3.8. In section 3.5, we pay closer attention to the employment prospects of the less skilled and how they are influenced by wage policy.

3.4   Wage Policy, Skill Formation, and Skill Allocation

Swedish wage policy, implemented by collective bargaining, clearly has produced a different allocation of labor across industries and of workers across skills than would an unimpeded labor market. The incentives to invest in skills and to seek productive employment opportunities may be curbed by wage compression. Moreover, an explicit aim of Swedish wage policy has been to price some jobs out of the market. Thus, wage policy affects both ends of the (potential) skill distribution. The purpose of the next two sections is to look more closely at these two aspects of wage policy. We begin by looking at how incentives to invest can affect human capital formation. We follow by examining the effects at the lower end of the skill distribution.[20]

Having the right incentives is obviously important in a number of ways.

19. The wage measures for both the United States and Sweden deflate wages by a common price index for all skill groups. In the United States, this overstates change in relative welfare, because prices have risen less rapidly for goods purchased by low-income families. See Broda and Romalis (2008).

20. Throughout, we focus on wage policy and how it may influence wage returns and employment outcomes. Obviously, other institutional arrangements are also important if we want to understand the full difference between the employment rates, for example, of natives and immigrants. Note also that our basic approach is the narrative—establishing causality is a much more difficult issue.

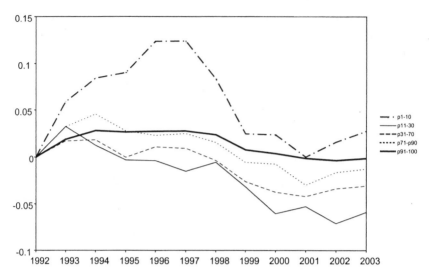

Fig. 3.10   Nonemployment by skill group, 1992 to 2003 (1992 = 0)
Source: Calculations based on LINDA.

They are essential for the acquisition of the (right) skills; they influence labor supply and are conducive for using the acquired skills in the most valuable way. Further, international migration is also affected by the return to skills. Measuring these various dimensions of the relationship between incentives and skills is of course difficult. But some aspects—such as the association between the returns to education and enrollment—are measurable.

In figures 3.11 and 3.12, we examine the relationship between the returns to university education and the university enrollment rate in Sweden and the United States, respectively. These graphs are constructed in a slightly different fashion—for Sweden, we report the fraction of the population aged nineteen to twenty-one attending universities, while for the United States, we show the fraction of high school graduates attending college—but the spirit of the calculations is the same.

Both figures convey the message that investments in this form of human capital respond to changes in the returns on such investments. Figure 3.11 shows two swings in the Swedish data. The returns to university education declined by roughly half—from 10.6 percent to 5.2 percent per year—between the early 1970s and the mid-1980s, concomitant with the decline in overall wage inequality in Sweden. Then, the return rebounded; by 2003, it had risen to about 8 percent. Importantly, the university enrollment rate mirrors this development, declining as the financial rewards to schooling fell and increasing as those returns subsequently rose.

This connection between rates of return and investment in human capital is also evident in the United States. Figure 3.12 shows corresponding

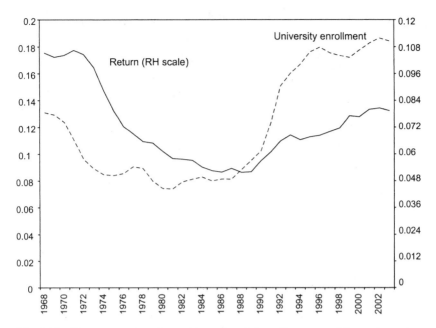

Fig. 3.11   Returns to university and the university enrollment rate (share of population) in Sweden, 1968 to 2003

Sources: Education and population statistics from Statistics Sweden (enrollment rate), and estimates based on LINDA (wage return).

Notes: The university enrollment rate is the number of university students less than twenty-two years of age as a fraction of the population aged nineteen to twenty-one. We have adjusted these data for the reform of university education in 1977. The return is measured in logs and is defined per year of university education. The return has been imputed using earnings regressions for years prior to 1992.

Fig. 3.12   Returns to college and the college enrollment rate (share of high school graduates) in the United States, 1963 to 2001

Source: Calculations based on the CPS.

patterns for investment and returns in the United States from 1963 onward. Here, the measurement of schooling investment is the fraction of high school graduates from a given cohort who report at least one year of college education. Figure 3.12 is slightly more compelling than figure 3.11, as in the United States, there is greater variation in the rate of return over time. The U.S. return per year of college bottomed out at about 7 percent in 1979, having declined by 5 percentage points since 1968. This corresponds closely with the trough in the fraction of eligible high school graduates with college training, which declined to 41 percent for the 1978/1979 cohorts of high school graduates. Then, the returns doubled to about 14 percent in the 1990s—far above anything observed in Sweden—which lines up with a 13 percentage point increase (from 41 percent to 54 percent) in the fraction of high school graduates who have completed some college. The implied elasticity of U.S. human capital investment with respect to the Mincerian return is about 0.40.

The evidence in figures 3.11 and 3.12 has important implications for Swedish productivity and economic growth. Egalitarian policies—which range from wage-bargaining institutions to redistributive taxes and publicly provided consumption—clearly compress wage, income, and consumption differences across skill groups. These differences *are* the returns to investing in productive skills, so the evidence is that wage compression impedes human capital formation. If we take the U.S. schooling data seriously, the elasticity of human capital with respect to wage returns is substantial. We have no evidence on how these policies affect investments in other forms of human capital, such as occupational choice, job-specific training, and the accumulation of other postschooling skills, but neither do we have reason to believe that these investments would respond differently than does schooling.

How large might be the effects of a slight increase in wage inequality on long-run productivity and welfare? Consistent with U.S. data, we assume the elasticity of human capital investment with respect to its return is 0.4. In Sweden today, the log of the 90/10 wage differential is about 0.70 (see figure 3.5), which, as we have noted, implies that a 90th-percentile Swede earns about double the wage of a Swede at the 10th percentile of the wage distribution. Reasonably, Swedish wage-setting and other institutions have compressed these returns to skill. Suppose that restrictions on wage setting were relaxed in such a way that the log 90/10 differential increased from 0.7 to 0.8, for an earnings ratio of 2.23. Few would argue that such a change has a major impact on egalitarian outcomes. This change implies a 14.3 percent ($0.10/0.70 = 0.143$) relative change in inequality.

Now suppose that the returns to skill rise in the same proportion. With a long-run elasticity of investment in human capital of 0.40, this yields a long-run change in the aggregate human capital stock of 5.7 percent ($0.143 \times 0.40 = 0.057$). In modern theories of economic growth, long-run productivity is proportional to human capital, so this change yields a permanent increase in national income of 5.7 percent. We are not expecting anyone to take the exact number very seriously. Still, this calculation indicates that there may be large gains from relaxing institutional restrictions on wage setting. (In other words, the efficiency costs of egalitarian policies may be quite large.)

Another dimension of economy-wide human capital formation concerns the skill content of international migration. While it is true that international migration flows are pretty low at present, even small flows may be a problem if the most talented leave the country. Moreover, international migration may be an increasingly important phenomenon as world market integration progresses.

Basic human capital theory suggests that high-ability immigrants should be attracted to countries that have more wage dispersion and greater returns to skills. This prediction is largely confirmed by comparing the immigration experiences of the United States and the European Union as a whole (see Wasmer et al. 2007). Figures 3.13 and 3.14 examine this issue in the context of Swedish/U.S. immigration flows. The figures show immigrant shares by percentiles of the wage distribution in the two countries. Immigrants to Sweden—see figure 3.13—are concentrated in the lower part of the wage distribution. Splitting the data by broad regions of origin, we see that this low-skill concentration is entirely due to non-OECD (refugee) immigrants being more prevalent at the lower end of the wage distribution; immigrants from Nordic and OECD countries are broadly distributed in the same way as native Swedes.

Figure 3.14 shows an analogous plot for the United States. In contrast to the low-skill concentration of Swedish immigrants, in the United States, immigrants are more prevalent at both extremes of the wage distribution. Splitting the data by ethnic origin (not shown) demonstrates that Asians are about as likely to be at the top as at the bottom of the wage distribution in the United States, while Hispanics look more like non-OECD immigrants to Sweden.

Given the nature of the recent immigrant inflow to Sweden, it is potentially misleading to compare Sweden and the United States without adjusting for the fact that the source countries are different, as are the reasons for immigration. The possible connection between skill content of immigration and the returns to skill is likely to be substantially weaker among refugee immigrants. To obtain a sharper comparison, we focus on immigrants from OECD-Europe (excluding the Nordic countries).[21] Notice that the distribution over source countries within this immigrant group is very similar

21. The reason for excluding the Nordic countries is that gravity is likely to be an issue here. Presumably, it is a much bigger step to move to the United States than to Sweden for Nordic immigrants. For analogous (but converse) reasons, we do not want to include immigrants from Central and South America in the comparison, who have much stronger ties to the United States.

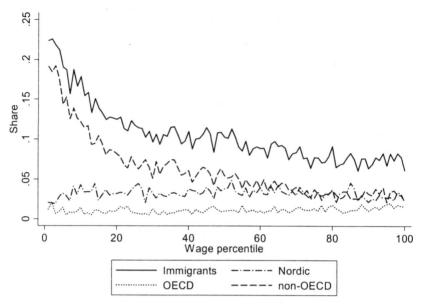

Fig. 3.13 Immigrants by wage percentile in Sweden, 2003
Source: Calculations based on LINDA.

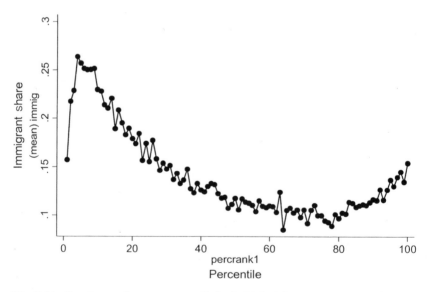

Fig. 3.14 Immigrants by wage percentile in the United States, 1999
Source: Calculations based on the CPS.

in the United States and Sweden, so such differences will not influence our comparisons.

In figure 3.15, we compare the distribution of OECD-European immigrants in the Swedish and U.S. wage distributions, respectively. While immigrants to Sweden from OECD-Europe are distributed roughly in the same way as native Swedes, the salient fact in the United States is that OECD immigrants are disproportionately high skilled, as indicated by market wages. Figure 3.16 further develops this point, comparing the ranking of immigrants from Nordic countries with the ranking of immigrants from OECD-Europe within the U.S. wage distribution. To smooth the data somewhat, we now show the cumulative fraction of immigrants at each percentile of the U.S. wage distribution—a sort of relative Lorenz curve.[22] Our finding is that Nordic immigrants to the United States are *more* heavily concentrated at the high end of the U.S. wage distribution than are other European immigrants. Most of this difference is above the 90th percentile—that is, Nordic immigrants to the United States are disproportionately concentrated in the upper decile of the U.S. wage distribution, where the returns to skill are much higher than in their home countries.

The question, then, is how we should interpret figures 3.15 and 3.16. One interpretation is that there is self-selection in the immigrant pool, and talented Europeans are attracted to the United States because of higher returns to skill (see figure 3.15). On this interpretation, the greater concentration of Scandinavian immigrants at the top of the U.S. wage distribution is due to greater returns to migration among the most talented, as wage distributions in their home countries are particularly compressed, even by European standards (see figure 3.16). There is a European brain drain to the United States, and the effects are most pronounced in Nordic countries, where wage compression is most severe.

Against this, one might argue that the average native-born Swede is more skilled than the average native-born American, so a given immigrant will have a lower rank in the Swedish than in the U.S. wage distribution. That there is some truth to this story is suggested by the IALS data (see OECD and Statistics Canada 1995). Among the countries listed in table 3.6, Sweden has the highest mean score, while the mean score in the United States is slightly below the other Nordic countries. The table also shows that an immigrant for any given OECD country would rank lower in the Swedish skill distribution than in the U.S. one.

So, let us narrow the comparison even more to try to separate the two explanations. In figure 3.17, we compare Nordic immigrants in the United States with German immigrants. We select German immigrants as the

22. There were not enough observations on Swedish immigrants (eighty) to do a reliable comparison, so Nordic countries include Norway, Finland, Sweden, and Denmark, yielding 204 immigrants. Non-Nordic countries are Austria, Belgium, France, Germany, Ireland, Italy, Luxembourg, the Netherlands, Portugal, Spain, Switzerland, and the United Kingdom.

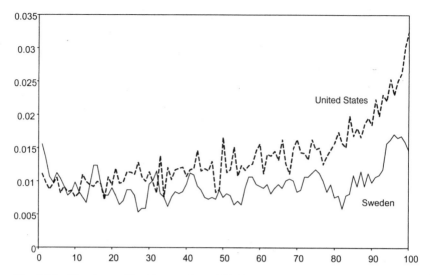

Fig. 3.15 The share of immigrants from OECD-Europe by wage percentile in the Swedish and U.S. wage distributions

Sources: Calculations based on LINDA (Sweden, 2003) and the U.S. Census Bureau Public-Use Microdata Samples (PUMS; United States, 1999).

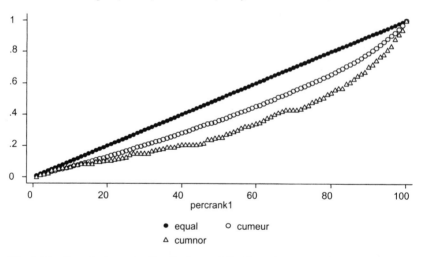

Fig. 3.16 Cumulative wage distributions of Nordic and other OECD-Europe immigrants by percentile of U.S. wage distribution

Source: Census PUMS, 1999.

Note: "cumeur" = OECD-Europe and "cumnor" = Nordic.

Table 3.6   **Test scores according to the International Adult Literacy Survey**

Country	Mean	Rank in Swedish distribution	Rank in U.S. distribution
Belgium	279	30	48
Denmark	289	37	56
Finland	289	37	56
Germany	287	36	55
Ireland	262	20	37
Italy	244	13	26
The Netherlands	288	36	55
Norway	296	43	62
Sweden	308	n.a.	69
Switzerland	285	34	53
United Kingdom	270	24	42
United States	284	33	n.a.

Notes: The sample pertains to natives aged sixteen to sixty-five in the respective countries. Sampling weights are used; "n.a." means not applicable.

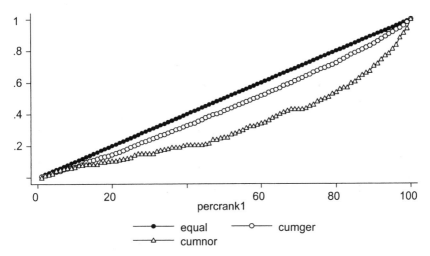

Fig. 3.17   Cumulative wage distributions of Nordic and German immigrants by percentile of U.S. wage distribution
Source: Census PUMS, 1999.
Note: "cumeur" = OECD-Europe and "cumnor" = Nordic.

comparison because they are most similar to Nordic immigrants—mean skills as measured by the IALS are only slightly below the averages in Finland and Denmark.

The conclusion is very similar to the one obtained from figure 3.16. Nordic immigrants in the United States are concentrated much more at the top of the U.S. wage distribution than are German immigrants. The evidence suggests that wage compression provides the strongest incentives to the most talented Swedes to migrate—a version of the brain drain—and that Sweden is relatively more attractive to less-skilled migrants. These effects on the composition of migrants are probably not alarming at present but may be a more pressing concern in the near future.

Another margin where wage policies may affect skill allocation concerns the utilization of human capital. The total amount of time spent in market work is substantially lower in Sweden (and in any other European country) than in the United States. In 2004, the average employee worked 1,585 hours per year in Sweden; the corresponding American worked 1,825 hours.[23] But if one compares the total amount of work—that is, the sum of market work and time spent doing household work—there is no difference across the two countries (Olovsson 2004). Different incentives thus imply that Swedes allocate less time to market activities—further evidence that welfare state policies distort incentives relative to unimpeded market outcomes. Of course, also in this instance, other features of the welfare state are relevant, as the total wedge between market and household activities is influenced by income taxes and transfers as well.

3.5   Wage Policy and Its Effects on Less-Skilled Workers

The fact that the total amount of work—particularly for females—is similar in Europe and the United States is consistent with the marketization hypothesis of Freeman and Schettkat (2005). The essence of their argument is that most European countries have wage-setting frameworks that include both a greater role for collective bargaining and higher payroll taxes than in the United States. This combination has raised the price of services that are intensive in low-skilled labor, so Europeans have lower market consumption of these services than do Americans. Freeman and Schettkat go on to argue that increased marketization of services would free up more time for women to engage fully in market activities and to make full use of their human capital investments. But this would require some relaxation of wage restraints among the least skilled.

Female employment rates in Sweden are closer to those in the United States than in continental Europe. An important reason for this is that services such as child care (see Kolm and Lazear, chapter 2 in this volume) and elderly care are publicly provided in Sweden rather than produced by the market and the household—as in the United States—or predominantly by the household—as in Germany. Nevertheless, some services, such as cooking and cleaning, are still home produced to a greater extent in Sweden than in United States. These facts imply that the private-service sector will be smaller in Sweden than in the United States—and it is (see table 3.7).

---

23. The numbers come from the OECD (2004).

Of course, the distribution of employment over industries is different in Sweden than in the United States for a variety of reasons. The first question we take up (section 3.5.1) is whether relative industry size is related to the employment prospects of workers with different skills. For instance, one may suspect that the employment opportunities of immigrants—who are disproportionately employed in low-wage services in all industrialized countries—are worse in a country where services are produced in the market to a lesser extent.

The distribution of industry employment in a given country depends on the entire institutional setup in that country. In addition to wage policy, tax and industrial policies have effects on the services and goods produced in the market (see Davis and Henrekson, chapter 7 in this volume). In section 3.5.2, therefore, we look directly at wage policies that are affecting the lower end of the skill distribution, with a focus on the impact of negotiated minimum wages on employment.

3.5.1 Industry Size and Employment of the Least Skilled

In 2000, the employment-to-population ratio of native Swedes was 17.6 percentage points higher than for immigrants. In the United States, the employment-to-population ratio of immigrants is slightly *higher* than for natives. A possible explanation for this gap is that the Swedish labor market offers scant employment opportunities for immigrants, especially less-skilled recent immigrants. Table 3.7 sheds light on this question by using the U.S. distribution of employment across broad industry categories as the counterfactual. In other words, we ask: if industry employment shares in Sweden were like those in the United States, what would happen to the demand for immigrant labor in Sweden? Would employment opportunities improve? We impute the immigrant distribution over industries using the U.S. distribution of industry employment, taking as given the concentration of immigrants in Swedish industries.

The first two columns report the distribution of employment in the overall population for the United States and Sweden, respectively. The share of manufacturing is smaller in the United States than in Sweden, while private services, in general, employ a greater fraction of individuals in the United States. The third column reports the distribution of employed immigrants in Sweden. Compared to Swedish natives and to the U.S. labor force, Swedish immigrants are disproportionately employed in manufacturing. Perhaps somewhat surprisingly, they are about as prevalent in trade, hotels, and restaurants as is the overall population. However, this simply is due to the aggregation of retail and wholesale trade and hotels and restaurants. A finer division of the data by industry also reveals that they are much more prevalent in hotels and restaurants but are less prevalent in retail and wholesale trade.

For the broad categories used in this calculation, the two industries that

Table 3.7   Employment by industry in Sweden and the United States in 2000

	United States All	Sweden Total employment per group (%)				
		Immigrants			Lowest quartile	
		All	Actual	Imputed using U.S.	Actual	Imputed using U.S.
Industry	(1)	(2)	(3)	(4)	(5)	(6)
Agriculture, forestry, and fishing	2.4	2.7	1.3	1.2	2.3	2.0
Mining and quarrying	0.4	0.2	0.0	0.1	0.1	0.1
Manufacturing	12.6	17.5	22.7	16.3	16.7	12.0
Power and water plants	0.6	0.7	0.2	0.2	0.3	0.3
Construction	5.7	5.2	2.7	2.9	2.1	2.3
Retail and wholesale trade; hotels and restaurants	24.7	15.5	15.6	24.9	25.1	40.0
Transport and communication	5.1	7	7.0	5.1	5.3	3.9
Finance, insurance, and real estate	16.8	13.4	13.1	16.4	11.9	14.9
Community and personal services	31.8	37.8	37.3	31.4	36.2	30.5
Total	100.1	100.0	100.0	98.5	100.0	106.0

Source: Calculations based on the OECD STructural ANalysis database (STAN) and LINDA.
Notes: The numbers in column (4) are calculated as column (4) = [column (3)/column (2)] * column (1). The numbers in column (6) are calculated in an analogous fashion. Lowest quartile columns pertain to individuals who are in the lowest quartile of the predicted wage distribution. This wage prediction was generated in the same fashion as in section 3.3.3.

account for the largest shares of Swedish immigrant jobs (manufacturing and community and personal services) are smaller in the United States than in Sweden. So, a shift to the U.S. distribution of industry employment would reduce the immigrant employment rate, holding constant the relative distribution of immigrants across industries. Immigrant employment would be reduced by 1.5 percent in this conceptual experiment—see column (4)—increasing the immigrant/native gap in the employment-to-population ratio to 18.3 percentage points. Having said this, we should note that this result is partly an artifact of the one-digit industry classifications used in table 3.7, which may mask the expansion of employment opportunities for immigrants.

The last two columns of the table report the results of an analogous exercise for individuals who are predicted to have a low wage. Column (5) thus reports the actual distribution of employment over industries for individuals that are predicted to be in the lowest quartile of the wage distribution. A comparison of columns (5) and (2) reveals that the major difference between these individuals and the overall population is that they are more likely to be employed in retail and wholesale trade and in hotels and restaurants relative to the overall population. The U.S. distribution of industry employment thus implies an increase in the employment rate for low-wage individuals. The U.S. counterfactual suggests that the employment-to-population ratio would increase by 6 percent, which would contribute to a decrease of the employment gap by almost 3 percentage points—from 22.9 to 20.1 percentage points—though we put more stock in the direction of this effect than in the particular magnitude estimated in this illustrative exercise.

3.5.2   Minimum Wages and Employment

As we noted earlier, minimum wages in Sweden are determined by the collective-bargaining process rather than by legislation; there is no legal minimum wage, though negotiated minima also apply to nonunion employees if there is a collective agreement at the workplace. So, minimum wages generally will vary by industry, as well as by age, occupation, and experience. And by most standards, they are high.

Table 3.8 shows the minimum wage bite by country in 2004, defined as the minimum wage divided by the median wage in manufacturing in each country.[24] Apart from Sweden, all countries reported in table 3.8 have legislated minimum wages. For Sweden, we report a range, because the minimum wage varies across collective-bargaining agreements. Among the countries covered in table 3.8, Sweden has the highest minimum wage bite. This reflects what seems to be an empirical regularity—minimum wages tend to be higher when they are subject to bargaining rather than to legislation. In 2001, minimum wages in Norway and Denmark were higher than in Sweden, while Finland's was slightly lower, and Germany's was much lower (Andersson, Kainelainen, and Reinbrand 2002).[25] Thus, the Nordic countries share the feature of having high minimum wages, just as they share many other features concerning wage dispersion and institutions.

Figure 3.18 tracks the evolution of Sweden's minimum wage bite, defined here as the minimum wage relative to the mean wage in each industry, since 1991 for a collection of industries. It is evident that the bite of the minimum wage is higher in the service sectors than in manufacturing, reflecting lower average wages in services. From 1994 to 2004, the minimum wage bite declined by roughly 8 percentage points (to 63 percent) in manufacturing. In

24. Much of the information on minimum wages in this section comes from Per Skedinger. We have also obtained some information on minimum wages from Albin Kainelainen. We thank them for supplying the data.
25. For countries with bargained minimum wages, Andersson, Kainelainen, and Reinbrand (2002) look at the minimum wage for dishwashers and relate that to the mean manufacturing wage. In 2001, the minimum wage bite defined in this way was close to 70 percent in Norway, slightly above 60 percent in Denmark, 60 percent in Sweden, roughly 55 percent in Finland, and 40 percent in Germany.

Table 3.8   **Minimum wage bite by country in 2004**

Country	Minimum wage bite (%)
Australia	59
Belgium	49
Canada	40
France	57
Greece	48
Ireland	52
Japan	34
The Netherlands	46
New Zealand	54
Portugal	38
Spain	30
Sweden	**60–72**
United Kingdom	43
United States	32

Source: Low Pay Commission (2005).

Notes: The minimum wage bite is defined as the minimum wage relative to the median manufacturing wage in each country. For the United States, we report the federal minimum wage; the number for Canada refers to a weighted average across regions.

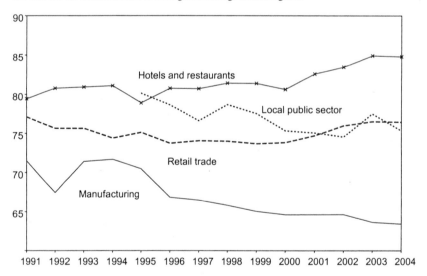

Fig. 3.18   Minimum wage bite for a selection of industries, 1991–2004 (%)
Source: Skedinger (2006b). Minimum wages come from the various wage settlements. Average wages pertain to unskilled workers and come from Statistics Sweden and the Swedish Municipal Workers' Union.

private services, on the other hand, the wage bite has been roughly constant (retail trade) or has increased (hotels and restaurants). It is clear that minimum wages have significant bite in hotels and restaurants—the bargained minimum stood at 85 percent of the average wage by 2003—so for practical purposes, the minimum contractual wage compresses the wage distribution in this sector substantially from below.

Of course, minimum wages have differential bite for various worker categories. Table 3.9 illustrates this by showing the minimum wage as a percentage of the mean wage for the native born, for the native born aged twenty to twenty-five, and for immigrants. Here, we focus on a single wage agreement—that pertaining to blue-collar workers in the local public sector. Minimum wages have substantial bite in these blue-collar occupations. The minimum wage bite varies in a rather obvious way across worker categories: immigrants and youths have lower wages than the average native born, and hence, the minimum wage amounts to a greater fraction of the mean wages of these two groups.

The interesting question is whether minimum wages reduce the employment prospects of the less skilled. This is a controversial issue in the empirical literature on minimum wages,[26] yet evidence from Sweden indicates a substantial effect. Edin and Holmlund (1994) used time series data to examine whether youth employment in manufacturing is related to the minimum wage bite. They found that the minimum wage is negatively related to youth employment. Skedinger (2006a) studied the consequences of minimum wages in hotels and restaurants, using individual wage and employment data. This allowed Skedinger to isolate those workers who were most likely to be affected by minimum wage changes. He then related the wage and employment experiences of this group to the experiences of a comparison group consisting of individuals with similar wages initially but who were less affected by minimum wage changes.[27] Like Edin and Holmlund, Skedinger also found negative employment effects of increases in the minimum wage, and the effect is substantial. His baseline estimates indicate that a 10 percent increase in the minimum wage reduced the relative employment rates of affected workers by 5 percent—a demand elasticity of about –0.5 among low-skill workers.

We previously noted that the employment-to-population ratio among immigrants is 17.6 points lower among Swedish immigrants than among natives, but in the United States, these ratios are roughly comparable. Given a demand elasticity of –0.5, it is reasonable to conclude that some of this immigrant/native employment gap in Sweden would close if bargained

26. In some notable examples, increases in minimum wages even have positive employment effects; see Card and Krueger (1995).

27. Of course, there is considerable difficulty in finding a comparison group that was not treated by the minimum wage. Most realistic theories predict that minimum wage changes will affect the entire wage distribution.

Table 3.9   Minimum wage bite by worker category, local public sector in 2003

Worker category	Minimum wage bite (%)
Natives, unskilled	79
Natives, semiskilled	72
Immigrants, unskilled	83
Immigrants, semiskilled	74
Aged 20 to 25, unskilled	83
Aged 20 to 25, semiskilled	79

Source: Calculations based on LINDA.
Notes: Unskilled occupations have no educational requirements. Semiskilled occupations normally require a vocational upper-secondary degree.

minimum wages in Sweden were to decline. It is highly unlikely, however, that the immigrant/native employment gap would disappear completely, as in the U.S. case, because the characteristics of the Swedish and U.S. immigrant populations are very different.

3.6   Conclusions

The original SNS-NBER study of the Swedish labor market was written in the midst of the economic crisis of the early 1990s. In this sequel, we have focused on the postcrisis performance of the labor market, emphasizing institutional and other changes that have affected wage determination, inequality, and employment. Our major conclusions are as follows:

1. *Changes in wage determination.* The institutional features of wage determination have changed since the beginning of the 1990s. The advent of the industrial agreement—and similar agreements in other sectors—appears to have reduced aggregate wage pressure. However, the impact of these agreements on the wage structure is likely to be limited. Wage differentials are more influenced by the decline of centralized bargaining and the consequent decentralization of negotiated wages. The tide toward decentralization is most evident among white-collar workers. Changes in the wage determination process for blue-collar workers are more minor. Bargained minimum wages are as prevalent as earlier, and the growth of minimum wages is largely on par with the growth of average wages. As a result, wage compression at the bottom of the skill distribution remains important.

2. *Changes in wage differentials.* Consistent with trends in other industrialized countries, wage dispersion in Sweden has increased since the early 1990s. This increase was concentrated among white-collar workers and in the upper tail of the wage distribution. The return to education and the wage gap between refugee immigrants and natives rose as well, indicating

that Sweden's modest move toward greater inequality reflects rising returns to human capital. Decentralization of wage determination probably has contributed to greater wage disparities, but decentralization may also be an effect, rather than a cause, of rising inequality. As argued by Edin and Topel (1997), rising returns to skill increased the distortions of centralized bargaining and likely prompted its demise. Decentralized wage setting added a layer of flexibility that better reflects market realities.

3. *Wage policy and efficiency.* In an unregulated market, the wage has an important allocative role. For instance, regional wage differences contribute to mobility, and skill differences in wages are the financial returns for acquiring human capital. Consistent with the latter effect, we have shown that university enrollment is positively associated with the return to education in both Sweden and the United States, indicating that a cost of Sweden's egalitarian policies may be to dampen investment in human capital. Similarly, we find that migrants *from* Sweden are likely to be highly skilled, while recent immigrants are concentrated heavily at the lower end of the Swedish skill distribution. All of this suggests dampened growth of human capital, which may have long-term effects on living standards.

4. *Wage policy and distribution.* Productivity growth has been high in Sweden since the beginning of the 1990s. Some of this reflects a recovery from crisis, but the evidence also suggests an improvement in long-term economic growth. Unlike the U.S. experience, where productivity growth appears to have been concentrated mainly among the most skilled, Sweden's productivity gains in the 1990s were more equally (though not equally) distributed across wage and income categories. It seems highly likely that this difference across the two countries is at least partly due to the difference in wage-setting institutions and other redistributive policies. But it also seems implausible that the gains that have accrued mainly to the most highly paid in the United States would have gone to others if American wage-setting institutions were different—it is also a matter of whose productivity has risen.

5. *Wage policy and employment.* Since the early 1990s, employment growth has been lower than average for those with the weakest position in the labor market. It is difficult tell to what extent this is due to wage policy. But wage policy has contributed to a different industrial structure in Sweden than in the United States. If Sweden's industrial structure would become more similar to the United States, employment prospects for the least skilled would improve. Minimum wages are likely to have especially hampered the employment prospects of immigrants and youths. These pressures are unlikely to abate, given the character of Sweden's recent immigration experience and the possibility of rising immigrant flows in the future. In this light, the employment distortions of minimum wages are likely to be greater today than earlier and possibly greater in the future than at present.

What can we take from this evidence? Ten years ago, in the midst of economic crisis, it was plausible to argue that a bit more inequality in wage outcomes would be a small price to pay for long-term improvements in economic performance. Whether causally or coincidentally, inequality in Sweden has risen, and economic performance has improved. But by almost any standard, inequality in Sweden remains remarkably low. Is the same prescription warranted today as ten years ago? In some part, this is a matter of values. Nevertheless, it seems to us that the market realities are pushing toward increasing wage differentials. In this environment, a given set of egalitarian outcomes will cause greater efficiency losses today than ten years ago.

What kinds of policy levers are available if one believes, for example, that minimum wages distort more today than ten or twenty years ago? Wage policy is in part a misnomer: it is not directly a tool of government economic policies. It reflects Sweden's collective bargaining institutions, and these are unlikely to change rapidly, if at all. But relevant wage differences for the most part are after tax and after transfers, which leaves some leverage for policy adjustments that could improve labor market performance and increase prosperity in Sweden.

Appendix

The purpose of this appendix is to describe our data construction efforts in more detail. Our data come from LINDA (see Edin and Fredriksson 2000). Throughout, we sample employees aged twenty to sixty-four whose educational attainment is not missing.

Weighting

The collection of the wage data has varied over time. Prior to 1998, the data have been collected by stratified sampling of the employed in the private sector. From 1998 and onward, the wage data are representative for the employed population.

When data were collected by stratified sampling, small firms were sampled with low probability (0.02 for firms with less than ten employees), and the sampling probability increased with firm size. (It is unity for firms with more than 500 employees.) Unfortunately, there is no information on the individual sampling probability in the data. However, we know the firm size distribution in each industry. Using these data together with the sampling probabilities, we calculate the average sampling probability for each two-digit industry. Pre-1998 private-sector data thus are weighted by the inverse of the sampling probability by industry to obtain estimates that are representative of the population. As a check on whether this procedure delivered sensible results, we used data from 2003. In the 2003 data, we know who would have been sampled under stratified sampling. Assuming that the difference in sampling procedure has a proportional effect on the measured standard deviation (for all years), we can calculate the adjustment necessary to go from the representative population to the population obtained by stratified sampling. Figure 3A.1 shows the standard deviation of the log wage distribution for different ways of adjusting the pre-1998 data. The line labeled "adjusted" reports the standard deviation obtained using this adjustment, and the line labeled "weighted" reports the estimated standard deviation using our weighting strategy. As shown by the figure, these two estimates more or less go together.

Trimming

In the wage data, there were some (albeit very few) obvious measurement errors in the lower tail of the wage distribution. Therefore, we trimmed the lower tail of the wage distribution by deleting those earning less than 17.45 SEK per hour (roughly $2.2 an hour at the 2005 SEK/dollar conversion rate). This had the effect of deleting 121 individuals in 1999 and less than five for all other years.

Years of Schooling

We have imputed years of schooling from attainment data. The attainment data come from registers that record the degrees of the individuals. This education register gradually has become more informative over time; in later years, it includes adult education and courses taken at the university level. The latest versions of the education register include measures of the

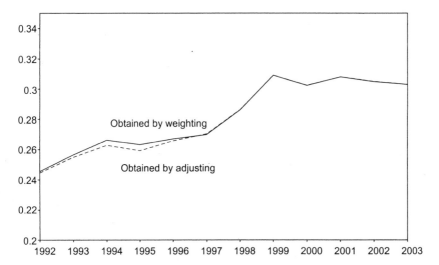

Fig. 3A.1   Standard deviation of log wages, different ways of adjusting pre-1998 data

normal time to degree for all attainment levels. For all years, there is also information on when the degree was obtained. We opt for an algorithm, where we assign the most informative measures of education also for the earlier years when it is obvious that the individual has not upgraded his or her education between these two time points.

Employment

We define employment on the basis of earnings data. Rather than opting for a single earnings limit applied to all individuals for each year, we calculate separate earnings limits for thirty-two cells based on gender, schooling, region, of origin, and experience. The reason for having several thresholds is that we wanted to avoid having all high-wage individuals automatically classified as employed. The exact procedure was the following: for each year, we divided the wage data into thirty-two cells based on gender, schooling, region of origin, and experience. Then, we identified the wages of the individuals on the 1st percentile and the 10th percentile for each cell, and we calculated average earnings for individuals within the interval defined by the first to the 10th percentile. All individuals with earnings above this threshold in each cell are defined as employed. The level of employment generated by this procedure differs somewhat from the one reported in the Labor Force Survey. But the evolution of employment over time corresponds reasonably well to the labor force surveys; see figure 3A.2.

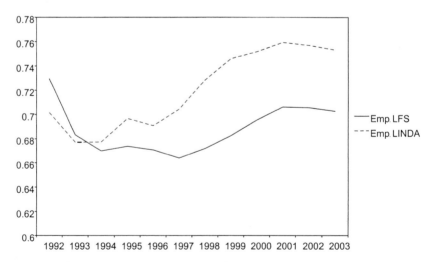

Fig. 3A.2   Different definitions of employment
Sources: Labor force surveys (LFS) and LINDA.

References

Andersson, D., A. Kainelainen, and J. Reinbrand. 2002. Lyfter floden alla båtar? Rapport. Stockholm: Landsorganisationen i Sverige.

Aronsson, T., and J. Walker. 1997. The effects of Sweden's welfare state on labor supply incentives. In *The welfare state in transition: Reforming the Swedish model,* ed. R. Freeman, B. Swedenborg, and R. Topel, 203–67. Chicago: University of Chicago Press.

Broda, C., and J. Romalis. 2008. Inequality and prices: Does China benefit the poor in America? Working Paper. University of Chicago, Department of Economics.

Burtless, G. 1987. Taxes, transfers, and Swedish labor supply. In *The Swedish economy,* ed. B. Bosworth and A. Rivlin, 185–250. Washington, DC: Brookings Institution.

Card, D., and A. Krueger. 1995. *Myth and measurement: The new economics of the minimum wage.* Princeton, NJ: Princeton University Press.

Edin, P.-A., and P. Fredriksson. 2000. LINDA: Longitudinal INdividual DAta for Sweden. Working Paper no. 19. Uppsala University, Department of Economics.

Edin, P.-A., and B. Holmlund. 1994. *Arbetslösheten och arbetsmarknadens funktionssätt,* bilaga 8 till LU94. Stockholm: Fritzes.

Edin, P.-A., and R. Topel. 1997. Wage policy and restructuring: The Swedish labor market since 1960. In *The welfare state in transition: Reforming the Swedish model,* ed. R. Freeman, B. Swedenborg, and R. Topel, 155–203. Chicago: University of Chicago Press.

Elvander, N. 2003. Avtalsrörelsen 2001: Den nya lönebildningsregimen på prov. *Ekonomisk Debatt* 31 (1): 15–27.

Freeman, R., and R. Schettkat. 2005. Marketization of household production and the EU-US gap in work. *Economic Policy* 20 (41): 5–39.

Granqvist, L., and H. Regnér. 2006. The outcome of individual wage bargaining and the influence of managers' bargaining power: Evidence from union data. SOFI Working Paper no. 3. Stockholm University, Swedish Institute for Social Research.

Gustavsson, M. 2004. Empirical essays on earnings inequality. *Economic Studies* 80. Uppsala University, Department of Economics.

Hibbs, D. 1990. Wage compression under solidarity wage bargaining in Sweden. Research report no. 30. Stockholm: Trade Union Institute for Economic Bargaining.

Holmlund, B. 2003. The rise and fall of Swedish unemployment. CESifo Working Paper no. 918. Munich: Center for Economic Studies and the Information and Forshung Institute for Economic Research at the University of Munich, April.

Juhn, C., K. M. Murphy, and R. Topel. 1991. Why has the natural rate of unemployment increased over time? *Brookings Papers on Economic Activity,* Issue no. 2: 75–142.

Katz, L., and D. Autor. 1999. Changes in the wage structure and earnings inequality. In *Handbook of labor economics,* vol. 3A, ed. O. Ashenfelter and D. Card, 1463–548. Amsterdam: North-Holland.

Le Grand, C., R. Szulkin, and M. Tåhlin. 2001. Lönestrukturens förändring i Sverige, ni SOU 2001:53, *Välfärd och arbete i arbetslöshetens årtionde.* Stockholm: Fritzes.

Leuven, E., H. Oosterbeek, and H. van Ophem. 2004. Explaining international differences in male wage inequality by differences in demand and supply of skills. *Economic Journal* 114 (495): 466–86.

Lindbeck, A. 2000. Swedish economic growth in an international perspective. *Swedish Economic Policy Review* 7 (1): 7–37.

Lindgren, B. 2005. Lönespridningen i näringslivet 2004. Unpublished manuscript, Svenskt Näringsliv.

Low Pay Commission. 2005. *National minimum wage: Low Pay Commission report 2005.* Available at: http://www.lowpay.gov.uk/lowpay/rep_a_p_index.shtml.

Lundborg, P. 2005. Individual wage setting, efficiency wages and productivity in Sweden. FIEF Working Paper no. 205. Stockholm: La Fédération Internationale pour l'Economie Familiale.

National Mediation Office. 2004. Avtalsrörelsen och lönebildningen 2004. Medlingsinstitutets årsrapport. Stockholm: Medlingsinstitutet.

Nickell, S., and R. Layard. 1999. Labour market institutions and economic performance. In *Handbook of labor economics,* vol. 3, ed. O. Ashenfelter and D. Card, 3029–84. Amsterdam: North-Holland.

Nordström Skans, O., P.-A. Edin, and B. Holmlund. 2006. Wage dispersion between and within plants. IFAU Working Paper no. 2006:9. Uppsala, Sweden: Institute for Labor Market Policy Evaluation.

Olovsson, C. 2004. Why do Europeans work so little? IIES Seminar Paper no. 727. Stockholm University, Institute for International Economic Studies, February.

Organization for Economic Cooperation and Development (OECD). 2004. *OECD employment outlook 2004.* Paris: OECD.

———. 2005. *OECD economic surveys: Sweden.* Paris: OECD.

Organization for Economic Cooperation and Development (OECD) and Statistics Canada. 1995. *Literacy, economy, and society: Results of the first International Adult Literacy Survey.* Paris: OECD and Statistics Canada.

Rosen, S. 1997. Public employment, taxes, and the welfare state in Sweden. In *The welfare state in transition: Reforming the Swedish model,* ed. R. Freeman, B. Swedenborg, and R. Topel, 79–109. Chicago: University of Chicago Press.

Skedinger, P. 2006a. Minimum wages and employment in Swedish hotels and restaurants. *Labour Economics* 13 (2): 259–90.

———. 2006b. Svenska minimilöner i den globaliserade ekonomin. *Ekonomisk Debatt* 34 (4): 63–77.

Söderström, M. 2006. Evaluating institutional changes in education and wage policy. *Economic Studies* 95. Uppsala University, Department of Economics.

Topel, R. 1997. Factor proportions and relative wages: The supply side determinants of wage inequality. *Journal of Economic Perspectives* 11 (2): 55–74.

Wasmer, E., P. Fredriksson, A. Lamo, J. Messina, and G. Peri. 2007. The macroeconomics of education. In *Education and training in Europe,* ed. G. Brunello, P. Garibaldi, and E. Wasmer, 1–140. Oxford: Oxford University Press.

Labor Supply, Tax Base, and Public Policy in Sweden

Thomas Aronsson and James R. Walker

4.1 Introduction

Sweden has long been at the forefront of creating innovative social insurance programs. For nearly as long, these programs have undergone intense scrutiny of effects on economic and social behavior. In terms of effects on hours of work, the consensus of opinion is that male work hours are relatively unresponsive to changes in the tax and transfer system, whereas female work hours appear to be (at least) slightly more responsive to economic incentives. Yet, this seeming nonresponsiveness of labor supply to tax and program incentives is surprising and unsettling. If incentive effects are so important, as many economists believe, why are the effects so elusive to recover empirically? Should one infer that there are *no* labor supply effects from Sweden's high marginal tax rates and generous (by U.S. standards) program benefits?

To address these and other questions, we continue the analysis of Aronsson and Walker (1997). Our earlier study gave a broad overview of incentives generated by the Swedish tax, transfer, and social insurance systems, as well as an overview of labor supply behavior, with an emphasis on studies based on Swedish data. We also related the incentive structure to existing empirical results by focusing attention on the tax and benefit reforms that took place in Sweden during the 1980s and early 1990s.

In this chapter, we consider labor supply trends and literature since our

Thomas Aronsson is a professor of economics at Umeå University. James R. Walker is a professor of economics at the University of Wisconsin-Madison and a research associate of the National Bureau of Economic Research.

The authors would like to thank Richard Freeman, Bertil Holmlund, Tomas Sjögren, Birgitta Swedenborg, and Robert Topel for helpful comments and suggestions. We thank Shiv Saini for able research assistance.

first study. Additional explanations emerge as possible reasons for the low responsiveness of work hours to taxes and transfers. We summarize this literature, and we review the related literature on why Swedes (and Europeans, in general) appear to supply much less market work than Americans do. Are differences due to higher tax rates in Europe and Sweden than in the United States, or are they due to the functioning of the labor market?

The last decade has witnessed an expansion from hours of work to consider the incentive effects on other dimensions of labor supply. Recent research considers the relationship between the tax system and before-tax income. Pretax income reflects hours of work, and it also reflects effort, occupational choice, wage formation, savings, and to some extent, tax avoidance (depending on the income measure used). Therefore, we combine the study of tax base determination with results from traditional labor supply studies in order to get a better understanding of the relationships between economic incentives and behavior. We also briefly address relationships, on the one hand between the tax system, and on the other, the union wage formation and tax avoidance. The incentives associated with unionized labor market are also relevant from perspectives other than just wage formation—for instance, for understanding international differences with regard to work hours.

The shift in focus from hours of work to broader measures of labor supply is complemented by a shift in interest from the effects of the income tax to the effects of social insurance, and notably for Sweden, of sickness insurance and pension problems. We review this literature and consider Sweden's major pension reform of 1999. The consequences of demographic changes (particularly in connection with pay-as-you-go social security systems) have become increasingly important. The reform of 1999 is the latest example of Sweden's innovative design of social insurance programs.

In summary, we will address the following questions:

- Why are the estimated effects of taxes and transfers on hours of work typically modest? In the light of empirical evidence for Sweden, we will discuss whether social norms and quantitative constraints contribute to this outcome, as well as augment the standard labor supply model with tax avoidance behavior.
- Why are the estimated effects of marginal tax rates on before-tax income typically larger than the corresponding effects on work hours? Are issues such as tax avoidance and wage formation important here?
- What factors determine cross-country differences with respect to work hours—in particular, differences between Sweden, other European countries, and the United States?
- How does the labor supply respond to health insurance and pension systems? The effects of the pension system are particularly interesting to analyze because of (a) the major reform implemented in 1999 and (b) the aging of the population.

Although estimated labor supply elasticities on hours of work are low, as we argued in Aronsson and Walker (1997), behavioral responses to income tax and social insurance programs appear in other dimensions of labor supply. So, our answer to the second question posed in the first paragraph is no—one cannot safely assume that labor supply does not respond to economic incentives. We agree that large responses do not appear in (reported) hours of work, but for reasons presented next, we believe substantial responses appear in other dimensions. As the Organization for Economic Cooperation and Development (OECD 2005) notes in a recent report, in light of these responses, Sweden faces important challenges regarding the structure of its social insurance programs and the tax programs necessary for their finance.

Before turning to this evidence, we first consider recent trends in labor supply.

4.2   Trends in Labor Supply

Over the last fifteen years, traditional measures of labor supply have been stable. Figure 4.1 presents labor force participation rates for three age groups by gender for Sweden and the United States for 1975 to 2004. Whereas labor force participation among Swedish youth equaled or exceeded that in the United States, since 1990, labor force participation in Sweden is 10 to 15 percentage points less than in the United States. Participation rates among prime-age men are nearly identical over this period in the United States and Sweden. Among the oldest age group of men, the secular pattern of participation is quite similar across the two countries. Participation rates for this group are higher in Sweden and have been for thirty years.

Participation rates between the older two age groups of women vary between Sweden and the United States. The role of Sweden's work-related social insurance programs produce high rates of participation, as labor market participation in Sweden is substantially higher for women aged twenty-five and higher. Also evident is the severe recession of the early 1990s, which was particularly harsh on the middle age group (aged twenty-five to fifty-four); participation rates fell sharply (approximately 10 percentage points) and had not yet fully recovered. Participation for women aged fifty-five to sixty-four increased in both countries; however, Sweden's recession depressed participation rates for this group but less so than for the younger age group.

Figure 4.2 presents the average hours of work per week (measured among those working) for three age groups by gender for the United States and Sweden for 1975 through 2004.[1] Among Swedish males, hours of work declined for all three age groups, with hours falling most sharply for the youngest

---

1. These are "usual weekly hours" as reported in the Current Population Survey (CPS) and "weekly hours of work" in the Labor Force Survey (AKU).

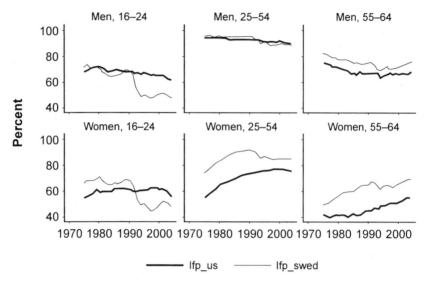

Fig. 4.1   Labor force participation by age and gender, United States and Sweden: 1975 to 2004

Note: Graphs by sex and age group.

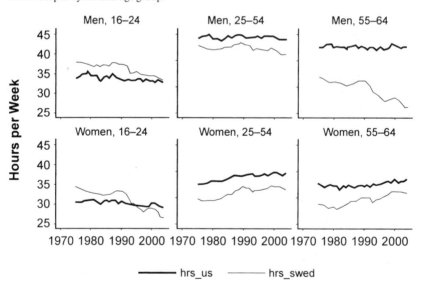

Fig. 4.2   Average hours worked per week by age and gender, United States and Sweden: 1975 to 2004

Note: Graphs by sex and age group.

group. Hours of work among prime-age workers (twenty-five to fifty-four) and mature workers (fifty-five to sixty-four) show little variation in the United States. However, in Sweden, hours of work fell during the recession in the early 1990s. Among women, hours of work declined for the youngest age group in Sweden and in the United States. For prime-age women, hours of work increased slightly in both countries. For mature women, average hours in Sweden increased and narrowed the difference with U.S. mature women.

The sector of employment changed substantially for Swedish women during the 1990s. Figure 4.3 reports the sector of employment from 1970 through 2002. Again, the recession in the early 1990s is visible, as the share of women in the local government sector declined precipitously at that time and never fully recovered. Employment in the local government sector stagnated, and women's employment increased in the second half of the 1990s as employment in the private sector increased.

Finally, figure 4.4—which is based on the OECD (2005) country report for Sweden—reports by gender the population share not at work from 1990 through 2003. Not at work includes individuals not in the labor force (e.g., those retired or in school full-time), the unemployed, and employed individuals absent from work. The last group includes individuals on disability insurance, sickness insurance, vacation, and temporary layoff.[2] We combine these different groups of nonworkers to avoid arbitrary labels of the different subpopulations.[3] The striking feature of this graph is the level of the curves—slightly more than 1 in 2.5 women and roughly 1 in 3 Swedish men are not actively working. And consistent with the trends in figures 4.1 and 4.2, the share of inactives increased during the recession of the early 1990s and stabilized at this higher level into the new century. The OECD (2005) country report for Sweden notes that Sweden has one of the highest levels of labor market inactivity levels (rivaled only by the other Nordic countries). This is an ominous trend for Sweden. Arguably, this increasing proportion of nonworkers provides long-run evidence of the work disincentives within the Swedish system that offers relatively generous (again by U.S. standards) income support with high rates of income taxation, which lessen the need of and the returns to market work.

4.3   Hours of Work: Some Evidence for Sweden and Extensions

To provide a starting point for the analyses, consider the simple labor-leisure model that forms the basis of empirical work on labor supply, where

---

2. The OECD (2005, 60) report notes that Sweden leads the OECD in the average number of days lost per year because of sickness. And Sweden has a relatively large share of potential workers who do not participate in the labor market because of medical reasons, especially among older age groups. Palme and Svensson (2002) report as well that sickness insurance and disability insurance systems serve as unofficial forms of unemployment insurance.

3. Thus, we want to avoid distinctions between unemployed and discouraged workers, neither of which is employed, and only the unemployed are considered in the labor force.

Numbers in 1000's   Women

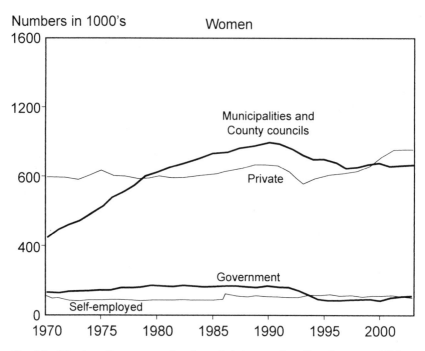

Fig. 4.3   **Number of women employed, aged sixteen to sixty-four, by sector: 1970 to 2003**

Source: Labor force surveys, Statistics Sweden.

the individual chooses the hours of work and the consumption of a single good to maximize utility subject to the budget constraint; that is:

$$\underset{h,c}{\text{Max }} u(c, h; z),$$

subject to $wh + y - T(wh, y_{tax}) - c = 0$, in which c is consumption, w is the gross wage rate, h is the hours of work, y is the nonlabor income, z is a vector of observable characteristics, y_{tax} (which is part of y) is the taxable nonlabor income, and $T(\bullet)$ is the tax payment net of transfers. The outcome of this problem can be written as a labor supply function:

(1) $h = g(w_n, y_n; z),$

where $w_n = w(1 - T')$ is the marginal wage rate, and $T' = \partial T(\bullet) / \partial(wh)$ is the marginal effect of the tax and transfer system, while y_n typically is referred to as the virtual nonlabor income (which we obtain by linearizing the budget constraint around the optimum point).

   The model serves to define the basic labor supply responses to changes in the budget constraint. The income effect, $\partial h / \partial y_n$, is the change in hours of work in response to an increase in the virtual nonlabor income. If leisure is a normal good, the income effect is negative (i.e., an increase in income induces

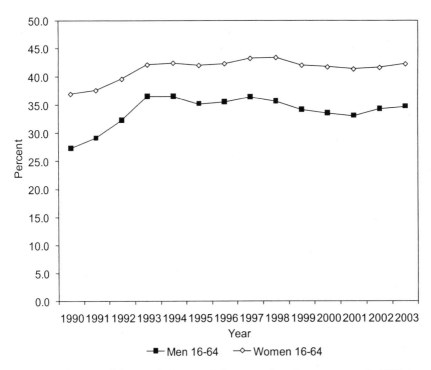

Fig. 4.4   Percent of the population, aged sixteen to sixty-four, not at work: 1980 to 2003

Source: OECD country report for Sweden (2005).

the individual to consume more leisure and thus to work less). The compensated wage effect, $\partial h / \partial w_n|_u$, measures the change in hours to an increase in the marginal wage rate, holding constant the consumer's utility. This effect captures the price or substitution effect. By the law of demand, the compensated wage effect is nonnegative. The compensated effect is important, because the welfare cost of taxes is proportional to the compensated wage effect. Finally, the uncompensated wage effect, $\partial h / \partial w_n$, summarizes the (net) change in hours with an increase in the marginal wage rate (which includes both the substitution and income effects).[4]

Blundell and MaCurdy (1999) summarize a large number of studies presenting estimates of the uncompensated labor supply elasticity with respect to the marginal wage rate (henceforth called wage elasticity) and the income elasticity. Estimates of the wage elasticity for men are typically small; most studies cover the interval from slightly negative point estimates to point

4. Readers interested in more thorough reviews of different labor supply models, as well as the econometric methods typically associated with them, are referred to Blundell and MaCurdy (1999).

estimates around 0.15. The estimates of the income elasticity are typically negative and relatively small in absolute value, although the variation between studies regarding the income elasticity appears to be greater than the corresponding variation with respect to the wage elasticity. For women, the picture is somewhat different; both the wage and the income elasticities are typically estimated to be larger in absolute value than the corresponding elasticities for men, suggesting that women's hours of work are generally more responsive to economic incentives than are male hours of work.[5] The higher wage elasticity for women may also reflect that women work fewer hours on average than men. Studies based on Swedish data yield a similar conclusion (see Aronsson and Walker 1997).[6] The appendix gives a brief summary of empirical results.

4.3.1   Responsiveness to Taxation and Programs

Clearly, one cannot infer the consequences of major reforms in the tax and transfer systems just by looking at the elasticity measures previously discussed. In this subsection, therefore, we briefly review some attempts to measure the labor supply responses to changes in the tax and transfer systems—again with a focus on results based on Swedish data. Aronsson and Palme (1998) estimate a household labor supply model using data from 1980. The model then is used to compute the desired hours of work for the husband and the wife, respectively, under three tax and transfer systems: 1980, 1989, and 1991, respectively (where the changes refer to the income tax, the value added tax, the housing allowance, and the child allowance).[7] Their results show an average 2.1 percent increase in the desired hours of work for the husband and a 0.7 percent increase for the wife due to the switch from the 1980 to the 1989 system. The main explanation for the seemingly small response in the wife's hours of work is a negative cross-wage effect (from the

5. Until recently, it was common to consider women as secondary workers, with men as primary workers. The greater labor supply responsiveness of women often was attributed to their movement in and out of the labor market.

6. See also the more recent studies of male labor supply by Blomquist, Eklöf, and Newey (2001) and Blomquist and Newey (2002) and the study of household labor supply by Flood, Hansen, and Wahlberg (2004). The own-wage elasticity of women's labor supply presented by Flood, Hansen, and Wahlberg is lower than the estimates presented in many earlier studies on labor supply based on Swedish data.

7. The most important changes refer to the income tax system. In Sweden, the income tax system contains two parts: a nonlinear national income tax and a proportional local income tax. (The local tax rate varies across local jurisdictions, and the average rate is slightly above 31 percent.) In the early 1980s, the national income tax was highly progressive with many tax brackets; for instance, in 1980, the tax rates of the national income tax schedule ranged from 0 to 58 percent, depending on the level of taxable income. In addition, labor income and capital income were taxed jointly, and capital losses were deductible from the labor income when computing the taxable income. Together with the local tax rate, an average earner may have faced a marginal income tax rate of around 50 percent, and the top rate exceeded 80 percent. The tax reform implemented during 1983 to 1985 meant splitting the national income tax into two parts: a basic part and a supplemental part. Nearly all income earners paid the basic tax, and this tax schedule had two brackets (with tax rates equal to 5 and 17 percent, respectively,

increase in the husband's marginal wage rate), accompanied by a relatively large income effect from the transfer system. The corresponding changes in desired work hours due to the shift from the 1989 to the 1991 system are 3.1 percent for the husband and 2.8 percent for the wife, respectively. Blomquist, Eklöf, and Newey (2001) use data from 1973, 1981, and 1991 to estimate the labor supply of married men aged twenty to sixty. The estimated model is used to simulate how the desired hours of work respond to the change in the tax and transfer systems between 1980 and 1991 (where the change refers to the income tax, the value added tax, the payroll tax, the child allowance, and the housing allowance). The average response in the desired hours of work is estimated to be 2.2 percent. (If evaluated in isolation, the changes in the marginal income tax rates cause the desired hours of work to increase by approximately 4 percent.) Our interpretation is that the estimated effects are relatively small, considering the magnitude of the reforms. We shall return to the 1991 reform in section 4.6, where we more fully explore the relationship between the marginal tax rate and the before-tax income.

Other types of policy-reform simulations based on Swedish data refer to combinations of deductions and transfer payments. This is interesting, because certain transfer payments may give rise to important marginal effects of relevance for the labor supply decision. Flood, Hansen, and Wahlberg (2004) estimate a household labor supply model using data from 1993 and 1999. Their model then is used to analyze the labor supply responses among married men and women to a substantial increase in the basic deduction, in combination with reduced housing allowances and welfare benefits (by 25 percent each). The results show very small (almost negligible) effects on the desired hours of work, except for low-income households (where the labor supply increase is substantial for women).

4.3.2 Does the Standard Model Capture All Relevant Effects?

As many studies on labor supply refer to time periods with increases in women's labor force participation, it is not surprising to find that women's hours of work are generally more responsive to economic incentives (measured in terms of the wage and income elasticities) than are the hours of work

---

in 1989). The supplemental tax, which contained higher tax rates, only was paid by those with sufficiently high income. Capital losses could still be deduced from the tax base for the basic tax, although it could not be deducted from the tax base associated with the supplemental tax (implying that the latter tax base was broader). The top rate for the national income tax was 42 percent in 1989. In 1991, an additional (and major) tax reform was implemented, which meant introducing a simpler national income tax system with two tax brackets for the labor income tax; the national tax rate was set to 0 for taxable incomes below 170,000 SEK (i.e., individuals with lower levels of income only paid the local income tax) and to 20 percent for higher incomes. It also implied a broader tax base by including some previously fringe benefits, as well as separate taxation of capital income (including capital gains) at 30 percent. By analogy, 30 percent of net capital losses were made deductible from the labor income tax payment. Another part of the reform was to increase the value added tax. For a more detailed discussion, see Aronsson and Walker (1997).

supplied by men. In addition, the labor supply results for women seem to vary more across studies than do the corresponding results for men, indicating (perhaps) that it is more difficult to reach a consensus regarding women's labor supply; more recent research—for example, Flood, Hansen, and Wahlberg (2004)—suggests a relatively low responsiveness of women's labor supply to economic incentives. The results from studies on male labor supply are surprisingly stable over time and across countries, in the sense that the estimates of the wage and income elasticities typically are found to be relatively small in absolute value. How can we explain this seemingly stable result? Does it mean there are no substantive responses to taxes and/or transfers?

To answer the second question, we first draw on Slemrod's (1992) behavioral hierarchy of response. This perspective recognizes that decisions involving transactions are the most responsive, followed by a variety of financial, accounting, and avoidance decisions. Real decisions involving savings, labor supply, and investment are the least responsive. In section 4.6, we consider some of the other responses to assess other possible effects of the tax. To answer the first question of why the real labor supply effects are so small, one possibility, of course, is that the standard labor supply model is correct, in which case the explanation has to do with the preferences for the trade-off between consumption and leisure. However, alongside this (unlikely) explanation, other studies try (at least in part) to attribute this finding to the character of the standard labor supply model by arguing that it neglects vital aspects of either the preferences or the choice set. We will discuss some of these approaches next by extending the standard model in order to capture quantitative constraints, social norms, and tax avoidance, respectively.

4.3.3   Quantitative Constraints

By quantitative constraints, we normally mean demand-oriented constraints, such that individuals facing them are off their labor supply curves. The presence of such constraints, at least in principle, can explain why the hours of work appear to be relatively unresponsive to small changes in the marginal wage rate and the virtual nonlabor income, respectively. Using Swedish data on prime-age married men from 1980, Sacklén (1996) addresses the issue of quantitative constraints. His study makes use of a question posed to the participants in the Level of Living Survey, where the respondents were asked to say whether they were satisfied with their work hours or if they wanted to increase or decrease their hours of work, given a corresponding change in their income. Those who claimed to be rationed in this sense were treated as if they were off their labor supply curves. This means that the labor supply of those who report rationing is treated as a latent variable. Therefore, a basic hypothesis is that once quantitative constraints are recognized and properly addressed, we may expect to find that the underlying (latent) labor supply is more responsive to economic incentives than in the standard model. However, the results do not show strong support for this hypothesis.

4.3.4   Social Norms

The standard labor supply model assumes atomistic behavior—that individuals make their labor supply decisions in isolation from one another. There is a growing literature that merges economic and sociological perspectives. One class of models incorporates social norms by augmenting individual preferences to depend on actions (and/or preferences) of others. Thus, utility declines as the individual's behavior deviates from the average choice within the group. Individual actions determine their own consumption but with possible spillover effects on others operating through the group choice. Moreover, multiple equilibria are possible and likely, as both Lindbeck, Nyberg, and Weibull (1999) and Brock and Durlauf (2001a, 2001b) show. Small changes of individual behavior operating through the social norm can magnify, leading to large changes in observed outcomes—at least over a longer time perspective. Thus, social multipliers may arise, much like the old investment multiplier of Keynesian economics in which the total effect of investment is larger than the individual marginal effect.

To exemplify, consider a slight modification of the utility function previously used, $u(c, h, \bar{h}; z)$, where $\bar{h}$ is interpretable as the average hours of work in the reference group with which the individual compares himself or herself. This variable may reflect a utility loss of deviating from a social norm regarding work hours (which here is assumed to be reflected in the average hours of work). In addition, to simplify the calculations, suppose that the utility function is such that the resulting labor supply function takes the form

$$(2) \qquad h = \alpha + \beta w_n + \gamma y_n + \delta \bar{h} + vz.$$

The parameters β and γ reflect the influence on hours of work of a change in the marginal wage rate and the virtual nonlabor income, respectively, conditional on $\bar{h}$. In the present context, these are only partial effects; a social multiplier exists, in the sense that if the marginal wage rate and the virtual nonlabor income facing all individuals would change (e.g., if the tax system is subject to reforms), so would the average hours of work in the reference group. Therefore, the total effect of a proportional increase in the marginal wage rate is $\beta / (1 - \delta)$, where $\delta \in [0,1)$, and $1 / (1 - \delta)$ is the social multiplier. If δ is large, we may expect substantial indirect effects via the presence of interdependent behavior. Therefore, in the standard labor supply model, if at least part of the effect of $\bar{h}$ is hidden in the constant, we may underestimate the total response to a change in the tax system.

The study of interdependent behavior in the context of labor supply models has a rich history.[8] Using Swedish data referring to prime-age married men, a variant of the model previously set out has been estimated by

8. See, for example, Kapteyn (1977), Alessie and Kapteyn (1991), and Woittiez and Kapteyn (1998). See also Manski (1993) for a thorough analysis of identification and Brock and Durlauf (2001a, 2001b) for a partial solution.

Aronsson, Blomquist, and Sacklén (1999). The results show that interdependent behavior is present and that it affects the labor supply. In addition, the effects are estimated to be sizeable; in terms of equation (2), the point estimate of δ is around 0.67. The partial wage and income elasticities evaluated at the mean of the data, $\beta \overline{w}_n / \overline{h}$ and $\gamma \overline{y}_n / \overline{h}$, are equal to 0.061 and –0.017, respectively, which resemble (or fall slightly short of) those found in earlier studies, which do not address interdependent behavior. The corresponding estimates of the full elasticities, $\beta \overline{w}_n / [(1 - \delta)\overline{h}]$ and $\gamma \overline{y}_n / [(1 - \delta)\overline{h}]$, are 0.187 and –0.052, respectively. Taken at face value, these results suggest that the effects of interdependent behavior are substantial and that the traditional labor supply model may imply considerable underestimation of the effects of taxation.[9] However, it is necessary to be careful in the interpretations, as we note the construction of social reference groups is arbitrary. The Monte Carlo simulations carried out by Aronsson, Blomquist, and Sacklén (1999) suggest that this is a potential problem; it may lead to the overestimation of δ, which is the parameter of main interest.

Although not formally addressed in the previous example, the time dimension is possibly very important here. As a consequence, there is no formal distinction between short run and long run. In the short run, social norms are likely to constrain behavior—suggesting moderate behavioral responses to policy—whereas social norms may evolve gradually in the long run as a result of the behavior of all individuals. If this argument is correct, then the long-run behavioral effects—which also incorporate the effects via changes in the social norm—will exceed those that follow in the short or medium run.

4.3.5   Tax Avoidance and the Choice of Assets

Clearly, many economists would expect the highly progressive income tax characterizing Sweden in the 1970s and 1980s to have caused serious disincentive effects in terms of work hours. Yet, these expected behavioral responses were not found in the empirical work based on data for that time period (at least not for men). Can asset trade, which is carried out for the purpose of avoiding taxation, explain the seemingly moderate influence taxes have on the labor supply? If it can, then the tax tables may exaggerate the effective degree of tax progression for certain groups of wage earners. We will formalize our argument by using a model developed by Agell and Persson (2000), which only requires a slight extension of the reference model previously set out. Consider an economy with two types of assets: a tax-exempt asset and a taxable asset, the returns on which now constitute the nonlabor income part of the reference model. Let e denote the initial endowment, x the tax-exempt asset, and d the taxable asset. Both assets are

9. Some normative implications of social norms and social interaction in the labor market are analyzed by Aronsson and Sjögren (2009).

risk free, and we give the rates of return r for the taxable asset and ρ for the tax-exempt asset. By using the wealth constraint, $d = e - x$, the optimization problem of a typical individual can be written as

$$\operatorname*{Max}_{h,c,x} u(c, h; z),$$

subject to $wh + \rho x + r(e - x) - T[wh + r(e - x)] - c = 0, x \geq 0$.

We assume that $T(\cdot)$ is such that $T'(\cdot) > 0$ and $T''(\cdot) > 0$ for $wh + r(e - x) \geq 0$. The tax system described here at least in part resembles the Swedish system before the 1983 tax reform, where negative asset income was fully deductible from labor income when calculating the taxable income. Examination of the first-order conditions suggests that when the pretax wage rate is sufficiently high, $x > 0$, whereas $x = 0$ for lower pretax wage rates. If the individual decides not to use the tax-exempt asset, then the labor supply takes the same form as in the reference model previously described. On the other hand, if the individual decides to place part of his or her endowment in the tax-exempt asset, the hours of work choice will obey the following condition:

$$(3) \qquad u_c(c, h; z)w\frac{\rho}{r} + u_h(c, h; z) = 0.$$

The labor supply implicit in equation (3) takes the form $h = h(w\rho / r, \hat{y}, z)$, where $\hat{y}$ denotes the virtual nonlabor income. This result has a very interesting implication; conditional on the ratio between the rates of return, ρ / r, a small tax reform will only give rise to an income effect. In other words, there is a distinction in terms of labor supply between tax avoiders and those who do not use the possibility to adjust their marginal income tax rate via the tax-exempt asset. For avoiders who lower their effective marginal income tax rate via avoidance behavior, the statutory marginal income tax rates exaggerate the distortions imposed by the income tax system. Therefore, avoiders in a sense will create their own labor supply incentives, suggesting that the work disincentives associated with the tax system may not have been as great as they may have appeared from the tax tables in the late 1970s and early 1980s.

Empirical research based on the Swedish tax system from the 1980s suggests that people responded to the incentives associated with tax avoidance; individuals with high labor income were found to be more inclined to have tax-favored assets than those with lower labor income (Edin, Englund, and Ekman 1995). Similarly, a decline in indebtedness seems to have taken place after the 1991 tax reform was implemented (Agell, Englund, and Södersten 1998). These results are interpretable as supporting the idea that individuals choose their portfolios in order to avoid taxation, which in turn may have implications for their labor supply behavior. In addition and perhaps even more important, if individuals respond to taxation via their portfolios, we may expect taxation to have a larger effect on taxable income than on hours of work.

4.4   Sickness Insurance and Family Policy

A distinguishing feature of the Swedish social insurance system is its two-part structure—nearly every program offers some minimal or guaranteed benefit and another component that replaces a fraction of earnings. For example, the sickness insurance, parental insurance, and unemployment insurance systems all have this feature. The work-conditioned benefits are distinctly more generous than the guaranteed benefits and offer a strong incentive for employment. Yet, the existence of the work-conditioned benefits requires that we distinguish between contract or paid hours of employment and active hours of work—hours spent working to produce a good or service. The 2005 OECD country report on Sweden does this, and the results are striking. Workers in Sweden were on the job and actively working an average 35.4 weeks per year, while the average for Europe was 40.7 weeks. The number of weeks away from work due to holidays varied little across countries in Europe. Hence, the primary difference in annual hours worked in Sweden versus the European average was in weeks absent for other reasons. In Sweden, the average number of weeks absent (excluding holidays) was more than twice the average for Europe (9.8 versus 4.5). We next explore some of the features of the social insurance programs that may give rise to this difference.

4.4.1   Sickness Insurance

Recent reforms that require increased medical documentation of illnesses and that require employers to pay sickness benefits for the first two weeks of absence were intended to increase the monitoring of usage and thereby to tighten control over benefit costs. Nevertheless, use of sickness insurance benefits continues to remain high in Sweden.

Using the conceptual framework presented in section 4.3, it is straightforward to explain the effect of sickness insurance benefits on labor supply. As we mentioned, demand-side considerations (e.g., setup costs and returns to coordination) may dictate the number of hours per period that must be supplied. Jobs can be seen as a tied sale of bundled attributes of which hours of work is only one of many attributes describing the working conditions and the nature of the job. Workers select the job that gives them the highest utility. Because it is cheaper to do so, employers have an incentive to offer job packages that workers prefer. Nevertheless, technology limits the choices available, and some workers may select jobs with required hours of work that are greater than desired (as defined by the labor supply function in equation [1]). Access to sickness insurance benefits permits workers to adjust their hours of work to more nearly equate desired and demanded hours. The qualifying period and less-than-full replacement rate means the adjustment will be less than complete. In this interpretation, there is nothing stochastic or unexpected about the use of sickness insurance—the worker accepts the job demanding a fixed number of hours, knowing he or she can adjust the level of effort downward through the use of sickness insurance.

Building on the same structure, we can view the labor supply function in equation (1) as implicitly defining the (unrestricted) supply price of labor. Inverting equation (1) gives $w_n = g^{-1}(h, y_n; z_n)$, where w_n is the worker's asking price (net of taxes and transfers) to supply h units of labor at a given level of effort or intensity. We can think that the effort required on the job may vary over the business cycle, with more effort requested in expansions and less in economic contractions. Once again, sickness insurance benefits permit the worker to moderate the demands over the cycle. This framework implies that we should see a procyclical use of sickness benefits—the number of sick days should increase when demand for labor is high and should decline when demand for labor is low. We reported in Aronsson and Walker (1997) that from 1967 (when the three-day qualifying period was reduced to a single day) through the early 1990s, usage of sickness cash benefits has been strongly procyclical, with the simple correlation of unemployment and sick days as high as –0.7.

Henrekson and Persson (2004) investigate the responsiveness of sick days to the major reforms of the sickness insurance system from 1968 to 2002. The National Insurance Board (RFV) reports sick days funded by the national sickness insurance system. These register data undercount the true number of sick days during the 1990s, as occupation sickness insurance plans offered additional coverage that partially offset the cost of the qualifying period and that covered earnings above the basic amount threshold of the national system. Henrekson and Persson's aggregate time-series data do not permit parameterizing the reforms in terms of their direct monetary incentives. Instead, the authors code the reforms by time-varying indicator variables and limit their analysis to only the major reforms. They adopt a distributed lag specification, with the number of sick days as the dependent variable, and they include controls for the age composition of the working population, the gender mix, and the unemployment rate as regressors. They find that sick days and unemployment are negatively related. Indeed, they find the 1991 reform, which increased the length of the qualifying period and reduced benefits, caused sick days to decline by 20 percent. The careful and thorough analysis provides compelling evidence of the link between the structure and generosity of the sickness insurance plan and the hours of work.

4.4.2   Social Norms and Transfer Programs

Recall our earlier discussion of social norms on hours of work, where we noted that social norms may moderate behavior in the short run, whereas over the longer run, they may generate larger effects. This is so for two reasons. First, the social multiplier may take time to work as individuals learn about reference group behavior. And second, social norms may evolve over time, providing an internal dynamic for changing behavior. Lindbeck and his coauthors (Lindbeck 1995; Lindbeck, Nyberg, and Weibull 1999, 2003) consider economies in which agents either work or receive a transfer payment and consume full leisure. Program participation entails a psychic cost (stigma), which is a decreasing function of the population living off benefits. As is common in models with social interaction, multiple equilibria exist. If the social norm for work is strong, with high psychic costs for those who deviate, then a good equilibrium with high program benefits and low free riding can be supported. Another bad equilibrium entails low benefits and high free riding. Lindbeck, Nyberg, and Weibull (1999) show that these extreme equilibria are stable compared to intermediate ones with moderate levels of program benefits and free riding. Shelling (1971) was the first to see that such economies may experience tipping, in which a small (exogenous) perturbation can shift the economy from one equilibrium to another.

Such extreme behavior has not been observed in Sweden, though its possibility is daunting. Consider the type of dynamic response in which the social norm depends on past program usage. An increased usage of program benefits today reduces the stigma of living off benefits tomorrow. Higher free riding tomorrow further lowers the cost. The tipping phenomenon is more gradual, but the system gravitates from the good equilibrium to the bad one.

The OECD (2005) reports that on an average day in Sweden, 14 percent of the working-age population is on sick leave or disability insurance. Figure 4.4 shows that the proportion of the population not at work increased dramatically during the early 1990s and remained at the higher level into the early 2000s. Disability claims show increases among women and those of younger ages. In our 1997 paper, we discussed intergenerational differences in the use of sick leave, where the results suggest that young people's usage of sick leave may be less related to medical need than to work preferences. All these figures point to a weakening of collective work ethic and to the decline of a social norm against free riding on social insurance programs. The OECD (2005) recognized this shift and called for a "change in the culture of sickness and disability" to one of "mutual obligation" to get the sick and disabled back to work as quickly as possible. If norms erode too much and a tipping point is reached, even more radical reforms will be needed.

All insurance programs face issues of moral hazard and adverse selection. Lindbeck, Nyberg, and Weibull (2003) note the difficulty of the insurance provider to develop objective criteria to distinguish between the deserving (unlucky) and undeserving (free riders) beneficiaries. When sufficiently strong, social norms may be a cost-efficient way of limiting free riding. Lindbeck, Nyberg, and Weibull (2003) argue that social norms are enforced tacitly by individuals who are close to the beneficiaries and who have better information than do program administrators. And enforcement of the social norms may operate through a variety of social channels, unconstrained by the formal rules and procedures that restrict program administrators. A hidden cost of weakening social norms against free riding on social insurance programs, especially sickness and disability insurance, will be increased administrative costs for additional monitoring and enforcement. In addition, stricter enforcement may imply that some of the truly needy will be denied benefits.

The social cost of continuing to allow easy access to generous social insurance programs is large. Getting people back to work has a twofold benefit of increased output and lower tax rates to cover the reduced program expenditure. Harder to measure are the reduced deadweight losses associated with the lower tax rates. We recognize these costs and realize the challenge encompasses the design of social insurance programs and their administration.

4.4.3 Parental Benefits

Historically, Sweden has been one of the leaders in offering benefits connected to childbearing and child rearing. Sweden offers subsidies to defray the medical costs of childbearing and child allowances to offset child-related expenditures necessary for young children and adolescents. As part of its family policy, parental benefits offer either parent subsidies to stay home with the child. It is important to recognize that parental benefits are one component of family policy and have the intended role of helping parents, primarily women, to balance the demands of family and the workplace. Thus, an evaluation of their effects requires a broader perspective than simply their incentive effects on labor supply. Even on labor supply, the effects are complicated and somewhat offsetting. Of course, upon childbirth, parental benefits offset the cost of leaving the market and will increase time away from work. Within the OECD framework previously described, absences while on parental benefits fall within the "absent for other reasons" category. However, guaranteed benefit levels are so low that prospective parents have an incentive to enter the labor market prior to *each* birth.[10] Empirical studies are few,[11] but the net effect for labor supply is likely to be negative, particularly as the entitlement period is substantially shorter than the benefit period.

The recent OECD country report on Sweden is critical of the level of parental benefits in Sweden, labeling the benefits as very generous and questioning their value on child development and welfare. We recognize the likely

10. See Mortensen (1977) for an elegant early analysis of entitlement effects that evaluates the employment effects of unemployment insurance within the United States.

11. See Walker (1996) for an (unsuccessful) attempt to measure the effects of parental benefits on fertility and female employment. Fertility is not completely controllable, and to the extent that births are unplanned, it weakens entitlement effects on employment.

disincentive effects on labor supply, but we are less critical of the current generosity of parental benefits. Households and individuals make decisions within the current and anticipated social insurance programs. For example, private-savings decisions are made with knowledge of the benefit levels of the public pension system, and fertility decisions are made when anticipating the programs and subsidies available to families with children. Reductions in child-related subsidies and programs that are interpreted as signaling the future policies to be even less supportive to families with children may decrease fertility. In light of Sweden's aging population, policies that may lower fertility merit further attention.

4.5 Public Pensions

Sweden retains its position as leader in innovative social insurance programs with its pension reform of 1999 that completely restructured the public pension system. The prereform pension system was a pay-as-you-go (PAYG) defined benefit system that had two components: a basic pension and a supplemental pension. The basic pension offered income security and established the minimum income floor for all workers. The supplement pension augmented the basic pension and targeted payments to replace about 60 percent of the worker's labor market earnings. Under the supplemental pension system, benefits were tied to the worker's highest earnings over fifteen years, and to obtain a full supplement benefit, an individual had to work thirty years. Over time, however, benefits became more generous, life expectancies rose, and birthrates fell. Thus, pensioners had to be supported for more years and were entitled to more generous benefits, with a declining worker base to support them. These changes necessitated either large tax increases or a significant cut in benefits.

4.5.1 The 1999 Reform

The Swedish pension reform of 1999 offers an innovative and in many ways radical solution to these problems.[12] The largest change is that the public pension system switched from a defined benefit to a *notional defined contribution* (NDC) system. In the new system, workers have an individual account, which receives each year a pension contribution equal to 18.5 percent of their pensionable income. Now, instead of guaranteed benefits upon retirement, workers have guaranteed contributions credited each year to their accounts. It is *notional* because workers' accounts are only credited; actual assets are not set aside. Balances in the account earn a rate of return each year equal to annual growth in average wages. Upon retire-

---

12. Like the previous system, the new pension system will be phased in over a number of birth cohorts; specifically, the birth cohorts of 1938 to 1953.

ment (after age sixty-one), the individual's accumulated notional wealth is converted into an annuity, dependent on the life expectancy of the individual's cohort.

A second innovation of the 1999 reform introduced limited individual control over the pension. Contributions equal to 16 percentage points go into the national public pension fund, which is managed by the government. The remaining 2.5 percent contribution is mandatory; however, these funds are under the individual's control. Hence, the government will collect all revenues and will disperse payouts, although the individual funds will be managed by private investment firms that are selected by the individual from an approved list of investment advisors. The last innovation is a significant broadening of the income base entering the public pension system. Besides earnings, the 1999 reforms recognized additional social insurance payments as part of the income base. This includes stipends to students pursuing postsecondary education and parental benefits. Indeed, child-rearing activities earn supplemental contributions, as does income while serving in the military.

The Swedish pension system remains a pay-as-you-go pension system, as tax contributions paid by those currently working are used to finance the pension payments of those currently retired. At an 18.5 percent contribution rate, the system's designers expect the new pension system to deliver pension benefits at about the same level as the old system. An interesting political compromise rests with the 18.5 percent contribution rate. Consensus estimates within the public debate was that a 16 percent contribution would suffice to maintain the (then) existing level of pension benefits. Yet, to ensure income security, a higher contribution rate was accepted, with the stipulation that the remaining funds were under individual control.

The new pension system represents a striking departure from Sweden's long history of guaranteed benefits and horizontal equity. Under the new system, different cohorts will receive different pensions for the same accumulated pension wealth as life expectancies change. Members of the same birth cohort will receive different pensions for the same life expectancy should the individuals retire in different years (and thus have the opportunity to accumulate different levels of pension wealth to annuitize at retirement). Finally, and the most individual specific, the individual accounts will accumulate wealth based on the individual's investment strategy. Individuals adopting more conservative portfolios may accrue less wealth than those who adopt more aggressive portfolios. Government oversight of the fund managers and restrictions on the types of investments permitted reduce this form of variability, and it may be more symbolic than real. Yet, within a social insurance system founded on the notion of horizontal equity in which alikes are treated alike, this source of individual-level diversity is a striking departure from the traditional Swedish social insurance system.

4.5.2   Pensions and Labor Supply

There is a vast empirical literature on the old pension system[13] and very little (because of its newness) on the 1999 pension reform. We note, however, that between 1999 and 2004, labor force participation rates increased among the elderly (fifty-five to sixty-four). Future research will determine whether the work incentives created by the 1999 pension reform increased these rates. We offer some observations that suggest it may have.

The shift from the old defined benefit PAYG system to the notional defined contribution system will induce both short-run and long-run effects on labor supply. In the long run, as Lindbeck (2002) and Feldstein and Leibman (2002) show, a notional or quasifunded benefit system can reduce the distortionary incentive effects caused by a tax on labor to finance benefits. That is, in a PAYG system in which there is *no* relationship between taxes paid and benefits eventually received, the implicit rate of return on tax contribution is minus 100 percent, and the deadweight loss reflects the entire pension tax on labor income. Under an NDC, taxes and benefits are related, as taxes paid are returned as future benefits, with an implicit rate of return equal to the growth rate of the population multiplied by the growth rate of labor income. If the implicit rate of return on pension contributions is close to the rate of return on other forms of savings the individual could make otherwise, the distortion of labor supply is much reduced. Indeed, if the implicit rate of return exactly equals the return on other forms of savings, then the distortion on labor supply is zero. Lindbeck and Persson (2003) show that for reasonable growth rates, the reduction in the tax wedge on labor income could be as much as 10 percentage points. The reduction in marginal tax rates should therefore increase labor supply (via participation, hours, and quality). The reduction of deadweight loss generated by the NDC may potentially improve welfare for both young and old generations.[14]

The short-term labor supply incentive effects are more transparent. The switch from a defined benefit to a defined contribution plan changes the nature of pension accruals. Under the NDC, another year of work will increase pension wealth because of the direct contribution from earnings, the return on accumulated contributions, and if the person is past normal retirement age, the increased annuity values for shorter benefit period. In the defined benefit system, the pension depends on years of employment and average earnings over the highest fifteen years of earnings. For someone with the same level of pension wealth and with fewer than thirty years of employ-

---

13. See the various studies by Mårten Palme; for example, Palme and Svensson (2004).

14. Importantly, the introduction of the defined contribution plan converts entitlements to contributions made rather than to benefits to be paid. Hence, the government is protected from having to guarantee benefits in the presence of increasing life expectancies and below-replacement birth rates.

ment or with earnings above their fifteenth-highest earnings, an additional year of employment thus would increase the annuity paid at retirement by increasing either the replacement rate or the average earnings (or both) used within the benefit formula. However, most workers near retirement age have worked for more than thirty years and thus under the defined benefit system have weak incentives to continue working. Therefore, the reformed Swedish pension plan now offers stronger work incentives, especially to those with persistent labor market attachment.

Yet, one cautionary remark is in order. Palme and Svensson (2002) estimate that approximately 20 percent of men and 27 percent of women exit the labor market via the social insurance programs. Under the 1999 reform, social insurance income is pensionable and thus may exacerbate this tendency. Moreover, recent work on social norms suggests that this problem is even more pernicious.

4.6   Other Aspects of the Tax Base

So far, we mainly have focused on hours of work. From a tax revenue perspective, it is of interest to understand how and why taxation affects before-tax income. In addition, by extending the analysis to before-tax income, several additional mechanisms will appear; for instance, in addition to hours of work, before-tax income also reflects effort, occupational choice, wage formation, and possibly also tax avoidance. By Seldrod's hierarchy of response, we may expect taxable income to respond differently to tax policy changes in comparison with hours of work.

4.6.1   The Relationship between Marginal Tax Rates and Before-Tax Income

The literature on tax base determination, initiated by Lindsay (1987) and further developed by Feldstein (1995), offers an interesting complement to the traditional study of labor supply, because it allows us to address several aspects of behavior simultaneously. In other words, although the framework for studying tax base determination typically resembles the traditional labor supply model, it does not restrict its attention solely to hours of work. Depending on the definition of income, it also (at least in principle) may capture avoidance, as well as the effects of tax policy on the gross wage rate, effort, occupational choice, and savings. Therefore, part of the difference in results among studies likely is to be due to differences regarding the way in which income is measured—for example, whether the analysis refers to taxable income or a broader income concept.

In their comprehensive study on tax base determination in the United States, Gruber and Saez (2002) make a distinction between two income concepts: taxable income and broad income, where the latter is defined as the sum of all items that compose total income less capital gains.[15] A basic hypothesis is that taxable income is more sensitive to marginal taxation than is broad income, because changes in taxable income also reflect (some aspects of) tax avoidance. Indeed, this is precisely what Gruber and Saez find. First, the elasticity of taxable income with respect to the net of tax rate (measured as one minus the marginal tax rate) is estimated to be around 0.4 on average.[16] The corresponding elasticity for broad income is 0.07. Second, income effects are very small, implying that the uncompensated and compensated effects on the before-tax income of a change in the net of tax rate are similar. Third, the effect on taxable income of a change in the net of tax rate appears to be strongest in the upper part of the income distribution.

There are several studies based on Swedish data dealing with the influence of marginal tax rates on before-tax income. Let us start by briefly discussing a paper by Ljunge and Ragan (2004). Instead of considering taxable income and broad income, respectively, as in the paper by Gruber and Saez, Ljunge and Ragan focus their attention on the determinants of labor earnings. Although this choice of dependent variable means neglecting some of the possible effects of taxation due to tax avoidance, it nevertheless will reflect the joint effect of taxation on several interesting aspects of behavior. As such, we may expect the behavioral responses to be different from those presented for work hours. Ljunge and Ragan use panel data and focus on individuals aged twenty-five to fifty-five during 1989. Their study period is from 1989 to 1994, meaning that attention is paid to the 1991 tax reform in terms of its effect on labor earnings. The results imply that the compensated elasticity of earnings with respect to the net of tax rate is around 0.33 on average, which is a relatively large response. (Recall that the corresponding elasticity for taxable income in the United States is measured to be around 0.4 by Gruber and Saez.) The uncompensated elasticity of labor earnings with respect to the net of tax rate is estimated to be in the interval of 0.25 to 0.33. In addition, there is considerable variation across groups. For instance, both low-income earners and high-income earners have higher estimated elasticities than income earners in the middle of the distribution. On average, the estimated behavioral response to the 1991 tax reform is an increase in earnings by 10 to 15 percent.

Using panel data for the years 1989 and 1992 and focusing on the group aged twenty-five to sixty in 1989, Hansson (2004) estimates the elasticity of

15. Broad income contains wages, salaries and tips, interest income, dividends, alimony received, business income, total Individual Retirement Account (IRA) distributions, total pensions and annuities, income reported on schedule E, farm income, unemployment income, and other income.
16. This number is an average estimate in comparison with earlier literature. Studies concentrating on the upper part of the income distribution typically estimate a higher number. On the other hand, some earlier studies that do not refer to the United States seem to imply a much weaker relationship between marginal tax rates and taxable income; see, for instance, Aarbu and Thoresen (2001) and Sillamaa and Veall (2001).

taxable labor income with respect to the net of tax rate to be 0.43 or 0.57 on average, depending on the choice of instruments for the net of tax rate. She also finds that the relevant elasticity may differ considerably across groups (with women being more responsive than men in at least one of the models). However, because she does not incorporate a measure of virtual income in the analysis, it is not clear whether the relevant elasticity estimate should be interpreted as a compensated or an uncompensated effect. The results also appear to be somewhat sensitive to the use of the estimation method (the choice of instrument for the marginal tax rate). Selén (2002) estimates a model similar to that of Gruber and Saez using data for the period from 1989 to 1992. He concentrates the analysis to men in the group aged twenty-five to fifty-five in 1989. His results imply a slightly lower estimate of the (compensated) elasticity of taxable income with respect to the net of tax rate, in the interval of 0.2 to 0.4. Finally, Blomquist and Sehlin (2008) estimate how taxable labor earnings as well as the hourly gross wage rate depend on the net of tax rate. By using data for 1981 and 1991, their preferred estimates imply that the elasticity of taxable earnings with respect to the net of tax rate is 0.26 for men and 0.75 for women (again indicating that women respond more to tax policy than do men), whereas the corresponding elasticities for the hourly gross wage rates are 0.20 and 0.33, respectively.[17] We will return to the relationship between gross wage rates and the tax system next.

Although we believe that the study of how marginal tax rates affect before-tax income is interesting in the sense that it provides a broader view of tax responses than the traditional study of labor supply, it is important to be careful when interpreting these results. This is so for at least two reasons. First, this research area is relatively new by comparison—at least when applied to Swedish data. To be useful for purposes of policy evaluations and recommendations, these studies should be supplemented by additional research.[18] Second, and more importantly, the theoretical foundations for the study of before-tax income is not always convincing; the income supply model by Gruber and Saez is only one possible model, and it resembles the

17. Blomquist and Sehlin also recognize that responses to tax policy are likely to be asymmetric; for instance, although a decrease in the marginal tax rate may lead to additional investments in human capital or a move toward jobs with higher wages, an increase in the marginal tax rate is not likely to lead to disinvestment in skills or moves toward jobs with lower pay. Indeed, when reestimating their models using similar data for other time periods, they obtain results that differ substantially from those referred to earlier.

18. As we previously mentioned, most earlier Swedish studies use the 1991 tax reform to identify the effects of marginal taxation on the before-tax income. An exception is Holmlund and Söderström (2008), who use data for the postreform period from 1991 to 2002; in addition, they consider a dynamic regression model, which allows them to distinguish between short-run and long-run effects of a change in the net of tax rate. For men, the estimates of the long-run elasticity of income with respect to the net of tax rate typically are found in the interval of 0.1 to 0.3, whereas the estimates for women are imprecise and statistically insignificant. They also calculate the fiscal consequences of a reform that reduces the top marginal income tax rate by 5 percentage points, and they find that this reform is likely to have only a minor effect on tax revenues.

labor supply model too much to provide a very interesting alternative. For instance, the income supply model itself is silent about important issues such as wage formation, as well as about the opportunities and constraints underlying avoidance behavior. As a consequence, we may not learn much about the mechanisms underlying behavior by studying only the relationships discussed here.

4.6.2   Wages, Taxes, and Tax Progression

One reason as to why marginal income taxation causes a larger response in the tax base than in the hours of work was discussed in section 4.3, where we argued that individuals may adjust to taxation via tax avoidance, which in turn tends to diminish the effects of taxation on hours of work. Alongside this explanation, empirical evidence also suggests that the wage formation system may contribute to explain the apparently large effect on the tax base following the 1991 tax reform. If the pretax wage rates are determined by bargaining between unions and firms, which is common in European labor markets, standard models for wage setting, as well as some of the empirical evidence associated with them, predict that an increase (a decrease) in the marginal tax rate with the average tax rate held constant leads to decreased (increased) pretax wage rates.[19] The intuition is based on a tradeoff (which the trade union is assumed to be facing) between the consumption wage per employed member and the number of employed members: a higher marginal tax rate tends to increase the opportunity cost of wage increases in terms of lost employment. On the other hand, a change in the average tax rate with the marginal tax rate held constant may either increase or decrease the pretax wage rate.

Let us discuss studies based on Swedish data. Holmlund and Kolm (1995) use data from the Swedish income distribution surveys (HINK) which include time series data for different income groups, as well as microlevel panel data.[20] In the panel data regressions, the results suggest that an increase in the marginal tax rate of 10 percentage points will reduce the pretax wage by about 4 to 6 percent for the average worker with the average tax rate held constant, whereas the corresponding number in the time series regression is around –2.5 percent. There is also evidence suggesting that this effect is stronger among the highest income earners. Aronsson, Wikström, and Brännlund (1997) estimate a union wage model based on panel data at the firm level for the Swedish pulp and paper industry. Their results imply that with the average tax rate held constant, the elasticity of the pretax wage rate with respect to the marginal tax rate is –0.5 on average. The corresponding elasticity with respect to the average tax rate (with the marginal tax rate held constant) is estimated to be 0.5.

19. Normative implications of unionized labor markets are analyzed, for example, by Fuest and Huber (1997) and Aronsson and Sjögren (2004a, 2004b).
20. Their model essentially is based on the seminal work by Lockwood and Manning (1993).

Despite arguments for caution,[21] it is tempting to compare the results on tax progression and wage formation with those discussed earlier on the determinants of the hours of work and before-tax income, respectively. Such a comparison provides at least one possible explanation as to why the labor earnings most likely increased more than the hours of work as a result of the 1991 income tax reform. In addition, this argument is further strengthened (from yet another perspective) by Blomquist and Sehlin (2008), who show that the difference between the tax base elasticity and the wage rate elasticity for men previously referred to is very close to the typical labor supply elasticity estimated in earlier studies (indicating that the study of tax base determination gives results that are consistent with the labor supply literature). Interestingly, therefore, their results suggest that the response in labor earnings to a change in the marginal tax rate that is due to the response in the wage rate is more important than the response in the hours of work—at least for men.

4.7   Cross-Country Comparisons

Most earlier studies on work hours, and particularly on how hours of work respond to taxation, transfer payments, and social insurance, are based on within-country microdata. More recently, however, several studies[22] have emerged with the explicit purpose of explaining cross-country differences, with a focus on differences between Europe and the United States. These differences have increased in general since the early 1970s and are now substantial: Americans tend to do much more market work than Europeans do. An important question is whether the differences in work hours between Europe and the United States can be explained by differences in taxation and transfer programs or whether they are (mainly) attributable to other factors, such as labor market institutions and legislation.

Differences between Europe and the United States with respect to work hours per person have been analyzed, for example, by Prescott (2004) and Olovsson (2004) in the context of numerical general equilibrium models. From our perspective, the study by Olovsson is particularly interesting, as it deals explicitly with a comparison between Sweden and the United States. Olovsson makes a distinction between market work and household production: the main difference between the two countries refers to how the households divide their time between market work and household production (more time is spent on market work and less time in household production in

21. Note that these strong results are not confirmed fully by more recent research based on data for other countries. For instance, by using Danish data, Lockwood, Slök, and Tranaes (2000) find evidence suggesting that the effects of higher tax progression on the pretax wage rate is income dependent. Similarly, Brunello, Parisi, and Sonedda (2002) use Italian data and find the opposite effect in comparison with the Swedish studies previously referred to: tax progression works to increase the pretax wage rate.

22. See, for example, Davis and Henrekson (2004), Prescott (2004), Olovsson (2004), and Alesina, Glaesen, and Sacerdote (2005).

the United States in comparison with Sweden), whereas the total time spent working is about the same in both countries. Olovsson uses an intertemporal model of a competitive economy, where preference and production parameters are set to reflect Olovsson's assessment of estimates in the empirical literature, whereas the policy parameters are chosen either to reflect Sweden or the United States. This enables him to compare how differences in public policy between the two countries affect the time spent in market work and household production, respectively. Adopting a long-run perspective of comparing steady states, Olovsson shows that differences in public policy (and in particular, income taxation) between the two countries can explain the differences with respect to how the households divide their time between market work and household production: high marginal tax rates in Sweden induce individuals to substitute from market to nonmarket production, with the total hours of work virtually equal between the United States and Sweden. His model predicts a gradual reduction in the hours spent in market work in Sweden between 1960 and 1980, the direction of which is consistent with the observed behavior, although it overestimates the hours of market work per person at the beginning of the period (implying that the predicted reduction is greater than the reduction that actually took place).

Although it is likely that differences in tax policy between Sweden (or Europe, in the paper by Prescott) and the United States give rise to differences in the hours of work per person, there are at least three problems with the preceding analyses. First, the expenditure side of the government's budget is dealt with in a somewhat superficial way; neither Olovsson nor Prescott allow public consumption to enter the utility function, and both of them give the tax revenues (net of the useless public consumption) back to the consumers in the form of lump-sum transfers. The latter weakens the income effect so that the substitution effect becomes dominant for the behavioral response to tax policy. Clearly, if the government spending (or part thereof) were not treated as a perfect substitute for private consumption, the income effect would tend to offset the behavioral responses to tax policy—an argument also put forward in a comment by Ljungqvist (2006). Second, the social insurance system gives rise to its own incentives, which are likely to contribute to differences in the hours of work per person. For instance, differences between countries with respect to the generosity of unemployment benefits may imply differences in the incentives among the unemployed to actively search for employment. This aspect is particularly interesting in light of how the difference between Europe and the United States with regards to the hours of work per person refers to differences in terms of employment-to-population ratios. Although employment-to-population ratios are generally lower in Europe than in the United States, the differences appear to be particularly large for the youngest and oldest age groups (see Gordon 2006). Generous unemployment benefits are likely to increase the reservation wage rates. Therefore, if human capital depreciates with unemployment, it becomes more difficult for the unemployed to find acceptable jobs. This in turn may contribute to reduce the search intensity. (See also Ljungqvist and Sargent [2005], as well as their chapter 6 in this volume.) As it is less beneficial for older individuals than for younger individuals to reinvest, this also suggests that generous unemployment benefits may have a relatively strong effect on the incentives facing the unemployed elderly. It is also consistent with the estimates by Palme and Svensson (2002) that unemployment is an important pathway to early retirement in Sweden. Third, the literature focusing on differences in tax policy between Europe and the United States as an explanation to differences in terms of the hours of work is often silent about the labor market structure—an issue to which we turn next.

4.7.1   Market Structure and the Role of Unions

Is there econometric evidence in favor of the hypothesis that differences (between countries) in economic policy, and particularly in tax policy, are related to differences in hours of market work? The answer is yes; there are studies showing a negative correlation between hours of work per person and the (average) marginal income tax rate. Alesina, Glaeser, and Sacerdote (2005) discuss the possibility that these observed correlations to some extent may be due to a missing variables problem. Their study focuses on differences in labor market institutions between the United States and Europe: European labor markets are often characterized by trade unions—which have a strong influence on wage formation and/or serve as a pressure group behind the economic policy—whereas the influence of trade unions is much weaker in the United States. They use panel data for the OECD countries for the period from 1960 to 1995. If they disregard the differences in labor market characteristics previously discussed (in a way similar to earlier literature in this area), their results show a negative and significant relationship between the marginal tax rate and the hours of work per person, which is consistent with the results previously mentioned. However, by adding a measure of union density (the fraction of union members in the labor force) and a measure of employment protection, this significant result disappears; instead, both the union density and the employment protection variable show negative and significant relationships with hours of work. Therefore, it seems as if unionization and regulations better explain differences between Europe and the United States than does the tax system.

The idea that unions are able to affect work hours (either directly or indirectly via wage formation) becomes more plausible with stronger trade unions. Unions may engage in pressure group activities; due to differences in membership and/or political strength, the expected return from doing so is likely to have been greater in some of the major European countries than in the United States. As such, unions may have had greater opportunity to affect market outcomes, as well as legislation, in Europe.

We do not want to draw strong conclusions from these results. This is so for several reasons. First, studies based on country-level data cannot provide as detailed descriptions of incentive effects as the microstudies discussed before, meaning that direct comparisons are difficult. Second, although union wage setting and measures of regulations may correlate with hours of work per person at the country level, so does the marginal tax rate, according to the results presented by Alesina, Glaeser, and Sacerdote (2005). Therefore, it very well may be the case that the tax and transfer systems, the social insurance system, and the institutional characteristics of the labor market all contribute to explain the differences with regard to work hours, and we are not yet able to establish which aspect is most important.

4.8   Summary and Discussion

Sweden's diverse set of social insurance programs provides a high safety net for its citizens but requires a high rate of taxation. Social insurance programs create their own disincentives for market work. Historically, Sweden's programs have been robust to individual malfeasance, yet there is emerging evidence that malfeasance is on the rise. The large and growing proportion of the near-retirement population on disability and sickness insurance benefits is disturbing and may mask other structural problems in the labor market. Equally worrisome, it seems that the disability and sickness insurance programs are now entitlements rather than insurance.

The high tax rates necessary to fund the social insurance programs also create incentives against market work. The 1991 tax reform reduced marginal tax rates, but tax rates in Sweden remain high compared with non-Nordic European countries and particularly the United States. The econometric literature finds little evidence that high marginal tax rates are reducing hours of work in Sweden. The literature offers a variety of reasons to explain why the distorting effects of high tax rates may not appear in hours of work. However, while taxes may not have very large effects on hours of work, there is emerging evidence that the high marginal tax rates do influence other choices that affect before-tax income. In the absence of any behavioral effects, an increase in the marginal income tax should have no effect on before-tax income. Recent estimates using Swedish data suggest that a 10 percent increase in marginal tax rate reduces before-tax income by 3 to 4 percent.

International comparisons reveal that Swedes work fewer hours in the market than Americans do. The income guarantees offered by the social insurance programs and high marginal tax rates are certainly part of the explanation, though there is far from a consensus on their relative importance. And it is easy to recommend that tax rates be lowered or that social insurance programs be reduced, but doing so would miss the Swedish perspective on the right level of social insurance. A fruitful approach is to inquire whether the social insurance programs meet their original intent with the least social cost.

Sweden's 1991 tax reform and the 1999 pension reform increased incentives for market work. These reforms addressed politically contentious problems and illustrate Sweden's remarkable ability to find pragmatic public policy solutions. The challenge facing the Swedish welfare system is to keep enough people working enough hours to fund its generous benefits. To preserve its high safety net, Sweden will need to increase self-insurance of small (short-term) risks and may need to increase the monitoring of benefits to limit the free riding that stems from the apparent shift in norms away from market work.

Appendix

Table 4A.1

Study	Description	e_w	e_y
	Results for men		
Blomquist (1983)	LNU 1973, married men aged 25–55	0.08	−0.04
Blomquist and Hansson-Brusewitz (1990)	LNU 1981, married men aged 25–55	(0.08, 0.12)	(−0.13, 0.02)
Flood and MaCurdy (1992)	HUS, married men aged 25–55	(−0.24, 0.2)	(−0.10, 0.04)
Aronsson and Palme (1998)	LNU 1981, married couples aged 25–55	0.12	−0.03
Flood, Hansen, and Wahlberg (2004)	HINK 1993, 1999, married couples, each spouse younger than age 56	0.05	—
Blomquist, Eklöf, and Newey (2001)	LNU 1973, 1981, and 1991, married men aged 25–55	0.075	−0.04
	Results for women		
Blomquist and Hansson-Brusewitz (1990)	LNU 1981, married women aged 25–55	(0.38, 0.79)	(−0.24, −0.03)
Aronsson and Palme (1998)	LNU 1981, married couples aged 25–55	0.44	−0.12
Flood, Hansen, and Wahlberg (2004)	HINK 1993, 1999, married couples, each spouse younger than age 56	0.1	—

Note: The variable e_w measures the elasticity of the labor supply with respect to the own marginal wage rate, whereas e_y is the labor supply elasticity with respect to the virtual nonlabor income. In some of the studies, the authors estimate several variants of the model, and the numbers refer to the intervals for the point estimates. LNU = Level of Living Survey; HUS = Swedish Panel Study on Market and Nonmarket Activities; HINK = Swedish Household Income Survey.

References

Aarbu, K., and T. Thoresen. 2001. Income responses to tax changes: Evidence from the Norwegian tax reform. *National Tax Journal* 54 (June): 319–35.

Agell, J., P. Englund, and J. Södersten. 1998. *Incentives and redistribution in the welfare state: The Swedish tax reform.* Basingstoke, U.K.: Macmillan Press.

Agell, J., and M. Persson. 2000. Tax arbitrage and labor supply. *Journal of Public Economics* 78 (1/2): 3–24.

Alesina, A., E. Glaeser, and B. Sacerdote. 2005. Work and leisure in the U.S. and Europe: Why so different? NBER Working Paper no. 11278. Cambridge, MA: National Bureau of Economic Research, April.

Alessie, R., and A. Kapteyn. 1991. Habit formation, interdependent preferences and demographic effects in the almost ideal demand system. *Economic Journal* 101 (406): 404–19.

Aronsson, T., S. Blomquist, and H. Sacklén. 1999. Identifying interdependent behaviour in an empirical model of labour supply. *Journal of Applied Econometrics* 14 (6): 607–26.

Aronsson, T., and M. Palme. 1998. A decade of tax and benefit reforms in Sweden: Effects on labour supply, welfare and inequality. *Economica* 65 (1): 39–67.

Aronsson, T., and T. Sjögren. 2004a. Efficient taxation, wage bargaining and policy coordination. *Journal of Public Economics* 88 (12): 2711–25.

———. 2004b. Is the optimal labor income tax progressive in a unionized economy? *Scandinavian Journal of Economics* 106 (4): 661–75.

———. 2009. Optimal income taxation and social norms in the labor market. *International Tax and Public Finance,* forthcoming.

Aronsson, T., and J. R. Walker. 1997. The effects of Sweden's welfare state on labor supply incentives. In *The welfare state in transition: Reforming the Swedish model,* ed. R. Freeman, B. Swedenborg, and R. Topel, 203–67. Chicago: University of Chicago Press.

Aronsson, T., M. Wikström, and R. Brännlund. 1997. Wage determination under non-linear taxes: Estimation and an application to panel data. *Oxford Economic Papers* 49 (3): 404–18.

Blomquist, S. 1983. The effect of income taxation on the labor supply of married men in Sweden. *Journal of Public Economics* 22 (2): 169–97.

Blomquist, S., M. Eklöf, and W. Newey. 2001. Tax reform evaluation using non-parametric methods: Sweden 1980–1991. *Journal of Public Economics* 79 (3): 543–68.

Blomquist, S., and U. Hansson-Brusewitz. 1990. The effect of taxes on male and female labor supply in Sweden. *Journal of Human Resources* 25 (3): 317–57.

Blomquist, S., and W. Newey. 2002. Nonparametric estimation with nonlinear budget sets. *Econometrica* 70 (6): 2455–80.

Blomquist, S., and H. Sehlin. 2008. Hourly wage rate and earnings responsiveness to changes in marginal tax rates. Working Paper no. 2008:16. Uppsala University, Department of Economics, November. Available at: http://www.nek.uu.se/Pdf/wp2008_16.pdf.

Blundell, R., and T. MaCurdy. 1999. Labor supply: A review of alternative approaches. In *Handbook of labor economics,* vol. 3A, ed. O. Ashenfelter and D. Card, 1559–695. New York: North-Holland.

Brock, W., and S. Durlauf. 2001a. Discrete choice with social interactions. *Review of Economic Studies* 68 (2): 236–60.

———. 2001b. Interactions-based models. In *Handbook of econometrics,* vol. 5, ed. J. Heckman and E. Leamer, 3297–380. New York: North-Holland.

Brunello, G., M. Parisi, and D. Sonedda. 2002. Labor taxes and wages: Evidence from Italy. CESifo Working Paper no. 715. Munich: Center for Economic Studies and the Information and Forshung Institute for Economic Research at the University of Munich, May.

Davis, S., and M. Henrekson. 2004. Tax effects on work activity, industry mix and shadow economy size: Evidence from rich-country comparisons. NBER Working Paper no. 10509. Cambridge, MA: National Bureau of Economic Research, May.

Edin, P.-A., P. Englund, and E. Ekman. 1995. Avregleringar och hushållens skulder. In *Bankerna under krisen*. Stockholm: Bankkriskommittén.

Feldstein, M. 1995. The effect of marginal tax rates on taxable income: A panel study of the 1986 Tax Reform Act. *Journal of Political Economy* 103 (3): 551–72.

Feldstein, M., and J. Liebman. 2002. Social security. In *Handbook of public economics,* vol 4, ed. A. Auerbach and M. Feldstein, 2245–324. New York: North-Holland.

Flood, L., J. Hansen, and R. Wahlberg. 2004. Household labor supply and welfare participation in Sweden. *Journal of Human Resources* 39 (4): 1008–32.

Flood, L., and T. MaCurdy. 1992. Work disincentive effects of taxes: An empirical analysis of Swedish men. *Carnegie-Rochester Conference Series on Public Policy* 37: 239–77.

Fuest, C., and B. Huber. 1997. Wage bargaining, labor-tax progression, and welfare. *Journal of Economics* 66 (2): 127–50.

Gordon, R. 2006. Issues in the comparison of welfare between Europe and the United States. Unpublished manuscript. Northwestern University, Department of Economics.

Gruber, J., and E. Saez. 2002. The elasticity of taxable income: Evidence and implications. *Journal of Public Economics* 84 (1): 1–32.

Hansson, Å. 2004. Taxpayers' responsiveness to tax changes and implications for the costs of taxation. Working Paper no. 2004:5. Lund University, Department of Economics, February.

Henrekson, M., and M. Persson. 2004. The effects on sick leave of changes in the sickness insurance system. *Journal of Labor Economics* 22 (1): 87–113.

Holmlund, B., and A.-S. Kolm. 1995. Progressive taxation, wage setting and unemployment: Theory and Swedish evidence. *Swedish Economic Policy Review* 2 (2): 424–70.

Holmlund, B., and M. Söderström. 2008. Estimating dynamic income responses to tax reforms: Swedish evidence. IFAU Working Paper no. 28. Uppsala, Sweden: Institute for Labor Market Policy Evaluation.

Kapteyn, A. 1977. A theory of preference formation. PhD diss., Leiden University.

Lindbeck, A. 1995. Welfare state disincentives with endogenous habits and norms. *Scandinavian Journal of Economics* 97 (4): 477–94.

Lindbeck, A. 2002. Pensions and contemporary socioeconomic change. In *Social security and pension reform in Europe,* ed. M. Feldstein and H. Siebert, 19–49. Chicago: University of Chicago Press.

Lindbeck, A., S. Nyberg, and J. Weibull. 1999. Social norms and economic incentives in the welfare state. *Quarterly Journal of Economics* 114 (1): 1–35.

———. 2003. Social norms and welfare state dynamics. *Journal of the European Economic Association* 1 (2/3): 533–42.

Lindbeck, A., and M. Persson. 2003. The gains from pension reform. *Journal of Economic Literature* 41 (1): 74–112.

Lindsay, T. 1987. Individual tax payer response to tax cuts: 1982–1984, with implications for the revenue maximizing tax rate. *Journal of Public Economics* 33 (2): 173–206.

Ljunge, M., and K. Ragan. 2004. Who responded to the tax reform of the century? Working Paper. University of Chicago, Department of Economics.

Ljungqvist, L. 2006. Comment on "Work and leisure in the U.S. and Europe: Why so different?" by A. Alesina, E. Glaeser, and B. Sacerdote. In *NBER macroeconomics annual 2005,* ed. M. Gertler and K. Rogoff, 65–77. Cambridge, MA: MIT Press.

Ljungqvist, L., and T. Sargent. 2005. The European unemployment experience: Uncertainty and heterogeneity. Unpublished manuscript. New York University, Department of Economics. Available at: http://homepages.nyu.edu/~ts43/RESEARCH/europe_employment_1.pdf.

Lockwood, B., and A. Manning. 1993. Wage setting and the tax system: Theory and evidence for the United Kingdom. *Journal of Public Economics* 52 (1): 1–29.

Lockwood, B., T. Slök, and T. Tranaes. 2000. Progressive taxation and wage setting: Some evidence from Denmark. *Scandinavian Journal of Economics* 102 (4): 707–23.

Manski, C. 1993. Identification of endogenous social effects: The reflection problem. *Review of Economic Studies* 60 (3): 531–42.

Mortensen, D. 1977. Unemployment insurance and job search decisions. *Industrial and Labor Relations Review* 30 (4): 505–17.

Olovsson, C. 2004. Why do Europeans work so little? IIES Seminar Paper no. 727. Stockholm University, Institute for International Economic Studies, February.

Organization for Economic Cooperation and Development (OECD). 2005. *OECD economic surveys: Sweden.* Paris: OECD.

Palme, M., and I. Svensson. 2002. Pathways to retirement and retirement incentives in Sweden. Arbetsrapport no. 2002:9. Stockholm: Institute for Future Studies.

———. 2004. Income security programs and retirement in Sweden. In *Social security and retirement around the world: Micro-estimation,* ed. J. Gruber and D. Wise, 579–642. Chicago: University of Chicago Press.

Prescott, E. 2004. Why do Americans work so much more than Europeans? *Federal Reserve Bank of Minneapolis Quarterly Review* 28 (1): 2–13.

Sacklén, H. 1996. Essays on empirical models of labor supply. PhD diss., Uppsala University.

Selén, J. 2002. Taxable income responses to tax changes: A panel analysis of the 1991 Swedish tax reform. FIEF Working Paper no. 177. Stockholm: La Fédération Internationale pour l'Economie Familiale.

Shelling, T. 1971. Dynamic models of segregation. *Journal of Mathematical Sociology* 1:143–86.

Sillamaa, M.-A., and M. Veall. 2001. The effects of marginal tax rates on taxable income: A panel study of the 1988 tax flattening in Canada. *Journal of Public Economics* 80 (3): 341–56.

Slemrod, J. 1992. Do taxes matter? Lessons from the 1980s. *American Economic Review* 82 (2): 250–6.

Walker, J. R. 1996. Parental benefits, employment and fertility dynamics. In *Research in population economics,* vol. 8, ed. T. P. Schultz, 125–72. Greenwich, CT: JAI Press.

Woittiez, I., and A. Kapteyn. 1998. Social interaction and habit formation in a model of female labour supply. *Journal of Public Economics* 70 (2): 185–205.

5

Did Active Labor Market Policies Help Sweden Rebound from the Depression of the Early 1990s?

Anders Forslund and Alan Krueger

5.1 Introduction

In the early 1990s, the Swedish labor market was hit by the worst shock it had experienced since the 1930s, with the unemployment rate rising to 10 percent. This development stands out in light of Sweden's performance in the postwar period. Between the mid-1940s and the crisis of the 1990s, the Swedish unemployment rate oscillated between 1 percent and just under 4 percent (figure 5.1). Unemployment even remained low in the 1970s, despite oil price shocks that led to persistently high unemployment elsewhere in Europe. A natural question is, what, if anything, in Swedish institutions and policies explains why Sweden's unemployment rate did not follow the same pattern as in most Western European countries? A factor often mentioned for this envious performance is Sweden's active labor market policies (ALMPs; e.g., cf. Layard, Nickell, and Jackman 1991).

The United States also avoided the persistently high unemployment rates of the Western European countries. Admittedly, the U.S. unemployment rate rose at about the same time as in Western Europe during the downturns of the 1970s and early 1980s. However, it also declined rapidly as the business cycle improved. The U.S. unemployment rate has also been lower than Sweden's during most years since the early 1990s. A common explanation of the more favorable development in the United States was its flexible labor market and modest social safety net, giving rise to high job search intensity, lower reservation wages,

Anders Forslund is the assistant director-general and an associate professor at the Institute for Labor Market Policy Evaluation. Alan Krueger is the Bendheim Professor of Economics and Public Affairs at Princeton University and a research associate of the National Bureau of Economic Research.

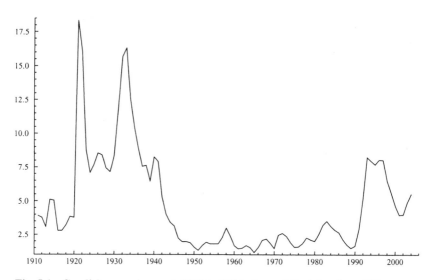

Fig. 5.1   Swedish unemployment, 1911 to 2004, share of the labor force (%)
Note: 1911 to 1955: unemployed union members; 1955 to 1961: unemployed registered at the Public Employment Service; 1961 to 2004: Statistics Sweden, labor force surveys.

and consequently, to considerably shorter unemployment spells than in Europe.

The steep increase in unemployment in Sweden did not reflect in any obvious way a reduced commitment to ALMPs (see figure 5.2). Extensive ALMPs, however, could not prevent the Swedish unemployment rate from rising in the early 1990s. Yet, this was not unexpected—the rapid increase in unemployment primarily reflected a rapid increase of the inflow into unemployment that could not reasonably be prevented by ALMPs.

In a previous paper (Forslund and Krueger 1997), we questioned whether ALMPs actually could have been a main explanation of the earlier low levels of unemployment. We showed that the scientific support for the view that ALMPs had played a key role in keeping Swedish unemployment low was fragile. We found that relief work crowded out regular jobs in some sectors (so that the net effect on unemployment was considerably smaller than the number of program participants). We also found that the evidence from cross-country studies of the kind that Layard, Nickell and, Jackman (1991) used to support the view that large-scale ALMPs lead to lower unemployment rates was not robust to the time period studied. Furthermore, it was hard to argue that the benefits of labor market training were large enough to offset the high costs. We also voiced concern that the generous social safety net and ALMPs in Sweden could lead to hysteresis. Indeed, to an outsider, it was puzzling that Sweden was able to maintain such low unemployment as it did before 1991 with its generous benefits for the nonemployed. Presumably, social stigma discouraged excessive use of public programs. We feared that

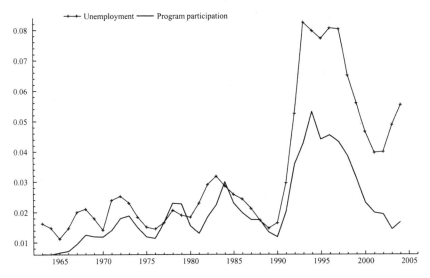

Fig. 5.2   Unemployment and program participation, 1963 to 2004 (shares of labor force)

this stigma could erode as a result of widespread unemployment in which weakness in the overall economy rather than shortcomings in individual initiative could be blamed for unemployment, leading to greater reliance on social benefits and ALMPs for years to come. At the same time, we did not find any obvious signs that the Swedish labor market suddenly worked less well and that this could explain the high unemployment rate of the early 1990s.

The fact that ALMPs were not sufficient to prevent the crisis of the early 1990s and that they probably were not important for the previous low unemployment rates does not imply that they were ineffective at combating the unemployment crisis of the 1990s.

Hence, in the following, we investigate whether ALMPs facilitated the recovery from the high unemployment rates of the early 1990s. To remove all suspense, we conclude that ALMPs probably played a minimal role in reducing total unemployment since the early 1990s. Although the programs may have maintained high labor force attachment, unemployment was slow to decline compared with past shocks, and cycling through programs and participation in unemployment insurance (UI) was common. The main function of ALMPs has been to cushion the blow of unemployment for those who become unemployed, not to speed reemployment or to increase overall employment. While the former is clearly important and salutary, interest in finding a combination of policies to raise employment remains high. Indeed, Sweden's commitment to supporting the unemployed *and* to reforming the mix of ALMPs when they do not seem to be as efficient as possible is admirable. The optimal formula, however, appears to be a work in progress.

5.2 The Swedish Labor Market Since the Early 1990s

In figure 5.2, we saw that the Swedish unemployment rate increased very rapidly between 1990 and 1993, from 1.5 percent to just above 8 percent, or from just under 3 percent to fully 13 percent as measured by total unemployment (the sum of open unemployment and program participation). Subsequently, the unemployment rate remained high until the business cycle upturn of the late 1990s. The decrease in unemployment was rapid, but by the time the unemployment rate increased again in 2003, it had never dropped below approximately 4 percent, twice the level of typical business cycle peaks during the decades preceding the 1990s. This could indicate a change for the worse in the workings of the Swedish labor market since the 1980s.

As we have already pointed out, the rise in unemployment was accompanied by a rapid increase in participation in labor market programs; in the mid-1990s, program participation amounted to around 5 percent of the labor force (figure 5.2).

Although dramatic, the increase in unemployment and program participation actually downplays the magnitude of the shock to the Swedish labor market. This is clear from figure 5.3, figure 5.4, and figure 5.5, where the evolution of labor force participation and employment in Sweden is compared with that in the United States.

The steep increase in unemployment reflected both an increased inflow and a longer duration (figure 5.6) of unemployment spells. Indeed, inflow and duration covary quite closely from the early 1990s on.

The observation that unemployment rates have not fallen to the pre-1990s levels may indicate deterioration in the functioning of the Swedish labor market. A common way to diagnose such problems is to examine the Beveridge curve—the relationship between vacancies and unemployment—for outward shifts. In Forslund and Krueger (1997), we concluded that there were no signs of a significant outward shift of the Swedish Beveridge curve over the period from 1981 to 1991; on the contrary, we detected a significant inward shift.

Looking at more recent data, there possibly may be an outward shift of the Beveridge curve, both in terms of open unemployment (figure 5.7) and in terms of total unemployment (figure 5.8). This impression is also supported by a more formal analysis. We estimated Beveridge curves using data for the period from 1970 to 2004, and an included time trend was significant and positive, confirming the visual impression from the plots. In a bookkeeping sense, this shift probably reflects the increased inflow into unemployment displayed in figure 5.6.

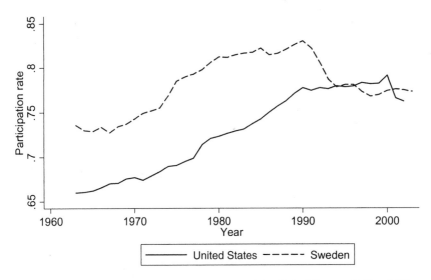

Fig. 5.3   Labor force participation in Sweden and the United States, 1963 to 2003 (share of population in active ages)

Source: OECD labor force statistics.

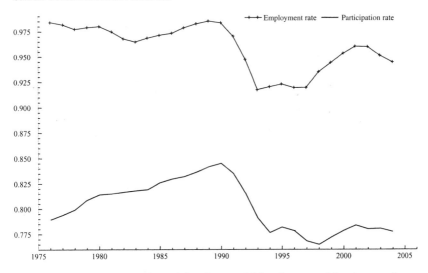

Fig. 5.4   Employment relative to labor force and labor force participation rate in Sweden, 1976 to 2004

Source: Statistics Sweden, labor force surveys.

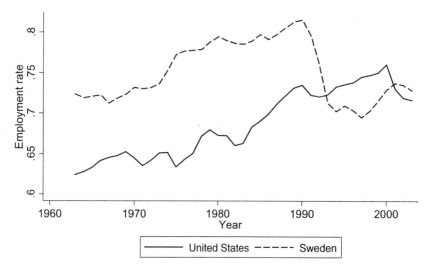

Fig. 5.5 Employment-to-population rate, 1963 to 2003, in Sweden and the United States (share of active population)

Source: OECD labor force statistics.

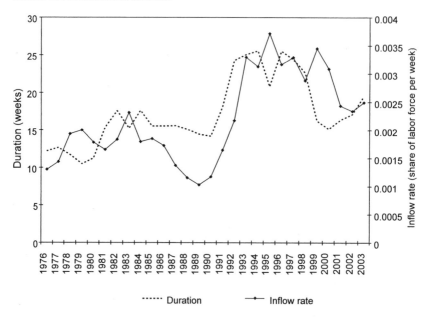

Fig. 5.6 Inflow to unemployment (right-hand scale) and the duration of unemployment (left-hand scale), 1972 to 2002, aged sixteen to sixty-four years

Source: Computations by Bertil Holmlund based on Labor Force Survey data.

Note: The inflow is given as weekly inflow as a share of the labor force (%). The values are running three-year averages.

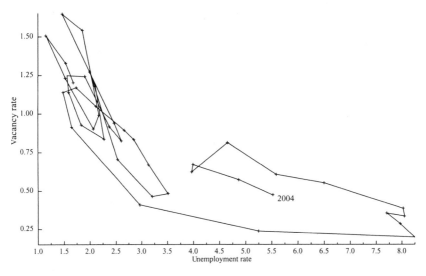

Fig. 5.7   The Swedish Beveridge curve, 1963 to 2004

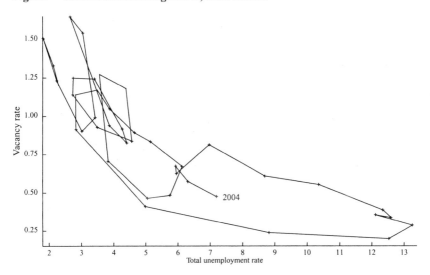

Fig. 5.8   The Swedish Beveridge curve, 1963 to 2004, in terms of total unemployment

Another way to check for changes in the functioning of the Swedish labor market is to see if the evolution of unemployment in the 1990s can be described satisfactorily by a model estimated on data ending before the crisis. To explore this idea, we have estimated an autoregressive model for unemployment.

In figure 5.9, we plot the actual unemployment rate from 1993 to 2004,

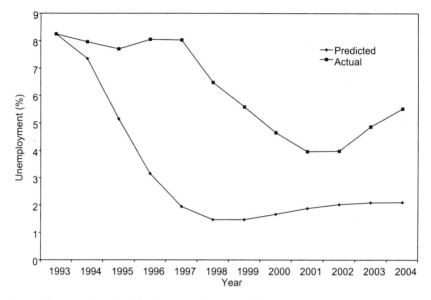

Fig. 5.9   Actual and predicted unemployment and impulse-response function for the period from 1993 to 2004

along with dynamic forecasts from this simple model estimated on unemployment data for the period from 1945 to 1990.[1] The model systematically underpredicts the actual rate of unemployment, and most notably, it predicts the unemployment rate to fall four years earlier than it actually does. According to this evidence, it seems that something happened with consequences for the persistence of unemployment in the 1990s. This would seem to bear out our concern that ALMPs were unlikely to prevent persistently high unemployment from taking root and that generous safety net programs could lead to hysteresis if the stigma associated with program participation was eroded.

There is an extensive research literature on possible explanations as to why high unemployment rates may become persistent. One such factor, often discussed in connection with the Western European unemployment problem, is that the average length of unemployment spells tended to increase hand in hand with the higher unemployment rates. If unemployment has a causal negative effect on the probability that the unemployed find jobs, and if this effect tends to increase with the duration of unemployment spells, then this mechanism is one way to explain why high unemployment may become persistent. This situation could be exacerbated if high unemployment causes people to take more advantage of the panoply of safety net programs.

The increase in duration of the survey-based measure of Swedish unem-

---

1. This estimation period is chosen because unemployment seems to have followed a reasonably stable process over this period; see figure 5.1.

ployment shown in figure 5.6 is not that dramatic: duration grew from some fifteen weeks to about twenty-five weeks in the mid-1990s and then fell again. However, there is reason to believe that this measure understates the extent of the problem, because many spells of open unemployment ended in a labor market program. Hence, in figure 5.10, we use information from the registers at the National Labor Market Board to compute the average duration of both ongoing spells of open unemployment and continuous spells of open unemployment and program participation.

Using the information in figure 5.10, the development is much more ominous: the average length of spells increased more or less continuously from around 400 days in 1994 to around 700 days (one hundred weeks) in 2000.[2] At the same time, the average duration of spells of open unemployment was only about one hundred days (fifteen to sixteen weeks; see figure 5.6).

Hence, the long continuous spells of open unemployment and program participation, on average, entail significant variation. Because the average spells of open unemployment are much shorter, a large number of unemployment spells end after only a few weeks. At the same time, there must be a number of spells that are significantly longer than the average. This is shown in figure 5.11, which shows the distribution of spells of different lengths in the stocks of the registered at the Public Employment Service (PES) on December 31, 1999, and February 28, 2005.

At both dates, a vast majority had relatively short spells: between 60 and 70 percent of the spells had durations of no longer than a year. But we also see that a significant proportion (just above 14 percent, or about 62,000 persons in 1999, and just above 7 percent, or about 32,000 persons in 2005) had been registered for at least three years. Comparing the two years, we see that spells were generally shorter in 2005, but the difference was not striking. We have also computed the average number of programs per person, conditional on participation in at least one program. This average was between 2.5 and 3 at both points in time, and around 10 percent had at least six program spells.

In our previous paper, we investigated whether the stability of the Beveridge curve (atypical for most European countries) and the low Swedish unemployment rates prior to the 1990s could be attributed to an expansion of public employment, but we did not find strong support for this hypothesis.

However, it is interesting to note that the share of public employment has developed quite differently in the 1990s than in the previous decades. This is evident from figure 5.12, which shows the evolution of the public employment share for the period from 1970 to 2004. If the increasing share contributed to lower unemployment in previous decades,[3] then the sharp

2. To some extent, this increase is an artifact, reflecting the fact that the registers only date back to August 1991. However, the level in the late 1990s is probably well measured.

3. We are a bit reluctant to push this point, however, given that we found no strong support for this hypothesis in our previous paper.

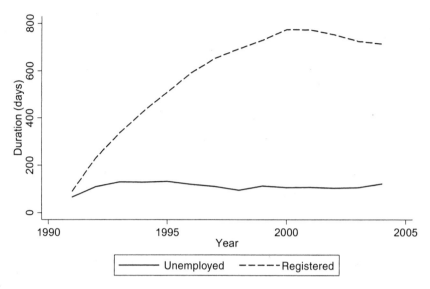

Fig. 5.10 Duration of ongoing unemployment and register spells at the Public Employment Service, averages

Source: National Labor Market Board.

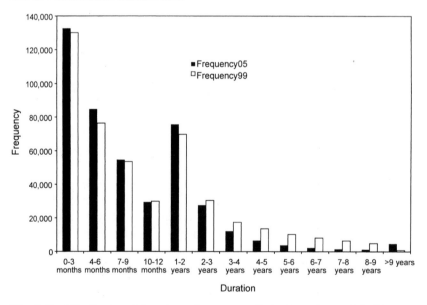

Fig. 5.11 Distribution of durations of ongoing spells in the registers of the National Labor Market Board: February 28, 2005, and December 31, 1999

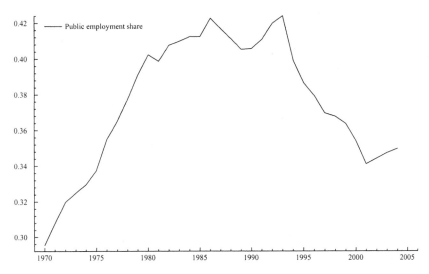

Fig. 5.12   The share of public employment, 1970 to 2004

decline in the 1990s may have contributed to the relatively high unemployment rate later.

We have estimated autoregressive models for private- and public-sector employment. The estimation samples cover the years from 1970 to 1992. Using these autoregressions to forecast employment from 1993 to 2004 gives rise to the results plotted in figure 5.13 and figure 5.14. Although these should not be given any causal interpretation, it is evident that private-sector employment evolved in a way that is fairly well described by the model estimated on data for the 1970s and 1980s, whereas the path of public-sector employment is radically different in the 1990s—the model overpredicts public-sector employment significantly in every single year from 1993 on. It is also notable that there has been no recovery in public employment since the mid-1990s. The difference to previous decades in this respect is striking.

5.2.1   Regional Adjustments

The evidence presented in Forslund and Krueger (1997) suggested that Swedish regional employment dynamics resembled those in other European countries, whereas the pattern of regional unemployment dynamics was more similar to that in the United States.

Fredriksson (1999) estimated regional values at risk (VARs) to analyze the dynamic adjustment to regional employment shocks. His main results were that a region-specific negative employment shock in the long run lowers employment in that region. The reduction was smaller than what is found for a typical U.S. state. In this respect, it was found that Sweden resembled the rest of Europe. Looking instead at the short-run dynamics, most of the

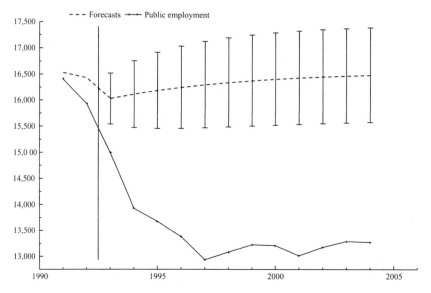

Fig. 5.13   Public-sector employment and dynamic forecast from autoregression model

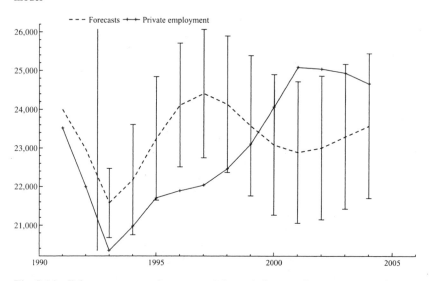

Fig. 5.14   Private-sector employment and dynamic forecast from autoregression model

adjustment is brought about by migration and very little by unemployment, wages, or labor market programs. In this respect, Sweden was found to be rather similar to the United States. The results do not suggest that ALMPs played any major role for mobility.

A number of studies have estimated the effects of labor market policies on geographical mobility more directly. There is a small number of studies of various mobility-enhancing programs (Storrie and Nättorp 1997; Harkman 1988; Westerlund 1998). These studies suggest that the mobility-enhancing measures have had minor or no effects on mobility between counties or local labor markets. A larger number of studies have estimated the effects of placement in different programs on mobility (McCormick and Skedinger 1991; Nilsson 1995; Westerlund 1997; Edin, Heiborn, and Nilsson 1998; Westerlund 1998; Widerstedt 1998; Fredriksson and Johansson 2003; Lindgren and Westerlund 2003). Most studies suggest that programs lock in participants and hence that increasing program participation decreases mobility. An interesting insight into possible mechanisms is provided by the analysis in Fredriksson and Johansson (2003), where it is shown that the negative program effect on mobility reflects a decreased job-finding rate among participants. Given the lower job-finding rate, the propensity to move by program participants is not significantly different from the propensity to move among nonparticipants.

5.3   Swedish ALMPs Since the Early 1990s

5.3.1   The Program Menu: New and Old Medicine

The labor market programs can be subdivided into three main categories: training, subsidized employment, and practice. During the 1990s, many new programs were launched, and the following description is not exhaustive.

For a long time, *labor market training* was equivalent to vocational training, but over time, it also came to involve more prep courses. More recently, it also has involved *computer activity centers,* as well as an *information technology (IT) training program* organized jointly with the Confederation of Swedish Industries. Between the late 1980s and the early 2000s, participation in training programs enabled participants to renew UI benefit eligibility. This system was abolished for all labor market programs in 2000 in connection with a reform in the UI system and the introduction of the activity guarantee (see the following).

Subsidized employment has taken many forms, with the provision of relief jobs a prominent historical approach. In the 1990s, however, relief jobs were used to a small extent (and were abolished in 1998). They largely were replaced by so-called *work experience schemes,* where participants were supposed to be placed in jobs that would otherwise not have occurred in order to avoid crowding-out effects. In 1998, *employment subsidies,* which entail wage subsidies to employers for hiring unemployed (mainly long-term unemployed) workers, replaced recruitment subsidies, introduced in 1981. In most respects, employment subsidies are similar to the previous program, the main difference being that the new program is targeted more heavily at the long-term unemployed.

Work practice programs are supposed to involve both work and training. Normally, the participant is paid an amount corresponding to his or her level of UI compensation. A number of *programs targeted toward youth* belong to this category (youth teams, schooling-in slots, youth practice, municipality youth programs, youth guarantee). There were also practice programs targeted at other groups—immigrants and unemployed school graduates. Many of the practice programs were replaced by a more general work placement program in 1995.

Resource jobs were introduced in 1997. This program was a subsidy to employers for temporarily hiring unemployed workers. Participants were supposed to both work and to undergo training. The wage rate was capped at 90 percent of the participant's previous income.

Trainee replacement schemes, used between 1991 and 1997, involved subsidizing employers who paid training for an employee and who hired a replacement from the PES. Hence, this program was a mixture of training and subsidized employment.

In August 2000, a new type of program, the *activity guarantee,* was inaugurated (Forslund, Fröberg, and Lindqvist 2004). The activity guarantee was (and is) targeted at persons at risk of becoming long-term registers at the PES or at those with expiring UI benefit eligibility. Participation is supposed to be full-time, and the participants receive the equivalent of UI benefits. The activity guarantee is a framework within which the participant is supposed to search for a job, to participate in a regular labor market program, or to be engaged in some training program. There are only three ways to leave the guarantee: by finding a regular job lasting at least six months, by participating in regular education, or by leaving the labor force.

The inauguration of the activity guarantee was synchronized with changes in the rules in the UI system, taking place in February 2001. The main changes introduced were that first, participation in labor market programs no longer qualifies for renewed UI benefit eligibility—the only way to renew eligibility is through an ordinary job; and second, if an unemployed worker has not found a job within the fourteen months of UI benefits, a case worker at the PES office decides whether the individual is to be transferred to the activity guarantee, or if the case worker assesses that the unemployed individual has a good chance of finding a job, he or she may award the individual another period (fourteen months) of UI benefits. If the unemployed has not found a job after a second period of UI benefits, he or she will be transferred to the activity guarantee or will lose all income support (possibly apart from means-tested social assistance).

Looking at the changes in ALMPs and UI from a bird's eye view, one can distinguish an increased focus on job search: a main feature of the activity guarantee is supposed to be full-time job search. One can also detect an increased focus on the long-term unemployed: several forms of the employment subsidies that have been in use since 1998 have been targeted explicitly at the long-term unemployed.

5.3.2 A Quantitative Description

In figure 5.15, we show the evolution of the different types of labor market programs since the early 1960s. Both training programs and subsidized employment trended up until the mid-1990s. Training programs had more participants than subsidized employment during most of this period. Practice programs were of a rather limited importance throughout the 1980s. A number of observations can be made concerning the 1990s. First, the measure of first resort to meet the rise in unemployment was training programs, which were expanded rapidly during 1991. This is a contrast to previous decades, when relief jobs were used as the primary countercyclical measure. Second, after some time, participation in subsidized employment programs reached very high levels at the same time that practice programs expanded and training programs decreased in volume. When the labor market improved in the late 1990s, participation in all kinds of programs declined, and in the early 2000s, the three types of programs were of approximately equal size.

5.3.3 Interactions between UI and ALMPs

A generous[4] unemployment insurance creates incentives that are likely to cause long unemployment spells. A number of reforms in the Swedish UI system have facilitated an analysis of the effects of changes in the level of compensation on the flow from (insured) unemployment to employment.

Carling, Holmlund, and Vejsiu (2001) studied a change in the replacement rate from 80 percent to 75 percent that was introduced on January 1, 1996. This reform only affected a subsample of the unemployed. The authors estimated the effect of the reform by comparing job-finding rates before and after the reform of those affected and unaffected. The estimates suggested that the cut in the replacement rate resulted in an increase in the job-finding rate by about 10 percent.

Bennmarker, Carling, and Holmlund (2007) investigated the effects of several changes in the unemployment insurance system introduced in 2001 and 2002. In 2001, a two-tiered benefit system was introduced. The new system entails a higher compensation during the first twenty weeks of an unemployment spell. In 2002, benefits were raised both for spells exceeding

---

4. This is in terms of compensation levels and duration, as well as in terms of the level of control the system has in ensuring that the unemployed who is receiving benefits actually is looking actively for a job. We described the basics of the Swedish system in Forslund and Krueger (1997).

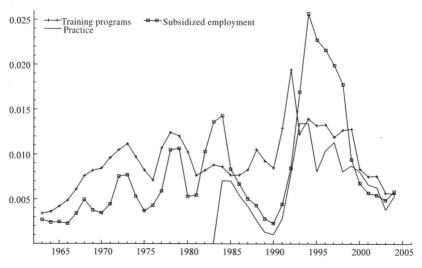

Fig. 5.15   Different ALMPs, 1963 to 2004 (shares of labor force)

twenty weeks and for the first twenty weeks of spells. The changes applied, as was the case in the 1996 reform, only to subsamples of the unemployed. Once again, this was used to identify effects on job-finding rates. Somewhat surprisingly, there is a striking difference between the results for males and females. The female job-finding rate was increased, whereas the male job-finding rate (in accordance with theoretical expectations) was reduced. There was no significant effect on the aggregate job-finding rate. The authors speculated that the difference between males and females was due to a reform in child care that took place simultaneously. The expected effect of this reform was to increase female labor supply.

A peculiarity of Swedish labor market policies in the 1990s was the opportunity to renew UI benefit eligibility through participation in labor market programs.[5] Given the generous Swedish UI system for unemployed members, this feature is likely to have affected both the efficacy of program participation and the work disincentives associated with the combined system of UI and labor market programs by lengthening benefit receipt. Indeed, there is accumulating evidence suggesting that the system led to cycling between unemployment and program participation and that this adversely affected the results of program participation.[6]

First, Ackum Agell, Björklund, and Harkman (1995) showed that long spells in the registers of the National Labor Market Board (including both

5. Provided that the program lasted long enough, participation in any program counted as employment and hence gave renewed benefit eligibility. Before 1986, only participation in job-like programs, such as relief jobs, qualified.

6. In Forslund and Krueger (1997), we presented some evidence consistent with these results, but we concluded that there was no direct conclusive evidence.

UI and program periods) were common in the early 1990s. Carling et al. (1996) showed that UI-compensated unemployment spells close to benefit exhaustion were significantly more likely to lead to program participation than were uncompensated unemployment spells. Sianesi (2001) found that program participation increased the probability of future benefit-compensated unemployment, as well as subsequent program participation. These effects were both nontrivial in size and long lasting. Finally, Hägglund (2000) found that both employment durations and the length of program spells were affected by changes in UI eligibility criteria.

Second, Sianesi (2001) found that the treatment effect (in terms of a number of different outcomes) of programs was among the worst for those individuals who were joining the programs around the time of UI benefit exhaustion, although it is hard to rule out that unobserved personal factors that lead to program participation late in the spell of unemployment, rather than the opportunity to participate itself, caused this result, absent a randomized experiment. In either interpretation, this result is consistent with the finding in Regnér (1997) and Harkman (2002) that unemployed job seekers often entered programs just to renew UI benefit eligibility.

Therefore, the evidence suggests that the system promoted cycling between periods of (UI-compensated) unemployment and program participation and hence longer periods of nonemployment. In countries that prohibit long-term cycling between open unemployment and labor market programs, it typically is found that shorter durations of compensated unemployment spells are associated with shorter unemployment spells.[7]

The possibility to renew benefit eligibility was removed in August 2000, when the activity guarantee[8] was introduced. Apart from other possible effects of the activity guarantee, this reform should be expected to improve the results of the active labor market programs.

5.3.4   Research Results on Swedish ALMPs: A Survey

Evaluations of ALMPs may be divided into micro- and macrostudies. The microstudies establish program effects for participants, whereas macrostudies consider general equilibrium effects of the programs (i.e., also consequences for nonparticipants). Typical microstudies estimate effects of program participation on subsequent income or employment; the macrostudies cover more diverse topics such as displacement effects, effects on matching efficiency, or effects on unemployment or wages.

Microevaluations depend on good data. In the United States, the modest amount of resources allocated to ALMPs has been accompanied by a fairly large amount of experimental evaluations. In Sweden, there still has been

---

7. Moffitt (1985), Meyer (1990), and Katz and Meyer (1990) for the United States; Ham and Rea (1987) for Canada; Dormont, Fougere, and Prieto (2001) for France; and Ahn and Garcia-Perez (2000) and Jenkins and Garcia-Serrano (2000) for Spain.
8. See section 5.3.1 for a description of the activity guarantee.

only one small experiment carried out for evaluation purposes (in 1974). Instead, Swedish evaluations have to rely on register data. This effort has been aided by the fact that the supply of register data has grown remarkably since the early 1990s, when the National Labor Market Board initiated an event database with information on all job applicants registering as job seekers at the Public Employment Service. Subsequently, these data have been matched with other register data from Statistics Sweden, giving rise to extremely rich observational databases for evaluation purposes. In the wake of the better data supply and the large program volumes in the 1990s, the number of high-quality evaluations of Swedish ALMPs has grown significantly since our previous paper. The number of macroevaluations, in contrast, has grown only marginally. We continue to think that it is unfortunate that Sweden still has not initiated randomized controlled evaluations of its labor market programs. Absent controlled studies, it is impossible to know if the programs or some other factors that are correlated with program participation are responsible for the measured success or failure of the programs in observational studies.

We begin by reviewing microevidence for different programs. Then, we take a closer look at some selected macrotopics.

Training Programs

In Forslund and Krueger (1997), we concluded that based on the available evidence, we could neither rule out that the returns to labor market training were 0, nor that they exceeded 3 percent, which were roughly the returns needed to make the investment worthwhile. Since then, a number of new evaluations of training programs have been published, and some patterns have emerged that may be used to refine the previous conclusions.[9]

The main impression conveyed by the studies is that there was a difference in the effects of training when comparing the 1980s and the 1990s, where the estimated effects generally looked more favorable in the 1980s. Indeed, most studies pertaining to (especially) the early 1980s point to nontrivial positive effects, whereas studies pertaining to the 1990s indicate insignificant results at best.[10]

There is no hard evidence available to account for these differences, but there are many possible explanations. First, for training to be effective, there should be easily identified bottlenecks for which to train. This is less likely in a deep recession (like in the 1990s) than in a more normal labor market (like in the 1980s). Second, the number of participants was much larger in the 1990s than in the 1980s, and the growth rate in the number of participants in the early 1990s was remarkable. (The number of participants doubled during the second half of 1991.) Such high volumes and growth rates may

9. Most studies are reviewed in some detail in Calmfors, Forslund, and Hemström (2004).
10. The studies either estimate effects on subsequent income or on the hazard to work.

have had detrimental effects on quality. Third, in the early 1990s, as opposed to in the early 1980s, participation in a (sufficiently long) training program could be used to renew UI benefit eligibility. To the extent that a fraction of the participants were motivated by a desire to renew benefit eligibility rather than to acquire useful skills, this is another possible explanation of the difference in estimated effects.

In 1997, a new program was introduced—the so-called adult education initiative (AEI). The program was targeted at unemployed workers with low levels of education, who were given the opportunity to take part in regular adult education while receiving the equivalent of unemployment benefits. It was a major program: between 1997 and 2000, more than 10 percent of the labor force participated. A number of studies (Albrecht, van den Berg, and Vroman 2004; Axelsson and Westerlund 2004, 2005; Ekström 2003; Stenberg 2003, 2005; Stenberg and Westerlund 2004) have estimated various types of effects of the program. The evidence on effects for the treated is mixed and depends on both the outcome measures and the methodology applied. Albrecht, van den Berg, and Vroman (2004) calibrated a general equilibrium search model and found positive effects for the treated but negative effects for the nontreated low-skilled workers.

Time Use of the Unemployed

To further examine how ALMPs affect the experience of unemployment in Sweden and the United States, we used Swedish time-use data for 2000 to 2001 and the American Time-Use Survey (ATUS) for 2003 to 2005 to examine how the unemployed spend their time in the two countries. Ideally, we would prefer to examine years that are at more comparable points of the business cycle, but these are the only data we have available at this time. There is also a question as to how comparable the data are. The Swedish data are based on tabulations from the Harmonized European Time-Use Surveys, which only summarize results in categories. Job-search activities for Sweden are represented in the category "activities related to employment," which includes some activities in addition to job search.

The ATUS has an activity category for job search and related activities. Unemployed American workers spend 0.55 hours per day on weekdays and 0.4 hours per day on weekends engaged in searching for a job or in related activities. The corresponding figures for Swedish workers are much lower: just six minutes per day on weekdays and one minute on weekends. Thus, the Swedish unemployed devote very little time to job search compared with the Americans. In addition, a smaller proportion of unemployed Swedes engage in job search on any given day than do Americans. Interestingly, both the American and Swedish unemployed workers report spending about one-third of an hour per day involved in education of some form. Surprisingly, we do not see much of a difference in the amount of time spent on training. While these results should be taken with a grain of salt, given the difficulties inherent in international comparisons of time use—and other factors that matter for job search intensity, such as the extent of variability in wages across comparable jobs—one plausible implication of this pattern is that Swedish ALMPs and unemployment compensation may have discouraged search effort as compared with American job seekers.

The outward shift of the Beveridge curve in Sweden suggests that the unemployed have become less likely to fill available vacancies. This shift is consistent with reduced job search activity by the unemployed in Sweden, although we do not have time series data on job search time. In any event, this comparison indicates that time-use data can provide useful insights into the behavior of the unemployed.

Other Microevaluation Results

A number of recent evaluation studies either have compared the effects of participation in different programs or have compared program participation to continued job search of the openly unemployed.[11]

A simple generalization of the results boils down to two conclusions. *First,* the more a program resembles an ordinary job, the more efficient it is in bringing the participant to work. This suggests that the most effective programs involve subsidizing employers to hire unemployed workers. It also implies that many of the low-budget programs used during the 1990s have proved to be the least effective in bringing unemployed persons back to work. *Second,* only employment subsidies (and perhaps subsidized self-employment for unemployed workers) have proved to be more effective than job search assistance. Hence, most programs, including training programs, are dominated by job search assistance, according to the available evidence.

The second result at first glance may seem counterintuitive. However, to the extent that it does, this may derive from the fact that time spent on job search may be at least as well spent as time in a program, where survey studies show that search activity goes down significantly. Against this background, the recently increased policy focus on job search seems warranted.

Direct Displacement Effects

Direct displacement takes place if employers substitute program participants for ordinary employment. In Forslund and Krueger (1997), we estimated displacement effects of relief jobs and found displacement to be high in building and construction but not significantly different from zero in health and welfare. Since then, much new evidence has accumulated. This evidence is surveyed in Calmfors, Forslund, and Hemström (2004), on which we base the following brief summary of results.

In a fairly large number of surveys, employers, program participants, and employment officers have been asked whether they believe that the tasks

11. See Calmfors, Forslund, and Hemström (2004) for a survey.

performed by program participants would have been performed also in the absence of the program. The results in the survey studies, almost without exception, suggest that all programs are associated with substantial displacement effects, but rarely are they above 50 percent. Another main result in these studies is that displacement effects are larger when the program more closely resembles an ordinary job. These findings must be taken with a grain of salt, however, as the public's opinion of the presence or absence of displacement opportunities is not proof that displacement actually takes place.

There are also several econometric studies of displacement, however. In most cases, these studies do not look at displacement effects for single programs. The results indicate larger displacement effects than those found in the survey studies; typically, displacement effects well above 50 percent are found in the econometric studies, whereas the estimated effects in the survey studies only in a few cases exceed 50 percent.

Why Do Employment Subsidies Work?

The purpose of employment subsidies is to facilitate the transition to regular jobs for the long-term unemployed. The job-finding rate among the long-term unemployed is significantly lower than among persons with shorter unemployment spells. This may have several explanations. One possibility is that employers perceive the long-term unemployed to be less productive than other persons with the same observed characteristics. So, the employment subsidy can be considered a subsidy to employers for the risk they are taking. If the long-term unemployed person in fact has lower productivity, this in turn may be due to either permanently lower productivity among the long-term unemployed (selection) or the fact that unemployment in itself has a negative effect on a person's ability to perform work tasks. If the latter is the case, the employment subsidy—that is, a temporary wage subsidy—is a reasonable policy measure; during the subsidized period, the employed can regain the working capacity lost during the unemployment spell. If, on the other hand, the productivity is permanently lower, a temporary wage subsidy is unlikely to solve the problem permanently.

We do not know with certainty whether employment subsidies primarily compensate employers for the risk taken when employing a long-term unemployed worker or for the cost of on-the-job skills upgrading. Also, some employees undoubtedly would have been hired absent the subsidy, just as some people who use coupons to buy milk would have bought milk anyway. However, it is clear from the estimates in Forslund, Johansson, and Lindqvist (2004) that a considerable part of the positive effect of employment subsidies derives from a large flow to work at the point in time when the subsidy expires. This indicates that a substantial fraction of the positive estimated treatment effect arises because subsidized employment turns into regular jobs. This pattern would not be expected if the subsidies to a large extent were given to employers who hire unemployed persons with permanently low productivity. To the extent that a nontrivial share of the long-term unemployed has permanently low productivity, the problem cannot be solved without permanent adjustments of wage costs for low-productivity workers. Such adjustments can come about in a number of ways, such as wage adjustments or various permanent subsidies through the tax system.

Other Macroevaluation Results

ALMPs may affect the wage-setting process. To the extent that ALMPs are perceived as a better alternative than open unemployment, large-scale ALMPs may weaken the incentives for wage restraint created by open unemployment. If, on the other hand, ALMPs contribute to job seekers that are more competitive, this creates incentives for wage restraint; if a union pushes for high wages, which then leads to members losing their jobs, the laid-off union members will face a tougher competition for the existing jobs. Hence, a priori, the sign of the net effect on wages is ambiguous.[12] A fairly large number of empirical studies have estimated the effect on wages of ALMPs.[13] Most studies have found that ALMPs increase the pressure for higher wages or have no effect at all. The uncertainty about the results, however, is considerable.

A few studies have estimated Swedish Beveridge curves (Jackman, Pissarides, and Savouri 1990; Calmfors 1993) or matching functions (Edin and Holmlund 1991; Hallgren 1996; Forslund and Johansson 2007) to determine the effects of ALMPs on matching efficiency, without finding evidence suggesting that ALMPs have actually improved matching.

One important objective of ALMPs in the 1990s was to promote labor force participation: even if programs did not have immediate effects on the transition from unemployment to work, it was claimed that they could prevent marginalization, and eventually, early retirement. There is a small number of studies dealing with the effects of ALMPs on labor force participation (Wadensjö 1993; Johansson and Markowski 1995; Johansson 2001; Dahlberg and Forslund 2005). All of them find significant positive effects. However, one should be careful when interpreting these results. If program participation, at least to some extent, was used to renew UI benefit eligibility, it is not clear to what extent the increased labor force participation reflected an increase in effective labor supply.

International Cross-Country Evidence on ALMPs

In Forslund and Krueger (1997), we claimed that much of the favorable impression of ALMPs was due to cross-country studies. In that paper, we

---

12. A formal analysis of this is presented in Calmfors and Lang (1995) and Forslund and Kolm (2004).

13. These studies are surveyed in Calmfors, Forslund, and Hemström (2004).

showed to some extent that these results were fragile. Calmfors, Forslund, and Hemström (2004) have surveyed this growing literature. They find that it seems to be a fairly robust result that ALMPs have contributed to lower rates of open unemployment. However, if this result should reflect that ALMPs improve the working of labor markets, one would expect that ambitious ALMPs also would contribute to lower rates of total unemployment (the sum of open unemployment and program participation). This, however, is less clear: some studies find that expanding ALMPs are associated with lower rates of total unemployment, while others find the opposite, and some studies find no significant effects at all. The implication of these two results is that ALMPs contribute to lower unemployment rates, whereas the effect on employment is unclear. Hence, the picture conveyed by the cross-country studies is rather similar to what we see in the studies of Swedish ALMPs. There are also results in the cross-country studies that are consistent with a positive effect of ALMPs on labor force participation—just as was the case for Sweden.

5.4   Recent Changes in Swedish ALMPs

The new right/center Swedish government replaced the Social Democrats after the 2006 general elections and rapidly introduced a number of changes in labor market policies. As of this writing, the new policies have been in place for less than a year, so there are no evaluations available. However, we can draw on evidence from similar programs and theoretical considerations to discuss expected effects.

The most fundamental changes have been introduced in the unemployment insurance program. First, replacement rates now are lowered from 80 percent to 70 percent after the first 200 days of unemployment. Second, the cap on the daily benefit, which was higher during the first one hundred days, is now constant over the entire unemployment spell. Third, the possibility of receiving more than one period (fourteen months) of UI benefits has been removed. Relatedly, compensation during time spent in labor market programs is no longer paid by the UI program. Previously, the UI clock stopped ticking during spells of program participation. This is no longer the case, meaning that periods paid either by UI or as compensation while in programs now have a maximum length of fourteen months, without exceptions. Previous theoretical and empirical research would indicate strongly that all of these changes should contribute to more rapid transitions from unemployment to work.

A fourth change involves membership fees for UI insurance fund members, which previously were independent of the level of unemployment among the members. The new government has introduced some elements of experience rating into the system by making membership fees dependent on the unemployment rate of each fund. However, the degree of experience rating is weak, so the expected effects should be small.[14] Government subsidization has also decreased, resulting in generally higher membership fees. This feature of the reforms seems to have given rise to a rather rapid decrease in UI fund membership.

Another reform that is closely related to the UI reforms is that the previous activity guarantee has been replaced by a *job and development guarantee*. This reform entails several changes vis-à-vis the former activity guarantee. First, the replacement rate in the new guarantee has been reduced to 65 percent; in the activity guarantee, it was the same as the (constant) UI replacement rate. Second, when eligibility for UI benefits expires after fourteen months of unemployment, entry into the job and development guarantee is mandatory. In comparison to the old system, this means that entry into the new program, on average, will take place earlier in an unemployment spell. Additional, mostly minor changes also were introduced. The lower replacement rate in the job and development guarantee is likely to speed up the transition to work compared with the old activity guarantee; the effects of the other changes are harder to predict.

The former employment subsidy programs have been replaced by the new-start jobs program. This program gives employers a tax subsidy—the employer does not have to pay any of the 33.42 percent payroll tax—for hiring an eligible worker. Workers become eligible by having a continuous period (at least twelve months long) of unemployment, sickness absence, or social assistance receipt, combined with nonemployment. The subsidy is in effect for a period equaling the duration of time in which the employee was not employed prior to starting the subsidized job.[15] The main innovation in this reform is that workers can acquire eligibility not only through a spell of unemployment but also through other spells outside the labor force. So, instead of targeting just the long-term unemployed, the new-start jobs program targets those who are more generally long-term nonemployed. It is hard to assess the importance of this reform, as well as of other differences between the old and the new programs, although Katz (1996) provides some evidence that targeted-jobs tax subsidies have increased employment in the United States in the past.

A few changes, specifically in youth programs, have also been implemented. First, payroll taxes are halved for all young workers (below age twenty-five). As a vast majority of youth qualifying for this benefit probably would have been employed anyway, this reform is likely to result in nontrivial tax transfers, causing deadweight costs due to lost tax revenue that will have be made up elsewhere. Second, the responsibility for providing the programs has been removed from the municipalities; youth programs,

14. In the Swedish system, the expected effects of experience rating primarily would be effects on wage setting; see, for example, Holmlund and Lundborg (1988). See Card and Levine (1994) for evidence of the effects of experience rating on unemployment in the United States.
15. There are exceptions for young people, old people, and immigrants.

like other programs, are now administered by the National Labor Market Board. This new program is called the *job guarantee for youth.* The available evidence suggests that transferring the responsibility away from the municipalities may have beneficial effects (Forslund and Nordström Skans, 2006). Third, according to the new policy guidelines, job search activities will be the main component of the first phase of the program. Evidence from the U.K. New Deal for Young People gives some support for this focus (see Blundell et al. 2000).

Some reforms outside of labor market programs are also likely to affect the labor market. For example, the new government has instituted tax reforms that are clearly designed to affect labor supply. We leave these issues for another chapter, as our focus is primarily on labor market programs.

5.5 Concluding Discussion

There are indications that the modus operandi of the Swedish labor market changed during the 1990s. Most importantly, we have documented that unemployment followed a different, less favorable pattern after the crisis of the 1990s than during the previous four decades. This could reflect the fact that some of those who lost their jobs in the early 1990s remained jobless during very long periods and became less employable in that process. This in turn could reflect the possibilities to renew UI benefit eligibility through participation in labor market programs. Labor market policies, in this respect, simply enabled people to remain jobless for a longer period of time. The possibility to renew UI benefit eligibility also seems to have had a negative influence on the treatment effect of labor market programs.

Available evaluations of labor market programs in the 1990s indicate that the only program that led to a job more rapidly than job search in open unemployment was employment subsidies (before 1998 recruitment subsidies). At the same time, such programs probably are associated with displacement effects, so the net effect on open unemployment may be small.

Altogether, these results suggest that the labor market policies of the 1990s were not well adapted to combat the unemployment that arose in the first years of the 1990s.

Was there an alternative? From an American perspective, it perhaps would seem natural to lower the levels of the social safety nets and in this way to make the unemployed persons seek, find, and accept new job offers more rapidly. Safety nets at the U.S. level, however, are not a realistic alternative in Sweden. For example, according to the OECD (2004), the level of compensation for an unemployed person was considerably lower in the United States than in Sweden (30 percent of previous income in the United States, compared to 77 percent in Sweden) counted over a long period (five years) of unemployment. An explanation of the big difference is that UI benefits normally are limited to six months in the United States. Thereafter, only time-limited means-tested support and disability insurance are available in the United States.

The finding that program participation generally was outperformed by job search, however, points to another alternative. If the social safety nets are kept at a high level, job search and job acceptance incentives must be provided in other ways. One such way is job search assistance and counseling. In the international evaluation literature, there is evidence that job search assistance is one of the few examples of successful measures.[16] While it is unclear why job search assistance is such a cost-effective strategy, one possibility is that such programs provide the unemployed with a more reasonable expectation for the type of jobs that they might be able to obtain (which has the economic effect of lowering reservation wages). The effectiveness of job search assistance partly may relate to our finding from time-use data that unemployed Swedes devote comparatively little time to job search.

In many circumstances, a distinction is made between active labor market policies (labor market programs) and passive labor market policies (UI benefits). This distinction seems to be based on a notion that UI benefits are paid as a compensation for not working. This is a misleading distinction for Sweden. In all existing UI benefit systems, there is a set of rules designed to ascertain that the unemployed person is available for work and is actively searching for a job in different ways. In Sweden, the Public Employment Service is the spider in this web. The PES is supposed to provide both counseling and monitoring to make sure that unemployed persons with UI benefits are available for work, according to the rules of UI. The activities of the PES in this perspective should be viewed as a (potentially) efficient labor market program. An alternative to the labor market policies pursued in the 1990s, therefore, would have been to allocate more resources to job counseling and monitoring and less to other programs.

From a perspective based on the experiences from the 1990s, the reforms in labor market policies in the early 2000s seem to be steps in the right direction. The activity guarantee involves an increased focus on measures to stimulate job search, and the new rules in UI have removed the problem of the 1990s of cycling between programs and open unemployment. The demise of relief jobs and the increased emphasis on employment subsidies is another development that is likely to lead to more efficient job creation. Of course, this does not mean that Swedes live in the best of all possible worlds. Unemployment is still high, and many problems of (potential) low-wage earners remain to be solved. In addition, the 1990s have left a legacy of long-term unemployed persons who have had only sporadic contacts with the regular labor market. As our discussion of wage subsidies suggests, traditional labor market policies probably can not solve all these problems. Yet, Sweden's commitment to improving labor market conditions and its policymakers'

---

16. See, for example, the survey in Martin and Grubb (2001).

willingness to experiment with different and innovative approaches when past approaches proved less effective than desired are positive signs.

References

Ackum Agell, S., A. Björklund, and A. Harkman. 1995. Unemployment insurance, labour market programmes and repeated unemployment in Sweden. *Swedish Economic Policy Review* 2 (2): 101–28.

Ahn, N., and J. I. Garcia-Perez. 2000. Unemployment duration and workers' wage aspirations in Spain. Working Paper no. 426. Universitat Pompeu Fabra, Department of Economics and Business, March.

Albrecht, J., G. J. van den Berg, and S. Vroman. 2004. The knowledge lift: The Swedish adult education program that aimed to eliminate low worker skill levels. IFAU Working Paper no. 2004:17. Uppsala, Sweden: Institute for Labor Market Policy Evaluation.

Axelsson, R., and O. Westerlund. 2004. Kunskapslyftets privatekonomiska effekter: Nybörjare höstterminen 1997. Umeå Economic Studies Working Paper no. 630. Umeå University, Department of Economics.

————. 2005. Kunskapslyftets effekter på årsarbetsinkomster. Umeå Economic Studies Working Paper no. 647. Umeå University, Department of Economics.

Bennmarker, H., K. Carling, and B. Holmlund. 2007. Do benefit hikes damage job finding? Evidence from Swedish unemployment insurance reforms. *Labour: Review of Labour Economics and Industrial Relations* 21 (1): 85–120.

Blundell, R., A. Duncan, J. McCrae, and C. Meghir. 2000. The labour market impact of the working families tax credit. *Fiscal Studies* 21 (1): 75–103.

Calmfors, L. 1993. Lessons from the macroeconomic experience of Sweden. *European Journal of Political Economy* 9 (1): 25–72.

Calmfors, L., A. Forslund, and M. Hemström. 2004. The effects of active labor-market policies in Sweden: What is the evidence? In *Labor market institutions and public regulation,* ed. J. Agell, M. Keen, and A. Weichenrieder, 1–63. Cambridge, MA: MIT Press.

Calmfors, L., and H. Lang. 1995. Macroeconomic effects of active labour market programmes in a union wage-setting model. *Economic Journal* 105 (430): 601–19.

Card, D., and P. B. Levine. 1994. Unemployment insurance taxes and the cyclical and seasonal properties of unemployment. *Journal of Public Economics* 53 (1): 1–29.

Carling, K., P.-A. Edin, A. Harkman, and B. Holmlund. 1996. Unemployment duration, unemployment benefits, and labor market programs in Sweden. *Journal of Public Economics* 59 (3): 313–34.

Carling, K., B. Holmlund, and A. Vejsiu. 2001. Do benefit cuts boost job-findings? Swedish evidence from the 1990s. *Economic Journal* 111 (474): 766–90.

Dahlberg, M., and A. Forslund. 2005. Direct displacement effects of labour market programmes. *Scandinavian Journal of Economics* 107 (3): 475–94.

Dormont, B., D. Fougère, and A. Prieto. 2001. L'effet de l'allocation unique dégressive sur la reprise déemploi. Théorie Economique, Modélisation et Applications (THEMA) Working Paper no. 2001-05. Paris: Université de Cergy-Pontoise.

Edin, P.-A., M. Heiborn, and C. Nilsson. 1998. Inter-regional migration in Sweden. In *Economic studies,* vol. 40, *Essays on demographic factors and housing markets,* ed. M. Heiborn. Uppsala University, Department of Economics.

Edin, P.-A., and B. Holmlund. 1991. Unemployment, vacancies and labour market programmes: Swedish evidence. In *Mismatch and labour mobility,* ed. F. P. Schi-oppa, 405–49. Cambridge: Cambridge University Press.

Ekström, E. 2003. Essays on inequality and education. PhD thesis, Uppsala University.

Forslund, A., D. Fröberg, and L. Lindqvist. 2004. The Swedish activity guarantee. OECD Social, Employment and Migration Working Paper no. 16. Paris: Organization for Economic Cooperation and Development, January.

Forslund, A., and K. Johansson. 2007. Random and stock-flow models of labour market matching: Swedish evidence. IFAU Working Paper no. 2007:11. Uppsala, Sweden: Institute for Labor Market Policy Evaluation.

Forslund, A., P. Johansson, and L. Lindqvist. 2004. Employment subsidies: A fast lane from unemployment to work? IFAU Working Paper no. 2004:18. Uppsala, Sweden: Institute for Labor Market Policy Evaluation.

Forslund, A., and A.-S. Kolm. 2004. Active labor market policies and real-wage determination: Swedish evidence. In *Research in labor economics,* vol. 23, *Accounting for worker well-being,* ed. S. Polachek, 381–441. Amsterdam: Elsevier.

Forslund, A., and A. Krueger. 1997. An evaluation of the active Swedish labor market policy: New and received wisdom. In *The welfare state in transition: Reforming the Swedish model,* ed. R. Freeman, R. Topel, and B. Swedenborg, 267–99. Chicago: University of Chicago Press.

Forslund, A., and O. Nordström Skans. 2006. Swedish youth labour market policies revisited. *Vierteljahrshefte zur Wirtshaftsforschung* 75 (3): 168–85.

Fredriksson, P. 1999. The dynamics of regional labor markets and active labor market policy: Swedish evidence. *Oxford Economic Papers* 51 (4): 623–48.

Fredriksson, P., and P. Johansson. 2003. Employment, mobility, and active labor market programs. IFAU Working Paper no. 2003:3. Uppsala, Sweden: Institute for Labor Market Policy Evaluation.

Hägglund, P. 2000. Effects of changes in the unemployment insurance eligibility requirements on job duration: Swedish evidence. IFAU Working Paper no. 2000:4. Uppsala, Sweden: Institute for Labor Market Policy Evaluation.

Hallgren, A. 1996. Job matching and labour market programmes in Sweden. Licentiate diss., Uppsala University.

Ham, J., and S. Rea. 1987. Unemployment insurance and male unemployment duration in Canada. *Journal of Labor Economics* 5 (3): 325–53.

Harkman, A. 1988. Arbetsmarknadspolitikens effekter på geografisk rörlighet: En tvärsnittsstudie av arbetslösa 20–29-åringar. AMS Rapport från utredningsenheten 1988:19. Stockholm: Swedish National Labor Market Board.

———. 2002. Vilka motiv styr deltagandet i arbetsmarknadspolitiska program? IFAU Rapport no. 2002:9. Uppsala, Sweden: Institute for Labor Market Policy Evaluation.

Holmlund, B., and P. Lundborg. 1988. Unemployment insurance and union wage setting. *Scandinavian Journal of Economics* 90 (2): 161–72.

Jackman, R., C. Pissarides, and S. Savouri. 1990. Labour market policies and unemployment in the OECD. *Economic Policy* 5 (2): 449–90.

Jenkins, S., and C. Garcia-Serrano. 2000. Re-employment probabilities for Spanish men: What role does the unemployment benefit system play? ILR Working Paper no. 55. University of Essex, Institute for Labor Research.

Johansson, K. 2001. Do labour market programs affect labour force participation? *Swedish Economic Policy Review* 8 (2): 215–34.

Johansson, K., and A. Markowski. 1995. Påverkar arbetsmarknadspolitik arbetskraftsdeltagandet? En empirisk studie. *Konjunkturläget maj 1995.* Specialstudier. Stockholm: Konjunkturinstitutet.

Katz, L. F. 1996. Wage subsidies for the disadvantaged. NBER Working Paper no. 5679. Cambridge, MA: National Bureau of Economic Research, July.

Katz, L. F., and B. Meyer. 1990. The impact of the potential duration of unemployment benefits on the duration of unemployment. *Journal of Public Economics* 41 (1): 45–72.

Layard, R., S. Nickell, and R. Jackman. 1991. *Unemployment: Macroeconomic performance and the labour market.* Oxford: Oxford University Press.

Lindgren, U., and O. Westerlund. 2003. Labour market programmes and geographical mobility: Migration and commuting among programme participants and openly unemployed. IFAU Working Paper no. 2003:6. Uppsala, Sweden: Institute for Labor Market Policy Evaluation.

Martin, J., and D. Grubb. 2001. What works and for whom? A review of OECD countries' experiences with active labour market policies. *Swedish Economic Policy Review* 8 (2): 9–56.

McCormick, B., and P. Skedinger. 1991. Why do regional unemployment differentials persist? In *Essays on wage formation, employment, and unemployment,* ed. P. Skedinger. Doctoral thesis, Uppsala University.

Meyer, B. 1990. Unemployment insurance and unemployment spells. *Econometrica* 58 (4): 757–82.

Moffitt, R. 1985. Unemployment insurance and the distribution of unemployment spells. *Journal of Econometrics* 28 (1): 85–101.

Nilsson, C. 1995. Den interregionala omflyttningen i Sverige: konsekvenser av arbetsmarknadsläge, arbetsmarknadspolitik och regionala levnadsomkostnader. EFA Rapport no. 33. Stockholm: EFA, Arbetsmarknadsdepartementet.

Organization for Economic Cooperation and Development (OECD). 2004. *Benefits and wages 2004: OECD indicators.* Paris: OECD.

Regnér, H. 1997. Training at the job and training for a new job: Two Swedish studies. PhD thesis, Stockholm University.

Sianesi, B. 2001. The Swedish active labour market programmes in the 1990s: Overall effectiveness and differential performance. *Swedish Economic Policy Review* 8 (2): 133–69.

Stenberg, A. 2003. An evaluation of the adult education initiative relative labour market training. Umeå Economic Studies Working Paper no. 609. Umeå University, Department of Economics.

———. 2005. Comprehensive education for the unemployed: Evaluating the effects on unemployment of the adult education initiative in Sweden. *Labour: Review of Labour Economics and Industrial Relations* 19 (1): 123–46.

Stenberg, A., and O. Westerlund. 2004. Does comprehensive education work for the long-term unemployed? Umeå Economic Studies Working Paper no. 641. Umeå University, Department of Economics.

Storrie, D., and B. Nättorp. 1997. Starthjälp: Geografisk rörlighet 1978–1995 och en utvärdering av starthjälpen. Stockholm: EFA, Arbetsmarknadsdepartementet.

Wadensjö, E. 1993. Arbetsmarknadspolitikens effekter på löner och priser. In SOU 1993:43, *Politik mot arbetslöshet.* Stockholm: Arbetsmarknadsdepartementet.

Westerlund, O. 1997. Employment opportunities, wages and interregional migration in Sweden 1970–89. *Journal of Regional Science* 37 (1): 55–73.

———. 1998. Internal gross migration in Sweden: The effects of mobility grants and regional labour market conditions. *Labour: Review of Labour Economics and Industrial Relations* 12 (2): 363–88.

Widerstedt, B. 1998. Moving or staying? Job mobility as a sorting process. Doctoral thesis, Umeå University.

6

How Sweden's Unemployment Became More Like Europe's

Lars Ljungqvist and Thomas J. Sargent

> The main difficulty with the Eurosclerosis hypothesis is one of
> timing. Although details can be debated, no strong case exists
> that Europe's welfare states were much more extensive or intru-
> sive in the 1970s than in the 1960s, and no case at all exists that
> there was more interference in markets in the 1980s than in the
> 1970s. Why did a social system that seemed to work extremely
> well in the 1960s work increasingly badly thereafter?
> —Krugman (1987, 68)

6.1 Introduction

Ljungqvist and Sargent (1997) applied an equilibrium version of a McCall
(1970) search model to explain the striking first graph in Lindbeck et al.
(1994). That graph shows that from the mid-1970s until the early 1990s, the
Swedish unemployment rate was lower than in other Organization of Economic Cooperation and Development (OECD) countries, and in the early
1990s, it jumped to the much higher level exhibited by an average of OECD
countries' unemployment levels since the early 1980s.[1] After noting that Sweden had no significant problem with long-term unemployment before 1990,
Lindbeck et al. (1994, 6) stated, "There is now an obvious risk that Sweden
will go the same way [as the rest of Europe]," and "It should be an overriding
task of economic policy to prevent creating a large group of permanently
unemployed citizens . . ." Ljungqvist and Sargent (1997) presented a model
that explained the set of policies that had allowed Sweden to attain its exceptionally low unemployment rates from 1975 to 1990 but that also posed a
nightmare scenario in which a macroeconomic shock would make one of
those policies become unsustainable; its absence then would make long-term
unemployment and a high unemployment rate persist in Sweden.

Lars Ljungqvist is a professor at the Stockholm School of Economics and a visiting professor
at New York University. Thomas J. Sargent is a professor of economics at New York University,
a senior fellow of the Hoover Institution at Stanford University, and a research associate of the
National Bureau of Economic Research.

Ljungqvist's research was supported by a grant from the Jan Wallander and Tom Hedelius
Foundation. Sargent's research was supported by a grant to the National Bureau of Economic
Research from the National Science Foundation. We thank Patrik Hesselius and Demian Pouzo
for research assistance.

1. But still, it remained below the average for OECD countries in Europe.

This chapter updates our earlier work in light of recent data about Swedish labor market outcomes. We read these data as saying yes, Swedish outcomes have become more like Europe's, as Lindbeck and his co-authors feared. To shed light on why, we describe extensions of our earlier theoretical work that are designed to understand some important factors that have contributed to the labor market outcomes in Europe since World War II. Important countries in Western Europe have experienced twenty-five years of high unemployment. Substantial fractions of their populations have been unemployed for long periods of time. But it was not like that in the 1960s, and it is very important for us to explain that, too, because ultimately, we shall attribute the persistently high level of European unemployment after 1980 to the higher safety nets and more generous unemployment benefits systems that prevail in Europe compared to the United States. The epigraph from Krugman (1987) concisely expresses the challenge confronting any such "high safety nets did it" explanation of high post-1980 European unemployment: European unemployment rates were lower than those in the United States during the 1950s and 1960s, despite the fact that Europe had more generous safety nets then, too. We explain higher-than-U.S. European unemployment in the 1980s and 1990s after lower-than-U.S. European unemployment in the 1950s and 1960s by bringing to light the *macroeconomic* implications of a force whose presence we infer from diverse sources of evidence about how the *microeconomic* risks facing individual workers have increased over time. For short, we label as turbulence the confluence of forces that have increased those risks over time. Our explanation of European unemployment stresses how safety nets influence how workers should cope with the emergence of a more challenging and turbulent economic environment after the early 1980s. Within a model that captures precise notions of *frictional* and *structural* unemployment,[2] we study how an increase in microeconomic turbulence on the one hand impinges on a welfare state economy with both high government-supplied unemployment insurance (UI) *and* strong government-mandated employment protection (EP) and on the other hand impinges on a laissez-faire economy with neither of those labor market institutions. We show that in times with low turbulence, the welfare state has lower unemployment, but in turbulent times, it has higher unemployment. We shall explain these outcomes in terms of how employment protection suppresses frictional but not structural unemployment.

This chapter is organized as follows. Section 6.2 briefly recalls recent patterns of Swedish unemployment and how we sought to explain them in

---

2. *Frictional* unemployment refers to the normal but time-consuming process of workers looking for jobs in an economy with search frictions. We let *structural* unemployment denote any additional unemployment that arises in a malfunctioning labor market. In our analysis, frictional and structural unemployment become synonymous with short- and long-term unemployment, respectively.

Ljungqvist and Sargent (1995a, 1995b, 1997). Section 6.3 describes facts about European and U.S. unemployment outcomes, labor market institutions, and earnings volatility that we use to frame the theoretical and computational work that we describe in sections 6.4 and 6.5. Section 6.6 interprets outcomes in Sweden in light of our model. Section 6.7 concludes by discussing proposals for reforming Swedish labor market institutions.

6.2   Our Mid-1990s Analysis of Sweden

6.2.1   Salient Facts about Sweden

We synthesized our quantitative explanation for the intertemporal pattern of Swedish unemployment portrayed in that first graph of Lindbeck et al. (1994) by building a model that could incorporate the following empirical patterns that we detected in the Swedish experience.

- The Swedish UI system had offered generous benefits to insured male blue-collar workers since the beginning of our time series, but the replacement ratio for all unemployed workers started to increase in the mid-1970s and had almost converged with the generous replacement ratio of insured male blue-collar workers by the mid-1980s.
- Swedish income taxes became substantially more progressive—marginal tax wedges went above 70 percent for both blue-collar and white-collar workers in the 1970s.
- The Swedish government was exceptional among European countries in intervening in workers' search processes by monitoring them to make sure that they accepted job offers that the government deemed to be acceptable.

To us, the search model of McCall (1970) seemed an ideal vehicle for bringing in these features.[3]

6.2.2   Our Mid-1990s McCall Search Model for Sweden

The classic single-worker search model of McCall (1970) envisioned an infinitely lived, risk-neutral unemployed worker who discounts the future at a constant factor $\beta \in (0, 1)$. At the beginning of each period that he or she is unemployed, the worker draws one offer to work forever at a wage w from a cumulative distribution function (c.d.f.) F. If the worker accepts the offer, he or she receives present value $w/(1 - \beta)$. If the worker rejects the offer, he or she receives unemployment compensation c this period and must wait one period until getting a new draw. The value of taking this option is $c + \beta Q$,

---

3. While we accepted what we understood to be a consensus view that other active labor market programs had minimal effects on labor market outcomes, we decided to highlight the government's monitoring program in our theoretical work.

where Q is the expected value for the problem of an unemployed worker at the beginning of a period *before* he or she has drawn a wage offer. Successive draws from F are statistically independent.

The McCall worker optimally rejects offers less and accepts offers greater than a reservation wage $\overline{w}$. Key implications of McCall's model are that $\overline{w}$ increases with increases in unemployment compensation c and also with mean-preserving increases in the spread of the offer distribution F.

Ljungqvist and Sargent (1995a, 1995b, 1997) adapted and extended McCall's model to create an equilibrium model of the Swedish unemployment experience. We added the following ingredients to the basic McCall model: (a) each period, a worker makes a search intensity decision that affects the probability that he or she succeeds in drawing an offer from F; (b) instead of drawing a single wage forever, a job offer entitles a worker to work at a wage that occasionally will be reset by drawing from some distribution G; (c) there is a fixed rate of exogenous job destruction, so all jobs eventually end; (d) a progressive tax system transforms the pretax distributions of wages F and G into posttax distributions that are more compressed;[4] (e) the government terminates UI benefits to all workers who reject offers above a government-set minimum acceptable wage w_g; and (f) a government budget condition and appropriate stationary conditions for the aggregate state of the economy that determine equilibrium rates of employment and unemployment complete the model.

Items (a) and (e) created avenues by which unemployment compensation c and the government-mandated acceptable wage w_g influenced search intensities and reservation wages. Item (b) created an avenue for endogenous job destruction. The acceptable wage w_g in (e) allowed us to turn on and off a program that earlier researchers had observed to be an unusual aspect of Swedish labor market policies.

This is a model in which countervailing forces combine to determine an equilibrium unemployment rate. Ceteribus paribus, more generous unemployment compensation raises the worker's reservation wage, the duration of a typical unemployment spell, and the equilibrium unemployment rate. By decreasing the option value of searching, an increase in the progressivity of taxes causes the reservation wage, the duration of unemployment, and the equilibrium unemployment rate all to fall. By decreasing the reservation wage, a decrease in the government-mandated acceptable wage w_g causes the unemployment rate and the duration of unemployment to fall.

This theory gives the government enough empirically plausible handles for us to explain the previously mentioned chart in Lindbeck et al. (1994). Our story is that the tendency for unemployment to increase caused by

---

4. Pissarides (1983) studied how income taxes influence reservation wages by compressing the pertinent after-tax wage distribution confronting a worker searching for a job. In our analysis, we applied that same logic to employed workers who face stochastic upgrades or downgrades on the job and who must decide whether to quit and search for a new job.

Sweden's increasingly generous system of government-supplied UI before 1990 was offset by the increased progressivity of income taxes and the government's stringent monitoring of workers' acceptance policies (represented by our w_g). The nightmare mentioned earlier is that when we computed an equilibrium with a much higher w_g as a computational experiment to represent a loosening of the government's monitoring program, unemployment exploded, making the Sweden in our computer no different from the average OECD country with its high unemployment rate.

This completes our summary of the situation in Sweden up to the mid-1990s as we interpreted it in Ljungqvist and Sargent (1995a, 1995b, 1997). We now turn to describing unemployment outcomes in Western Europe and how we think we can explain them.

6.3   Salient Facts about Europe's Unemployment Experience and Turbulence

We divide our brief exposition of the facts into two parts. First, in section 6.3.1, we summarize how unemployment outcomes and labor market institutions varied over time and between Europe and the United States. Then, in section 6.3.2, we describe a body of microeconomic evidence that provides the smoking gun that explains the puzzle posed in the epigraph by Krugman. We interpret that evidence in light of a model in section 6.5.

6.3.1   Salient Facts about Unemployment

Research surveyed by Ljungqvist and Sargent (2008) can be summarized in terms of the following broad findings. First, we state some facts about unemployment and government labor market interventions:

- Because there were higher rates of inflow into unemployment in the United States, in the 1950s and 1960s, unemployment rates were systematically lower in Europe than in the United States.
- After the 1970s, unemployment became persistently higher in Europe.
- Within both Europe and the United States, inflow rates into unemployment remained roughly constant between the 1950s and 1960s, on the one hand, and the 1980s and 1990s, on the other hand.
- In Europe, in the 1950s and 1960s, average durations of unemployment spells were low. Throughout Europe, they became high after the 1970s.
- In the United States, after the 1970s, the average duration of unemployment spells stayed at their low levels of the 1950s and 1960s.
- In Europe, after the 1970s, hazard rates of leaving unemployment fell with increases in the duration of unemployment. The long-term unemployed in Europe constitute a very diverse group, but as noted by Machin and Manning (1999, 3093), "In all countries there is a higher

incidence of [long-term unemployment] among older workers and a lower rate among young workers."

- Government-supplied unemployment compensation has been generous in amount and long in duration in Europe throughout both periods, but it has been stingy in amount and short in duration in the United States.
- Government-mandated employment protection was stronger in Europe throughout both periods.

6.3.2   Salient Facts about Turbulence

In this section, we refer to some findings of microeconomists that indicate to us that there has been an increase in what we call turbulence since the late 1970s.

While the volatility of many macroeconomic variables has declined since the 1980s (see, for example, McConnell and Perez-Quiros [2000] and Stock and Watson [2002]), there is extensive evidence of increased volatility of individual workers' earnings in the United States.[5] In an influential early study, Gottschalk and Moffitt (1994) found that the permanent and transitory variances of log annual earnings both rose by approximately 40 percent between the periods of 1970 to 1978 and 1979 to 1987. Their findings have proven to be robust across a variety of studies and data sets, as reviewed by Katz and Autor (1999).[6]

Another strand of literature relevant for our notion of turbulence consists of studies of displaced workers. Early contributors such as Topel (1990), Ruhm (1991), and Jacobson, LaLonde, and Sullivan (1993) estimate that displaced U.S. workers suffer persistent earnings losses that range from 15 to 30 percent, even five years after displacement.[7] Besides administrative data,

5. Other studies have documented increased firm-level volatility (see, e.g., Campbell et al. [2001] and Comin and Philippon [2005]). Davis et al. (2006) offer a qualification by showing that the increased volatility pertains to publicly traded firms, while the volatility among privately held firms, in contrast, has fallen significantly since the 1980s and has almost converged to that among publicly traded firms.

6. In a recent study by the Congressional Budget Office (2007), Social Security records are shown to be consistent with earlier findings that are based on publicly available survey data. The administrative records confirm that workers have experienced substantial earnings variability, which has remained roughly constant between 1980 and 2003. Likewise, there is evidence that the earnings volatility increased for men between 1960 and 1980 (when computed for the bottom two quintiles of the earnings distribution, because recorded earnings in 1960 were truncated at the Social Security maximum taxable income, which was relatively low). However, the increase in earnings variability among men was offset by a decrease among women. Note that if the latter observation reflects a secular increase in the persistence of women's labor force participation, it needs not contradict our hypothesis of increased turbulence between the 1960s and 1980s.

7. There are fewer studies available in Europe. But a common finding seems to be that both earnings losses *and* reemployment probabilities of displaced workers are smaller in Europe than in the United States. For Germany, Burda and Mertens (2001, 38) remark, "As only around 80% of all displaced workers [in Germany in 1986] are observed in socially insured employment

the most comprehensive source of information about the incidence and costs of job loss in the United States is the Displaced Workers Survey (DWS), a biennial supplement to the Current Population Survey since 1984. (See Farber [1997, 2005] for summaries of DWS studies.) We acknowledge that the substantial earnings losses experienced by displaced U.S. workers since the 1980s by themselves say nothing about *increased* turbulence between the 1950s and 1960s and the post-1980s, as that would require evidence from similar displaced worker studies from the 1950s and 1960s, which unfortunately do not exist. Perhaps the lack of interest among both academic researchers and the popular press suggests that worker displacements were less disruptive in those days, but this cannot be known without the historical data.

The central question is whether disruptive labor market experiences have become more common since the 1980s. Evidence that they have is provided by Kambourov and Manovskii (2008), who document a substantial overall increase in occupational and industry mobility in the United States over the period from 1968 to 1997.[8] Citing an earlier study by Rosenfeld (1979), who showed that occupational mobility was constant in the 1960s, Kambourov and Manovskii argue that a more turbulent economic environment is a phenomenon of the last thirty years.

Our view that turbulence has increased since the late 1970s is not universally accepted; for example, Layard, Nickell, and Jackman (1991) offer one skeptical voice.[9] But others such as Heckman (2003) find the evidence of increased turbulence persuasive, as summarized in his wide-ranging talk at the 2003 Munich Economic Summit:

> A growing body of evidence points to the fact that the world economy is more variable and less predictable today than it was 30 years ago. . . . [There is] more variability and unpredictability in economic life . . . (30–31)

---

even 4 years afterwards, it seems that lower displacement wage losses in Germany come at the cost of lower reemployment probabilities."

8. For another study that uses a different technique but reaches the same conclusion that occupational and industry mobility has increased in the United States, see Parrado, Caner, and Wolff (2007).

9. Layard, Nickell, and Jackman (1991, 46) used measures of sectoral reallocation when they asked and answered the question, "Has turbulence increased since the 1960s in a way that could help to explain increased unemployment? The answer is a clear no." They computed the proportions of jobs in each industry in adjacent years and then took the changes in each proportion. After summing the positive changes to get a measure of the proportion of employment switching industries, they found that turbulence had not increased enough to explain the emergence of high European unemployment. However, we think that their definition of turbulence is not the appropriate one from the perspective of individual workers. The restructuring of the U.S. steel industry in the 1980s can serve as an example. While the decline and subsequent recovery of that industry might have left a small imprint on measures of sectoral reallocation, the consequences for workers initially employed in that industry were dramatic. As studied by Shaw (2002), the restructuring led to new hiring standards that meant workers laid off at older, declining steel mills were not considered for employment at the newer steel mills.

In our theoretical model, we define an increase in *turbulence* as an increase in the probability that an involuntarily displaced worker loses human capital. We have used the microeconomic evidence of increased earnings variability and earnings losses of displaced workers described in Gottschalk and Moffitt (1994) and Jacobson, LaLonde, and Sullivan (1993), respectively, as checks on the realism of the model that we constructed to explain the macroeconomic outcomes about inflows and outflows, durations, and levels of unemployment described in section 6.3.1. We report some results of these checks in section 6.5.4.

6.4 Extensions of the Basic Search Model for Analyzing Europe

To construct a theory of European unemployment, we again started from the basic McCall model, then added the following features:

1. *Age.* A worker moves stochastically through four age groups, with transition probabilities calibrated to represent the following age groups: twenty to forty-five, forty-five to fifty, fifty to fifty-five, and fifty-five to sixty. We use only four age groups to control the dimension of the state for an unemployed worker. We want to include age as a state variable, and we use a finer grid for older workers, because adverse welfare state dynamics that we describe later threaten to affect older workers especially.

2. *Job termination and stochastic wages on the job.* We retain the features from Ljungqvist and Sargent (1995a, 1995b) that a previously employed worker faces a probability λ that the job ends exogenously, and his wage rate on the job evolves stochastically, with occasional new draws from the distribution F resulting in job upgrades or downgrades.

3. *Human capital or skills.* We make earnings depend on a worker's human capital or skills, and we let human capital appreciate when the worker is employed and depreciate gradually during spells of unemployment. Their levels of human capital differentiate workers. Unemployed workers set reservation wages and search intensities that depend on their skill levels, because the option values of search and the rewards to more intensive search depend on skill.

We specify H potential skill levels, ordered from lowest to highest. We also specify two sets of transition probabilities that describe the motion over time of skills. One set of transition probabilities applies when a worker is *employed* and probabilistically impels skills upward. Another set of transition probabilities applies when a worker is *unemployed* and probabilistically causes skills to deteriorate.

We set a worker's total earnings equal to the product of a base wage, drawn from the exogenous distribution F and the worker's skills. During a spell of employment, a worker who starts from a low level of skills can expect his earnings gradually to grow because his or her skills grow, subject to the caveat that the base wage also might change on the job. The worker takes into account the likely growth of earnings in formulating his reservation wage and search intensity. The worker also takes into account the way unemployment compensation depends on past earnings.

4. *Earnings-dependent unemployment compensation.* The basic McCall model has a fixed level of unemployment compensation that is independent of the worker's earnings during his previous employment spell. To be more realistic, we modify this feature by linking unemployment compensation to earnings attained on the previous job. This substantially affects the option value of search and makes it depend on the worker's current skill level, the law of motion of those skills, and the worker's previous earnings. How unemployment compensation alters this option value and its dependence on past earnings is an essential part of our analysis.

5. *Employment protection.* To represent a government-mandated employment protection concisely, we impose a tax on all job destruction, except when a worker retires by exiting the highest age group and leaving the labor force.

6. *Representing economic turbulence.* Our model contains two types of parameters that can be used in principle to represent labor market turbulence: the firing or job dissolution parameter λ, and parameters governing the rate at which human capital depreciates while unemployed. We choose to use one particular parameter from the latter set to measure turbulence; namely, a parameter that sets the one-time depreciation in skill level that an employed worker experiences upon an exogenous job termination. In tranquil times, we let such a worker experience no *immediate* depreciation in human capital, but in turbulent times, we expose that worker to a risk that there is a one-time reduction in human capital. This is our way of capturing the disparity in skills used in different jobs. In tranquil times, skills are more transferable across jobs than in turbulent times—turbulent times are ones with more rapidly changing job descriptions.

6.4.1 Consequences of the Additional Features

The modifications of the basic model alter the incentives that an unemployed worker faces. An unemployed worker's choices of search intensity and reservation wage depend on his skill level, his current entitlement to UI benefits—which in turn depend on his skill level at the time his previous job was terminated—and his age. Because his job may terminate, the unemployed worker takes into account not only his current unemployment compensation, which is linked to his *past* earnings, but also the fact that his *future* unemployment compensation will be linked to his *future* earnings, which in turn depends on his base wage and his human capital level. The present value of these future compensations depends on the worker's age. Because his human capital level deteriorates with the passage of time spent unemployed, the worker will balance the benefits of waiting for a higher base wage against the prospects of further deterioration of human capital while unemployed.

High unemployment compensation sets the following trap. Consider a worker who had relatively high earnings before he was dismissed and who therefore qualifies for a high level of unemployment compensation. This person's reservation base wage and search intensity both depend on his human capital level. Early in a spell of unemployment, the worker searches intensively and sets a reasonable reservation base wage, because his earnings are the product of that wage and the human capital level, and even for typical wages, the associated earnings compare favorably to unemployment compensation. However, if the worker remains unemployed for a while and finds himself with a lower level of human capital, the incentives confronting him change adversely. His unemployment compensation remains high (because it is tied to his previous earnings), but for any given prospective draw from the base wage distribution, his earnings are lower because of his diminished human capital. Because the benefits of searching have declined relative to the compensation for remaining unemployed, the worker will tend to search less intensively *and* to set a higher reservation base wage. Both of these types of behavior will diminish the worker's probability of leaving unemployment and will increase the mean duration of unemployment. The likelihood that a worker falls into this trap depends on his age, the risk being greater that an older worker will become discouraged from making the kinds of search intensity and wage acceptance choices that would be likely to return him to work soon.

Human capital acquisition can also provide a source of quits or voluntary separations. It can occur that a worker with low human capital accepts a lower base wage than one who has higher human capital. Having accepted a low base wage job but then experiencing growth in human capital, the worker can find it optimal to quit his job and to search for a higher base wage to capitalize on his higher human capital.

The dynamics coming from human capital are too difficult to work out analytically, but they can be worked out with the computer, which is what we have done in Ljungqvist and Sargent (2008).

6.4.2   An Equilibrium as a System of Lakes and Streams

The search model is about the experiences of an individual worker as time and opportunities pass. We can use it as a building block to model the behavior of a large number of ex ante identical but ex post diverse workers composing a complete labor market. The key step in building a model of the labor market is to reinterpret the search model's *individual* descriptive statistics—average duration of unemployment, average accepted wage, average times between incidents of quitting or being laid off—as applying to the average at any point in time of a large number of statistically identical individuals.

Imagine the labor market as a set of lakes connected by inlet and outlet streams (see figure 6.1). The volume of water in each lake represents the number of people in a particular labor market state (e.g., employed, unemployed and having quit a previous job, unemployed and having been laid off from a previous job, unemployed because of having just entered the labor force), and the flows between lakes represent rates of hiring, laying off, and quitting. The system is in a stationary equilibrium when all lake levels are constant over time, which means that inflows just balance outflows for each lake. The rates of inflow and outflow are evidently the critical determinants of the lake levels. The individual search model lends itself to becoming a model of these inflow and outflow rates. For example, simply reinterpret the

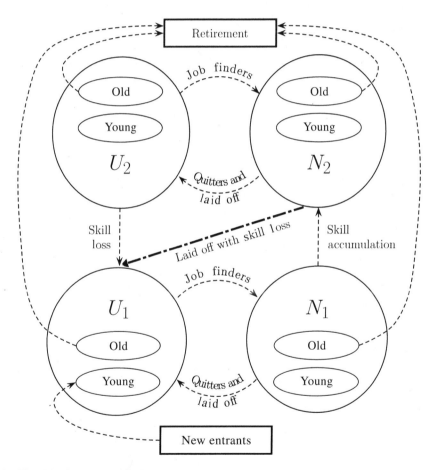

Fig. 6.1   Search model of the labor market

Note: The variables U_i and N_i refer to pools of unemployed and employed, respectively, where the subscript denotes the skill level of workers in a particular pool, with skills increasing in the index i.

probability of job acceptance as determining the *rate* of flow from a state of unemployment to a state of employment.

Within such a model, government-supplied unemployment compensation gives rise to expenditures that must be financed. In particular, the size of the unemployment lake (or lakes) determines the total volume of government unemployment compensation payments. We suppose that these are financed from income taxes. In a stationary *equilibrium,* government expenditure rates and tax rates must be set so that the government budget balances.

6.4.3   Some Parameters

We report some of the results for the calibrated versions of our model reported in Ljungqvist and Sargent (2008) for two types of economies: one that we call laissez-faire (LF) and another that we call the welfare state (WS). The laissez-faire economy has no UI and no EP. The welfare state economy has UI that is set to approximate a replacement ratio of 0.6 times earnings on the last job and layoff tax that is set at what amounts to fourteen weeks of the average productivity of all employed workers. We intend LF to represent a stylized version of the United States and WS to stand in for Europe.[10] Other parameters are calibrated in ways that Ljungqvist and Sargent (2008) describe.

Unemployed workers draw base wages from the same truncated normal distribution with range [0, 1]. A worker's skill level can assume one of eleven possible levels inside the range [1, 2], among which he moves according to calibrated transition matrices. To represent economic turbulence, we expose a newly involuntarily displaced worker to an instantaneous reduction in his human capital, modeled as a draw of a new skill level from a truncated left half of a normal distribution with specified variance, where the right end point of the distribution is the displaced worker's skill level in the latest period of employment just before being laid off. We use this specification to study six different degrees of economic turbulence (with the variance of the underlying normal distribution in parenthesis): T00 (variance 0), T03 (variance 0.03), T05 (variance 0.05), T10 (variance 0.1), T20 (variance 0.2), and T99 (uniform distribution). Only during tranquil times (T00) does the

---

10. While unemployment insurance is typically of limited duration, Layard, Nickell, and Jackman (1991) emphasize the fact that in Europe, further benefits are often available for an indefinite period once unemployment compensation has been exhausted. For example, Hunt (1995) describes the German policy in 1983 when unemployment compensation ("Arbeitslosengeld") replaced 68 percent of an unemployed worker's previous earnings and could be collected up to a maximum of twelve months. And if those benefits were exhausted, means-tested unemployment assistance ("Arbeitslosenhilfe") paid a replacement rate of 58 percent for an indefinite period. Although a cap was imposed on the amount that one could receive, it affected less than 1 percent of the unemployed. For additional evidence on generous replacement rates and long benefit durations in Europe, see Martin (1996). Regarding our assumption of costly layoffs in Europe, quantitative measurements are fraught with difficulties, but the account of Myers (1964) in note number 14 suggests a long-standing difference between Europe and the United States.

worker retain his skill level from the latest period of employment when laid off. In tables 6.2 and 6.3 (which we discuss later), we use these T labels to denote different levels of turbulence.

6.5   Computational Results

We have computed equilibria of our model under the WS and LF settings of government policy for different settings of the turbulence parameter. But before examining the effects of increased turbulence, we first scrutinize equilibrium outcomes in tranquil economic times when there is no turbulence.

6.5.1   Tranquil Economic Times

Table 6.1 displays the equilibria of the WS economy and the LF economy when there is no economic turbulence. The WS economy has significantly lower unemployment than the LF economy because of a lower inflow rate into unemployment, while the average duration of unemployment is similar across the two economies. As a result, lower unemployment in the WS economy is accompanied by much longer average job tenures than in the LF economy. Ljungqvist and Sargent (2008) explain these outcomes with the aid of a detailed analysis of decision rules for job destruction and a worker's choice of his or her reservation wage and search intensity. We provide a brief summary as follows.

In tranquil times (denoted by an index of turbulence equal to T00), table 6.2 shows that the layoff cost in the WS economy is responsible for the lower unemployment rate. If the LF economy were to impose the same layoff cost, it would have an even lower unemployment rate than the WS economy. The reason for layoff costs being an effective tool for holding down unemployment is simply that such costs make it expensive to lay off workers, and as a result, there is much less worker turnover in the economy. The lessened turnover translates into a lower rate of frictional unemployment. Thus,

Table 6.1   **Equilibrium values for the welfare state (WS) economy and the laissez-faire (LF) economy (under no economic turbulence)**

	WS	LF
Unemployment rate	3.83%	5.70%
Inflow into unemployment per month[a]	2.06%	3.39%
Average unemployment duration[b]	7.73 weeks	7.13 weeks
Percentage of unemployed with spells so far ≥ 6 months	2.87%	1.73%
Percentage of unemployed with spells so far ≥ 12 months	0.08%	0.02%

[a]The monthly inflow into unemployment is expressed as a percentage of employment.
[b]The average unemployment duration is computed by dividing the unemployment rate by the inflow rate, when both rates are expressed as percentages of the labor force.

Table 6.2 | Unemployment effects of layoff costs with different degrees of economic turbulence

	WS economy			LF economy		
Layoff cost[a]	0	5	10	0	5	10
Turbulence						
T00	5.85	4.77	3.83	5.70	4.43	3.51
T03	5.65	4.74	4.18	5.24	4.14	3.23
T05	5.76	5.03	5.06	5.18	4.06	3.16
T10	6.01	5.92	6.75	5.11	4.03	3.19
T20	6.31	7.00	8.76	5.07	4.00	3.19
T99	6.60	8.08	10.95	5.02	3.98	3.24

Note: Tranquil times have an index of turbulence equal to T00.
[a]A layoff tax of 5 (10) corresponds to roughly seven (fourteen) weeks of the average productivity of all employed workers.

the analysis dispels a common argument that layoff costs should increase unemployment because firms that anticipate the future payment of layoff costs find it too costly to hire workers, which should cause employment to fall. The problem with this argument is that it is *partial* equilibrium rather than *general* equilibrium in nature. The argument apparently treats the payment to a worker as a constant, while it is endogenous and changes in our general equilibrium analysis. In particular, payments to workers must adjust downward to restore firms' profitability in response to the introduction of layoff costs. The lower payments to workers do not only reflect the future payments of layoff costs but also the fact that layoff costs interfere with efficient separations in the labor market; that is, layoff costs give rise to a less efficient allocation of labor in the economy. Hence, we can say that the workers in an economy with layoff costs enjoy longer job tenures at the cost of a less efficient allocation or that the workers pay for more job security with lower earnings.[11]

The government's policy of paying unemployment benefits in the WS economy does increase unemployment relative to the LF economy. In table 6.2, it can be seen that unemployment in the WS economy is higher for any level of turbulence and any level of layoff costs relative to the corresponding entry for the LF economy. But it is important to understand why the upward pressure that the benefit system exerts on unemployment in the WS economy

11. The outcome that layoff costs reduce equilibrium unemployment is not unique to our analysis. Despite countervailing forces in search and matching models, Ljungqvist (2002) shows that there is a quantitative presumption that layoff costs reduce unemployment in these models of frictional unemployment. Exceptions in the literature, notably of Millard and Mortensen (1997), arrive at the opposite conclusion by making the nonstandard assumption that firms incur layoff costs not only when laying off workers but also after encounters with job seekers whom they do not hire.

is not strong enough to overwhelm the downward pressure from layoff costs in tranquil times; that is, the WS unemployment rate is lower than the LF unemployment rate in table 6.1. The reason is that in tranquil times, workers do not incur any immediate skill losses at the time of layoffs, and hence, they can search for new job opportunities with pay comparable to their last earnings. So, while unemployment benefits do make unemployed workers search a little less diligently than they otherwise would, they are still relatively eager to recoup their full earnings potential in the market place rather than to collect benefits that amount to 60 percent of their last earnings.

It is instructive to take a closer look at an unemployed worker's decision rule for the choice of a reservation base wage (per unit of skill), as defined in section 6.4. The arguments entering the decision rule are the state variables that describe circumstances relevant for making an optimal decision: the worker's age, last earnings, and current skills. The age determines the worker's time left in the labor force, last earnings determine the benefits to which he or she is entitled, and current skills determine his or her earnings potential. Recall that the earnings in a new job is the product of the worker's skills and the base wage that he or she draws from the wage offer distribution. As an illustration, figure 6.2 depicts the reservation base wage of workers in the group aged fifty-five to sixty as a function of their last earnings and current skills. For example, consider a recently laid-off worker who has high last earnings, which would indicate that this worker is likely to have attained a high skill level in his last job. Such a worker also should have high current skills, because layoffs in tranquil times are not associated with any instantaneous loss of skills. Our argument implies that recently laid-off workers are likely to be found on a diagonal in figure 6.2, with a positive relationship between last earnings and current skills. It is interesting to note that the reservation base wage lies on an almost flat plateau for these unemployed workers—a plateau that extends below the diagonal, where lower last earnings mean less generous benefits. It follows that all these workers with similar reservation wages will find jobs at similar rates, and the implied average duration of unemployment spells turns out be close to that of the LF economy (as also reported for the aggregates of all unemployed in table 6.1). In this sense, we can say that the workers in the WS economy have reasonable wage demands.

We find an important hint about what will happen in the WS economy in turbulent times in figure 6.2. Workers who experience instantaneous skill losses upon layoffs will be positioned above the described diagonal, where their benefits are high because of high last earnings, while their current earnings potentials are low because of low current skills. Figure 6.2 suggests that these skill losers will choose much higher reservation wages; that is, before giving up their generous benefits, they want to find jobs that pay very well per unit of remaining skills. Furthermore, it turns out that because these high reservation wages are hard to find and the generous benefits make

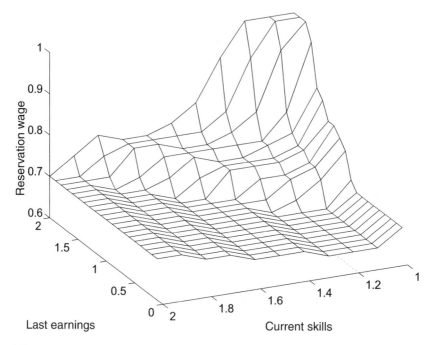

Fig. 6.2   Reservation base wage of the unemployed in age group fifty-five to sixty who are eligible for unemployment compensation in the WS economy (under tranquil economic times)

it less costly to remain unemployed, an unemployed worker in these circumstances invests less in search by choosing a relatively low search intensity. Ljungqvist and Sargent (2008) show that these adverse incentive effects of generous benefits are most pronounced for the highest age group, fifty-five to sixty.

Fortunately, in tranquil economic times, it turns out that there are hardly any unemployed workers with low skills who are entitled to high benefits based on high last earnings, so the WS economy sustains a low equilibrium unemployment rate in table 6.1.

6.5.2   Turbulent Economic Times

When we increase the turbulence parameter in table 6.3, the WS economy posts an ever higher unemployment rate, while unemployment is practically flat (with some drift downward) in the LF economy. The emergence of high, long-term unemployment in the WS economy is due both to generous unemployment benefits and to high layoff costs.

The decision rules of unemployed workers in turbulent economic times are qualitatively the same as in times of tranquility. But the adverse incentive effects of unemployment compensation in the WS economy are exacer-

Table 6.3   **Equilibrium values for the WS economy and the LF economy with different degrees of economic turbulence**

	Index of economic turbulence[a]					
	T00	T03	T05	T10	T20	T99
Unemployment rate (%)						
WS	3.83	4.18	5.06	6.75	8.76	10.95
LF	5.70	5.24	5.18	5.11	5.07	5.02
Inflow into unemployment[b] (% per month)						
WS	2.06	2.05	2.03	2.00	1.99	1.97
LF	3.39	3.33	3.30	3.27	3.25	3.23
Average duration of unemployment[c] (in weeks)						
WS	7.73	8.53	10.52	14.47	19.34	25.00
LF	7.13	6.64	6.63	6.59	6.57	6.56
Percentage of unemployed with spells so far ≥ 12 months						
WS	0.08	9.67	23.53	41.10	54.14	62.64
LF	0.02	0.01	0.01	0.01	0.01	0.01

[a]A higher index of economic turbulence is associated with a higher variance of skill losses at layoffs.
[b]The monthly inflow into unemployment is expressed as a percentage of employment.
[c]The average unemployment duration is computed by dividing the unemployment rate by the inflow rate, when both rates are expressed as percentages of the labor force.

bated in turbulent times, because there are now laid-off workers who suffer significant amounts of instantaneous skill loss, and they will choose high reservation wages (as suggested by the decision rule depicted in figure 6.2). Because these workers' depreciated skill levels are low relative to their recent earnings history, their unemployment benefits, based as they are on their high previous earnings, are very attractive when compared to their current labor market prospects. Therefore, these workers demand a high wage per unit of remaining skill before they are willing to give up those generous benefits. Moreover, such high wages are hard to come by, so workers under these circumstances tend to become discouraged and to choose low search intensities. Older laid-off workers have a shorter horizon until retirement and therefore less time for any accumulation of new skills, so they are choosier than younger workers before accepting a job and giving up their benefits. These adverse incentive dynamics are absent from the LF economy, because past earnings are not a state variable for unemployed workers. Therefore, any laid-off worker in the LF economy who experiences an instantaneous skill loss will immediately adjust to the new situation and will search diligently for a suitable job, given the change in circumstances.

We now briefly examine the effects of layoff costs in the WS economy. Ljungqvist (2002) showed that in a search model like ours, higher layoff costs lower the unemployment rate by reducing frictional unemployment.

However, table 6.2 shows that in turbulent times, the effect is reversed in the WS economy, because in turbulent times, unemployment has both frictional and *structural* components. The structural component contains the long-term unemployed who have chosen to become less active in the labor market. In turbulent times, when agents think about withdrawing from the labor market, both the higher turbulence and the higher layoff cost make labor market participation less attractive by reducing the equilibrium wage. But in the absence of generous benefits, not participating in the labor market is not a viable option. In fact, the negative relationship between layoff costs and unemployment is a robust feature in the LF economy, even in the face of variations in the degree of economic turbulence, as shown in table 6.2 (even though it *isn't* such a robust feature of the WS economy).

6.5.3   Summary of Macroeconomic Findings

Interactions among employment protection (EP), unemployment insurance (UI), and turbulence constitute the smoking gun that solves the puzzle summarized in the epigraph from Krugman. With our calibration, in tranquil times, most unemployment is *frictional,* in the sense that it consists of workers who are actively searching and who expect to find new jobs quickly. In tranquil times, there is little *structural* unemployment consisting of discouraged workers who have already been unemployed for a long time and who do not expect to find jobs soon. The imposition of strong EP serves to suppress frictional unemployment by reducing the inflow of workers into unemployment, thereby lengthening the durations of existing jobs by reducing churning.

Strong EP also reduces frictional unemployment in turbulent times, but now frictional unemployment is not the main problem. In turbulent times, the adverse welfare state dynamics coming from generous UI indexed to past earnings trap a significant minority of workers who have experienced skill losses into structural unemployment. The frictional unemployment fighting tool of EP does nothing to encourage the discouraged workers who have been unemployed for a long time.

This is our explanation for how generous UI benefits led to benign outcomes under a low-turbulence environment but contributed to forming pools of discouraged workers, especially among older workers, when times became turbulent.

6.5.4   Implications about Earnings Heterogeneity

So far, we have described the implications that our way of introducing increased turbulence has for equilibrium aggregate outcomes within the WS and LF regimes. But the computations used to obtain those results contain a rich set of implications about the ex post heterogenous workers who inhabit the various versions of the model. We can form artificial panels of these workers and apply to them the same procedures that microeconomists used to ferret out the implications summarized in some of the studies mentioned in section 6.3.2. This is an independent check on our calibration of the turbulence parameter and other parameters of the model, because those microeconomic observations were not among the targets that we used to calibrate the model. It is encouraging to us that by using our model in this way, we have been able to replicate important aspects of earnings dynamics described by Gottschalk and Moffitt (1994) and Jacobson, LaLonde, and Sullivan (1993). We describe that exercise in detail in Ljungqvist and Sargent (2008) and summarize it briefly here.

Using the LF economy with economic turbulence indexed by T10 and T20, we generate artificial versions of Gottschalk and Moffitt's Panel Study of Income Dynamics (PSID) panels for 1970 to 1978 and 1979 to 1987, respectively. As our counterparts to their figures 2 and 4 (reproduced here in our figure 6.3 [panels A and B]), we arrive at figure 6.4 (panels A and B) after applying their method for decomposing each panel's earnings into permanent and transitory components. Evidently, an increase in our turbulence parameter spreads the distributions of both components of the Gottschalk-Moffitt decomposition in the direction observed. However, there are differences in the ranges of the distributions. The fact that our distribution of permanent earnings in figure 6.4 (panel A) spans a smaller range than the Gottschalk-Moffitt data is not surprising. Our artificial panel contains a group of homogeneous individuals who are ex ante identical, while the PSID used by Gottschalk and Moffitt comprises a diverse group of American males with different educational backgrounds. It is also noteworthy that the increased earnings variability in the more turbulent period in our figure 6.4 (panel B) occurs at lower standard deviations than Gottschalk and Moffitt's. In this respect, the increase in economic turbulence in our parameterization for the 1980s falls short of the changes documented for the United States.

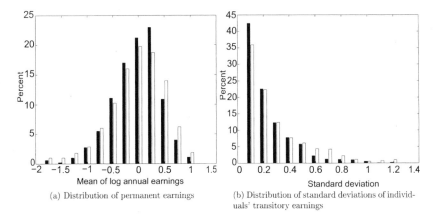

(a) Distribution of permanent earnings

(b) Distribution of standard deviations of individuals' transitory earnings

Fig. 6.3   Reproduction of Gottschalk and Moffitt's (1994) figure 2 (panel a) and figure 4 (panel b)

Note: The black bars correspond to 1970 to 1978, the white bars to 1979 to 1987.

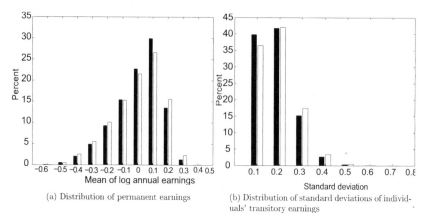

(a) Distribution of permanent earnings

(b) Distribution of standard deviations of individuals' transitory earnings

Fig. 6.4   Simulated laissez-faire economy

Note: The black bars and the white bars correspond to degrees of economic turbulence indexed by T10 and T20, respectively.

As reported here in our figure 6.5, our figure 6.6 reproduces figure 1 of Jacobson, LaLonde, and Sullivan (1993). It shows earnings losses experienced by displaced workers in Pennsylvania in the first quarter of 1982. Using artificial data from the LF economy with economic turbulence indexed by T20, we produce a counterpart of their graph in figure 6.6. The surprisingly good fit here is obtained for our subsample of separators who have experienced skill losses of at least 30 percent. These separators constitute roughly one-third of all separators in our artificial data set.

6.6   Recent Swedish Outcomes

An essential question as posed by Lindbeck et al. (1994) was whether Sweden had succeeded in permanently setting itself apart from Europe starting in the 1980s, when the Swedish unemployment rate remained low, while Europe experienced sustained higher unemployment. Was the episode in the early 1990s in Sweden only a temporary departure from Sweden's exceptionally low unemployment rate? Or, was the higher Swedish unemployment rate in the early 1990s the start of a reversion of Sweden's unemployment rate to a permanent level more typical of most other Western European countries?

We answered this question by using a particular theory of the European unemployment experience. We constructed a model that attributes the historically low European unemployment rates to welfare state institutions that tend to suppress frictional unemployment, such as employment protection. This part of our theory aligns well with our earlier analysis of the Swedish unemployment experience, and after adding the system of monitoring the unemployed in Sweden, our theory can rationalize why unemployment until

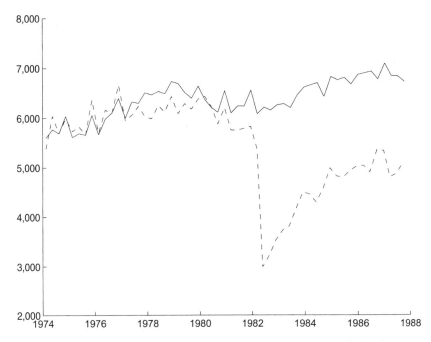

Fig. 6.5   Quarterly earnings of high-attachment workers separating in the first quarter of 1982 and workers staying through 1986

Note: The solid line refers to stayers, the dashed line to separators. This is a reproduction of figure 1 in Jacobson et al. (1993), omitting their last observation because it was based on an insufficient sample.

the 1970s was lower in Europe, and especially in Sweden, as compared to the United States. Next, our theory attributes the outbreak of persistently higher unemployment in Europe in the 1980s to generous unemployment benefits in times of microeconomic turbulence that increase the volatility of individual workers' earnings prospects. We allege that such turbulence is driven by worldwide developments such as new information technologies and competitive pressures coming from globalization. So, how has Sweden fared in this context?

Recent economic events that are unfolding in Sweden have made it clear that the national economy has changed and that repercussions from the global marketplace are greater than ever. As an example, the restructuring of the global automobile industry has reached Sweden with far-reaching implications for its former domestically owned car makes, Volvo and SAAB, and their many local subcontractors. Edling (2005) uses this restructuring of the automobile industry to support his argument that the increased specialization associated with the new global economy is here to stay and that it necessitates a more adaptive Swedish labor force in which individual workers are better prepared to make career changes.

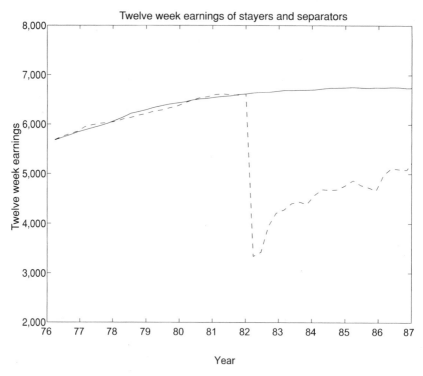

Fig. 6.6   Simulated quarterly earnings of high-attachment workers separating in the first quarter of 1982 with skill losses exceeding 30 percent and workers staying through 1986

Note: The solid line refers to stayers, the dashed line to separators. The simulation is based on the LF economy, with economic turbulence indexed by T20. The earnings numbers are multiplied by a factor of 700 to facilitate comparison with the empirical study by Jacobson et al. (1993).

To illustrate further the loss of Swedish innocence in the new global market economy, consider the changing fortunes of another heirloom in the Swedish economy—Ericsson, an international supplier of telecommunications. The company lost considerable public goodwill in 1997 because of cost-cutting measures that involved mass layoffs in the Swedish city Norrköping. In a public speech that year, the party secretary of the governing Social Democratic Party suggested that Swedish consumers should consider boycotting the company's mobile phones because of its apparent disregard for workers' welfare (Dagens Nyheter 1997). It was not a domestic boycott but rather a weakening international demand for its mobile phones, and ultimately worldwide difficulties in the telecommunications industry, that threatened Ericsson's survival as an independent company. Compared to the high that its share price attained in 2000, the value of the company's equity had tumbled more than 98 percent two years later

(Ericsson 2005). Since then, Ericsson has regained ground in an intensively competitive international industry, and its comeback in mobile phones has fittingly been undertaken as a joint venture with the large Japanese company SONY.

What has happened to Swedish unemployment in this new economy?

6.6.1   Two Views of Swedish Unemployment

The lower solid line in figure 6.7 represents the official Swedish unemployment rate that excludes participants in labor market programs. The unemployment rate explodes during the economic crisis in 1992/1993 and remains high for a few years before starting to come down at the end of the 1990s. Since then, unemployment seems to have settled down to a somewhat higher level than the historically low Swedish unemployment rate.

The lower dashed line is the unemployment rate when participants in labor market programs are also included in the ranks of unemployed.[12] The difference between the lower dashed line and the lower solid line is fairly constant, with less than 2 percentage points of the labor force in labor market programs at any point in time. An exception occurred in the 1990s, when the economic crisis caused enrollment in labor market programs to increase. Since then, enrollment apparently has returned to precrisis levels.

Edling (2005, 41) offers a different view of Swedish unemployment by asking whether "unemployment is hidden in accounts other than those originally intended for the unemployed." Edling documents that the numbers of early retirees and the long-term sick in different geographic regions in Sweden seem to vary with labor market conditions in those regions. The correlation between unemployment and early retirement in local municipalities is especially strong for the older labor force in the group aged fifty-five to sixty-four. Edling concludes that early retirement to a large extent is used as a measure for labor market policy rather than only for its original purpose of providing insurance against disability.

To impart a time dimension to Edling's argument, we make the following calculations. After summing up all the employed, unemployed including labor market program participants, and early retirees in the year 1963, we estimate that the early retirees made up 3.5 percent of that base. For now, suppose that this fraction constitutes the true fraction of disabled workers in the labor force in 1963 and in all subsequent years. Under this

---

12. Participants in labor market programs are involved in (a) subsidized employment, (b) education, or (c) work practice. The first group is counted as employed when computing the official unemployment rate, represented by the lower solid line in figure 6.7, while the latter two groups are completely left out from the labor force. Hence, starting from the official unemployment rate, the unemployment rate that includes labor market program participants, represented by the lower dashed line in figure 6.7, is computed by transferring the first group of program participants from employment to unemployment and by adding the latter two groups that are involved in education and work practice to both the labor force and the ranks of the unemployed.

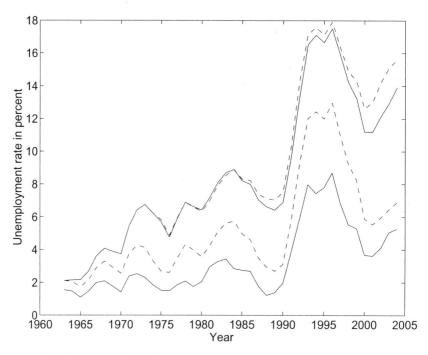

Fig. 6.7   Measures of Swedish unemployment

Sources: Openly unemployed (yearly average): Labor Force Survey, Statistics Sweden (AKU, SCB); participants in labor market programs (yearly average): National Labor Market Board (AMS); early retirees and long-term sick (in December): Swedish Social Insurance Agency (Försäkringskassan).

Note: The lower solid line is the official unemployment rate, and the lower dashed line is the unemployment rate after adding participants in labor market programs. The upper solid line is an adjustment of the latter unemployment rate that includes also excessive enrollment in early retirement, defined as early retirees in excess of the fraction of early retirement that prevailed in the year 1963 (i.e., 3.5 percent of the labor force). The upper dashed line is yet another adjustment of the unemployment rate that adds the excessive number of long-term sick who have received benefits for more than a year, defined as long-term sick in excess of the fraction of long-term sick in year 1974 (i.e., 0.5 percent of the labor force).

maintained assumption that 3.5 percent are truly disabled in every year, we can ask what has been an adjusted Swedish unemployment rate in the period from 1963 to 2004 after adding to the number of unemployed the excessive enrollment in early retirement. The upper solid line in figure 6.7 depicts our answer.

Using sickness insurance data available from 1974, we can make a similar adjustment to the unemployment rate for the number of long-term sick; that is, those who have received sickness insurance benefits for more than one year. The long-term sick can be found both in the labor force and out of the labor force. As a first approximation, if we assume that all long-term sick have employment, we find that in 1974, there was 0.5 percent long-term sick out of the previous base. Under the assumption that 0.5 percent are truly long-term sick in every year, we can ask how the previous adjusted unemployment rate would look like in the period from 1974 to 2004 if we add the excessive number of long-term sick. The upper dashed line in figure 6.7 depicts this adjusted unemployment rate that includes both early retirees and long-term sick in excess of their fractions prevailing in 1963 and 1974, respectively.

Our alternative measure of unemployment conveys a very different picture of Swedish unemployment than the official measure, represented by the lower solid line in figure 6.7. According to the alternative measure in the upper dashed line, Sweden's unemployment has indeed become more like Europe's since the beginning of the 1990s. But instead of classifying the long-term unemployed as unemployed, Sweden has relabeled many of them as early retirees and long-term sick. Admittedly, unemployment rates in general would have to be adjusted upward to reflect hidden unemployment in social welfare programs other than unemployment insurance.[13] In any case, when the activity of unemployment is properly measured, the fear of Lindbeck et al. (1994) that there would become a large group of permanently unemployed citizens in Sweden seems to have been realized.

6.6.2   Swedish Outcomes through the Camera of Our Model

Some observers of the Swedish economy might argue that turbulence is nothing new, because in the 1960s, there were large migratory flows from the northern to the southern parts of the country, as well as an accelerated urbanization. But such restructuring of the economy is not necessarily associated with the kind of turbulence described in our theory. In fact, workers in the 1960s were moving to regions where expanding industries in the manufacturing sector offered better-paying jobs than could be found where they came from. Hence, the circumstances in the 1960s were actually the opposite to our theory of *negative* shocks to individual workers' earnings potentials.

---

13. Autor and Duggan (2003) argue that reduced screening stringency since 1984 and rising replacement rates of the disability insurance program in the United States have led to a higher propensity of workers facing adverse shocks to exit the labor force to seek disability benefits. Because of the progressive (i.e., concave) benefit formula, they find that these incentive effects apply foremost to high school dropouts who have also experienced adverse demand shifts for their skills in recent decades. Autor and Duggan suggest that the measured unemployment rate in the United States would be about half a percentage point higher if the excessive enrollment in the disability insurance program were to be included. Hence, their reasoning is qualitatively the same as our argument for Sweden, but the magnitudes are different. According to Autor and Duggan, 3.7 percent of Americans aged twenty-five to sixty-four received disability insurance benefits in 2001, while Edling (2005) reports that for the Swedish population aged twenty to sixty-four, early retirees comprised 10 percent in 2004, and another 2.4 percent had received sickness insurance benefits for more than a year in 2003. For further evidence on significant increases in early retirement and enrollments in disability insurance programs in several European countries since the 1980s, see the country studies compiled by Gruber and Wise (2004).

Other observers of Sweden might argue for alternative theories that attribute current unemployment problems to the *macroeconomic* shock of the early 1990s. A similar reason that has been offered for the European unemployment dilemma has been that the oil price shocks of the 1970s served as the catalyst for high European unemployment. But as time has gone by, that view has become less and less tenable, because the transient response to that shock should not have lasted so long. Likewise, our theory suggests that the high incidence of long-term unemployment and early retirement in Sweden of today has little do with the macroeconomic shock of the early 1990s.

An open question is why Sweden seemed to have been spared the European unemployment problem until the 1990s. One also could ask why Belgium was the first country to experience the problem of long-term unemployment as early as the 1960s (see Sinfield [1968]). This is not puzzling in the light of our theory and for the fact that there was an economic upheaval in Belgium with massive layoffs in mining and a faltering steel industry. In hindsight, the Belgian experience signaled what the future had in store for the rest of Europe.

Our analysis raises concerns about Swedish labor markets that were not present in our earlier analysis (Ljungqvist and Sargent 1997), where we proceeded under the assumption that *macroeconomic* shocks had given rise to an increase in the Swedish unemployment rate in the early 1990s, which was exogenous to our model. The implication of our earlier model was that Sweden could revert to its historically low unemployment rate if the government could restore its monitoring of unemployed workers and make them accept suitable wage offers. Our present analysis that attributes high European unemployment to increased turbulence complicates the policy problem: what constitute suitable wage offers now depends on shocks to individual workers' earnings potentials that cannot be verified easily by unemployment agencies, making it likely that benefit levels become misaligned relative to those unobserved diminished earnings potentials.

Wages serve as signals that induce workers to find jobs that value their skills highly. Markets award pay increases when workers' skills increase but also make workers accept pay reductions when their skills become economically obsolete. Generous unemployment benefits do not interfere with the former but make the latter more difficult. A worker who has experienced adverse labor market conditions might have to leave a long-tenure job and seek employment in a new industry where the pay is lower and where valuable skills must be reconstructed. Needless to say, such transitions are especially difficult for older workers who have shorter horizons and therefore have less time to accumulate skills. The challenge of a welfare state with generous unemployment benefits is to provide incentives to workers who have experienced adverse labor market conditions to return to employment. Questions about incentives in social insurance systems are now common in the Swedish policy debate.

6.7   Concluding Remarks

In this second generation of the Center for Business and Policy Studies-National Bureau of Economic Research (SNS-NBER) project, we have extended our analysis of the Swedish unemployment experience in a model that extends our earlier framework. We have widened our inquiry to contrast the experience of Sweden, in particular, and of European welfare states, in general, to outcomes in a more laissez-faire economy like that of the United States. Our research strategy has remained one of identifying and analyzing institutions and factors that tend either to decrease or to increase the equilibrium unemployment rate in a welfare state relative to that of a laissez-faire economy. Among welfare state institutions that tend to decrease equilibrium unemployment in tranquil economic times, our analysis focuses on employment protection that makes it costly for firms to lay off workers. Because government-mandated employment protection has been much stronger in Europe since World War II, our model can explain why unemployment rates in the 1950s and 1960s were systematically lower in Europe than in the United States.[14] The lower rates of inflow into unemployment in Europe are consistent with this prediction, because employment protection reduces churning of workers in the labor market and locks workers into their current employment. The result is a reduction in frictional unemployment in tranquil economic times that allows transferability of workers' skills between jobs. The ease with which unemployed workers can find jobs, comparing favorable ones in pay and other benefits, ensures that the average duration of unemployment spells remains low in a welfare state, despite generous unemployment benefits, as in Europe in the 1950s and 1960s.

Concerning the outbreak of high European unemployment after the late 1970s, our analysis starts from *microeconomic* evidence that labor market prospects facing workers have become more variable and less predictable. Our model explains why such turbulent times should cause unemployment to increase in welfare states with generous benefits; our model also says that increase should take the form of long-term unemployment—structural unemployment—with an especially high incidence among older workers.

---

14. Our explanation mirrors the insight developed by Myers (1964, 180–1), Deputy Commissioner at the U.S. Bureau of Labor Statistics, when thinking about possible reasons for the low European unemployment rate in the 1950s and 1960s: "One of the differences [between the United States and Europe] lies in our attitude toward layoffs. The typical American employer is not indifferent to the welfare of his work force, but his relationship to his workers is often rather impersonal. The interests of his own employers, the stockholders, tend to make him extremely sensitive to profits and to costs. When business falls off, he soon begins to think of reduction in force. . . . In many other industrial countries, specific laws, collective agreements, or vigorous public opinion protect the workers against layoffs except under the most critical circumstances. Despite falling demand, the employer counts on retraining his permanent employees. He is obliged to find work for them to do. . . . These arrangements are certainly effective in holding down unemployment."

Notwithstanding the apparent delay in the onset of these adverse welfare dynamics in Sweden, we argue that the analysis also pertains to Sweden, where the growing numbers of long-term unemployed and early retirees should be a source of major concern.

Our analysis attributes the unemployment problems of Europe, in general, and of Sweden, in particular, to the adverse incentive effects in a welfare state when workers encounter unfavorable developments in the labor market. While we have modeled those unfavorable developments as negative shocks to laid-off workers' earning potentials, it is important to keep in mind that workers' job opportunities can also deteriorate in other ways because of the multidimensional character of employment. Thus, the dilemma of the welfare state becomes the question of how to increase job acceptance rates among workers who have encountered unfavorable labor market conditions in one way or another and who are entitled to generous benefits while staying unemployed. Although it is outside the scope of our chapter to suggest a solution to this dilemma, it is useful to comment on various proposals from the perspective of our theoretical framework. Many of the proposals fall within one of two categories: (a) measures that attempt to increase the return to work, and (b) measures that reduce the return to being unemployed.

6.7.1 Proposals for Reducing Unemployment in the Lens of Our Model

If government programs for retraining had proved effective in raising the marketable skills of the unemployed, they could be a potent measure for reducing unemployment in our model. But the accumulated empirical evidence on the returns to government-arranged retraining programs is not promising. The latest major initiative in Sweden, called the "Knowledge Lift," does not seem to have been an exception. Albrecht, van den Berg, and Vroman (2004) provide an evaluation of this massive program: in the period from 1997 to 2000, more than 10 percent of the labor force had participated in it. While the study detects a positive employment effect for young men, it finds no evidence of an income effect from the program, and hence, older men and the average female participant seemed to have fared no better than nonparticipants. For a further discussion and a summary of studies finding at most minor effects of labor market programs, see Forslund and Krueger (chapter 5 in this volume). Our model embodies a stark version of this empirical evidence by assigning no role to public expenditures on retraining and relief jobs. In our model, displaced workers who incur losses of earnings potential are left to seek employment opportunities where new skills can be accumulated. Our model incorporates an empirically based skepticism about government-mandated programs and abstracts from initiatives by individual workers who acquire formal education in response to perceived market opportunities.

Other measures aimed at increasing the return to work include proposals to subsidize employment of long-term unemployed workers. Such measures would certainly reduce unemployment in our model, because the subsidies would come on top of the return to the workers' marketable skills, and because in a competitive labor market, the subsidies would be reflected in workers' pay. Hence, a policy-induced artificial increase in workers' earnings potentials would motivate them to search more intensively and to be more willing to accept new employment. We have two doubts about targeted employment subsidies. First, there would be incentives for both firms and workers to try to qualify for these temporary subsidies. Such behavioral responses are well known for policies that attempt to single out and subsidize some marginal actions like new hires by firms. Second, the risk that subsidies distort competition in the marketplace is always a concern. An illustration of the latter would be a case where an unemployed worker gets a subsidy to cover some of his or her pay when opening a new coffee house. Needless to say, existing coffee houses in the same community would be at a disadvantage in the competition with the new subsidized entrant. Therefore, as an alternative to targeted subsidies, one might want to consider measures aimed at improving the return to work for low-income workers, in general, such as recent proposals to reduce taxes at lower-income levels. Such labor supply inducements for low-income workers necessarily would be more costly than targeted employment subsidies, but they could also be seen as serving the overall workfare goal espoused by Björklund and Freeman (chapter 1 in this volume).

A reduction in benefit levels is the most obvious measure that reduces the return to being unemployed, and it clearly would reduce unemployment in our model. However, proposals prescribing benefit reductions for the long-term unemployed have been criticized for abandoning the European welfare model and for advocating a stinginess resembling that of social insurance systems in the United States. It is probably safe to say that there is a strong European sentiment that the low benefit levels for the long-term unemployed in the United States would not be acceptable in Europe. The question then becomes how to reform the unemployment insurance system so that it provides proper incentives while preserving the social fabric of Europe. After recognizing that the task is to reduce the return to being unemployed *relative* to being employed, one shortcoming of our model stands out—the value of leisure enters only in the workers' decision to search for jobs, whereby a choice of higher search intensity is associated with exerting more effort; that is, a loss of leisure. The model incorporates no disutility of working relative to the enjoyment of leisure while not working. If this feature were to be added to our model, proposals to reduce the return to being unemployed would not necessarily have to take the form of reduced benefits but could also be accomplished by reducing the amount of leisure available to the unemployed.

Requiring that the long-term unemployed perform social work commensurate to the number of hours in a regular full-time job could markedly reduce the return to unemployment compared to employment.[15] If the states of unemployment and employment are not that different in terms of hours devoted to either social work or regular work, unemployment benefits would become much less attractive when compared to earning a wage in the marketplace. In addition to providing incentives for the unemployed to return to regular employment, social work requirements would address concerns about the mental health of the unemployed. Jahoda (1982) identifies a number of psychological benefits from working, including the joy of participating in useful social activities and the daily structure that regular activities provide. Apart from the economic hardship of being unemployed, Nordenmark and Strandh (1999) document from a longitudinal survey of unemployed Swedes that a standard measure of poor mental health is correlated with the extent to which individuals feel socially deprived by not having a job. It seems that unemployed workers "who have, or manage to find, alternative roles and identities to the role of employee fare quite well" (583). In this perspective, social work requirements would aid those who have lost jobs and who yearn to join a social context with the ultimate goal of securing regular employment and also would provide work incentives for those who have become complacent in a life of benefit dependence. From a budgetary perspective, the measure would not cost anything in terms of payments to the unemployed, because they already receive benefits, and the social needs that could be met when the unemployed perform social work assignments presumably would outweigh the administrative costs of the program.

A new Swedish labor market program called the "activity guarantee" was introduced in 2000 with the goal of strengthening labor market prospects of UI recipients who are at risk of becoming long-term unemployed. The program participants are entitled to unemployment benefits, but participation also is supposed to imply full-time activity. The unemployment agencies are instructed to organize both individual and group activities for the participants to be engaged in job search, regular labor market programs, and studies or activities arranged by firms, municipalities, and other government agencies. Implementation of the program has encountered difficulties, as reported by Forslund, Fröberg, and Lindqvist (2004). More than half of interviewed supervisors at the unemployment agencies complain about insufficient information concerning how to organize the activities, and the

---

15. Ljungqvist (1999, section 6) discusses a number of conditions that a social work program for the unemployed should satisfy. A key condition is that the assignments should fall within a well-delimited range of work that would not distort competition in the rest of the economy. Because of high turnover rates, the tasks should require minimal skill requirements. The fact that social work would not earn a market wage qualifies it as a labor market program rather than an alternative to regular employment.

lack of manpower is cited as an explanation to why one-quarter of the agencies have been unable to offer full-time activities. It can also be noted that only a small fraction of those with long unemployment spells have entered the program—the fraction was less than 3 percent among those with spells of at least two years. Despite the rather negative assessment of the program to date by Forslund, Fröberg, and Lindqvist, we see this measure as a potential tool for implementing the social work requirement previously discussed.[16]

6.7.2   Jobs Are Not the Bottleneck

Whether there are enough jobs available in the economy is a question that is often raised in discussions of reforms aimed at reducing unemployment. In our search model, there is no lack of jobs, because the unemployed search against a wage offer distribution, where one worker's decision to accept a job does not impinge on the ability of other workers to find jobs commensurate to their earnings potentials. Both historical evidence and economic theory support the notion that market economies will create jobs in response to workers' aspirations that reflect their marketable skills. For example, Blanchard (2006, 24) notes that "even in economies with high unemployment, exogenous movements in the labor force—due to demography or repatriation, such as the return of European nationals after the independence of former colonies—translate fairly quickly into movements in employment." In their treatise about European unemployment, Layard, Nickell, and Jackman (1991, 73) also refute the view that the available work in an economy is given—the "lump-of-output fallacy." As a consequence, they forcefully argue that early retirement and work sharing are not solutions to Europe's problem but rather are "excellent way[s] of making a country poorer." Against this background, a recent Swedish initiative called the "free year," which furloughs gainfully employed workers into a sabbatical year so that their vacant positions can be offered to the unemployed, seems perverse.

6.7.3   Reform Is Imperative

Measures that facilitate job creation, such as those aimed at improving the conditions for entrepreneurs and small firms, as discussed by Davis and

---

16. In addition to the considerations mentioned in note number 15, Ljungqvist (1999) argues why social work requirements should be imposed in a gradual fashion over unemployment spells. First, as in the analysis of optimal unemployment insurance by Shavell and Weiss (1979), the foremost purpose of imposing work requirements or reducing benefits is to provide the unemployed with correct incentives in their choice of search intensities and reservation wages. The anticipation of a future imposition of a work requirement, like the anticipation of a future reduction in benefits, induces an unemployed person to adjust his or her search behavior so that the probability of gaining employment increases today. Second, the gradual imposition is warranted, because in contrast to reductions in benefits, work requirements reduce the time left for the unemployed to search for regular employment.

Henrekson (chapter 7 in this volume), certainly would be helpful when try-
ing to reduce the ranks of the unemployed and early retirees in Sweden.
However, we would like to emphasize that real success hinges critically upon
reforms that increase the returns to employment relative to unemployment
for workers who have experienced unfavorable labor market outcomes.
Reform here is imperative, because a culture of nonemployment is not only
difficult to reverse but is also unfair to individuals who are lured into prolonged periods of nonactivity. They are exposed to the political risk that the
rules of the game ultimately will change and that they will have to return
with much diminished skills to a harsher labor market. The difficulties that
France and Germany are having in implementing labor market reforms
after decades of long-term unemployment ought to serve as an early warn-
ing and to spur reform efforts that could spare Swedish workers future
hardships.

6.7.4   Post Scriptum: A New Swedish Government and Policy

Most observers of the Swedish national election in September 2006 attribute the defeat of the incumbent Social Democratic government and the vic-
tory of the center-right coalition to differences in labor market policies. While
the former government promised to raise the cap on labor income, below
which the social insurance system replaces lost earnings during joblessness,
the opposition offered a different vision in which benefit dependency and the
ranks of the jobless should be reduced, among other things, by increasing
the relative return to work over nonemployment. Besides tax breaks on labor
income, the new center-right government has decided to reduce replacement
rates over unemployment spells and to impose activity/work requirements
(see Swedish Government [2007a, 2007b]). The replacement rate in the UI
system becomes 80 percent during the first 200 days of an unemployment
spell, 70 percent during the next 100 days, and 65 percent thereafter. (Parents
with children are allowed longer benefit durations at the higher replacement
rates.) After 300 days of unemployment, benefit recipients are entitled and
obliged to participate in a "job and development guarantee" that replaces
the "activity guarantee" discussed earlier.

There are quite a few overlaps between these measures of the new Swedish
government and our own proposal for reducing unemployment. Because the
government's lowest replacement rate of 65 percent is likely to be close to
what is socially acceptable in Sweden, we believe for the reasons previously
stated that the way the "job and development guarantee" is designed in practice will be vital. The Swedish Government (2007b, 34) lays out three phases
for an unemployed worker who enters this program: the first phase focuses
on assistance with intensified job search; the second phase involves a battery
of instruments including retraining, trainee work, subsidized employment,
and other activities aimed at raising the level of competence; and the final
third phase prescribes that "someone who has failed to gain employment

after 450 days under the Job and Development Guarantee, is assigned lasting socially valuable work that corresponds to the participant's full labor supply." We might quarrel about the duration and timing of the different phases, but we prefer to reiterate on our previous comment that the last phase will be crucial for successfully reducing the ranks of the nonemployed. Properly designed, what we called social work will provide potent incentives to those nonemployed who are able to return to regular employment and will also serve as a meaningful source of activity for those who are unable or unwilling to make that transition.

References

Albrecht, J., G. J. van den Berg, and S. Vroman. 2004. The Knowledge Lift: The Swedish adult education program that aimed to eliminate low worker skill levels. IFAU Working Paper no. 2004:17. Uppsala, Sweden: Institute for Labor Market Policy Evaluation.

Autor, D. H., and M. G. Duggan. 2003. The rise in the disability rolls and the decline in unemployment. *Quarterly Journal of Economics* 118 (1): 157–205.

Blanchard, O. 2006. European unemployment: The evolution of facts and ideas. *Economic Policy* 21 (45): 5–59.

Burda, M. C., and A. Mertens. 2001. Estimating wage losses of displaced workers in Germany. *Labour Economics* 8 (1): 15–41.

Campbell, J. Y., M. Lettau, B. Malkiel, and Y. Xu. 2001. Have individual stocks become more volatile? An empirical exploration of idiosyncratic risk. *Journal of Finance* 56 (1): 1–43.

Comin, D., and T. Philippon. 2005. The rise in firm-level volatility: Causes and consequences. In *NBER macroeconomics annual 2005,* ed. M. Gertler and K. Rogoff, 167–201. Cambridge, MA: MIT Press.

Congressional Budget Office. 2007. *Trends in earnings variability over the past 20 years.* Washington, DC: CBO.

Dagens Nyheter (Stockholm). 1997. Politikerna skyr inga medel [Politicians stop at nothing]. May 5.

Davis, S. J., J. Haltiwanger, R. Jarmin, and J. Miranda. 2006. Volatility and dispersion in business growth rates: Publicly traded versus privately held firms. In *NBER macroeconomics annual 2006,* ed. D. Acemoglu, K. Rogoff, and M. Woodford, 107–56. Cambridge, MA: MIT Press.

Edling, J. 2005. *Alla behovs: Blott arbetsmarknadspolitik skapar inga nya jobb* [Everybody is needed: Labor market policies alone do not create any new jobs]. Stockholm: Timbro. Available at: http://www.timbro.se/pdf/Alla_behovs_2.pdf.

Ericsson. 2005. *Arsrapport 2004* [Annual Report 2004]. Stockholm: Telefonaktiebolaget LM Ericsson.

Farber, H. 1997. The changing face of job loss in the United States, 1981–1995. *Brookings Papers on Economic Activity, Microeconomics:* 55–128. Washington, DC: Brookings Institution.

———. 2005. What do we know about job loss in the United States? Evidence from the Displaced Workers Survey, 1984–2004. *Federal Reserve Bank of Chicago Economic Perspectives* 29 (2): 13–28.

222   Lars Ljungqvist and Thomas J. Sargent

Forslund, A., D. Fröberg, and L. Lindqvist. 2004. The Swedish activity guarantee. OECD Social, Employment and Migration Working Paper no. 16. Paris: Organization for Economic Cooperation and Development, January.

Gottschalk, P., and R. Moffitt. 1994. The growth of earnings instability in the U.S. labor market. *Brookings Papers on Economic Activity,* Issue no. 2: 217–72. Washington, DC: Brookings Institution.

Gruber, J., and D. A. Wise. 2004. *Social Security programs and retirement around the world.* Chicago: University of Chicago Press.

Heckman, J. J. 2003. Flexibility, job creation and economic performance. *CESifo Forum* 4 (2): 29–32.

Hunt, J. 1995. The effect of unemployment compensation on unemployment duration in Germany. *Journal of Labor Economics* 13 (1): 88–120.

Jacobson, L. S., R. J. LaLonde, and D. G. Sullivan. 1993. Earnings losses of displaced workers. *American Economic Review* 83 (4): 685–709.

Jahoda, M. 1982. *Employment and unemployment: A social-psychological analysis.* Cambridge: Cambridge University Press.

Kambourov, G., and I. Manovskii. 2008. Rising occupational and industry mobility in the United States: 1968–1997. *International Economic Review* 49 (1): 41–79.

Katz, L. F., and D. H. Autor. 1999. Changes in the wage structure and earnings inequality. In *Handbook of labor economics,* vol. 3, ed. O. Ashenfelter and D. Card, 1463–555. Amsterdam: Elsevier.

Krugman, P. R. 1987. Slow growth in Europe: Conceptual issues. In *Barriers to European growth: A transatlantic view,* ed. R. Z. Lawrence and C. L. Schultze, 48–99. Washington, DC: Brookings Institution.

Layard, R., S. Nickell, and R. Jackman. 1991. *Unemployment: Macroeconomic performance and the labour market.* Oxford: Oxford University Press.

Lindbeck, A., P. Molander, T. Persson, O. Peterson, A. Sandmo, B. Swedenborg, and N. Thygesen. 1994. *Turning Sweden around.* Cambridge, MA: MIT Press.

Ljungqvist, L. 1999. Squandering European labor: Social safety nets in times of economic turbulence. *Scottish Journal of Political Economy* 46 (4): 367–88.

———. 2002. How do layoff costs affect employment? *Economic Journal* 112: 829–53.

Ljungqvist, L., and T. J. Sargent. 1995a. The Swedish unemployment experience. *European Economic Review* 39 (5): 1043–70.

———. 1995b. Welfare states and unemployment. *Economic Theory* 6 (1): 143–60.

———. 1997. Taxes and subsidies in Swedish unemployment. In *The welfare state in transition: Reforming the Swedish model,* ed. R. B. Freeman, R. Topel, and B. Swedenborg, 299–314. Chicago: University of Chicago Press.

———. 2008. Two questions about European unemployment. *Econometrica* 76 (1): 1–29.

Machin, S., and A. Manning. 1999. The causes and consequences of longterm unemployment in Europe. In *Handbook of labor economics,* vol. 3, ed. O. Ashenfelter and D. Card, 3085–139. Amsterdam: Elsevier.

Martin, J. P. 1996. Measures of replacement rates for the purpose of international comparisons: A note. *OECD Economic Studies* 26 (October): 99–115.

McCall, J. J. 1970. Economics of information and job search. *Quarterly Journal of Economics* 84 (1): 113–26.

McConnell, M. M., and G. Perez-Quiros. 2000. Output fluctuations in the United States: What has changed since the early 1980's? *American Economic Review* 90 (5): 464–76.

Millard, S. P., and D. T. Mortensen. 1997. The unemployment and welfare effects of labor market policy: A comparison of the USA and the UK. In *Unemployment policy: Government options for the labor market,* ed. D. Snower and G. de la Dehesa, 545–75. Cambridge: Cambridge University Press.

Myers, R. J. 1964. What can we learn from European experience? In *Unemployment and the American economy,* ed. A. M. Ross, 139–54. New York: John Wiley and Sons.

Nordenmark, M., and M. Strandh. 1999. Towards a sociological understanding of mental well-being among the unemployed: The role of economic and psychosocial factors. *Sociology* 33 (3): 577–97.

Parrado, E., A. Caner, and E. N. Wolff. 2007. Occupational and industrial mobility in the United States. *Labour Economics* 14 (3): 435–55.

Pissarides, C. A. 1983. Efficiency aspects of the financing of unemployment insurance and other government expenditures. *Review of Economic Studies* 50 (1): 57–69.

Rosenfeld, C. 1979. Occupational mobility during 1977. *Monthly Labor Review* 102 (12): 44–48.

Ruhm, C. 1991. Are workers permanently scarred by job displacements? *American Economic Review* 81 (1): 319–23.

Shavell, S., and L. Weiss. 1979. The optimal payment of unemployment insurance benefits over time. *Journal of Political Economy* 87 (6): 1347–62.

Shaw, K. 2002. By what means does information technology affect employment and wages? In *Productivity, inequality, and the digitial economy,* ed. N. Greenan, Y. L'Horty, and J. Mairesse, 229–69. Cambridge, MA: MIT Press.

Sinfield, A. 1968. *The long-term unemployed: A comparative survey.* Employment of Special Groups, no. 5. Paris: Organization for Economic Cooperation and Development.

Stock, J. H., and M. W. Watson. 2002. Has the business cycle changed, and why? In *NBER macroeconomics annual 2002,* ed. M. Gertler and K. Rogoff, 159–218. Cambridge, MA: MIT Press.

Swedish Government. 2007a. *Regeringens proposition 2006/07:89.* Stockholm: Swedish Government Offices.

———. 2007b. *Regeringens proposition 2006/07:100.* Stockholm: Swedish Government Offices.

Topel, R. 1990. Specific capital and unemployment: Measuring the costs and consequences of job loss. *Carnegie-Rochester Conference Series on Public Policy* 33: 181–214.

Economic Performance and Market Work Activity in Sweden after the Crisis of the Early 1990s

Steven J. Davis and Magnus Henrekson

7.1 Introduction

Since emerging from a severe contraction in the early 1990s, the Swedish economy has accumulated a strong record of output growth, outpacing the average growth rate in the Organization for Economic Cooperation and Development (OECD) and in the European Union (EU-15). The performance of the Swedish labor market has been less impressive. By 2005, hours worked per person were still 10.5 percent below the 1990 peak and a mere 1 percent above the 1993 trough. Employment rates tell a similar story.

We more fully describe Swedish developments with respect to output and market work activity in the balance of this section. We then turn to several aspects of the Swedish institutional setup that repress market work activity. Our discussion highlights the role of high tax rates on labor income and consumption expenditures, wage-setting arrangements that compress relative wages, and business tax policies that disfavor labor-intensive industries and technologies. We describe these features of the Swedish institutional setup and provide evidence of their consequences based on Swedish outcomes

Steven J. Davis is the William H. Abbott Professor of International Business and Economics at the Booth School of Business, University of Chicago, and a research associate of the National Bureau of Economic Research. Magnus Henrekson is a professor and director of the Research Institute of Industrial Economics, Stockholm.

We thank Robin Douhan, Martin Flodén, Tino Sanandaji, and participants in the September 2006 Center for Business and Policy Studies/National Bureau of Economic Research (SNS/NBER) conference on *Reforming the Welfare State* for helpful comments. We also thank Erik Hurst for assistance with the American Time-Use Survey and Richard Rogerson for data on hours worked in a number of countries. Robin Douhan, Martin Olsson, and Per Thulin provided excellent research assistance. We gratefully acknowledge financial support from the Jan Wallander and Tom Hedelius Foundation. Needless to say, we are responsible for any remaining errors and shortcomings.

and international comparisons. We also identify some noteworthy policy changes since 2006 and their potential effects on market work activity in Sweden.

7.1.1   Output Growth

Beginning in the mid- to late 1960s, Swedish gross domestic product (GDP) growth slowed relative to earlier decades and relative to other rich countries. Income per capita fell from third or fourth place among OECD countries in 1970 to seventeenth place in 1993, dropping some 20 percentage points relative to the OECD average (Lindbeck 1997; Henrekson 2001). Since the 1993 trough, the Swedish growth record has greatly improved relative to the contemporaneous performance in other rich countries and relative to the previous two decades. Sweden's output grew almost 3 percent per annum from 1994 to 2005, well above the average pace in the EU-15 and the OECD. In terms of per capita GDP growth, Sweden even outperformed the United States over this period. No doubt, rapid growth after 1993 partly reflects a rebound from an unusually deep contraction in the early 1990s. Nevertheless, the Swedish economy had not experienced such rapid growth on a sustained basis since the 1960s, a decade often seen as the golden age of the Swedish model.[1]

Sweden's rapid output growth in recent years has not translated into comparable gains in relative income because of deterioration in its terms of trade (Håkansson and Lindbeck 2005). The industry composition of Swedish output growth in recent years is also noteworthy. As reported in table 7.1, manufacturing accounts for 41 percent of the real output gains in Sweden's private sector from 1994 to 2005.[2] Nearly half of the output growth within manufacturing took place in electrical and optical products. This aspect of Swedish output growth is particularly striking in light of manufacturing's falling share of output, and especially of employment, in the world's rich countries in recent decades. The terms-of-trade deterioration has probably helped stimulate the growth of Sweden's manufacturing output (measured at constant prices).

Outside manufacturing, the greatest contributions to the growth of Sweden's private sector occurred in trade, transportation and communication, real estate, and business services. Output grew relatively rapidly in education, health and community, and personal services, but from a very modest base. We will return to the performance of market-based services in our analysis of Sweden's institutional setup.

---

1. The average GDP growth rate in Sweden was 4.1 percent in 1966 to 1970, 5.2 percent in 1961 to 1965, and 3.4 percent in 1951 to 1960 (Statistics Sweden).
2. When measuring GDP from the production side, Statistics Sweden calls this "total market producers and producers for own final use." This roughly corresponds to total production, excluding government production. However, it should be noted that incorporated production units wholly owned by the government, such as the postal service, housing owned and run by local governments, and incorporated public hospitals are classified as market producers.

7.1.2   Market Work Activity

Figure 7.1 displays cumulative changes in Sweden's employment and population since 1950. As stressed in our original study, the second half of the twentieth century saw almost no net job growth in Sweden's private sector, even though the working-age population expanded by roughly one million persons. In contrast, government employment grew more than one for one with the working-age population until 1990.

The early 1990s marked a pronounced departure from employment patterns in earlier decades in two respects. First, government and private employment fell sharply relative to the working-age population. The employment-population ratio fell by roughly 10 percentage points within a few years, and the open unemployment rate soared to levels not seen since the Great Depression. Second, the partial employment recovery after 1993 occurred almost exclusively in the private sector. In fact, private-sector employment exceeded its previous peak in Sweden by 2001, while government employment remains well below the levels of the 1980s. Private-sector employment fell again after 2001, however, and aggregate employment in 2005 remained well below its peak in 1990.

Despite the impression given by figure 7.1, the extent to which the Swedish private sector has rediscovered a capacity for job creation is unclear. Some of the measured gains in private-sector employment reflect changes in the legal form of organization rather than new job creation within the private sector. For example, when a regional government incorporates its hospitals, employment at these hospitals is reclassified into the private sector. As a somewhat different example, when a publicly funded private school substitutes for a municipal school, the effect is to boost measured employment in the private sector.

Relative to population, employment was much higher in Sweden than in the United States and the rest of the OECD until the deep contraction of the early 1990s. It then fell below the value in the United States and greatly narrowed the gap relative to the average of other countries in the OECD.

Table 7.1 also presents a breakdown of employment and employment growth in Sweden's nongovernment sector from 1994 to 2005. Nongovernment employment grew by 11.3 percent, and all of the net gains occurred in the service sector. Sizable contributions to nongovernment employment growth occurred in wholesale and retail trade, real estate, renting and business services, and education, health, and social work. Manufacturing employment fell by 3 percent, despite a 95 percent gain in real value added.

Although widely studied, employment and unemployment statistics have serious limitations as measures of overall work activity. Definitions of employment and unemployment are seldom straightforward, and they change over time and differ among countries in ways that defy easy comparisons. These data are especially problematic when used as measures of labor market performance and work activity levels in Sweden.

Table 7.1   Decomposition of Swedish nongovernment GDP and employment growth, 1994 to 2005

	Share of total value added, 1994 (%)	Contribution to real value added growth, 1994–2005	Share of employment, 1994	Contribution to employment growth, 1994–2005
Total market producers and producers for own final use	**100.0**	**49.7**	**100.00**	**11.30**
Producers of goods	40.9	21.9	42.0	-0.8
Producers of services	59.1	23.4	58.0	12.1
Producers of goods	**40.9**	**21.9**	**42.0**	**-0.8**
Agriculture, forestry, fishing	3.5	0.0	5.2	-1.4
Mining and quarrying	0.4	0.1	0.3	0.0
Manufacturing	26.6	20.6	27.2	-0.8
Electricity, gas, and water works	4.3	0.2	1.2	0.2
Construction industry	6.1	0.8	8.0	1.2
Producers of services	**59.1**	**23.4**	**58.0**	**12.1**
Wholesale and retail sale	14.3	6.1	20.1	1.4
Hotels and restaurants	1.8	0.6	4.1	0.7
Transport, storage, and communication	9.5	3.8	10.3	0.1
Financial institutions and insurance companies	7.3	2.0	3.2	0.2
Real estate, renting, and business service companies	22.8	6.7	12.6	6.4
Educational, health, and social work establishments	1.6	1.5	3.3	2.6
Other community and personal service establishments	1.8	1.0	4.4	0.7
Manufacturing	**26.6**	**20.6**	**27.2**	**-0.8**
Food product, beverage, and tobacco industry	2.3	0.3	2.6	-0.4
Textiles, clothing, and leather industry	0.4	0.0	0.6	-0.2
Wood and wood products	1.2	0.8	1.4	0.0
Pulp and papers; publishers and printers	4.3	0.2	4.0	-0.9
Coke and petroleum products	0.2	0.2	0.1	0.0
Chemicals	2.6	2.3	1.3	0.0
Rubber and plastic products	0.7	0.3	0.9	0.0
Other nonmetallic mineral products	0.6	0.1	0.7	-0.1
Basic metals; fabricated metal products	3.5	1.0	3.7	0.5
Machinery and equipment n.e.c.	3.5	1.3	3.6	0.1
Electrical and optical products	3.0	9.7	3.1	-0.3
Transport equipment	3.6	3.0	3.2	0.7
Manufacturing industry n.e.c.	0.6	0.2	2.1	-0.3

Source: Statistics Sweden (SCB) and own calculations.

Note: Growth figures are based on constant prices; reference year 2000. Due to different weights and variations in the value added growth between industries, the subparts will not add up to the total market when accounting for the contribution to total real value added growth. Employment is defined as number of persons; n.e.c. = not elsewhere classified.

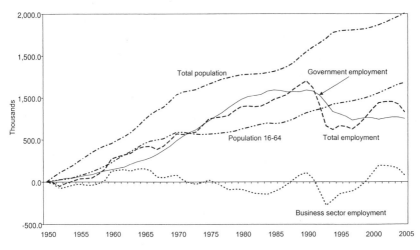

Fig. 7.1   Cumulative employment and population changes in Sweden, 1950 to 2005
Source: Statistics Sweden and own calculations.

Official statistics for Sweden show high rates of employment in the working-age population. For example, Statistics Sweden reports an employment rate of 77 percent in 2004 for persons twenty to sixty-four years of age. This figure reflects many employed persons who are not actually working— including those on sick leave, some students and conscripts, some persons on unpaid leave, people on paid parental leave, and people on temporary leave to care for a sick child. Sickness leave, in particular, is a major source of absenteeism in the Swedish economy. Because official employment statistics make no adjustment for sickness leave and other factors just mentioned, they overstate Sweden's aggregate labor input. The OECD (2005, 82) estimates that the number of persons actually at work in Sweden is 10 percentage points lower than the employment rate for men and 15 percentage points lower for women.

Official unemployment measures in Sweden also paint an overly strong picture of labor market performance. The open unemployment rate in Sweden was 5.5 percent as of 2004, according to Statistics Sweden, but several more comprehensive measures of unemployment have been suggested. They generally include all or part of the following categories: people on sick leave, parental leave, leave to care for family members, and unpaid leave; participants in labor market programs; discouraged workers; people on welfare; and early retirees. It is virtually impossible to agree on an exact number, but expansive concepts of Swedish unemployment yield figures in the range of 18 to 24 percent of the labor force (Edling 2005).

As a broad measure of labor input, hours actually worked per person is a more useful indicator and one that sidesteps some of the conceptual and measurement issues that arise with employment and unemployment measures. At a minimum, hours-based measures of work activity shed additional light on the behavior of aggregate labor inputs. Hours worked per person aged sixteen to sixty-four years fell by 11 percent from 1990 to 1993 (from 1,325 to 1,178 hours).[3] The recovery from 1993 to 2005 is only a tiny eight hours. Hours worked per person of working age in 2005 are 10.5 percent below the level of 1990.

These data on hours worked derive from self-reported measures in samples of persons. As of 2004, average reported hours of work per employed person is 1,630. This figure may well be an overstatement, given the incidence of part-time work, sick leave absenteeism, parental leave, training, and so forth among those counted as employed in Sweden. Some support for this view comes from a survey of 500 firms collected by the Confederation of Swedish Employers. According to this source, the average number of actual hours worked among *full-time* employees in the private sector was 1,554 hours in 2005.[4] In comparison, the average of self-reported hours worked for *all* employees in 2004 was about 5 percent higher. In this regard, it should be noted that absenteeism of every kind, as well as part-time work, is more prevalent in the public sector. Additional evidence comes from OECD estimates for average hours by full-year equivalent workers in 2002, accounting for various kinds of absences. According to the OECD (2005, table 4.1), the estimate for Sweden is only 1,349 hours, dramatically lower than self-reported hours. (The corresponding European average is 1,567 work hours.) In short, these comparisons suggest that official statistics substantially overstate market work activity in Sweden.

Figure 7.2 shows average hours per person of working age from 1956 to 2003 in Sweden and the United States.[5] Average work time evolves along remarkably different paths in the two countries, with Americans working much less than Swedes in the 1950s and much more by the 1990s. Among Swedes aged fifteen to sixty-four years, work time fell by more than 200 hours per year from 1956 to 1972. Swedish work time then fluctuated in a narrow band for fifteen years, before recovering somewhat in the late 1980s

---

3. Measures of hours worked are also subject to errors and interpretation difficulties. In this regard, we note that Statistics Sweden revised their estimates of the annual number of hours worked per employed person upward in the early 2000s. For example, the figure for 1997 (as reported in the OECD *Employment Outlook*) was revised upward by seventy-eight hours.
4. See *Svenskt Näringslivs Tidsanvändningsstatistik,* a quarterly publication. The data on work and absenteeism cover 200,000 employees at 500 firms with roughly 2,500 establishments. Reporting firms have chosen to participate, so the response rate is 100 percent.
5. We rely on international data on average hours worked per person of working age supplied by Richard Rogerson (2006), who compiled the data from OECD sources and from data made available by the Groningen Growth and Development Center, available at: http://www.ggdc .net/. The Groningen data on annual hours worked are "intended to include paid overtime and exclude paid hours that are not worked due to sickness, vacation and holidays, etc." Nevertheless, since the Groningen data rely heavily on official national sources, they are subject to the same concerns expressed in the text regarding inaccurate reports of hours actually worked. These concerns apply to the data for all countries, but they may be more serious for Sweden.

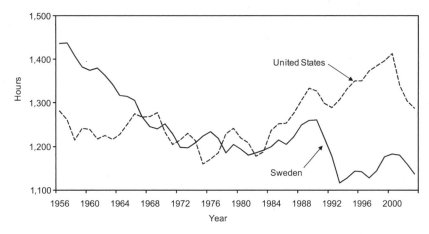

Fig. 7.2   Average hours worked per person aged fifteen to sixty-four, 1956 to 2003, Sweden and the United States

Source: Rogerson (2006), as compiled from OECD sources and the Groningen Growth and Development Center.

and plummeting to new lows in the 1990s. Hours per working-age Swede dropped by 11.5 percent, from 1,261 in 1990 to 1,116 in 1993. In contrast, average hours among working-age Americans rose rapidly, from 1,179 in 1982 to 1,413 in 2000, and then fell sharply after 2000 from a very high base. According to these data, as of 2003, Americans spend 150 hours more per year in market work activity than Swedes.

Large national differences in the level and time path of average hours worked hold more broadly among rich countries, as Rogerson (2006) effectively highlights. Compared to other rich countries, the United States experienced unusually large gains in average hours worked after the early 1980s, but Australia, Canada, and New Zealand had similar experiences. Austria, Denmark, Finland, Portugal, and the United Kingdom, among other countries, experienced large declines in average work time from high levels in the 1950s and 1960s, much like Sweden. Average hours fell even more sharply in Germany, France, and Italy. They fell by smaller amounts from higher starting points in Switzerland and Japan. Greece, Ireland, the Netherlands, and Spain experienced large increases in average work hours after the late 1980s, partly reversing declines in previous decades. The overall picture is one of remarkable heterogeneity among rich countries in the evolution of average work time.

Figure 7.3 displays the joint evolution of average work hours and per capita output in Sweden and the United States. The prevailing longer-term pattern in Sweden is one of output gains accompanied by decreases in average work hours. In sharp contrast, the prevailing pattern in the United States is one of output gains accompanied by increases in average hours. Judging by

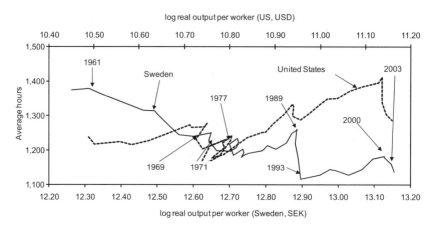

Fig. 7.3   The joint evolution of average work hours and per capita output in Sweden and the United States, 1960 to 2003

Source: Authors' calculations on data from Rogerson (2006) and OECD sources.

Note: Average hours is average annual hours worked among persons fifteen to sixty-four years of age. Real output is measured in 2000 Swedish kronor (SEK) and U.S. dollars (USD), respectively.

the experience of these two countries in recent decades, there is no natural tendency for the amount of time devoted to market work activity to either rise or fall as per capita output rises. Instead, the long-term response of market work activity appears to depend greatly on country-specific features.

7.1.3   Time-Use Surveys

The preceding section draws on standard sources for data on employment and hours worked in the market sector. Time-use surveys allow for a broader view of work activity that includes time devoted to (unpaid) work activity outside the market sector. We draw on evidence from time-use surveys to briefly address three questions. First, how much time do Swedish and American adults devote to work activity outside the market sector? Second, how does the composition of time spent outside paid employment differ between the two countries? And third, how do trends in the amount of time devoted to overall work activity compare to those for market work activity?

Table 7.2 addresses the first two questions, drawing on time-use data for persons between twenty and seventy-four years of age in Sweden (2000 to 2001) and the United States (2004). On average, Americans spend 138 more hours per year in paid employment than Swedes according to the time-use data, an amount very similar to the extra 150 hours per year according to labor force surveys. However, Swedes spend an extra 95 hours per year in domestic household work, excluding child care. In other words, the U.S.-Swedish difference in time spent on overall work activity, inclusive of domestic household work, is less than one-third the difference in time devoted to

Table 7.2   **Time-use breakdown, Sweden and the United States compared**

Men and women, 20–74 years old Time-use category	Hours per day		U.S.-Swedish difference	
	United States (2004)	Sweden (2000–2001)	Hours per day	Hours per year
1. Study	0.21	0.28	–0.07	
2. Travel (excluding travel during work)	1.30	1.44	–0.15	
2a. Commuting to and from work	0.32	0.33	–0.01	
3. Free time	15.51	15.55	–0.04	–13
3a. Personal care	10.29	10.43	–0.14	
3b. Leisure activities	5.22	5.12	0.10	37
4. Work	6.38	6.26	0.12	43
4a. Paid employment	3.90	3.53	0.38	138
4b. Domestic work (excluding child care)	2.47	2.73	–0.26	–95
Food prep, dishwashing	0.55	0.89	–0.35	–126
Cleaning dwelling	0.36	0.38	–0.02	
Laundry	0.20	0.17	0.03	
Construction and repairs, gardening, pets	0.56	0.59	–0.03	–12
Shopping and services	0.53	0.43	0.10	35
Other	0.28	0.27	0.01	
5. Child care (unpaid)	0.50	0.38	0.13	47
6. Unspecified time use	0.11	0.10	0.00	
Domestic work + child care	2.98	3.11	–0.13	–48
Leisure activities + child care	5.72	5.49	0.23	84

Sources: Sweden: Harmonised European Time-Use Survey (HETUS) Pocketbook, available at: http://circa.europa.eu.int/Public/irc/dsis/tus/library?l=/comparable_statistics/sweden_25_01xls/_EN_1.0_&a=d. United States: authors' calculations on microdata from the American Time-Use Survey, available at: http://www.bls.gov/tus/datafiles_2004.htm.

Note: Personal care includes sleeping, eating, and other personal care activities. Leisure includes unpaid volunteer work outside the household and care of adults who do not reside in the household. Large breaks at work (e.g., time spent on lunch break) are classified as part of paid employment under work-related activities, but short breaks are treated differently for the two countries. They are classified as work time for Sweden and as leisure time for the United States.

paid employment.[6] If unpaid child care is treated as part of domestic work activity, then the extra time devoted by Swedes to nonmarket work activity falls by half.

Remarkably, table 7.2 indicates that Americans enjoy more leisure time than Swedes—an extra 37 hours per year or an extra 84 hours per year if unpaid child care is treated as leisure. Another striking feature of the

6. Olovsson (2009) reaches a similar conclusion from tabulations in Juster and Stafford (1991) of time devoted to nonmarket work activity in Sweden and the United States in the 1980s. Freeman and Schettkat (2005) report similar differences between the United States and Germany.

comparison pertains to time devoted to meals in the domestic household sector. Swedes spend an extra 126 hours per year, roughly 2.4 hours per week, on food preparation and cleanup. These patterns in the data are consistent with a theory of tax effects on task assignment and time allocation, which we describe in section 7.3.2. They are also consistent with evidence described later of how taxes on consumption expenditures and labor income alter the mix of market production activities.

Turning to trends in time use, Aguiar and Hurst (2006) document changes in time devoted to leisure and work activity from 1965 to 2003 by Americans aged twenty-one to sixty-five, excluding students and early retirees. They find very large increases in leisure time of six to nine hours per week for men and four to eight hours per week for women. The precise figure depends on the exact definition of leisure and the variables used to control for shifts in demographic structure. Among men, the rise in leisure mainly reflects a decline in time devoted to paid employment. Among women, it reflects a large decline in time devoted to domestic work that more than offsets rising time in paid employment. Total work time—paid employment plus domestic work—declined by about eight hours per week for both men and women over the period covered by the study. In sum, working-age Americans enjoyed large gains in leisure time after 1965, with no decline in time devoted to paid employment (figure 7.2). Because Americans spend a larger portion of their adult years in retirement now than in decades past, the gains in leisure time among all adults are even larger than suggested by the findings of Aguiar and Hurst. We are unaware of a comparable study for Sweden, but Statistics Norway reports very similar trends in time use from 1971 to 2000.[7]

7.1.4   Expansion in Market Work Activity from 2006 to 2008

There has been a significant increase in Swedish employment and hours worked since 2006, particularly in the private sector. For instance, since the second quarter of 2006, the number of hours worked per person aged sixteen to sixty-four increased by 6.7 percent in the private sector, and employment increased by 6.4 percent. We discuss recent developments in market work activity and the potential role of recent policy reforms in section 7.4.

7.1.5   Summary

We summarize the main points of this section. First, despite Sweden's rapid output growth since 1993, there was little net job creation and almost no gain in market work hours per person through 2005. As of 2005, Swedes aged sixteen to sixty-four spent 10 percent fewer hours in market work activity than in 1990. Second, Sweden has experienced a considerable shift away from public-sector employment since 1990. It is unclear how much of this

7. Available at: http://www.ssb.no/english/subjects/00/02/20/tidsbruk_en/.

shift reflects newly created jobs in the private sector rather than a reclassification of existing employment positions. Third, the time path of market work hours is strikingly different in Sweden and the United States over the past several decades. Fifty years ago, Swedes spent 200 more hours per year than Americans in market work activity; today, they spend 150 fewer hours. Fourth, broader measures of work activity that encompass time spent on unpaid domestic work show a much smaller gap between Swedes and Americans. Based on a comparison of recent time-use surveys, we find that American adults spend an extra 43 hours per year in overall work activity. Swedes spend considerably more time than Americans in unpaid domestic work, especially in food preparation and cleanup, and Americans actually enjoy greater leisure time. Fifth, the Swedish private sector has experienced a significant increase in employment and hours worked from 2006 to 2008.

7.2   Main Thesis and Lessons from Earlier Work

Our earlier work holds that institutional arrangements strongly influence national economic performance. In line with this broad thesis, we developed evidence and analysis that country-specific institutional arrangements have important effects on work activity, industry structure, activity shares of smaller and younger businesses, and the size of the underground economy.

7.2.1   Tax Burdens on Consumption and Labor

Taxes on labor income and consumption expenditures encourage substitution from the legal market sector to home production and the underground economy. To appreciate the power of taxes to depress employment and distort production decisions, consider the choice between market provision and home production in the simple case with no capital inputs. The household opts for the least-cost source of supply. In the absence of taxes, we can express the household's decision rule as

$$(1) \qquad \text{Choose market provision if: } W^B H^B > W^P H^P \Leftrightarrow \frac{W^B H^B}{W^P H^P} > 1,$$

where W^P is the wage rate of the professional supplier in the market, H^P is the production time required by the professional, W^B is the opportunity cost of household time, and H^B is the time input required in household production. According to equation (1), the law of comparative advantage governs the choice of production sector. The household opts for self-supply when it has comparative advantage at the production activity in question and opts for market provision when the professional has comparative advantage. This decision rule is socially efficient in the sense of minimizing the value of scarce time resources used up in production.

Taxes break this link between privately optimal decisions and socially efficient outcomes. To see this point, let t denote the tax rate on the household's labor income, let s denote the payroll tax rate on the professional's compensation, and let m denote the tax rate on consumption expenditures. The decision rule for the choice of production sector becomes

$$(2) \qquad \text{Choose market provision if: } \frac{W^B}{W^H} \frac{H^B}{H^P} > \frac{(1 + s)(1 + m)}{1 - t}.$$

As seen in equation (2), higher tax rates raise the threshold comparative advantage ratio at which the market solution dominates. The private choice of production sector is now governed by a tax-distorted law of comparative advantage.[8] Too few tasks are carried out in the market sector because of taxes, and too little time is spent working in the market. Conversely, too many tasks are carried out in the household (or underground) sector, and too much time is spent working outside the formal market sector.

As tax rates rise, marginal producers in the market sector are displaced by less-efficient producers in the household sector. This displacement effect lowers average productivity computed over the market and household sectors, but it raises official productivity measures, because they do not encompass the household sector.[9] Hence, the displacement effect also leads official statistics to overstate true productivity in high-tax societies relative to that of low-tax societies. This effect operates even when all workers have the same productivity and earnings ability in market-based activities. Thus, the productivity effect identified here is distinct from the idea that the tax and transfer system has bigger disemployment effects on the least productive workers.

To assess whether tax rates in the relevant range significantly alter the composition of market-based activity, Davis and Henrekson (2005a) consider fourteen rich countries with comparable data on tax rates and on the industry distribution of market activity. They identify tax-sensitive industries on a priori grounds, then investigate whether such industries have lower employment and output shares in high-tax countries. Employment and output shares are markedly lower in a broad group of tax-sensitive industries that includes retail trade, hotels and restaurants, and consumer repair services. An increase in the tax-distorted comparative advantage ratio by 25 basis points lowers the employment share in this industry group by

8. Davis and Henrekson (2005a) derive analogous decision rules when production requires capital and labor.

9. If firms differ in their ability to evade taxes, then taxes need not crowd out the least productive firms. In this case, taxes can lower average productivity and raise average pretax production costs within the formal market sector. See Palda (1998) for an analysis of this issue. Strand (2005) analyzes the efficiency consequences of taxation in a model with three production sectors—the above-ground market economy, the black market economy, and production for own use in the household. He also provides an extensive set of references to other work on the efficiency effects of income and consumption taxes in models with taxed and untaxed production sectors.

2.4 percentage points, or by 12 percent of industry employment evaluated at the mean. Similarly, a 25 basis point rise lowers the value added share by an estimated 1.9 points (13 percent). Davis and Henrekson also find that the share of market activity accounted for by eating, drinking, and lodging establishments is twice as sensitive to taxes as the broader industry group. In contrast, the share of employment in manufacturing shows a positive, statistically insignificant relationship to the tax-distorted comparative advantage ratio. These cross-country patterns support the view that taxes on labor and consumption distort the choice of production sector, and in the process, depress employment in the formal market economy.

These results also help to explain certain aspects of Sweden's industry structure. In particular, compared to countries with lower tax burdens on consumption expenditures and labor income—for example, Canada, Ireland, Switzerland, the United Kingdom, and the United States—Sweden has small employment and output shares in retail trade, consumer repair services, and eating, drinking, and lodging establishments. Production activity is relatively labor intensive in these industries and relatively easy to substitute between the market sector and home production (or the underground sector). Hence, high tax burdens push production activity in these industries out of the (legal) market sector. This interpretation finds additional support in table 7.2, which shows that Swedes devote considerably more time to domestic household work, especially meal preparation and dishwashing, than Americans.

Another type of evidence on tax-induced displacements of employment and production is available from official adjustments to Swedish GDP accounts. Statistics Sweden now makes upward adjustments to official measures of GDP in an effort to capture unrecorded black market activity. These adjustments go back to 1993, and they are largely based on an inquiry carried out in 1997 by the National Audit Office (1997). Table 7.3 reports the official adjustments by industry in 1996. The largest adjustments are for auto repair, restaurants, taxi services, and hairdressing, and the smallest are for industry and consulting. These patterns are consistent with the hypothesis that high tax rates and burdensome regulations shift the mix of (above-ground) market production away from labor-intensive activities (e.g., restaurants and hairdressing) and toward capital-intensive and skill-intensive activities (e.g., industry and consulting). A new comprehensive inquiry conducted in 2005/2006 by the Swedish National Tax Board (2006) found results consistent with the 1997 study. Total black market work is estimated at 4 to 5 percent of GDP.[10] An estimated 13 percent of all persons aged eighteen to seventy-four engaged in black market work within the previous year, an increase of 2 percentage points compared to the 1997

10. Indirect methods for estimating the size of the black market economy in Sweden tend to produce much larger numbers. See, for example, table 4.3 in Schneider and Enste (2002).

Table 7.3   **Adjustments to official GDP for black market activity by Statistics Sweden, 1996**

Industry	Black market activity, % of recorded value added
Agriculture	6.4
Forestry	8.5
Industry	0.3
Construction	10.4
Auto repair	26.4
Restaurants	16.2
Taxi services	19.2
Freight hauling	15.8
Consulting	4.0
Cleaning	5.2
Gambling	6.6
Hairdressing	34.8
Other	4.5

Source: SOU 2002:113 (Stockholm: Ministry of Finance).

study. Hours worked in the black market are estimated to have increased in roughly the same proportion.[11]

Our cross-country investigation in Davis and Henrekson (2005a) also finds that higher tax rates on labor income and consumption expenditures lead to less work activity in the formal market sector as a whole and to a larger underground economy.[12] Consider, for example, a 12.8 percentage point difference in the tax rate between two countries, which amounts to a unit standard deviation in the cross section of countries. Using data for the mid-1990s, we estimate that a tax increase of this size leads to 122 fewer hours worked per adult per year in the formal market sector, a drop of 4.9 percentage points in the employment-population ratio, and a rise in the underground economy equal to 3.8 percent of GDP. Evaluating at means in the cross-country sample, the implied elasticity of aggregate hours worked with respect to the combined tax rate on labor and consumption is −0.55. As we explain in our earlier work, our estimates reflect the direct effect of taxes

11. More specifically, a special inquiry into the underreporting of revenue in restaurants indicates an increase in black market activity in recent years: "The Swedish National Tax Board estimates, based on an extensive audit of the restaurant industry in the county of Dalecarlia, that the unreported revenue in the restaurant industry in 1995 nationwide amounted to 37 percent of total revenues of 20 billion kronor, or approximately 7 billion kronor. The degree of tax evasion has subsequently accelerated. More recent estimates suggest that unreported revenues amount to roughly double in 2002, i.e. 15 billion kronor" (Skatteverket, *Skattestatistisk Årsbok 2004*, 238; authors' translation). Fifteen billion kronor amounts to 102 percent of total value added in restaurants in 2002, according to the National Accounts.

12. Many other studies investigate the role of tax rates in cross-country differences in work activity and the size of the underground economy. Several recent studies in this area are motivated by the provocative work of Prescott (2004). See Alesina, Glaeser, and Sacerdote (2005), Davis and Henrekson (2005a), and Rogerson (2006) for references to this literature.

on labor supply and labor demand plus the effects of tax-funded welfare and social insurance programs on labor supply incentives.

Taxes on labor income and consumption expenditures also alter relative labor demands among workers in a potentially important manner. Tax-sensitive industries include eating and drinking establishments, laundry and cleaning services, child care, consumer repair services, domestic household help, and most personal services. As suggested by this list, tax-sensitive sectors tend to rely heavily on less-skilled workers with lower schooling and wages. Hence, uniform tax rates on labor income and consumption expenditures have disproportionately large negative effects on the demand for less-skilled workers, depressing their relative wages and employment opportunities.

The interaction of wage-setting institutions and high tax rates is also important in the Swedish case. Institutions that compress pretax wages reinforce tax-induced distortions in the choice between market provision and home production. To see this point, consider first the impact of institutional forces that raise wages for less-skilled, lower-wage workers. Because activities with easy substitution between home and market production rely heavily on less-skilled workers, wage floors for less-skilled workers raise the cost of production by a larger percentage in these activities. In this respect, wage floors for less-skilled workers reinforce the departures from comparative advantage induced by taxes on labor and consumption. Second, institutional forces that reduce wages for skilled workers affect their choice between home production and market provision in the same way as higher labor income taxes. Again, the effect is reinforced by tax-induced departures from the law of comparative advantage in the choice of production sector.

7.2.2   Business Tax Policy

The preceding discussion indicates that Sweden's compressed wage structure and high tax burdens on labor and consumption depress employment and output in industries that compete closely with the black market or unpaid household production. Some important aspects of Swedish business tax policy have reinforced these effects and have repressed further labor demand, as we now discuss.

Beginning in the early 1960s and continuing for three decades, effective tax rates on business income in Sweden differed tremendously by source of finance and ownership category. Debt was the most tax-favored form of financing, and new equity issues were the most penalized. Business ownership positions held directly by individuals and families were taxed much more heavily than other ownership categories. To illustrate the magnitude of these differences, table 7.4 presents effective marginal tax rates for different combinations of owners and sources of finance. Three categories of owners and three sources of finance are identified. The effective marginal tax rates

Table 7.4   Effective marginal tax rates on business income in Sweden by ownership category and source of financing, 1960, 1970, 1980, 1985, 1991, 1994, and 2005

	Debt	New share issues	Retained earnings
1960			
Households	27.2	92.7	48.2
Tax-exempt institutions	–32.2	31.4	31.2
Insurance companies	–21.7	41.6	34.0
1970			
Households	51.3	122.1	57.1
Tax-exempt institutions	–64.8	15.9	32.7
Insurance companies	–45.1	42.4	41.2
1980			
Households	58.2	136.6	51.9
Tax-exempt institutions	–83.4	–11.6	11.2
Insurance companies	–54.9	38.4	28.7
1985			
Households	46.6	112.1	64.0
Tax-exempt institutions	–46.8	6.8	28.7
Insurance companies	–26.5	32.2	36.3
1991			
Households	31.7	61.8	54.2
Tax-exempt institutions	–9.4	4.0	18.7
Insurance companies	14.4	33.3	31.6
1994			
Households	32.0/27.0[a]	28.3/18.3[a]	36.5/26.5[a]
Tax-exempt institutions	–14.9	21.8	21.8
Insurance companies	0.7	32.3	33.8
2005			
Households	27.9/22.9[a]	58.1/48.1[a]	42.7/32.7[a]
Tax-exempt institutions	–1.2	23.2	23.1
Insurance companies	18.2	44.6	42.6

Source: Calculations provided by Jan Södersten; see also Södersten (1984, 1993).

Note: The calculations assume a real pretax return of 10 percent, an asset holding period of 10 years, an asset composition identical to the actual composition in the manufacturing sector, and the following inflation rates: 3 percent in 1960, 7 percent in 1970, 9.4 percent in 1980, 5 percent in 1985 and 1991, and 2 percent in 1994 and 2005. The calculations conform to the general framework developed by King and Fullerton (1984).

[a]Excluding wealth tax; the wealth tax on unlisted shares was abolished in 1992. Hence, the higher figure applies only to the securities of listed companies.

are calculated assuming a 10 percent pretax real rate of return, an asset holding period of ten years, and an asset composition that matches the actual composition in manufacturing. A negative entry in table 7.4 means that the real rate of return is greater after tax than before tax.

Differences in effective tax rates on Swedish business income were especially large around 1980. For example, a debt-financed business investment in 1980 offering a pretax real return of 10 percent yielded an after-tax return of 18.3 percent for a tax-exempt institution such as a pension fund. The same business investment financed by a new equity issue purchased directly by households yielded an after-tax real return of −3.7 percent. More generally, debt financing was highly favored by the tax system throughout the period covered by table 7.4, and direct household ownership positions were heavily disfavored. King and Fullerton (1984) and Fukao and Hanazaki (1987) find that Swedish tax policy was extreme in these respects compared to other countries.

These differences in effective tax rates have potentially powerful effects on the organization of business activity and the industry mix of productive activity. A few examples serve to make this point. First, to the extent that debt financing is less costly and more readily available for larger and more firmly established firms, high statutory tax rates coupled with tax-deductible interest payments work to the disadvantage of smaller firms and potential entrants. Second, debt financing is more easily available to firms with ready forms of collateral. Hence, firms and sectors that intensively utilize physical capital reap greater benefits from tax code provisions that favor debt financing. This aspect of the tax system favors capital-intensive industries and modes of production relative to labor-intensive ones. Third, high tax rates on business income accruing directly to households represses many of the same activities as high tax rates on labor and consumption. Many economic activities that are highly substitutable between market provision and home production (e.g., cooking, cleaning, laundering, landscaping, home repairs) offer greater-than-average scope for self-employment, employment in small firms, start-ups, and family-owned businesses.

7.2.3 Summary

Key features of the Swedish institutional setup have depressed market work activity. Heavy tax burdens on labor and consumption repress the market provision of services with close substitutes in the black market and home production. Wage-setting institutions that compress pretax wage differentials reinforce this tax effect. International comparisons indicate that market work activity is particularly sensitive to tax rates and wage compression in labor-intensive, service-oriented activities. Many activities that fit this description also offer greater-than-average scope for self-employment, small businesses, start-ups, and family-owned businesses. In addition, Sweden's business tax policies have worked to the disadvantage of labor-intensive industries and modes of production.

7.3   Institutional Developments in the 1990 to 2005 Period

We now turn to Swedish institutional developments since the early 1990s. We consider these developments in the light of both our earlier analyses and Swedish economic performance since the deep crisis of the early 1990s.

7.3.1   Wage-Setting Arrangements

An important new wage-bargaining agreement was introduced in Sweden in 1997—namely, the Agreement on Industrial Development and Wage Formation (*Industriavtalet,* IA).[13] The IA is a further step toward more decentralized and individualized wage setting, a process that is often said to have started in 1983, when the metal workers' union defected from the centralized regime (Hibbs and Locking 2000). Under the IA, many agreements are reached that make no reference to centrally negotiated pay structures—everything is decided at the local level. Most agreements, however, still incorporate guarantees regarding minimum pay levels.

An important question is whether this new wage-setting regime also affected bargaining outcomes. After the demise of centralized bargaining in the mid-1980s, wage dispersion began to increase among blue- and white-collar workers (Edin and Topel 1997; Hibbs and Locking 2000; and Davis and Henrekson 2005b). As Lundborg (2005) documents, wage dispersion among blue-collar workers leveled off in the mid-1990s but began to rise even more sharply among white-collar workers in the private sector. Moreover, average real wages began to increase much faster among white-collar workers. From 1995 to 2005, average real wages rose by 43 percent for white-collar workers, as compared to 22 percent for blue-collar workers (based on a comprehensive wage measure that includes bonuses, paid overtime, and fringe benefits).[14] In short, the period from 1995 to 2005 saw a considerable widening of the wage gap between white-collar and blue-collar workers and a sharp increase in wage dispersion among white-collar workers (see also Fredriksson and Topel, chapter 3 in this volume).

7.3.2   Taxes on Labor and Consumption

The simple theory of task allocation sketched in section 7.2.1 identifies the tax-distorted comparative advantage ratio as a key determinant of market work activity and its composition. Motivated by this analysis, figure 7.4 plots the evolution of the tax-distorted comparative advantage ratio, or tax factor, for three types of Swedish workers. The values in figure 7.4 capture mandatory Social Security contributions, consumption taxes, and marginal tax rates on labor income.

Swedish workers faced modest tax factors in the early 1950s of around two for executives and lower for others. The tax factors rose steadily after 1952. By the late 1970s, they reached levels near four for industrial workers, above five for white-collar workers, and above eight for executives. The tax factors declined somewhat in the 1980s, dropped sharply with the tax

---

13. See Elvander (2002), Djerf et al. (2003), and Fredriksson and Topel (chapter 3 in this volume) for a more thorough description of the IA and its functioning.

14. Statistics Sweden and the Confederation of Swedish Enterprise (2006).

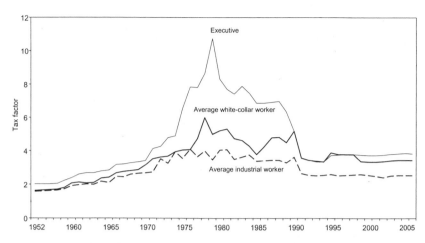

Fig. 7.4   Tax-Distorted comparative advantage ratios for three types of workers in Sweden, 1952 to 2006

Source: Du Rietz (1994) and new calculations supplied by Du Rietz.

Note: The tax factor for each category is evaluated at mean earnings each year. An executive is defined as an individual in the management group (below the CEO) in a private firm. The tax factor includes mandatory Social Security contributions paid by the employer or the employee, the marginal income tax, and the indirect taxes on private consumption. (All income is assumed to be spent for private consumption purposes.) Property taxes are excluded. The tax wedges for executives and average white-collar workers coincide between 1991 and 1998.

reform of 1990 and 1991, and crept upward in recent years as the result of higher tax rates at the local government level. As of 2006, Swedish tax factors stand at 2.54 for industrial workers, 3.44 for white-collar workers, and 3.85 for executives. The corresponding tax factors for the United States are in the interval of 1.4 to 2. While current Swedish tax factors are well below levels of the 1970s and 1980s, tax factors in the range of 2.5 to 3.9 still provide powerful incentives to shift production and employment out of the formal market sector. As a result, large parts of the service sector face harsh competition with unpaid work and the black market. These tax effects are amplified by institutions that compress the pretax wage distribution, as we explained in section 7.2.1.

Figure 7.4 does not account for some important tax-avoidance strategies. In particular, the income tax code in Sweden and many other countries provides significant opportunities for households to reduce effective tax burdens by shifting income to tax-favored sources, incurring tax-deductible expenses, and engaging in certain portfolio transactions. Before Sweden's tax reform in 1990/1991, high-income earners "could exploit a number of asset transactions to escape taxation" (Agell, Persson, and Sacklén 2004, 964). These transactions included "complex schemes of transforming corporate income into low-taxed capital gains" (964–5), an unlimited ability to subtract net negative asset income from labor income when calculating taxable income, tax-deductible interest payments, the purchase of tax-preferred assets with borrowed funds, and intrafamily debt transactions. Households also, within limits, could invest in untaxed pension funds and tax-favored savings accounts. Agell and Persson (2000) and Agell, Persson, and Sacklén (2004) present several pieces of evidence that high-income Swedish households used these tax-avoidance strategies to a significant extent.

For our purposes, the theoretical and empirical literature on these asset-based tax-avoidance strategies yields some cautionary lessons. First, effective tax factors are undoubtedly smaller than reported in figure 7.4. Second, the 1990/1991 Swedish tax reform engineered a smaller reduction in effective tax factors than suggested by figure 7.4 or by any other examination of statutory tax rates. In line with this conclusion, Malmer and Persson (1994) find that the discrepancy between taxable income and labor income declined substantially in the wake of the 1990/1991 tax reform. Similarly, Agell, Englund, and Södersten (1998) report that Swedish households initiated a rapid pay down of their debts in the early 1990s. Third, because the tax reform imposed new restrictions on asset-based tax-avoidance strategies, it is possible that the reform actually raised effective tax rates for many high-income earners. Hence, it is unclear whether and how much the tax reforms in 1990/1991 stimulated employment or how much they softened the incentives to shift certain production activities to the underground economy and unpaid household work.

7.3.3   Taxation of Business Income

The substantial tax preference for debt financing described in section 7.2.2 presupposed a policy of strictly regulated capital markets. However, the deregulation of domestic capital markets in the latter half of the 1980s greatly expanded credit availability, even as the tax system remained virtually unchanged and foreign exchange controls continued to limit investment abroad by Swedish households (Jonung 1994; Norrman and McLure 1997). Later, in 1991, the corporate tax rate was cut in half to its current value of 28 percent.[15] The conversion to a dual income tax system with a 30 percent flat tax rate on capital income in 1991 and the abolition of wealth taxation on unlisted stock in 1992 favored individual equity investments relative to the earlier situation.

The tax burden on Swedish individual ownership remained heavier than the tax burden on institutional ownership and individual ownership in most other countries (Henrekson and Jakobsson 2005). Globalization has also made it easier for large Swedish incumbents to shift their ownership stakes to foreign tax jurisdictions in order to reduce corporate tax burdens and to escape personal taxation on ownership (Henrekson and Jakobsson 2005).

---

15. At first, it was reduced to 30 percent. See Agell, Englund, and Södersten (1998) for a detailed examination of the tax reforms in the early 1990s.

Tax loopholes continue to channel individual wealth into institutional equity funds rather than owner-operated businesses. For closely held companies, there are restrictions on the payment of dividends—the so-called 3:12 rules. These rules were introduced in 1991 to prevent owners of profitable small businesses from saving on taxes by paying themselves dividends taxed at 30 percent rather than wages taxed at the marginal tax rate for labor income. The scope for dividend payments thereby was restricted to a relatively small percentage of the equity capital paid in by owners. To the extent that labor-intensive service-sector production tends to be more amenable to owner-operated businesses and operations by nonlisted firms, this is a mechanism by which market work activity is discouraged.

7.3.4   Government Production of Income-Elastic Services

On the surface, there appears to be substantial scope for private entrepreneurs in Sweden to compete with government production through public procurement programs and voucher systems in schooling, child care, and so forth. In practice, however, public providers are often insulated from competition with private business (Fölster and Peltzman, chapter 8 in this volume).

Due to the de facto public-sector monopolization of production in many income-elastic services, vast areas of the economy remain unexploited as sources of commercial growth. In particular, in the health sector, it is easy to imagine how a different organizational mode could provide a basis for the emergence of new high-growth firms. Instead, large-scale production in the manufacturing sector has been seen as a model for central parts of the production of highly income-elastic services such as health care, child care, elderly care, and education. This has had a profound effect on private-sector growth—from 1960 until the late 1990s, all net employment growth in Sweden took place in the local government sector (Rosen 1997).

These publicly produced services in many cases are highly suitable for production in private and often also small firms. The political decision to produce these services primarily through a public-sector monopoly has largely barred this area from both startup activity and the emergence of high-growth firms. To provide some evidence on this point, table 7.5 summarizes the share of private production for the major services that are fully or primarily tax financed. The private production share is very low in activities such as child care, care of the elderly, and after-school care, despite the fact that these activities are highly amenable to private, small-firm production.

7.4   Recent Policy Developments and Changes in Market Work Activity

The center-right government that took office after the September 2006 elections implemented several policy reforms aimed at increasing market work activity. In this connection, we briefly discuss the introduction of an

Table 7.5   **Sweden's private-sector production share for major services that are primarily publicly funded, 1996, 2000, and 2005 (%)**

Service	1996	2000	2005
Institutional child care (preschool)	12.5	11.8	16.7
Child care in the home (of the professional)	2.2	8.6	12.0
After-school care	4.5	—	9.2
Compulsory schooling	2.4	3.9	7.4
High school	1.9	4.4	13.4
Care of the elderly at nursing homes	8.3	10.0⎫	13.2
Care of the elderly in special apartments	5.1	11.0⎭	
Care of the elderly in their own home	2.6	7	9.7
Hospital care	4.3	—	7.3[a]
Medical consultations	28	—	28.7
Share of doctors privately employed	10	7.3	7.0[a]
Psychiatric wards	24	—	5.9
Children's dental care	5	—	9.8

Source: Werenfels Röttorp (1998) for 1996; Jordahl (2002) for 2000; Socialstyrelsen (2006) for care of the elderly in 2005; The Swedish National Agency for Education (www.skolverket.se/) for all schooling measures in 2005; and Jordahl (2006) for health and dental care in 2005.

Note: For 2005, the categories "care of the elderly at nursing homes" and "care of the elderly in special apartments" cannot be distinguished, so they comprise one category.

[a]2004. Dashed cells = data not available for that year and service.

earned income tax credit (EITC), cuts in Social Security tax rates, tax breaks for household services, and changes in job security mandates and unemployment insurance.

Sweden introduced an EITC in 2007 and modified the program in two later steps. Here, we consider the rules in effect from January 2009. The average and marginal tax rate is zero up to an annual labor income of 38,500 Swedish kronor (SEK).[16] From annual income of 38,500 SEK to 300,000 SEK, the marginal tax rate is lowered by roughly 5 percentage points (from roughly 31 percent to 26 percent). For labor income exceeding 364,000 SEK, there is no effect on the marginal tax rate, and the maximum rate is unchanged at roughly 56 percent. For older people, the taxation of labor income has been lowered even more by strengthening the effect of the EITC system for this group. The marginal tax rate is now 11.5 percent for annual labor income between 38,500 SEK and 100,000 SEK in this group.

Economic theory implies that the EITC lowers workers' gross wage demands, because they care about after-tax wages. The result is likely to be greater work activity by the affected groups. However, unions are pressing hard to undo this effect by pushing for increased minimum wages in the relevant industries. To the extent that they succeed in these efforts,

16. Using a purchasing power parity adjusted exchange rate of 9.2 SEK per U.S. dollar in 2008 (from the OECD), 38,500 SEK corresponds to about 4,200 dollars.

they will undo the positive effects of the EITC program on market work activity.

Social Security (SS) rates have been reduced for several demographic groups.[17] There was an across-the-board reduction of 1 percentage point (down to 31.4 percent), plus a further reduction of 2 percentage points for self-employed persons who opt for a thirty-day waiting period in the sickness insurance system. Prior to 2007, the SS rate for pensioners was 24 percent, but it has now been reduced to 0 percent for people above age seventy and to 10.2 percent for those aged sixty-five to sixty-nine and for those aged sixty-one to sixty-four who withdraw their public pension (allowed from age sixty-one). In addition, the SS rate has been cut to 15.5 percent (half of the regular rate) for employees aged sixteen to twenty-five, to 0 percent for people coming off disability pensions or a paid sick leave of more than one year's duration,[18] and to 0 percent for refugees who get a job while they study Swedish.

In 2007, the government also introduced a large tax break on household-related services. The maximum tax reduction is 50,000 SEK per person, amounting to 50 percent of the labor cost, including value added tax. The tasks must be performed at or in the immediate vicinity of the buyer's own home. Eligible tasks include cleaning, washing, cooking, child care, and gardening. For a household of two adults, services eligible for a subsidy of up to 200,000 SEK per year can be purchased. This is a huge reduction in the effective tax rate on many market-mediated substitutes for own-household production. Given prevailing market wages for this type of work, the tax break can be applied to roughly 800 to 1,000 hours per year of purchased services.

As an example, suppose the buyer faces the highest marginal tax rate of 56.5 percent, and the seller of household services is an older person who faces a Social Security tax rate of 10.2 percent under the new regime. In this example, the tax factor falls from 3.9 under the 2005 tax code to $(1 + 0.102)(1 + 0.25)/(1 - 0.565) \times 1/2 = 1.58$ under the 2007 regime. For persons who qualify for the zero percent tax rate under the new regime, the effective tax factor falls to 1.44. Based on the analysis and evidence previously reviewed in section 7.2.1, we anticipate that this change in the tax law will eventually stimulate a large increase in the market provision of household services. At this writing, however, there is little evidence of such an increase. Based on the experience of Finland, it takes some time for a system like this to gain momentum.[19] Moreover, families who employ help in the black market may

---

17. These reductions in SS tax rates described in this paragraph are partly offset by the fact that an earlier reduction of up to 5 percentage points on wages up to 740,000 SEK per year was rescinded in 2007 (which had been in effect since the late 1990s).

18. The 0 percent SS rate applies for a period of time that matches the duration of the previous spell of disability or paid sick leave.

19. See Niilola and Valtakari (2006).

continue to do so. In some cases, families may be unwilling to fire helpers who lack a valid work permit. In other cases, they may make payments off the books to persons who receive social welfare benefits and who, if the income were declared, would face an effective tax rate of 100 percent.

From July 1, 2007, Swedish job security mandates were relaxed, in that firms are now allowed to employ anyone for up to twenty-four months without granting tenure rights, as long as the term of employment is prefixed. A host of measures have also made it more difficult to be eligible for unemployment benefits. Examples include a requirement to accept jobs outside one's immediate expertise and an obligation to relocate for a new job if there are suitable openings. The retention rate in the unemployment insurance has been reduced from 80 percent to 70 percent of the former wage (up to a cap). Finally, the maximum number of days that one can receive unemployment benefits has been lowered. Altogether, these measures are likely to increase search intensity among jobless persons.

It is premature to quantify the impact of recent tax and labor market reforms on Swedish work activity. However, our analysis suggests that the reforms described here will stimulate market work activity, perhaps by a significant amount. Recent changes in employment and market work hours are consistent with this prediction. Figure 7.5 shows a continuing increase in employment and hours worked per person aged sixteen to sixty-four through the second quarter of 2008 (the latest available data). Since the second quarter of 2006, the number of hours worked per person aged sixteen to sixty-four rose 6.7 percent in the private sector, and employment rose 6.4 percent. These are sizeable increases, consistent with what we would expect from the recent policy reforms. However, to what extent these employment effects can be attributed to the reforms and to what extent they are due to business cycle effects is too early to tell.

7.5 Concluding Remarks

After the deep economic contraction in the early 1990s, Sweden enjoyed strong output growth relative to the 1970s and 1980s and relative to contemporaneous experience in much of the OECD and EU. However, relatively rapid output growth failed to produce much recovery in employment or market work hours. Thirteen years after the trough in 1993, hours worked per person of working age remained roughly 10 percent below their peak in 1990. International comparisons indicate that Swedes spend considerably less time in market work activity than Americans and the average for European countries.

One possible reaction to these outcomes is a shrug of complacency. If Swedes choose to enjoy the fruits of economic progress in the form of more leisurely lifestyles and a more robust social safety net, that is a perfectly reasonable, even sensible, path to follow. We think this view is too sanguine on

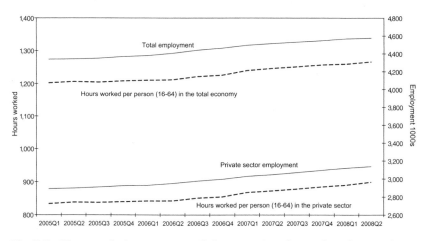

Fig. 7.5   Hours worked per person aged sixteen to sixty-four and employment in the total economy and in the private sector, Sweden 2005:I–2008:II.
Source: Statistics Sweden.
Note: All data are seasonally adjusted, and hours worked are annualized.

several counts. First, the dramatic drop in Swedish work activity in the early 1990s coincided with a sharp contraction in output and real incomes. Moreover, low work time is not taken by individuals with high income; rather, it mainly reflects persons of relatively modest means who work little or not at all (Björklund and Freeman, chapter 1 in this volume). These time-series and cross-sectional patterns do not fit a story of rising real incomes used to purchase additional leisure.

Second, the inference that low market work hours means plentiful leisure is unwarranted. Data from time-use surveys indicate that working-age Swedes devote nearly as much time to work as Americans, once domestic household work is factored into the comparison. Working-age Swedes actually enjoy less leisure than their American counterparts, according to our comparison of recent time-use surveys. The time-use evidence squares neatly with evidence that Sweden and other high-tax countries have comparatively small output and employment shares in sectors that produce time-saving goods and services.

Third, recent international studies find evidence of a sizable elasticity of aggregate work hours with respect to the combined tax rate on labor income and consumption expenditures.[20] Our own work based on cross-country variation in a sample of rich countries in 1995 yields an estimated hours elasticity of –0.55. Dew-Becker and Gordon (2006) estimate an elasticity of –0.4 based on within-country time-series variation from 1960 to 2004. We

20. See Davis and Henrekson (2005a), Dew-Becker and Gordon (2006), and Rogerson (2006).

interpret these estimated elasticity values as reflecting the combined effects of high tax rates on labor supply and demand, plus the effects of tax-funded welfare and social insurance programs on labor supply incentives. Tax and spending effects of this magnitude are likely to generate sizable welfare losses in a country with a public sector as large as Sweden's (Aronsson and Walker, chapter 4 in this volume).

Several recent policy changes have created a favorable environment for the expansion of market work activity in Sweden. The introduction of an earned income tax credit, sharp reductions in Social Security tax rates for certain demographic groups, big drops in effective tax burdens on the market provision of household services such as cooking and cleaning, the relaxation of job security mandates, and the tightening of eligibility requirements for unemployment benefits are noteworthy developments in this regard. While it is too early to confidently assess the impact of these reforms, our analysis and evidence suggest that they will raise market work activity over time, perhaps substantially. Increases in private-sector employment and work hours from 2006 to 2008 are consistent with this view.

References

Agell, J., P. Englund, and J. Södersten. 1998. *Incentives and redistribution in the welfare state: The Swedish tax reform.* London: Macmillan.

Agell, J., and M. Persson. 2000. Tax arbitrage and labor supply. *Journal of Public Economics* 78 (1): 3–24.

Agell, J., M. Persson, and H. Sacklén. 2004. The effects of tax reform on labor supply, tax revenue and welfare when tax avoidance matters. *European Journal of Political Economy* 20 (4): 963–82.

Aguiar, M., and E. Hurst. 2006. Measuring trends in leisure: The allocation of time over five decades. NBER Working Paper no. 12082. Cambridge, MA: National Bureau of Economic Research, March.

Alesina, A., E. L. Glaeser, and B. Sacerdote. 2005. Work and leisure in the United States and Europe: Why so different? In *NBER macroeconomics annual 2005,* ed. M. Gertler and K. Rogoff, 1–64. Cambridge, MA: MIT Press.

Confederation of Swedish Enterprise. 2006. *Fakta om löner och arbetstider 2006.* Stockholm: Svenskt Näringsliv.

Davis, S. J., and M. Henrekson. 2005a. Tax effects on work activity, industry mix and shadow economy size: Evidence from rich-country comparisons. In *Labour supply and the incentives to work in Europe,* ed. R. Gómez-Salvador, A. Lamo, B. Petrongolo, M. Ward, and E. Wasmer, 44–104. Cheltenham, U.K.: Edward Elgar.

———. 2005b. Wage-setting institutions as industrial policy. *Labour Economics* 12 (3): 345–77.

Dew-Becker, I., and R. J. Gordon. 2006. The slowdown in European productivity growth: A tale of tigers, tortoises and textbook labor economics. Paper presented at the National Bureau of Economic Research (NBER) Macroeconomics and Productivity Workshop. 20 July 2006, Cambridge, MA.

Djerf, O., H. Frisén, L. Hagman, and H. Ohlsson. 2003. Köpkraft och konkurrensk-raft: tredje avtalsrörelsen med Industriavtalet. *Ekonomisk Debatt* 31 (8): 16–26.

Du Rietz, G. 1994. *Välfärdsstatens finansiering.* Stockholm: City University Press.

Edin, P.-A., and R. Topel. 1997. Wage policy and restructuring: The Swedish labor market since 1960. In *The welfare state in transition: Reforming the Swedish model,* ed. R. B. Freeman, R. Topel, and B. Swedenborg, 155–203. Chicago: University of Chicago Press.

Edling, J. 2005. *Alla behövs: Blott arbetsmarknadspolitik skapar inga nya jobb.* Stockholm: Timbro. Available at: http://www.timbro.se/pdf/Alla_behovs_2.pdf.

Elvander, N. 2002. The new Swedish regime for collective bargaining and conflict resolution: A comparative perspective. *European Journal of Industrial Relations* 8 (2): 197–216.

Freeman, R. B., and R. Schettkat. 2005. Marketization of household production and the EU-US gap in work. *Economic Policy* 20 (41): 5–39.

Fukao, M., and M. Hanazaki. 1987. Internationalization of financial markets and the allocation of capital. *OECD Economic Studies* 8 (Spring): 35–92.

Håkansson, C., and A. Lindbeck. 2005. Korpi vilseleder igen: Replik. *Ekonomisk Debatt* 33 (1): 58–65.

Henrekson, M. 2001. Swedish economic growth: A favorable view of reform. *Challenge* 44 (4): 38–58.

Henrekson, M., and U. Jakobsson. 2005. The Swedish model of corporate ownership and control in transition. In *Who will own Europe? The internationalisation of asset ownership in Europe,* ed. H. Huizinga and L. Jonung, 207–47. Cambridge: Cambridge University Press.

Hibbs, D. A., and H. Locking. 2000. Wage dispersion and productive efficiency: Evidence for Sweden. *Journal of Labor Economics* 18 (4): 755–82.

Jonung, L. 1994. The rise and fall of credit controls: The case of Sweden, 1939–89. In *Monetary regimes in transition,* ed. M. D. Bordo and F. Capie, 346–73. Cambridge: Cambridge University Press.

Jordahl, H. 2002. *Vad har hänt med de enskilda alternativen?* Stockholm: Reformin-stitutet.

———. 2006. Konkurrensutsättning av offentlig verksamhet: Hur stor är effektiviseringspotentialen? IFN Policy Paper no. 8. Stockholm: Research Institute of Industrial Economics.

Juster, T., and F. P. Stafford. 1991. The allocation of time: Empirical findings, behavioral models, and problems of measurement. *Journal of Economic Literature* 29 (2): 471–522.

King, M. A., and D. Fullerton. 1984. *The taxation of income from capital: A comparative study of the United States, the United Kingdom, Sweden, and West Germany.* Chicago: University of Chicago Press.

Lindbeck, A. 1997. The Swedish experiment. *Journal of Economic Literature* 35 (3): 1273–319.

Lundborg, P. 2005. Individual wage setting, efficiency wages and productivity in Sweden. FIEF Working Paper no. 205. Stockholm: Trade Union Institute for Economic Research.

Malmer, H., and A. Persson. 1994. Skattereformens effekter på skattesystemets drifts-skostnader, skatteplanering och skattefusk [The effects of the tax reform on compliance costs, tax planning, and tax fraud]. In *Århundradets skattereform,* ed. H. Malmer, A. Persson, and Å. Tengblad, 5–364. Stockholm: Fritzes.

Niilola, K., and M. Valtakari. 2006. The effect of the tax deduction scheme for household services on the market for household services and new employment. Publication no. 310. Helsinki, Finland: Finnish Employment Office.

Norrman, E., and C. E. McLure. 1997. Tax policy in Sweden. In *The welfare state in transition: Reforming the Swedish model,* ed. R. B. Freeman, R. Topel, and B. Swedenborg, 109–55. Chicago: University of Chicago Press.

Olovsson, C. 2004. Why do Europeans work so little? Seminar Paper no. 727. Stockholm University, Institute of International Economic Studies.

Organization for Economic Cooperation and Development (OECD). 2005. *OECD Economic Surveys: Sweden.* Paris: OECD.

Palda, F. 1998. Evasive ability and the efficiency cost of the underground economy. *Canadian Journal of Economics* 31 (5): 1118–38.

Prescott, E. 2004. Why do Americans work so much more than Europeans? *Quarterly Review of the Federal Reserve Bank of Minneapolis* 28 (1): 2–13.

Rogerson, R. 2006. Understanding differences in hours worked. *Review of Economic Dynamics* 9 (3): 365–409.

Rosen, S. 1997. Public employment, taxes, and the welfare state in Sweden. In *The welfare state in transition: Reforming the Swedish model,* ed. R. B. Freeman, R. Topel, and B. Swedenborg, 79–109. Chicago: University of Chicago Press.

Schneider, F., and D. H. Enste. 2002. *The shadow economy: An international survey.* Cambridge: Cambridge University Press.

Socialstyrelsen. 2006. Äldre: vård och omsorg år 2005. Statistik Socialtjänst no. 2006:3. Stockholm: Socialstyrelsen.

Södersten, J. 1984. Sweden. In *The taxation of income from capital: A comparative study of the United States, the United Kingdom, Sweden, and West Germany,* ed. M. A. King and D. Fullerton, 87–149. Chicago: University of Chicago Press.

———. 1993. Sweden. In *Tax reform and the cost of capital: An international comparison,* ed. D. W. Jorgenson and R. Landau, 270–300. Washington DC: Brookings Institution.

Strand, J. 2005. Tax distortions, household production, and black-market work. *European Journal of Political Economy* 21 (4): 851–71.

Swedish National Audit Office. 1997. Svart arbete. RRV 1997:59. Stockholm: Riksrevisionsverket.

Swedish National Tax Board. 2006. *Svartjobb och svartköp i Sverige.* Rapport no. 2006:4. Stockholm: Skatteverket.

Werenfels Röttorp, M. 1998. Den offentliga sektorns förnyelse: vad har hänt under de senaste 15 åren? In *På svag is,* ed. H. Lundgren, B. Falk, E. Jannerfeldt, T. Svensson, and M. Werenfels. Stockholm: Timbro.

8

Competition, Regulation, and the Role of Local Government Policies in Swedish Markets

Stefan Fölster and Sam Peltzman

8.1 Introduction

In a previous analysis of competition in Sweden (Fölster and Peltzman 1997), we concluded that Sweden's high price levels and low productivity growth in the 1970s and 1980s partly could be explained by a history of lax competition policy and a shortfall of new entry into many markets. Since then, a number of markets have been at least partially deregulated. For most goods, there is now intense competition from imports. Imports have increased from 29 to 48 percent of gross domestic product (GDP) over the period from 1990 to 2005. While this largely may be an effect of globalization, changes in competition policy and deregulation have probably contributed. Competition policy has now been strengthened in line with EU policy.

In this chapter, we begin by describing the dramatic changes in competition policy, the deregulations that have been implemented, and the effects that have been found in various studies. To broaden the perspective, we relate the Swedish experience to developments in other European countries, in general, and in the United States, in particular. Our survey suggests that by and large, the Swedish policy changes have been successful. Prices are lower and/or productivity has improved in deregulated industries. Also, the aggregate productivity growth has picked up, and Swedish prices have converged to those in other countries.

In one sector of the Swedish economy, however, competition is still the exception. Local government monopolies control a large share of the

Stefan Fölster is chief economist of the Confederation of Swedish Enterprise. Sam Peltzman is the Ralph and Dorothy Keller Distinguished Service Professor of Economics Emeritus at the Booth School of Business, University of Chicago.

economy, providing a wide array of social services, schools, health care, and local utilities. This may affect prices and efficiency in these services. In addition, anticompetitive practices by local governments may inhibit the growth of local business and thus have wider consequences for local economic development. The second part of the chapter is an empirical analysis of how local government intervention affects income and employment. The analysis makes use of panel data for 290 local municipalities to examine how political economy variables such as unfair competition, cumbersome bureaucracy, small share of private competition, and high tax rates affect economic performance. The relationships are descriptive rather than causal, but the consistent pattern suggests that much more attention should be paid to local government policies in any analysis of Swedish economic performance.

8.1.1   Productivity Growth Has Picked Up

Many countries have deregulated markets in recent decades. Swedish markets initially were regulated more than most, but around 1990, Sweden embarked on a more ambitious policy of deregulation than many other countries. At the macrolevel, these policies appear to have been successful. Since the deregulation began, Sweden's productivity growth has increased relative to both the European Union and the United States. Of course, how much of this improvement can be ascribed to deregulation is an open question. Several other factors have undoubtedly contributed, among them being better macroeconomic policies and technological improvements, especially in the telecommunications industry, which is relatively important in Sweden.

8.1.2   Prices Not as High as They Were

In 1990, Sweden's overall price level was among the highest in the developed world. This is no longer the case. High-income countries tend to have higher price levels, but Sweden's 1990 price level was roughly 40 percent higher than would have been expected, given Sweden's level of GDP per capita. In 1992, Sweden abandoned its fixed exchange rate regime, and the krona was allowed to float. After a sizable depreciation, Sweden moved to roughly 20 percent above the value motivated by its per capita GDP and has since inched down to about 15 percent above that value.

Accordingly, while the combination of macro- and regulatory policies may have reduced Sweden's high price level, Sweden remains a relatively expensive country. The remaining price gap between Sweden and the Organization for Economic Cooperation and Development (OECD) average is probably due to many causes. The Swedish Competition Authority[1] concluded that about half of the difference between Swedish and OECD price

1. For example, in Konkurrensverket (2000).

levels can be explained by population size, GDP per capita, tax levels, labor costs, consumption patterns, and exchange rates. They surmised but did not present evidence that part of the unexplained difference might reflect a lack of competition.

8.1.3   Competition Policy Has Been Sharpened

Sweden's competition policy was extensively revised in the 1990s. In earlier decades, this policy had been extremely lax. Until 1993, cartel agreements were legal. Firms were free to enter agreements on price fixing, sharing of markets, and allocation of retail outlets among manufacturers. Only resale price maintenance agreements and joint tendering on public contracts were prohibited. Around 1990, there were over one thousand cartel agreements registered, affecting about 15 percent of total sales of goods and services.[2]

In our previous analysis of the Swedish manufacturing sector over the period from 1976 to 1990, we found that cartels had a substantial negative effect on output, but it was hard to find a corresponding effect on prices once the effect of regulation was accounted for.[3]

In 1993, Sweden's law on competition was brought in line with rules of the European Community. Cartel agreements and other forms of horizontal price fixing and market-sharing agreements became illegal per se. Fines were increased considerably. In 1995, Sweden joined the European Union.

The state of competition did not change immediately. Previous legal arrangements continued as informal arrangements in some cases. A number of cartels of this sort have been uncovered by the competition authority in recent years. Furthermore, it is unclear how effective competition policy has been, or for that matter, can be. An analysis of U.S. antitrust policy reveals that there is little evidence that antitrust policy has actually had much effect on consumer welfare. The reason is that market changes have worked faster against anticompetitive practices than antitrust policy (Crandall and Winston 2003).

8.1.4   Increased Competition in Retail Trade

Entry has become easier in a number of areas, from financial services to retail stores and chimney sweepers. In retail trade apart from food, foreign chains have entered on a large scale and in many cases now hold considerable market shares.

Our previous analysis showed that the food sector was an especially important example of the price-increasing effects of regulation. Prior to 1992, protection against imports was even greater than in the European Union. Entry at the food retail level was also subject to municipal zoning regulation, which was often used to protect the biggest chains. These

---

2. SPK (1992).
3. It should be noted, however, that output was more accurately measured than prices.

laws remain in place today. However, many municipalities have adopted less restrictive regulation, which has led to a gradually increasing market share for low-price stores and to some entry by new food-store chains and foreign chains. The Swedish Competition Authority found that in the period from 1997 to 2000, municipalities with a restrictive implementation of zoning regulation had less food stores per inhabitant and that a more liberal regulation appeared to lower food prices.[4] Reduced import protection in combination with increased competition in food retailing appears to have had a measurable impact on prices. From 1991, when the reforms began, to 2003, consumer prices for food increased only 5 percent, compared to an increase of more than 30 percent in the overall Consumer Price Index.

8.1.5   Natural Monopolies Have Been Deregulated

Many of the traditional natural monopolies have been deregulated rather more in Sweden than the European average, and in some cases, the United States. Comparisons made by the European Union show that all European countries have opened their aviation and telecommunications markets. Most countries, but not Sweden, still retain a partial monopoly for postal services (letters). About half of the European countries have not yet opened their electricity markets to competition. Taxi regulation prevents entry in many countries, but not in Sweden (Bekken 2003). And railways seem to be more liberalized in Sweden than in most European countries.

Nevertheless, there remain quite a number of unresolved regulatory issues in all these markets. We will give a brief account of how Sweden has tried to tackle these issues and of what the outcome has been. Comparisons with the U.S. experience of deregulation, which often predated Sweden's, provide supplementary evidence and sometimes suggest lessons for both countries.

Electricity

The electricity market was previously vertically integrated. The large producers regulated the market in various clubs under the chairmanship of the dominant state-owned Vattenfall. After deregulation in 1996, the market has been divided into three segments: generating, distributing, and trading firms. Only distribution firms are now regulated monopolies. In addition, the Nordic market has opened up so that the export and import of electricity have become easier. It is quite common now for trading firms to sell imported electricity directly to households. Consumers are billed separately by the distribution firm.

One concern in the wake of deregulation has been that the larger groups have bought up small and medium-sized networking and trading firms.

---

4. Lundvall and Odlander (2001).

State-owned Vattenfall remains a dominant actor, which increasingly has invested in other countries as well. A recent investigation by the Regulatory Reform Commission also claims that the supervising Energy Agency needs to be strengthened and given more independence.

Electricity prices are lower in Sweden than in many other European countries. In one study of the effects of deregulation on prices, Green and Damsgaard (2005) show that costs and prices are lower than they would have been without deregulation. The largest gains, due to cost savings, have accrued to the electricity-producing companies and industrial customers. Households, after an initial period of lower prices, have ended up paying higher prices. This may be due to environmental taxes, increasing demand, and integration of the Swedish electricity market with pricier markets in neighboring countries.

The vertical separation of generation from distribution in Sweden parallels developments in other countries such as the United Kingdom. In the United States, the trend toward vertical separation has been slowed considerably in the aftermath of a poorly designed restructuring in California and the scandalous collapse of Enron, which had been a major participant in the California wholesale market. The well-publicized supply shortfalls and price increases in California and the association of regulatory restructuring with a major corporate scandal have made further restructuring politically impossible for the time being. However, a gradual trend toward vertical separation continues. In retrospect, it is clear that California's experiment failed because of poor regulatory design—the uncertainty induced by the long delay between the decision to restructure and implementation of changes, the slavish devotion to spot markets at wholesale, and the frozen retail rates. Nevertheless, the experience has slowed moves toward further market liberalization elsewhere in the United States.

Aviation

Aviation has been deregulated in the same way as in most European countries and in the United States. The market is still dominated by Scandinavian Airlines System (SAS), which is partly state owned. A considerable number of entrants have come into the market, and some have left again. Profit levels are generally low. Most airports are state owned and are not exposed to competition. There are complaints of how they charge fees for their services and allocate slot times. Fees have increased considerably since 1993.

Prices have risen more than the Consumer Price Index since deregulation. But an international comparison seems to indicate that Sweden has about the same price level as many European countries for business tickets but lower prices for private tickets (Luftfartsverket 2004).

In the United States, domestic aviation has been deregulated since 1978. There has been considerable entry and exit since then. Most of the new entrants have tried to attract passengers with low fares, and this has put pressure on the established carriers. The result has been inconsistent profitability for the carriers but substantially lower prices for most consumers. For example, the industry's average yield (revenues per passenger kilometer) has declined by 55 percent in real terms since 1977. As in Sweden, the airports and airways are government monopolies, and their slot allocation and overall management policies have begun to constrain the industry's further growth.

Railways

Previously, the Swedish State Railways (SJ) had a monopoly. Since 1988, it has been merely a carrier, while the National Rail Administration operates the network. For goods, traffic entry is free, but for passenger traffic, SJ still has a monopoly on profitable traffic. Nonprofitable interregional and local traffic is procured by various authorities, often in a competitive tendering procedure.

In the railway market, prices fell for the transport of goods but increased for passenger traffic, in particular for nonsubsidized traffic. This partly is explained by new high-speed trains that were taken into operation. The subsidized traffic was often put out to tender and has seen smaller price increases. Some of the price increases are explained by the fact that the degree of subsidization has been reduced from 64 percent in 1990 to 42 percent in 2002. One study concludes that the most important competition to railways has come from long-distance bus traffic, which was also liberalized during the 1990s.[5]

The United States deregulated railway freight transportation in 1980. The industry has since consolidated from over one hundred firms into six major firms. Productivity has increased much faster than the economy-wide average, and prices have fallen considerably. For example, the cost per ton kilometer of freight has fallen 50 percent in real terms since 1980.

Postal Services

The state-owned postal service, Posten AB, has been exposed to intense competition in financial services and package delivery. At the heart of the monopoly, however, was letter delivery. Unlike the United States, this has been opened to competition, and up to one hundred firms entered. Only one firm, however, has been able to establish a large-scale operation. London Economics (2003) finds that Sweden has an average price level comparable to other European countries. Most European countries have also deregulated financial services and package delivery but retain a state monopoly in letter delivery. Swedish prices are considerably lower than still-regulated Norwegian prices.

5. Järnvägsgruppen (2003).

Telecommunications

Starting in 1993, the market gradually has been opened to more players than the former monopolist, the partly state-owned TeliaSonera. TeliaSonera also operates most of the fixed nationwide network, but it is required to allow access to other firms at regulated prices. Mobile services are provided by a number of competitors that operate their own network.

In the telecommunications market, an OECD comparison indicates that prices are relatively low in Sweden compared to other European countries.[6]

The United States began restructuring the telecommunications industry in the 1980s, when the traditional land-line long-distance market was opened to competition and deregulated. Prices, especially in long distance, have fallen considerably.

Other Markets

Apart from the network services, there have been a number of other deregulations. One example is taxis. Before deregulation, entry and prices were regulated, as they are in every sizeable U.S. city, except Washington, DC. There were often queues for taxis. After deregulation, the number of taxi companies and drivers increased considerably, but prices also increased. Burdett and Fölster (1994) analyze the effects of taxi deregulation and conclude that the decrease in waiting times of an average of four minutes per trip was well worth the price increase, given taxi customers estimated valuation of waiting time. More recently, Bekken (2003) shows that Stockholm has relatively low taxi prices compared to other European capitals.

8.1.6   Assessing the Overall Effects of Deregulation

A recent government investigation team, the Regulatory Reform Commission (2005), has attempted to evaluate the effects of deregulation in telecommunications, electricity, postal, domestic aviation, taxi, and railway markets. Their conclusion is that the number of firms has increased in all of the deregulated markets. Productivity has increased faster after deregulation in at least four of the six markets.[7] A sign of this also is that employment has decreased in all markets, except for the taxi market.

When it comes to price changes, the commission notes that prices after deregulation have increased relative to the Consumer Price Index in five of the six markets. The only exception is the telecommunications market, where prices have fallen substantially. From this, the commission infers that

---

6. OECD (2003).
7. For example, Falkenhall and Kolmodin (2004) show that labor productivity in the state-owned postal firm (Posten AB) increased by 30 percent after deregulation between 1993 and 2000. Veiderpass (2004) shows that total productivity in the electricity supply industry fell by 16.9 percent during the period from 1970 to 1995 but increased after deregulation by 19 percent.

deregulation has not had the effect of lowering prices. This is not a valid inference, however, because the relevant question is whether prices are lower than they would have been in the absence of deregulation. The studies referred to in the previous section suggest that they may be, as Sweden has relatively low prices in deregulated network markets. One explanation for these diverging conclusions is that many of the network markets have been subject to industry-specific cost increases. Electricity and aviation, for example, have been burdened with various environmental taxes. Railroads have had to pay higher electricity prices. Furthermore, prices in network markets have not increased faster than domestic services, in general. This may be a more relevant comparison than the Consumer Price Index, which is affected by falling prices for imported goods. Another aspect, however, is that competition in network markets, even after deregulation, remains far from perfect. Therefore, prices in network markets hardly can be expected to follow the same pattern as in consumer markets, where competition is unfettered. On average, consumer prices have increased 1.2 percent per year over the period from 1994 to 2004. The partially deregulated network industries previously reviewed have seen price increases of 3 percent a year during this period. Finally, completely regulated sectors such as health care and municipal services have seen price hikes of 6 percent a year.

It is possible to examine the relation between the degree of competition and the average annual price increases a bit more closely. In figure 8.1, eighteen industries have been ranked in terms of a competition index that is based on the extent of product market regulation, new entry, and a number of other factors.[8] There seems to be a surprisingly good correlation with average annual price increases. Bergman (2004) plots the unexplained (by differences in labor costs, wage tax wedges, and consumption taxes) price differences between Sweden and the European Union against our competition index and also finds a close correlation.

Even these correlations are quite crude, however, and we view them as merely suggestive.

While there is no similar data for the United States, the overall pattern is reasonably clear. All of the transportation industries that were deregulated in the late 1970s—air, truck, and rail—experienced substantially lower prices. In telecommunications and electricity, which have been partly deregulated, the picture is more mixed. The decline in telecommunications prices has been substantial, but part of this is due to technological advances rather than regulatory changes. The partial restructuring of electricity has had

8. The competition index is based on eleven variables that are graded on a scale from one to five for each branch. The variables are horizontal and vertical integration, import competition, rate of entry, industry concentration, regulation, share of private production, productivity growth, subsidies, existence of a black market, and the profit margin. The variables are weighted equally. The exact calculation is shown in Svenskt Näringsliv (2005).

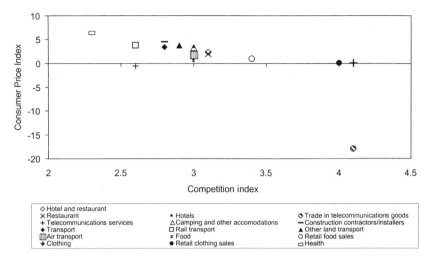

Fig. 8.1   The competition index and the average annual price increase, 1994 to 2004

effects similar to those in Sweden: declining prices for large users and little change for small users.

8.1.7   Pervasive Local Monopolies

The one area where monopolies are pervasive is in services provided by the local government sector. Local governments finance and are the main providers of health care, schools, child care, and care of the elderly. Competition in this sector is quite limited, although private provision has increased since 1990. Now, 9 percent of local public consumption is purchased from private providers, up from about 4 percent in 1990. In child care, 13 percent is produced by private providers; in elderly care, the figure is 12 percent; and in schools, it is 5 percent. School vouchers were introduced in 1991, and nearly 6 percent of all pupils use them to attend nongovernment schools.

The gradual increase in competition for local government services has had some success. For example, costs for local bus services decreased considerably in the early 1990s, as most municipalities began procuring these services in open tendering.[9] In the United States, such public tendering remains the rare exception. Several studies indicate that voucher schools have had a positive effect on academic achievement in surrounding municipal schools.[10] In the United States, there has been much discussion of school vouchers, but only a few scattered experiments have focused on poor households, and no strong conclusions about their effects have emerged thus far. Education through high school remains essentially a public monopoly in the United

---

9. Alexanderson, Fölster, and Hultén (1998).
10. For example, Bergström and Sandström (2002, 2005).

States, with 90 percent of students attending a public school usually tied to residence. The important competition in this system traditionally has come from the thousands of local school districts financed mainly by taxes tied to local property values, which might be eroded by dissatisfaction with the schools as people move to districts with better schools. However, this interjurisdictional competition has weakened. A greater proportion of school revenues now comes from outside the local school districts (states and the federal government), and recently, all school districts have come under substantially increased federal regulation.

8.1.8   Concluding Remarks

A main theme in our 1997 study was that poor productivity growth and high prices in Sweden were related to the lack of competition in regulated industries. Developments since then are supportive of that theme. Although we cannot quantify the relationship between deregulation and increased competition on one hand and higher productivity growth and lower prices in the overall economy on the other, the evidence from microstudies surveyed here suggests that these policy reforms have had a considerable effect on productivity growth and prices. This largely mirrors the experience with similar deregulations in the United States that most often were implemented a few years ahead of those in Sweden. In both countries, there is scope for further competition and an improved regulatory framework—for example, in aviation and electricity markets.

The fact that Swedish industry has been exposed to more international competition and to much stricter competition law since the early 1990s undoubtedly also has contributed to improved productivity and lower prices. The lack of new entry remains a problem in many sectors, however. In our previous study, an important finding was that the lack of new entry was a greater barrier to competition than was industry concentration. At a macroeconomic level, Sweden still has relatively few people engaged in starting new firms. Regardless of whether one compares the rate of start-ups, the share of self-employed, the number of registered firms, or other measures of entrepreneurship, Sweden appears to have less entrepreneurial activity than the European Union and much less than the United States. (See, for example, Henrekson and Stenlund 2006). Even though it is impossible to know what the optimal rate of entry is, Sweden's exceptionally low rate of entrepreneurial activity suggests that insufficient entry may inhibit competition. It is therefore of interest to examine also how competition policy affects new entry and establishment of new businesses, in general.

In the next section, we take a closer look at the competition problems in the local public sector. Specifically, we analyze the relationship between local government policies and the growth of local business, employment, and incomes.

8.2   Local Government Policies and the Private Sector in Sweden

Local governments play an important role in Sweden's public finances. Their expenditures amount to around 25 percent of GDP, and they also employ about a quarter of all Swedish workers. These are around double the comparable figures for the United States. Because of their large economic role, the tax, expenditure, and regulatory policies of these local governments can have important effects on the private sector, and that connection is the subject of this section.

Sweden's political system consists of twenty-one counties (län), which are the rough equivalent of U.S. states in terms of political geography. Each county is divided into municipalities (kommun), which are similar to a combination of U.S. counties and cities. There are 290 municipalities. Here, we focus on the municipalities, which account for around 80 percent of local government employment and 70 percent of expenditures. Our goal first is to describe some aspects of the municipalities' political economy that we can measure and then to explore the connection between those measures and the larger local economy. The analysis is in two parts. The first uses a panel of municipalities in the 2001 to 2004 period. The second part focuses on growth over the last decade. The short panel has a greater variety of data than the longer cross section, but the latter covers perhaps the more interesting data.

8.2.1   The 2001 to 2004 Panel

This part of our analysis extensively uses the results of an annual survey conducted by the Confederation of Swedish Enterprise (SN) of approximately 37,000 Swedish business owners. The survey includes two questions about the government of the municipality in which the business operates: (a) what is your experience with unfair public competition from your municipality? and (b) what is your experience with bureaucracy and regulation in the municipality? The responses are on a one to six scale, where higher numbers mean a better experience. We have municipality averages of these responses for no fewer than 273 of the 290 municipalities for 2001 to 2004.

The questions principally are about different aspects of a business owner's relations with municipal government. The first question reflects the extensive involvement of the government in local enterprises. Specifically, the 290 municipalities operate a total of 1,400 firms, with combined revenues of about 130 billion SEK per year. Around half the revenues come from housing firms. Municipality-owned utilities are common, and many municipalities also operate hotels, restaurants, retail outlets, repair shops, or other kinds of businesses that are typically privately owned. This government activity raises a concern about constriction of the private sector, either through unfair methods of competition or through more general policies.

In a survey by the Swedish Competition Authority, two of three firm owners claimed to be exposed to competition from government services.[11]

In the SN survey that we use later, firm owners were also asked about the problems they encountered in competing with their municipality. The most commonly mentioned problems are as follows:

- *Sales below costs.* Municipal agencies frequently sell at marginal cost, because fixed costs are already covered by tax revenue. For example, the municipal park administration frequently sells excess plants to the general public at low prices.
- *Subsidies to some actors on the market.* Municipal agencies provide subsidies to municipal sport facilities or provide free labor in unemployment programs to municipal firms.
- *Tendering.* Competition between municipal and private companies is rigged in favor of the municipal firms.
- *Conflict of interest.* An example is that a municipal agency that controls fire-security standards also sells consultancy services on fire security.

At the state and county levels, there are also a large number of government agencies and state- and county-owned firms that affect competition. In one survey of government agencies, one-fourth of all agencies were found to be active producers in private markets (Bergdahl 2000). The government is thus both a competitor and a potential source of contracts for the private sector. In the context of the survey question, a private business person would give low marks to a municipality that favored or subsidized a government-owned competitor or foreclosed a market entirely to private supply.

The second question in the SN survey, which is about bureaucracy and regulation, would apply to all businesses, not just those facing government competition. We will soon see, however, that there is a large common element—call it perceived business friendliness—in the answers to these two questions.

Swedish municipalities have been increasingly privatizing some activities. In the aggregate, the share of municipally financed services that is provided by private contractors has increased from 4 percent to 9 percent since 1990. There are, however, large regional differences. In Stockholm, about 20 percent is purchased from private providers, and private contracting is extensive in the rest of the Stockholm region. However, in about half of all municipalities, the share is close to zero. We use the percentage of a municipality's budget spent on private contracts as another indicator of the local political economy.

Finally, we use two broad measures: one political, the other fiscal. Politically, municipalities are governed by municipal councils. These have anywhere from 31 to 101 members, depending on population, and they are

---

11. Konkurrensverket (2004).

elected every four years. The last election occurred in 2002, which is conveniently in the middle of the 2001 to 2004 period that we analyze. The allocation of seats among parties is determined by proportional representation. We use a simple right-left summary of this allocation. The right-wing share is based on the seats held by the four main right-of-center parties (Moderates, Center Party, Liberals, and Christian Democrats), while the left-wing share is based on representation of the three main left parties (Greens, Social Democrats, and Left Party). Together, the seven main parties hold 95 percent of the seats, but the minor parties can be important locally.[12]

Our fiscal measure is the local tax rate. Most revenue for county and municipality government is raised by a tax on individual income (after exemptions and deductions). The rates reflect the division of spending between the two levels of government, with the municipality tax around twice the county tax. The combined local tax rate averages around 25 percent of unadjusted income and over 30 percent of taxable income.

Our goal is to see if local public policies plausibly affect the size of the local economy, with particular reference to the private sector. For example, does a municipality's private sector grow if it adopts policies that are friendly to the private sector? Does any private-sector growth enlarge the overall economy, or does it just replace government activity? To answer such questions, we employ a variety of measures of the municipality's macroeconomy. These include the following:

- Employment—total and private sector: these are for workplaces located within the municipality.
- Individual income and individual plus enterprise income: these are the amounts assessed for collection of local and national taxes. Individual income approximates wage and salary payments in the national accounts. Each municipality taxes its own residents.[13] Accordingly, one municipality is credited with income that may have been earned by its residents at a workplace in another municipality. The enterprise income principally is the capital income that is generated at workplaces in the municipality (and that is taxed at the national level).
- The private-sector share of household income: the numerator is wages and benefits received from the private sector. The denominator adds to these wages and benefits from the public sector plus publicly financed transfers.
- Private workplaces in the municipality: a workplace is similar to an establishment in U.S. data (i.e., the basic microunit for industry

analysis). Total private-sector activity equals activity per workplace multiplied by the number of workplaces. Accordingly, an increased number of workplaces need not imply a larger private sector if there are many small new workplaces.

None of these measures directly captures activity in the unreported shadow economy. By some measures, this may comprise 5 to 15 percent of GDP. Accordingly, municipality policies that negatively affect private business activity may be partly offset by greater activity in the shadow economy.

Tables 8.1 through 8.3 provide some descriptive data and correlations. They are mainly self-explanatory, but some highlights deserve mention. Table 8.1 shows the business community to be faint in its praise of the local public sector. The scores hover below the middle of the one to six range, and there is no discernible trend. By contrast, as mentioned previously, private contracting is growing rapidly, with the private share of municipal budgets having nearly doubled over the 1997 to 2003 period. Politically, municipalities tilt slightly left. There was small but nontrivial party turnover in the 2002 elections, which led to slightly more right-left polarization than before. Both tables 8.1 and 8.2 highlight again the importance of Sweden's public sector: over half of household income in the average municipality comes from public-sector employment or transfers.

Table 8.3 provides descriptive correlations (panel A) and regressions (panel B). The variables in the latter are chosen somewhat arbitrarily, and no causal inferences should be drawn from them (especially the between-municipality regressions in part 1 of panel B). Our goal here is to give the reader a sense of the important regularities (and nonregularities) in the makeup of the political economy of Swedish municipalities. Panel A, which is dominated by between-municipality effects, shows that the municipalities most friendly to business (high survey scores, relatively low tax rates, high private-contract shares) tend to have relatively large private sectors and lean to the right politically. The between-regressions in panel B suggest that both these factors (and where relevant, lower tax rates) contribute independently. The one wrinkle here is with private contracting. This has gone furthest in large, high-income cities and in the Stockholm area, where the private-contract share is over double the national average. Neither city size nor income nor location seems consistently related to the other indicators.

The within-municipality regressions (panel B.2) confirm some of the cross-sectional patterns. So, a tilt to the right in the 2002 elections or an increase in tax rates tends to be associated with lower scores on the SN survey. However, these regressions are more interesting for what they do not show. For example, each includes among the regressors an estimate of the exogenous component of the size of the local economy. This is derived from the presample period industry composition of local employment and

Table 8.1   **Descriptive statistics: Political economy of Swedish municipalities, 2001 to 2004**

	Sample size	Mean	Standard deviation	Within SD	Notes
Confederation of Swedish Enterprise survey					
Unfair public competition?	1,142	3.19	0.48	0.24	1
(1 = big problem, 6 = no problem)					
2001	273	2.87	0.47		2
2002	273	3.11	0.40		2
2003	273	3.56	0.39		2
2004	273	3.19	0.39		2
Quality of bureaucracy and regulation					
(1 = bad, 6 = excellent)	1,142	2.66	0.27	0.14	1
2001	273	2.61	0.27		2
2002	273	2.64	0.28		2
2003	273	2.71	0.27		2
2004	273	2.69	0.27		2
Municipal council seats, shares					
Right-wing parties	580	0.45	0.12	0.03	3
Left-wing parties	580	0.50	0.11	0.03	3
2002 election transitions					
Right majority gained	18				4
Right majority lost	12				4
Left majority gained	20				4
Left majority lost	15				4
Local tax rates (%)					5
Total	1,158	31.32	1.13	0.42	
Municipality	1,158	21.25	1.32	0.21	
County	1,154	10.10	0.54	0.33	
Private contracting (%)					6
2001 to 2003	868	6.11	4.81	1.32	
2001	289	5.51	4.19		
2002	289	6.21	4.94		
2003	290	6.62	5.20		
1997	287	3.57	3.11		7

Notes: Subsequent regressions may use transformations of these variables. "Within SD" is the standard deviation within municipalities, across years, and net of year fixed effects. 1 = sample includes municipalities with missing data for some years. 2 = sample includes only municipalities with data in all years. 3 = share of seats in the 1998 and 2002 elections held by the main right-wing parties (Moderates, Liberals, Christian Democrats, Center). 4 = majority means that the coalition has over 50 percent of the seats. There are 580 potential transitions for the 290 councils in 2002. 5 = local tax or left-wing parties (Green, Social Democrats, Left). Other parties not classified. 6 = payments to private contractors as percent of municipality's total expenditures. 7 = shown for comparison only.

the within-sample period *national* trends in industry employment.[14] That expected employment variable has no consistent relation to the political

14. Specifically, we have a roughly one-digit industry breakdown of employment by municipality. We take the 1999 composition as a base year. Then, we multiply the base-year employment in each industry in each municipality by an index (1999 = 1.0) of total Swedish

Table 8.2   Descriptive statistics: Economic variables, Swedish municipalities, 2001 to 2004

	Observations	Mean	Standard deviation	Within SD	Notes
Aggregate indicators (per capita)					
Personal income (SEK 000)	1,157	141.18	16.79	2.070	1
Personal + enterprise income (SEK 000)	1,157	152.09	25.13	7.290	1
Employment (2001 to 2003)	868	0.40	0.09	0.009	2
Private sector					
Share of household income (2001 to 2003)	868	0.49	0.08	0.007	3
Share of employment (2001 to 2003)	869	0.62	0.08	0.015	4
Private workplaces per 1,000	1,158	107.46	29.96	3.280	

Notes: Subsequent regressions may use transformations of these variables. "Within SD" is the standard deviation within municipalities, across years, and net of year fixed effects. 1 = assessed income before deductions and exemptions for assessing local and national taxes. Local taxes are assessed only on personal income. 2 = employment at workplaces located in the municipality. 3 = household income from privately financed wages and benefits/(private + public wages and benefits + public transfers). 4 = employees at privately owned workplaces/employees at all workplaces.

economy variables. Thus, we can rule out, for example, that incipient good times become reflected in business peoples' praise for the local government or in a rightward tilt politically. Also, the last within-regression suggests that business perceptions of unfair competition do not move significantly in the short run when the private sector receives more municipal contracts.

Finally, all of the correlations and regressions suggest that the two elements of the SN survey may be measuring much the same thing. The two are highly correlated across and within municipalities, and they share similar coefficients in the between-regressions. Accordingly, we henceforth will work with an average of the two elements, which we chose to regard as an overall indicator of probusiness policies.

8.2.2 The Local Economy and Political Economy

Table 8.4 contains a more systematic look at the data. It shows results of within- and between-municipality regressions in which the dependent variable is some economic outcome and in which one of the political economy variables is on the right-hand side. This procedure in effect treats the political economy measures as alternative depictions of similar underlying local policies, a view which is roughly consistent with the data in table 8.3. We also include a couple of regressions with two of the political economy variables on the right-hand side to indicate that nothing much hinges on our estimation strategy. The within-regressions are identified from movements, net of fixed-year effects, over three or four years within each of the 290 munici-

employment in that industry for each year. The result is an estimate of what total employment in the municipality would have been if employment in each of its industries had grown at the national average rate after 1999. This estimate is unaffected by any municipality policy change or political shift after 1999 (that differs from the national average).

Table 8.3　　　　Correlations and descriptive regressions: Political economy variables

Notes	Unfair public competition (1)	Municipal bureaucracy and regulation (2)	Local tax rate (3)	Right-wing seat share (4)	Private contract (%) (5)
	A Correlation coefficients, political and economic variables				
Municipal bureaucracy/regulation	.61				
Local tax rate	−.23	−.27			
Right-wing seat share	.37	.33	−.37		
Private contract (%)	.24	.13	−.46	.34	
Personal income per capita	.28	.14	−.31	.15	.66
Private-income share	.35	.35	−.55	.36	.49
Private-employment share	.34	.39	−.39	.33	.21
Private workplaces per capita	.12	.01	.15	.33	−.08
Population (log)	−.15	−.06	−.38	.06	.42
Stockholm region = 1	.15	.05	−.36	.18	.69
	B Descriptive regressions				
	1. Between-municipalities coefficients				
1　Unfair public competition			−.019[a]		.369[a]
1　Municipal bureaucracy			−.380		
Local tax rate	−.186	−.156			−.714
Right-wing seat share	1.649	1,435	−.658[a]		7.559
Private contract (%)	.015[a]	−.001[a]	−.061		
Per capita income (log)	.028[a]	.099[a]	.941[a]	−.242	14.315
Private-income share	3.842	4.370	−3.768	.706	−9.356
Population (log)	−.390	−.222	−.271	−.002[a]	.854
Stockholm region	−.151[a]	−.634	.109[a]	.038[a]	7.459
Between R-square	.53	.28	.48	.17	.69
Number of observations (municipalities)	851 (289)	851 (289)	851 (289)	578 (289)	851 (289)
2	*2. Within-municipalities coefficients*				
3　Expected employment (log)		−6.427[a]		−.366[a]	10.054[a]
Unfair public competition					.035[a]
4　Municipal bureaucracy and regulation	.82				
Local tax rate		−.153		−.008	.385
Right-wing share		.169[a]			1.098[a]
Private contract (%)		.003[a]			
Within R-square		.55		.07	.15
Number of observations (municipalities)	1,142 (290)	851 (289)		578 (289)	851 (289)

Notes: 1 = expressed as a standardized (0,1) variable. 2 = all regressions include year and municipality dummies. Standard errors (not shown) are clustered by municipality. 3 = predicted employment, given presample industry composition of municipality and national trends in industry-specific employment. See text. 4 = first column gives within-municipality correlation between "unfair public competition" and "municipal bureaucracy/regulation." Subsequent results on this line and for the next column are for a standardized (0,1) average of the two standardized variables.

[a]Coefficients have *P*-value > 0.05. All others have *P*-values < 0.05.

palities. The between-regressions are just cross-municipality averages with added controls for municipality population and the Stockholm region.[15] As expected, the within-results tend to be weaker, but the presumed direction of causality is perhaps a bit easier to swallow than for the between-regressions.

15. In the Swedish context, this region is an outlier. Per capita income here is around 20 percent above the sample average, as is the private share of household income and employment. We also tried dummies for Sweden's far north, which lies at the other end of these distributions, but these never proved significant. Table 8.4 does not show any of the results for these controls, because they are peripheral to our inquiry. In summary, larger municipalities, and of course the Stockholm region, have above-average incomes, employment, and private-income

Table 8.4   Local public policies and the local economy and private sector, 2001 to 2004

| | | Political economy variable | | | | | | |
| | | SN survey[a] (1) | | Tax rate[a] (2) | | Private contracts[a] (3) | | Right-wing share[a] (4) | |
Notes	Economic outcome[b]	Coefficient	t	Coefficient	t	Coefficient	t	Coefficient	t
	Total (per capita, logs)								
	Individual + enterprise income								
1	Within	.004	0.9	−.011	2.7	.001	1.1	.034	0.9
1	Between	.022	3.1	−.024	4.0	.008	3.8	.059	1.2
	Within (multi)[a]	.003	0.6	−.013	3.3				
	Between (multi)[a]	.015	2.0	−.017	2.5				
2	Employment (net of expected)								
	Within	.004	1.7	.008	2.8	.002	2.1	−.062	1.2
	Between	.013	4.0	−.008	3.5	.002	2.0	.103	5.2
	Private-sector shares of								
3	Household income								
	Within	.002	2.3	−.002	2.2	−.0001	0.4	.024	1.6
	Between	.042	10.8	−.032	9.2	.004	3.1	.194	6.2
	Within (multi)[a]	.002	2.0	−.002	2.5				
	Between (multi)[a]	.033	7.6	−.016	4.4				
	Employment								
	Within	.002	1.2	−.001	0.5	.0004	0.6	.023	0.8
	Between	.047	9.2	−.035	7.9	.005	3.1	.228	5.8
2	Employment (net of expected)								
	Within	.001	0.8	−.0003	0.1	.0001	0.8	.011	0.4
	Between	.016	5.4	−.017	6.9	.005	5.4	.153	7.5
	Private workplaces (per capita, log)								
	Within	.003	0.9	.007	3.4	.002	2.0	−.062	1.1
	Between	.006	0.3	−.003	0.2	.016	3.2	.958	8.4

Notes: 1 = Each "within" regression includes year and municipality dummies, and standard errors are clustered by municipality. Each "between" regression includes the log of population and a dummy for the Stockholm region. Coefficients for all these controls and regression summary statistics are not shown. Sample sizes vary according to the variables: total income, the SN survey, right-wing seat share, and tax rates are available for most municipalities for 2001 to 2004. Employment, private workplaces, private contracts, and private-household income shares are available for 2001 to 2003. There are 290 municipalities. 2 = Expected employment is computed as described in text. We have a similar but noisy measure for private employment. It is the expected employment in industries with mainly private employers (all one-digit industries, except government, health, and education). For total employment, we deduct the log of expected employment from the log of actual employment. For the private-employment share, we use our noisy measure of expected private employment to construct an expected private-employment share and deduct that from the actual private-employment share. All employment data are for workplaces in the municipality. Thus, per capita employment can and does occasionally exceed 1.0. 3 = household income from privately financed wages and benefits/(private + public wages and benefits + public transfers). The denominator includes government transfers, as well as government wages and benefits.

[a]Dependent variable in each regression is the indicated economic outcome. The political economy variable in each column is entered separately, except for regressions denoted (multi), where both indicated variables are entered

[b]Economic outcomes under "total" are municipality totals divided by population. "Private-sector shares" are the fraction of the total originating in the private sector. The "SN survey" is a standardized (0,1) variable that averages the standardized values of "unfair public competition" and "municipal bureaucracy and regulation" as described in table 8.3. Other variables are as described in tables 8.1 through 8.3.

All of the results need to be taken with some caution: undoubtedly, causality runs both ways, and these data are too crude to do much more than state

shares. Private-employment shares are unrelated to population (but higher around Stockholm). Private workplaces per capita are more numerous in the smaller municipalities (but there is no regional difference).

that caveat.[16] Accordingly, we try to emphasize the more-or-less consistent patterns in the data.

While individual results vary in strength, the broad pattern can be gleaned from the first two columns of table 8.4. Municipalities that business people perceive as friendly and that have lower tax rates tend to have higher incomes, which are generated in larger private sectors. That pattern shows up in both the short-run (within) and long-run (between) relationships. The only wrinkle is the significant positive within-coefficient of local tax rates, combined with the equally strong negative between-effect, in the total employment regressions. One inference is that public-sector expansion raises employment in the short run but reduces it in the long run.

Some of the magnitudes in the between-regressions are quite substantial. Consider, for example, the –0.024 between-coefficient for local tax rates at the top of column (2). This is an estimate of the effect of a +/–1 point move in the local tax rate on the log of per capita income. A 1-point move in local tax rates is around 3 percent, so the –0.024 coefficient implies that about three-fourths of the potential revenue from a tax increase ultimately is lost because of erosion of the tax base.[17] While this estimate of the reduction of the tax base may seem large, we would suggest that the result not be dismissed lightly. A reason for doubt would be that the tax rate is proxying for some force that makes intrinsically low-income municipalities adopt high tax rates. If that is true for Sweden, it is certainly not generally true. For example, while we have not done the same simple between-state exercise for the United States, we suspect it would show, if anything, results opposite to those we find for Sweden: the high tax rate states in the United States (New York, California, Massachusetts) include some with the highest per capita incomes. It is not the case that low-income Swedish municipalities need to have higher tax rates in order to provide the services they are mandated to offer. A state redistribution scheme fully compensates municipalities for most structural causes (such as demography) of lower tax revenue or higher spending on services.

The between-tax coefficients for the private-sector income and employment shares are even more startling. While some of the variables are not directly comparable, it is worth tracing through the implications of a 1-point local

16. We gave into the usual temptation to search for instruments. For example, we tried using the results of the 2002 municipal elections to instrument for some of the other policy variables. However, as table 8.3 suggests, the connection here is too weak for this kind of strategy to be useful.

17. For example, suppose a municipality with income of 100 now has a local tax rate of 31.32 percent (the sample average of the municipality, plus county tax rate). So, it collects 31.32 in taxes. Now the municipality wants to raise revenue by 1.00, so it raises its tax rate to 32.32. However, the regression implies that a 1-point tax increase will reduce income by approximately 0.024 percent. So ultimately, the tax base will decline from 100 to 97.60. The 32.32 percent tax on the 97.60 income will yield 31.54 in revenue, which is only 0.22 higher than the original revenue of 31.32. So, 0.78 of the potential revenue will be lost due to the erosion of the tax base following the tax increase.

tax rate increase for the size of the private sector if the between-coefficients are causal: as mentioned, total income would fall 2.4 percent. Now read down column (2) to the –0.032 between-coefficient for the private share of household income, and note from table 8.2 that this share averages just under half (0.49). So, the 1-point tax rate increase would reduce the private share to around 0.46. All in all, these results imply that private-sector-based incomes would fall by nearly three times the percentage increase in the tax rate.[18] The same exercise for private employment yields a percentage decline that ranges from the same to twice the percentage tax rate increase.[19]

The between-coefficients in the SN survey also imply sizeable effects. Again, the caveat about causality is in order (as is the counter-implication of U.S. experience, where low-income states and cities often adopt business friendly policies to attract businesses to their area). For example, the 0.022 coefficient near the top of column (1) suggests that per capita income will rise by 4.4 percent if a city moves from moderate hostility (1 standard deviation below the mean) to moderate friendship toward business (1 standard deviation above the mean) on this survey.[20] This may not sound like much, but

18. Consider the municipality in the previous footnote that raises its tax rate by 1 point and thereby suffers a reduction in its tax base of 2.4 percent, from 100 to 97.60. According to table 8.2, 49 percent of the average municipality's household income is derived from the private sector. Though the tax base includes enterprise income as well as household income, we will assume for simplicity that 49 of the 100 of initial income came from the private sector, and the remaining 51 came from the government sector. After the tax increase, not only does the income decline to 97.60, but a smaller percentage also comes from the private sector. Specifically, the –0.032 regression coefficient in the private-income share regression implies that the private-income share declines from 0.49 to 0.458. Thus, private-sector income will be 45.8 percent of the 97.60 total income, or 44.70. This is almost 9 percent (8.78 percent) below the pretax increase private-income level of 49. In sum, a tax increase of just over 3 percent (+ 1/31.32) reduces private-sector incomes by a percentage almost three times as great.

19. The larger estimate is based on the –0.035 between-coefficient in column (2) in the private-employment share regression. The smaller estimate is based on the –0.017 coefficient in the regression immediately below that. We will illustrate the larger estimate by supposing that a municipality has 1,000 employees prior to a 1-point increase in the local tax rate, from the sample average of 31.32 percent to 32.32 percent. Of these 1,000 workers, 620 work in the private sector (based on the sample average private-sector share in table 8.2). The between-coefficient in the total employment regression (–0.008) implies that the tax increase will reduce total employment by 0.8 percent to 992 workers. The –0.035 coefficient in the private-employment share regression implies that the 1-point tax increase will reduce the private-sector employment share from 0.62 to 0.585. Accordingly, after the tax increase, 58.5 percent of the 992 workers, or 580 workers, will be employed in the private sector. This is 6.5 percent fewer private-sector workers than the 620 who were employed prior to the tax increase. The 6.5 percentage reduction in private employment is around twice the percentage increase in the tax rate.

20. Note that the SN survey variable is scaled to have a mean of 0 and standard deviation of 1. So, the coefficient of 0.022 measures the effect of a 1-standard-deviation change in the survey score. The 2-standard-deviation move described here would therefore raise income by twice the coefficient, or approximately 4.4 percent.

But the reader should not take the estimate literally. The coefficient is measuring a variety of forces summarized in one variable—the SN survey. When we enter both the SN survey variable and the tax rate in the same between-regression, the coefficient of the survey declines around 40 percent (and the –0.024 tax coefficient drops by around a fourth).

in egalitarian Sweden, it is around a fourth to nearly a half of the standard deviation of per capita income across Swedish municipalities.[21] The implications for the size of the private sector of the relevant between-regressions are even more dramatic.[22]

The remaining political economy variables—private contracting and party shares in the municipal council—mostly echo the preceding results. Generally, higher aggregate incomes and greater private-sector shares tend to be associated with municipalities that have more private contracting or that lean to the right politically. However, the effects here tend to be measured a bit less precisely than the tax rate and SN survey effects.[23]

The private workplace variable behaves differently than the other measures of the private sector. There is no robust evidence that business friendly policies are associated with more private businesses. Indeed, the short-run (within) tax rate effect is significantly positive. Recall, however, that the number of private workplaces can increase, even if the private sector contracts in the aggregate. Thus, the results in column (2) of table 8.4 hint that new workplaces opening in the wake of a tax increase are smaller than average and make up for only part of the reduced activity at established workplaces. To some extent, this apparently odd stimulus to private workplaces from a tax increase may reflect the greater ease with which small workplaces can evade taxes by operating partly in the shadow economy.

On the whole, we think the results in table 8.4 should encourage a broader investigation into the impact of local public policies on economic activity, in general, and on private-sector activity, in particular. Some of the individual results are weak, and we would reiterate caution about interpreting each result as a causal effect of a particular policy. However, we would emphasize the broad pattern in the data: municipalities that show up well on most any probusiness metric or that move in that direction also tend to have better-performing local economies and larger private sectors. These results

21. From table 8.2, note that the mean of the per capita income variable is around 150,000 SEK, with a standard deviation of around 25, or 17 percent. So, 4.4 percent is around a fourth of this latter figure. Note, however, that the between-regression includes controls for population and Stockholm, which reduce the unexplained standard deviation to around 10 percent. Accordingly, a 4.4 percent income gain would be nearly half a standard deviation for average-sized municipalities, either within or outside the Stockholm region.

22. For example, if a municipality with income of 100 raises its survey score by 2 standard deviations, the between-coefficient in the total income regression (0.022) implies that total income will rise by twice the coefficient, or 4.4 percent, to 104.40. Prior to the score improvement, 49 of the 100 income was from the private sector (based on the 0.49 private-sector share mean in table 8.2). According to the between-coefficient in the private-income share regression (0.042), the private-income share would rise from 0.49 to 0.532. Private income would then be 53.2 percent of the 104.40 total, or 55.54. This is 13.3 percent more than the initial level of 49, or in percentage terms, three times as much as the increase in total income.

23. They also tend to be smaller numerically. For example, the results imply that only a small part of the effects of raising the tax rate by 1 percentage point would be offset by devoting all of the revenue to private-sector contracts.

for Sweden are similar to those found for the United States and India, where the probusiness metric in both cases concerned labor legislation.[24]

8.2.3   Long-Term Growth and Local Public Policies

In tables 8.5 through 8.8, we look at the connection between local policies and growth rates rather than the level of local economic activity. Specifically, we first ask how the policies that a municipality had in place in the early 1990s are related to the municipality's growth over the subsequent decade or so. We think the answer to that query reinforces the previous hints about the effects of local policies. Then, we ask how policy changes within a municipality during the decade are related to growth within the period, and this adds still more weight to the preceding results.

We focus on the period from the early 1990s and forward rather than using an even longer period, because prior to the 1990s, municipalities were subject to a form of state subsidies that may have given rise to quite different relations.[25]

We have only two measures of the local political economy available to us for the early 1990s. These are the local tax rate[26] and the party distribution of seats resulting from the 1991 municipal election.[27] Accordingly, the growth measures and policy indicators are summarized in table 8.5, and table 8.6 investigates whether growth in a municipality's economy over the subsequent decade is related to these two indicators of the initial conditions in the political economy of the municipality.

Because of the decade-long time frame, we drop the assumption implicit heretofore that population is exogenous, and we treat it as endogenous, along with other aggregates such as employment and income. Indeed, resource mobility over long periods suggests that much of the impact of one municipality's policies will show up in such aggregates rather than, say, in wage rates or in the size of the private sector. For example, a positive demand shock to the size of one municipality's private sector may raise per capita wage and business incomes in the short run, but that will induce migration of resources

24. Holmes (1998) found that U.S. counties (similar to Swedish municipalities) on the probusiness side of a state border grew substantially faster than adjacent counties on the antibusiness side of the border. Besley and Burgess (2004) found that Indian states that amended their labor laws in a prolabor direction experienced subsequent decreases in (formal) economic activity compared to states that did not change their labor laws.

25. During the 1970s and 1980s, municipalities received state transfers as a share of their expenditure. This meant that municipalities that raised taxes received matching state funding and could increase their expenditure and employment by about twice the increase in tax revenue. This was a main engine for the large increase in public-sector employment in the period from 1970 to 1990. It also meant that municipalities that raised taxes faster may well have seen greater increases in employment during that period.

26. At that time, this included a small parish tax in addition to the municipal and county tax. The parish tax was eliminated in the mid-1990s.

27. The next election occurred in 1994. When the initial year of any growth rate is 1994 or later, we use the 1994 results as the initial condition.

Table 8.5   **Growth rates and initial conditions: Swedish municipalities, 1993 to 2004, summary statistics**

Growth rate variables	Mean	Standard deviation	Unit
A. Size of the economy			
Population	−0.30	0.78	% per year
Employment	0.36	1.05	% per year
Income (individuals + enterprises)	3.88	1.03	% per year
Income per capita	4.17	0.52	% per year
B. Private sector			
Employment share	0.603	0.508	parts of 100 per year
Income share	0.474	0.273	parts of 100 per year
Workplaces per capita	0.78	1.08	% per year
Initial conditions			
1993 local tax rate	31.66	1.22	% points
1991 right-wing party share	0.497	0.107	share

Note: Growth rates are measured over the decade 1993 or 1994 to 2003 or 2004, except workplaces for which initial year is 1997 and private share of household income for which initial year is 1995. Income is nominal SEK. Deduct approximately 1.3 percent per year for real growth rates.

to the municipality. The migration will expand aggregates such as employment and population while bringing per capita incomes back down. The tax base and hence tax revenues will also expand, offsetting some of the effects of the demand shock on the relative size of the private sector.

A long-run adjustment process such as this seems consistent with the results in table 8.6, which reveals substantial effects of the initial conditions on subsequent growth. The direction of these effects is entirely consistent with the previous analysis of the first few years of the new millennium, where the political climate in the early 1990s was friendlier to business (low taxes, high right-wing party seat shares) growth over the subsequent decade. This holds true for most every variable examined, including per capita and private-sector share variables.[28] But the largest effects numerically, and the most reliable statistically, tend to show up, as expected, in the overall size of the local economy. The results are robust to controls for the expected growth of the local economy, for the Stockholm region, and for the initial size of the municipality.[29]

The magnitudes of some of the effects implied by table 8.6 are surprisingly

28. The only exception is the marginally significant negative coefficients of the right-wing seat share in the private-employment share regression.

29. Usually, adding the Stockholm region dummy results in a smaller estimated tax rate effect. This reflects the fact that the Stockholm region had lower initial tax rates and higher subsequent growth rates than the rest of Sweden. It is not clear to us that this average difference between the Stockholm region and the rest of Sweden should be treated as exogenous, which is implicitly what we are doing by adding the Stockholm area dummy to the regression.

Table 8.6   Growth of Swedish municipalities, 1993 to 2004 and initial conditions

Dependent variable: Annual growth rate or change	Beginning of period value of				Expected growth of				Other controls		R-square	Root mean square error
	Right-wing share		Local tax rate		Employment		Private share of employment		Stockholm area	Population		
	Coefficient	t	Coefficient	v	Coefficient	t	Coefficient	t				
Total economy												
1. Population	1.498	4.1	−0.330	9.4							.40	.61
	2.053	7.8	−0.146	4.7	0.578	3.2			P	P	.65	.47
	2.341	8.5	−0.122	4.0	1.645	7.1			P	P	.66	.46
2. Employment	3.918	7.5	−0.156	2.9					0	P	.40	.82
	3.862	7.3	−0.115	2.1					0	P	.42	.81
(net of expected growth)	3.782	7.5	−0.122	2.4							.30	.83
3. Income (individual + enterprise)	3.028	6.7	−0.415	9.9	1.161	3.6					.47	.75
	3.977	9.0	−0.280	6.6	1.458	7.9			P	P	.55	.69
	3.883	9.4	−0.213	4.7	0.685	3.2					.61	.65
4. Income (individual + enterprise) per capita	1.529	5.6	−0.085	3.0							.19	.47
	1.536	5.4	−0.084	2.6	.010	0.1			0	0	.19	.47
	1.488	5.5	−0.095	2.7							.19	.47
Private sector												
1. Employment share (× 100)	−758	2.1	−0.056	1.9							.03	4.96
	−677	1.8	−0.058	2.1			0.966	3.3			.06	4.90
	−634	1.7	−0.002	0.1			0.713	2.8	P	0	.11	4.76
2. Household income share (× 100)	0.239	1.6	−0.056	3.3							.09	0.26
	0.290	2.1	−0.052	3.4			0.059	3.3			.13	0.26
	0.317	2.4	−0.011	0.7			0.026	1.4	P	P	.22	0.24
3. Private workplaces per capita	0.819	1.5	−0.235	4.5							.10	1.02
	1.186	2.0	−0.175	3.2			0.700	2.4	P	0	.12	1.02
	0.616	1.1	−0.087	1.7			0.047	0.2			.24	0.95

Notes: Dependent variable is an annual percentage growth rate (100 × annual log change), except for share variables, which are in annual point changes (100 × annual share change). Beginning-period value of right-wing share is usually the seat share from the 1991 municipal election, and the initial local tax rate is for 1993. However, for private-income share and private workplaces, the initial year is taken as 1995 (1994 election results and 1995 tax rates). Expected growth variables are constructed as described in text. Other controls are a dummy for the Stockholm area (twenty-six municipalities) and the log of the 1993 population. "P" means the coefficient of the variable is positive at $P < 0.05$; 0 means insignificant ($P > 0.05$). There are 286 to 290 municipalities in each regression.

(to a non-Swede) large. Table 8.7 summarizes a few of these effects by comparing growth in a hypothetical probusiness environment (right-wing party shares above and tax rates below the sample averages by one standard deviation) to growth in an antibusiness environment (vice versa). The aggregates (income, employment) grow over 1 percent per year faster in the probusiness municipality. While this may not sound like much, it is substantial relative to the growth rates Sweden has experienced over this period. It is the difference between declining employment and modestly growing employment. In terms of cumulative real income growth, the probusiness environment generates 80 percent more growth by 2003 than the antibusiness environment.

The growth effect is also large in the sense that it tends to corroborate the previous finding that higher tax rates may substantially erode a municipality's tax base. The regressions in table 8.6 suggest that well over half of the potential tax revenues from any tax increase is ultimately lost through slower growth of the tax base. To see this, focus on aggregate income, which is the ultimate tax base for the local public sector.[30] We will consider only the tax component of the policy-growth nexus (which, as indicated on line 6 of table 8.7, is under half the total effect of the counterfactual policy shift that the table analyzes.) So, imagine that in 1993, a municipality (with the national average party makeup of its municipal council) raised the local tax rate by 1 point, from 31.66 percent (the sample average) to 32.66 percent. That should increase the municipality's revenue by (1/31.66), or 3.16 percent, if there is no erosion of the tax base. However, the tax coefficient in table 8.6 (–0.213) suggests that income will grow 0.213 percent less per year than it would without the tax increase. By 2004, the smaller tax base engendered by this slower income growth would produce only 0.8 percent more revenue from the tax increase—not the 3.16 percent that might have been expected.[31] The slowdown of income growth after the tax increase is enough to offset around three-fourths of the potential revenue gain. This figure is quite consistent with some of the larger estimates of the tax effects in table 8.4. The two tables also tend to reinforce the view that higher tax rates are reducing

30. The capital income component is not taxed locally, but growth in capital contributes to taxed income in the long run.

31. To see this, consider two municipalities, A and B, which are average in every respect, except that B raises taxes by 1 point in 1993, from the sample average of 31.66 percent to 32.66 percent. Municipality A keeps its tax rate at 31.66 percent. Assume income is 100 in 1993 for both municipalities. So, both municipalities have 31.66 in local government revenue in 1993 before B raises the tax rate. In the ensuing eleven years ending in 2004, income in A will grow at a nominal rate of 3.88 percent per year, or 2.58 percent per year in real terms (see table 8.5). Accordingly, real (1993 SEK) income in A will have increased from 100 to approximately 132.34 ($= 1.0258^{11} \times 100$). The unchanged tax rate of 31.66 percent would produce 41.90 of local tax revenues from the 132.34 in income in A in 2004.

Now we wish to estimate how much more than this benchmark of 41.90 in local taxes B will collect in 2004, a decade or so after having raised its tax rate by 1 point, or 3.16 percent, from 31.66 to 32.66 percent. The answer will be less than 3.16 percent more, because according to the regressions in table 8.7, B's tax base will grow more slowly than A's in the next eleven years. We will use the most conservative estimate of this effect, which is the –0.213 coefficient on the last line of panel A.3 in table 8.7. This means that income in B will grow at a real rate

Table 8.7   Estimated impact of initial conditions on growth rates, Swedish municipalities, 1993 to 2003

		Annual growth rate or change in			
Notes and lines	Initial conditions	Total income (%/year) (1)	Total employment (%/year) (2)	Per capita income (%/yr) (3)	Private share of income (pts of 100/year) (4)
1	Probusiness	4.56	0.91	4.45	0.521
2	*Average*	*3.88*	*0.36*	*4.17*	*0.474*
3	Antibusiness	3.20	−0.19	3.90	0.427
4	Probusiness advantage (1 to 3)	+1.36	+1.10	+0.55	+.047
5	in standard deviation units	+1.2	+0.52	+1.06	+0.34
6	percent due to tax rate	38.2	25.5	42.2	28.6

Notes: All estimates are based on coefficients of right-wing party share and tax rates in regressions with controls for expected growth of employment (or the private share of employment), log of population, and the Stockholm region. 1 = a municipality with a right-wing municipality council seat share of 0.607 (1 standard deviation above the average) and a local tax rate of 30.44 percent (1 standard deviation below average). 2 = a municipality with a right-wing municipality council seat share of 0.497 and a local tax rate of 31.66 percent, which are the sample averages. 3 = a municipality with a right-wing municipality council seat share of 0.393 (1 standard deviation below the average) and a local tax rate of 32.88 percent (1 standard deviation above average). 5 = the probusiness advantage on line 4 divided by the standard deviation of the growth rate or change in the sample. 6 = the part of the probusiness advantage on lines 4 or 5 due to the difference in tax rates assumed for lines 1 and 3. The rest of the advantage comes from the assumed difference in right-wing party seat shares.

income rather than the other way around.[32] That is, we see high taxes in the past, followed by low subsequent growth that eventually leads to the below-average income levels we found in the panel analysis.

We hesitate to do a similar counterfactual exercise for shifts in the makeup of the municipal council, because we think of that variable as a proxy for a whole set of policies that we cannot measure. Indeed, we would caution against too literal a reading of the tax increase counterfactual for the same reason.[33]

We also need to emphasize again the preliminary and suggestive character of the results. Public policies in Swedish municipalities tend to be highly persistent, even over long periods. Thus, a municipality with a high tax rate

---

of only 2.367 percent per year, or 0.213 percent per year less than A's 2.58 percent growth rate. Thus, instead of the 132.34 tax base in A, municipality B's 2004 income will be only 129.35 (= $1.02367^{11} \times 100$), which is 2.26 percent below A's income. Municipality B's tax rate of 32.66 percent produces revenues of 42.25 on this 129.35 of income. This exceeds A's tax revenues of 41.90 by 0.35, or 0.84 percent. Thus, most of the potential revenue gain of 3.16 percent—more precisely, 73.4 percent of it (= (3.16−0.84) / 3.16)—has not been realized by B because of the subsequent erosion of the tax base.

32. If it is income that is causing tax rates, the story linking tables 8.4 and 8.6 would have to be that municipalities with poor unobserved growth prospects for the future also have a high current demand for public spending. Then, we would see high taxes correlated with low subsequent growth and eventually lower-than-average income levels.

33. Municipal council party shares and tax rates in 1993 are related to subsequent policies that we can measure. For example, a regression of the average SN survey responses for 2001 to

at the beginning of the 1990s very likely has a high tax rate now. Accordingly, the correlation between tax rates in 1993 and subsequent growth does not imply a causal link between the two.[34] Had we regressed the same growth rate on 2004 tax rates, the same negative correlation would be observed, but neither would this imply a reverse causation—that the growth somehow led to high tax rates in 2004.

The persistence in growth rates and political economy variables at the municipality level raises a concern that the correlation between the two is driven by unobserved or unmeasured heterogeneity across municipalities. That is, something that we do not measure—call it the local culture for short—produces both high growth and business friendly policies. On this view, the persistence of both the policies and the growth would simply reflect the durability of the local culture, but this would not imply that the policies produced the growth.[35]

One way to try to account for unobserved heterogeneity across municipalities is to treat it as a fixed effect and then to estimate the model from within-period changes in each of the municipalities.[36] We implement this in table 8.8, and as we will see, the results there enable us to rule out (unchanging) unobserved heterogeneity as the only reason for our previous results.

Another advantage of the fixed effects model is that it allows us to specify the growth process more precisely than we could in table 8.6. Specifically, think of growth in any aggregate, such as population, as the closing of a gap between some current long-run equilibrium value (Y_t^*) and the actual value at the start of the period (Y_{t-1}); if the gap between the equilibrium and the starting actual values is positive, then growth is positive, for example.[37]

2004 or the average private-contract share of a municipality's budget in 1997 to 2003 on right-wing seat share and tax rates for 1993 yields positive coefficients for the former and negative coefficients for the latter. The coefficients are precisely estimated (t-ratios in the 4 to 6 range) and quantitatively important.

34. One difficulty with exploring this causal link is that until 1991, municipalities that raised taxes receive generous matching funds from the state. Therefore, it may well be that higher taxes increased incomes before 1991 but decreased incomes after 1991. This distinction would be lost in panel regressions over longer periods.

35. Nor would it rule out such a causal link. A local culture that values growth may also enact policies that enable growth. A further difficulty is to disentangle measures that capture the overall demand for public spending from those that reflect local preferences. For example, Torsten Persson informs us that adding the share of the population below age fifteen and above age sixty-five as an explanatory variable to regressions like those in table 8.6 sometimes rendered the estimated coefficients for the tax rate nonsignificant. The motivation for adding these variables is that the young and old are primary consumers of local government goods (education and health care). So, municipalities with many young or old people might be expected to have high taxes and possibly lower growth, simply because they have fewer people who work. However, this interpretation is not clear cut, because municipalities are fully compensated by state transfers for any demographic disadvantage. On the other side, if higher shares of the elderly and young increase the vote for spending programs, the extra variables may simply dilute the estimated tax effect by introducing a determinant of the tax rate as an independent control variable.

36. We thank Torsten Persson for suggesting this.

Table 8.8   Growth and political economy: Swedish municipalities, 1993 to 2004, fixed effects estimates

Dependent variable: change in natural log of	Political economy variable				Expected employment		Lagged level of dependent variable		R^2 (within)	Number of observations	
	Right-wing share		Local tax rate							Total	Municipality
	Coefficient[b]	t	Coefficient	t	Coefficient	t	Coefficient	t			
1. Population	.012	2.5	−.0016	3.4	.034	1.2	−.046	2.4	.15	3,146	286
Equilibrium effect[a]	*.256*		*−.035*		*.739*						
2. Employment (1991–2004)	.054	3.4	−.0025	1.8	.327	4.3	−.170	7.8	.62	3,716	286
Equilibrium effect	*.326*		*−.015*		*1.928*						
3. Income (individual + enterprise)	.076	3.3	−.0004	0.2	.752	6.0	−.389	7.4	.26	3,146	286
Equilibrium effect	*.195*		*−.001*		*1.932*						
4. Income (individual + enterprise) per capita	.053	2.7	.0011	0.5	.381	4.2	−.615	13.3	.37	3,146	286
Equilibrium effect	*.085*		*.002*		*.619*						

Notes: Dependent variable is the change from the previous year in the natural log of the indicated variable, or the approximate growth rate (0.01 = 1 percent) for each year. Independent variables: the political economy variables are the right-wing party shares (0.01 = 1 percentage point) of the municipal council for that year (as determined by the previous municipal council election) and the local tax rate (percentage points; 1 = 1 percent). Expected employment is constructed as described in the text and in the note to table 8.3. This shows what employment would be in the municipality if all industry sectors in that municipality experienced the national growth in employment starting in the base year (1992). The lagged level of the dependent variable is included to implement the adjustment model described in the text. Each regression includes municipality and year fixed effects (not reported), so all the coefficients are identified from year-to-year changes within a municipality (less the national average change). All standard errors are clustered at the municipality level.

[a] This is the long-run effect of a unit change in the independent variable on the level of the dependent variable, based on the adjustment model described in the text. It is calculated by dividing the regression coefficient just above by the absolute value of the coefficient of the lagged level of the dependent variable. See text for elaboration.

[b] Right-wing share has a range of 0 to 1. So, the equilibrium effects (e.g., the 0.256 in regression 1, or over 25 percent) are based on the implausible change from a 0 to 100 percent right-wing share. To obtain a more plausible value, these equilibrium effects can be divided by ten, which would give the effect of a 10-point swing in municipal county seat shares.

Specifically, ignoring an error term for a moment, the aggregate would change, according to

$$(1) \qquad \Delta Y_t = a(Y_t^* - Y_{t-1}),$$

where the delta is the change over the period, and a is an adjustment coefficient, which generally should be less than one to allow for partial adjustment over arbitrary time periods, such as a calendar year. In our application, the municipality's political economy affects growth by changing the equilibrium or target values of some Y variable, such as population or employment. That is, suppose for simplicity that there is one index, X, that summarizes any municipality's political economy and that it is related to the equilibrium Y in that municipality by

$$(2) \qquad Y_{it}^* = h_i + kX_{it},$$

where the i subscript denotes a specific municipality. Substituting equation (2) back into equation (1), multiplying through by the adjustment coefficient, a, and adding an error term gives

$$(3) \qquad \Delta Y_{it} = ah_i + akX_{it} - aY_{i,t-1} + e_{it}.$$

In this model, the error term includes a durable, municipality-specific fixed effect (the otherwise unmeasured heterogeneity). We also allow for macroeconomic effects on local growth with year fixed effects and add the usual mean-zero error term. This gives an error term like

$$(4) \qquad e_{it} = v_i + T_t + u_{it},$$

where the first and second terms are the municipality and year fixed effects, respectively. The parameters we are interested in are in equation (3). If the model makes sense, the estimated adjustment coefficient should be in the $(-1,0)$ interval, and we can recover the parameters of the equilibrium relation in equation (2) by dividing the coefficient of X in equation (3) by the absolute value of the adjustment coefficient.

Before discussing the estimates of the model in table 8.8, it is important to clarify how they can be compared to the results in table 8.6. Both sets of results describe the link between political economy and growth, but they answer different questions. In table 8.6, we ask whether municipalities that have more business friendly policies grow faster than other municipalities. In table 8.8, we ask whether any municipality—business friendly or not—experiences accelerated growth when it moves its policies in a more business friendly direction. The weight one chooses to give to each set of results involves a tradeoff: in our data, the substantial bulk of the variance—on

---

37. We couldn't implement a model like this in table 8.6, because it would require the untenable assumption that every municipality, for example, is gravitating toward the same equilibrium population.

the order of 90 percent of the total variance—in growth rates and political economy variables is cross-sectional. Once the municipality and the time fixed effects are accounted for, there is relatively little year-to-year movement in either growth or policies. Thus, table 8.8 removes the possible unmeasured heterogeneity across municipalities, at the cost of leaving little variation left to be explained. Table 8.6 describes a much greater range of variation than table 8.8, possibly at the cost of a less-clear interpretation of the estimates.

These caveats understood, the results in the two tables are broadly similar. For population and employment, both the right-wing share and tax rate variables have the same signs and hint at similar magnitudes of effects in the two tables.[38] For income and income per capita, there are statistically or economically meaningful effects from the right-wing share variable in table 8.8 but none for the tax rate. This absence of a tax rate effect on the income related measures in table 8.8 is the one clear difference between the two tables.

The other results in table 8.8 are sensible. The expected employment variable—a municipality-specific measure of the effect of national employment trends—always has the expected positive sign. The coefficient of the lagged dependent variable—the adjustment coefficient in equation (1)—always lies in the (–1,0) interval implied by the model.

We think that the overall message coming from the results in tables 8.6 and 8.8 tends to be mutually reinforcing: municipalities that either have or move toward business friendly policies tend to grow faster than they otherwise would. However, these results should be viewed as the beginning rather than the end of an important inquiry. We would again emphasize that the particular variables that we use to measure local policies in tables 8.6 and 8.8—tax rates and municipal council politics—were selected based on data availability and should be regarded as proxies for a wider range of policies that affect a municipality's growth. The first part of the empirical analysis tried to suggest what some of those policies might be. We hope that these results will stimulate further research into the connection between local policies and growth. For example, which specific policies are more or less important in stimulating growth? We think the answers to such questions

38. For example, consider the 2.34 coefficient on the right-wing share variable in the third population regression in table 8.6. This means that a municipality with a 10-point above-average right-wing share grew 0.234 percent faster per year over the eleven-year sample period. That faster growth would compound into approximately a 2.6 percent higher population in 2004 than it would otherwise. In table 8.8, the 0.256 equilibrium effect of the same variable also implies a 2.6 percent higher population in the long run from a 10-point shift to the right in the makeup of the municipal council.

For tax rates, the magnitudes implied by the two tables are also broadly similar. In table 8.6, the tax rate coefficients for population and employment are –0.122, which implies a compound reduction of 1.3 percent over the sample period. This is just about the same as the equilibrium effect of the same change in tax rates on employment in table 8.8 (–1.5 percent), but it is around 2 percentage points less than the equilibrium effect on population (–3.5 percent) in table 8.8.

might provide an important part of any progrowth strategy for Sweden as
a whole.

References

Alexandersson, G., S. Fölster, and S. Hultén. 1998. The effects of competition in
Swedish local bus services. *Journal of Transport Economics and Policy* 32 (2):
203–19.
Bekken, J.-T. 2003. *Taxi regulation in Europe: Final report.* Geneva, Switzerland:
International Road Transport Union.
Bergdahl, P. 2000. Staten som kommersiell actor. Statskontorets Rapport no. 16.
Stockholm: Statskontorets.
Bergman, M. 2004. Anpassas svenska priser till europeisk nivå? *Ekonomisk Debatt*
32 (7): 21–36.
Bergström, F. and M. Sandström. 2002. School vouchers in practice: Competition
won't hurt you! IFN Working Paper no. 578. Stockholm: Research Institute of
Industrial Economics.
———. 2005. School vouchers in practice: Competition will not hurt you. *Journal
of Public Economics* 89 (2/3): 351–80.
Besley, T., and R. Burgess. 2004. Can labor regulation hinder economic performance?
Evidence from India. *Quarterly Journal of Economics* 119 (1): 91–134.
Burdett, K., and S. Fölster. 1994. Analyzing the effects of taxicab deregulation: A
new empirical approach. IUI Working Paper no. 410. Stockholm: Research Insti-
tute of Industrial Economics.
Crandall, R. W., and C. Winston. 2003. Does antitrust policy improve consumer
welfare? Assessing the evidence. *Journal of Economic Perspectives* 17 (4): 3–26.
Falkenhall, B., and A. Kolmodin. 2004. Samhällsekonomisk analys av effekterna av
liberaliseringen av postmarknaden: Underlag och överväganden för Post- och
kassaserviceutredningen. ITPS-rapport till Post- och kassaserviceutredningen.
Stockholm: Swedish Institute for Growth Policy Studies.
Fölster, S., and S. Peltzman. 1997. The social cost of regulation and lack of compe-
tition in Sweden: A summary. In *The welfare state in transition: Reforming the
Swedish model,* ed. R. B. Freeman, R. Topel, and B. Swedenborg, 315–53. Chi-
cago: University of Chicago Press.
Green, R., and N. Damsgaard. 2005. *Den nya elmarknaden.* SNS förlag. Stockholm:
Studieförbundet Näringsliv och Samhälle.
Henrekson, M., and M. Stenlund. 2006. Företagsstruktur och nyföretagande. Bilaga
till Kris- och framtidskommission. Stockholm: Confederation of Swedish Enterprise.
Holmes, T. The effect of state policies on the location of manufacturing: Evidence
from state borders. *Journal of Political Economy* 106 (4): 667–705.
Järnvägsgruppen Kungliga Tekniska Högskolan (KTH). 2003. *Utveckling av utbud
och priser på järnvägslinjer i Sverige 1990–2003.* Stockholm: KTH Royal Institute
of Technology.
Konkurrensverket. 2000. Varför är de svenska priserna så höga? Konkurrensverkets
rapportserie no. 2000:2. Stockholm: Swedish Competition Authority.
———. 2004. Myndigheter och marknader. Konkurrensverkets rapportserie no.
2004:4. Stockholm: Swedish Competition Authority.

London Economics (LE). 2003. *Study of the consequences of further liberalisation of the postal market in Norway.* London: LE.

Luftfartsverket (LFT). 2004. *Flygets utveckling 2003: En sektorsredovisning.* Stockholm: LFT.

Lundvall, K., and R. Odlander. 2001. Kan kommunerna pressa matpriserna? Konkurrensverkets rapportserie no. 2001:4. Stockholm: Swedish Competition Authority.

Organization for Economic Cooperation and Development (OECD). 2003. *OECD communications outlook 2003.* Paris: OECD.

Regulatory Reform Commission. 2005. Liberalisering, Regler och Marknader. SOU 2005:4. Stockholm: Regulatory Reform Commission.

Statens Pris och Konkurrensverk (SPK). 1992. Horisontell prissamverkan och marknadsdelning. SPK rapportserie no. 1992:3. Stockholm: SPK.

Svenskt Näringsliv. 2005. *Svenskt konkurrensindex: åtta konsumentnära branscher granskade.* Stockholm: Svenskt Näringsliv.

Veiderpass, A. 2004. Avreglerad elförsörjning: Ökad konkurrens och ökad effektivitet. Rapport 1 och Rapport 2, Projektrapport no. 105/1999. Stockholm: Swedish Competition Authority.

9

What Have Changes to the Global Markets for Goods and Services Done to the Viability of the Swedish Welfare State?

Edward E. Leamer

9.1 Introduction

When we learned professors from America, together with our distinguished Swedish colleagues, examined Sweden a decade ago and reported our findings in Freeman, Topel, and Swedenborg (1997), we offered our heartfelt but dour prognostication: this dog will never win a race—not hobbled by its welfare state. But like real three-legged dogs, the performance of the Swedish economy since last we examined this patient has been in many ways superior, including a growth rate of real gross domestic product (GDP) per capita in the years 1995 to 2004 equal to 2.4 percent per year, compared with the Organization for Economic Cooperation and Development (OECD) average of 2.2 percent (OECD 2005).

This might be a surprise to Leamer and Lundborg (1997), who warned that there are deep inconsistencies between the egalitarian goals of a welfare state and the ongoing but largely incomplete task of integrating masses of low-wage unskilled third-world workers into the global trading system. "Not really so surprising," Leamer and Lundborg might reply, as their conceptual framework applies to the long run, and the performance over the last decade may have been dominated by short-run circumstances that mask the long-run problems. It is best to keep in mind that a free-market economic system cannot tolerate persistent vast geographical differences in prices of gold or wages of unskilled workers, unless those differences have a technological/cost basis. With that dogged persistence, I offer you my message again, updated to address two startling changes in the global economy

Edward E. Leamer is the Chauncey J. Medberry Chair in Management and a professor in economics and statistics at the University of California, Los Angeles, and a research associate of the National Bureau of Economic Research.

in the last decade: the remarkable growth of Chinese exports (more of the same, but lots more) and the communications revolution we call the Internet (a new and entirely different kind of threat).

9.1.1   Rise of China as a Manufacturing Powerhouse

It is not news that the liberalizations of China, India, Eastern Europe, Russia, and so on have increased the effective global supply of workers willing and able to do mundane manufacturing jobs at very low-wage rates under uncomfortable working conditions.[1] What is news is the remarkable speed at which millions of Chinese manufacturing workers are being integrated into the global trading system.

Part of the rise of China and other low-wage manufacturers comes from continued improvements in governance of global trade that have apparently reduced the risk of government interference in business transactions across national borders. That risk reduction plus improvements in transportation and communication have allowed firms to fragment supply chains, seeking the most cost-effective location for each point in the chain, in particularly by moving mundane labor-intensive assembly operations to low-wage locations. (According to the September 18, 2005 edition of the *Los Angeles Times,* 60 to 70 percent of the new Boeing 787 Dreamliner will be produced overseas, some of it in China.)

Meanwhile, at greater speed than ever before, standardization and mechanization are turning rooted innovative new products into footloose standardized commodities, where cost is the competitive driver. This has allowed Asian low-cost suppliers, particularly China, to enter markets in electronics and machinery that heretofore were completely controlled by the high-wage countries. To give a pertinent example, hardly any of the IBM mainframe computers were manufactured in low-wage countries, but the personal computer had a shelf life of only a few years as far as U.S. manufacturing workers were concerned.

9.1.2   The Transition to a Postindustrial Economy: The Personal Computer and the Internet

The fraction of the global workforce in manufacturing is under persistent pressure to contract because of the steady march of productivity, which allows fewer workers to do the tasks of many. This technological reduc-

---

1. The global competition for manufacturing jobs is made more intense because the high savings rates in Asia and other developing countries limit their demand for manufactured products. The transfer of manufacturing jobs from Northern Europe and North America to Eastern Europe and Asia thus tends to reduce the global total of manufacturing jobs, because the reduction in demand for manufactures in high-wage high-spending Europe and North America is not mitigated much by an increase in demand for manufactures in low-wage high-saving Asia and Eastern Europe. It's a less-than-zero sum game.

tion in the global number of manufacturing workers might be offset by new demand for new manufactured products and by increases in demand for existing products because of rising income levels and falling manufactured prices. But in the last three decades, the force of process innovation has outstripped the opposing forces of product innovation, rising income levels, and falling prices, and the fraction of the workforce in manufacturing has substantially fallen in Sweden and in every other OECD country. (The Swedish share of manufacturing has fallen from 26 percent in 1970 to 16 percent in 2003.[2])

This decline in manufacturing means that a rising fraction of the workforce has to be absorbed either by government or private services. It means that increasingly, the sources of growth will come from services. This is troubling, because in the last decade, the production of both mundane and creative intellectual services has been completely revolutionized by the Internet and the personal computer (PC). The Internet, which has been likened to the printing press in terms of its potential effects on the way we communicate, is increasing the intensity of price competition among manufactures and is allowing the costless delivery of some knowledge services across borders. The Internet and the PC are altering the labor markets' compensation for education and talent.

The transition from artisan shop to factory floor came with a great deskilling of manufacturing and good jobs for high school graduates. Education and natural talent had mostly additive effects on earnings, with decent returns to educational investments for almost everyone. With that structure of earnings, compensatory education could easily offset talent deficiencies—if you and I are both trained to operate a forklift, we will be equally productive, no matter your strength advantage over me. But in a postindustrial PC/Internet age, compensation in the intellectual service sector may be determined more by the *interaction* of talent and education, meaning that the rate of return to education depends substantially on the talent of the student—if you and I are both trained to operate a computer, one of us is going to do a lot better than the other. This creates a Hollywood kind of inequality for which compensatory education is ineffective—without the talent, you cannot be a star.

It's not just talent. It's also hard work. In the industrial age, the problem was capital scarcity. That capital scarcity was relieved by hiring workers who were willing to operate the equipment at a high pace for long hours, thereby spreading the fixed capital cost over a large total output. In order to get workers to operate the equipment at a high pace for long hours, workers had to have an incentive, which has meant higher wages in manufacturing than in agriculture or services and higher wages in capital-intensive manufacturing

2. OECD STAN database.

than in labor-intensive manufacturing. That wage inequality causes some difficulty for an egalitarian state, of course, though access for most to the high-pace high-wage jobs in capital-intensive manufacturing is a politically mitigating factor.

Compensation is very different in the creative intellectual services. In the intellectual services, talent, not capital or worker time, is the scarce input. An efficient postindustrial economy cannot afford to have idle talent for the same reason that an efficient industrial economy cannot afford to have idle capital. Efficiency thus requires that the most talented among us work longer hours than the less talented. The Swedish decline in hours worked that is described in Davis and Henrekson (chapter 7 in this volume) and the compression of wage rates may be incompatible with efficient production in the intellectual services sector. Extreme disparities in rates of compensation in Hollywood and on Wall Street properly encourage long hours of talented workers, and the combined effects of long hours for the talented with enormous hourly compensation creates in Hollywood vast inequality that is deeply inconsistent with an egalitarian state. It's not just Hollywood. It's also all the other professions—law, architecture, accounting, medicine, and even economics.

This isn't news for Sweden, which experienced the friction between its welfare state and the creative services sector when Ingmar Bergman, after being arrested for tax evasion in 1976, suffered a mental breakdown and then went into self-imposed exile in Germany. That may be an apocryphal story replayed quietly but repeatedly as creative Swedes make the difficult choice between staying at home with comfortable livelihoods versus moving abroad, where the compensation for their ideas and creative products may seem limitless.

These two problems—the rise of China and the transition to a postindustrial economy—are addressed in separate sections of this chapter. The rise of China as a manufacturing powerhouse can be entirely beneficial for Sweden. The force of Chinese competition falls on countries that produce the same products, and high-wage countries that compete in the same product space as low-wage competitors inevitably must suffer wage reductions and slower growth, but investments in skills, human capital, and product innovations can support a product mix unlike the ones made in China, in which case the lowering of prices for Chinese products is all to the good. The next section provides an answer to the question, which countries compete with Sweden? This question is related but not identical to the question that Leamer and Lundborg (1997) posed: are Swedish wages set in Beijing? This section assembles a large amount of information about Swedish exports in comparison with other countries. There are some ominous developments here, especially the rapid rise of Chinese exports and their move up the value added chain, but all in all, the locus of Swedish competition remains (happily) in high-wage Europe, the United States, and Japan.

In the third section, I offer some theory and evidence of the transition from industrial to postindustrial societies, a transition that is being experienced by all advanced developed countries. This section is largely speculative, because countries are at the beginning of their transitions from industrial to postindustrial societies, with relatively little clear evidence of what that transition entails. One clear symptom of this transition is the decline in the value added share of manufactures and the rise in the value added share of finance and other intellectual services—what I am calling neurofacturing. With that as the backdrop, I contrast earnings and hours in finance with earnings and hours in manufacturing, in the United States, and in Sweden. Finance in the United States is characterized by long hours and exceptional pay. Sweden seems to have adopted a different solution. But I do not provide any evidence that the extraordinary levels of compensation for the leaders of the U.S. financial system have anything to do with any special talent, other than being in the right place at the right time, and I do not provide evidence that U.S. finance is more efficient by virtue of it compensation system. The clearer cases of U.S. talent-driven compensation are in entertainment and sports. But I also don't provide evidence that the Ingmar Bergman experience is common in Sweden. This section is intended to be thought provoking, suggesting, but not proving, that the transition to a postindustrial economy will put greater strain on the egalitarian aims of the Swedish welfare system.

9.2   Who Competes with Sweden?

Our first item of business is to look closely at the structure of Swedish exports to determine if the source of competition for Swedish products remains in the high-wage countries or if it has shifted south toward low-wage developing nations. To do that, I will be proposing a new measure of the extent to which exports from other countries compete with Swedish exports. This new measure suggests that in the U.S. market, it is Japan and Canada that historically have been Sweden's greatest competitors, but the degree of competition with these two principal competitors fell sharply from 1989 to 2004, while the degree of competition with China, Korea, and Mexico rose substantially. This is highly suggestive of a shift southward of the center of Swedish competition in manufactures. Incidentally, no correction is made for the part of Chinese exports that originate in high-wage countries such as Japan, but cost advantages apply to any export from China, no matter the value added fraction that originates elsewhere.

9.2.1   The Distinctiveness Barrier to Factor Price Equalization

The factor price equalization theorem is often invoked to support the alarming idea that international trade soon enough will equalize wages in

Stockholm, Los Angeles, Mexico City, and Shanghai. This is a possibility but is by no means a sure thing.

One important reason why wages might not equalize across counties is differences in product mix. The force for factor price equalization comes through the product market, but that force is completely inoperable if Sweden and other countries produce no products in common. There are a great variety of barriers that support distinctive product mixes and that help to prevent the equalization of wages in Stockholm and Shanghai. A natural barrier is the economic distinctiveness that comes from natural resources and from climate. For example, a country that exports softwood lumber products in exchange for apparel and footwear need not fear the low wages paid for the production of apparel and footwear. On the contrary, the lower the wages, the better, because that supports a terms-of-trade improvement, providing more shirts and shoes for each cord of wood or ream of paper exported.

The role of product differences in preventing wage equalization is illustrated well by contrasting a Ricardian model with a Heckscher-Ohlin (HO) model of international trade. In a Ricardian equilibrium, distinctive abilities lead to complete specialization according to one's comparative advantage. Countries with different abilities produce different mixes of products and are partners that share the gains from specialization, not competitors. In a Ricardian model, the gains from trade raise wages everywhere.

But in a Heckscher-Ohlin model, comparative advantage is marginal and is eroded as countries move to specialize according to their comparative advantage. In a simple Heckscher-Ohlin equilibrium, comparative advantage at the margin is completely eliminated; all countries produce the same mix of products and are consequently competitors, not partners. Though the inframarginal gains from exchange raise aggregate incomes for all countries, the remaining marginal competition forces an equalization of the rewards to all factors of production, including labor. Countries abundant in labor with low pretrade wages enjoy increased wages as their abundant factor finds external demand, but countries scarce in labor with high pretrade wages suffer reduced wages as the scarcity rents are eroded by foreign competition.

What drives the factor price equalization theorem is a sequence of zero-profit conditions that equate the prices of products to their costs of production:

$$p_i = A_{Li} w + A_{Ki} r + \ldots, i = 1, 2, \ldots,$$

where p_i is the price of product i, A_{Li} and A_{Ki} are the amounts of labor and capital (and other factors) needed to produce a unit of the good, and w and r refer to the wage rate and the rental cost of capital. If there are enough of these zero-profit conditions (if the number of traded products equals the number of factors of production) and if the input intensities A_i are fixed, then it is a simple matter to solve this linear system for the wages and rental rates of capital as a function of the product prices.[3]

Thus, if international trade equalizes product prices, it also must equalize factor prices—wages and rental rates of capital. Trade in products is a complete substitute for trade in factors of production.

Lurking in the background behind the simple zero-profit equations that allow one to solve for factor prices given product prices are a number of critical assumptions that may not be fully met. These are conditions that are needed to assure (a) product price equalization and (b) identical input intensities. Here are some of the assumptions:

- Traded goods are commodities whose prices are set in global marketplaces. (Firms produce undifferentiated products and have no market power.)
- Transportation costs are zero. There are no other barriers to trade.
- The best methods of production are common knowledge; there are no first-mover advantages.
- The services of the factors of production—land, labor, and capital— are also undifferentiated internationally and are available in nationally integrated rental markets.
- The factors of production are costlessly mobile across firms/sectors.
- Production occurs at constant returns to scale; there are no benefits from agglomerations.

While violation of one or more of these conditions will allow sustained differences in (pretax) wages between Stockholm and Los Angeles, the substantial gap in wages between Stockholm and Shanghai may rely especially on the violation of another critical condition: all countries are sufficiently similar in factor endowments so that they produce the same mix of products.

Technically speaking, if different countries produce different mixes of products, they solve different sets of zero-profit conditions to determine wages and other factors of production, and factor-price equalization need not apply.

Though identical product mix and factor price equalization are often taken as implications of a Heckscher-Ohlin model, this HO framework is also capable of producing a Ricardian-like equilibrium, in which countries sort into distinct groups with different product mixes. Factor price equalization then operates within the groups but not between. As in the Ricardian model, countries are competitors within the groups defined by product

---

3. If the technology allows substitution among the factors and thus variable factor intensities, A_{Li} and A_{Ki}, the proof of factor price equalization is a bit more involved, requiring that the technologies do not exhibit factor-intensity reversals, which would allow two or more solutions to the system of zero-profit conditions.

mixes, but between groups, they are partners, mutually enjoying the gains from specialization. Then trade is a tide that lifts all boats.

What determines the product mix? In a Heckscher-Ohlin model, the product mix is dictated by the availability of land, labor, and capital. If countries are sufficiently similar in their supplies of these productive resources, then the equilibrium has all countries producing the same mix of products, but if countries are greatly different, the multicone equilibrium occurs with countries producing different product mixes. For example, capital-abundant countries might produce a capital-intensive mix of products and have high wages and low returns to capital, while labor-abundant countries might produce a labor-intensive product mix and have low wages and high returns to capital.

If an equilibrium with different wages in different countries does emerge, there are powerful forces that work to destroy it. Differences in factor prices create arbitrage opportunities that can be pursued by migration of labor and capital. If there is enough international factor mobility, then countries can become sufficiently similar so that the two-wage solution is unsustainable. Even without capital mobility, high savings and investment rates responding to the higher returns in capital-scarce countries can eliminate the dissimilarities in countries that are necessary to support the multicone equilibrium.

9.2.2   Empirical Measurement of Product Mix Similarities

The message of the HO model is that while ample stocks of human and physical capital historically have helped to create a high barrier to protect Swedish workers from low-wage foreign competition, those barriers will be constantly under assault as the low-wage countries invest heavily in physical and education assets and shift their product mix ever closer to the Swedish capital-intensive mix. In the face of capital accumulation in low-wage countries, the distinctiveness barriers protecting Swedish wages can be maintained only by the maintenance of Swedish distinctiveness through further investments in education and infrastructure that maintain Sweden as the preferred place to produce high-tech, human-capital-intensive products.

There are several ways to measure progress in the race to stay ahead of the emerging low-wage countries, none of which is perfect. One approach is to compare Swedish educational attainments and rates of investment in new capital with the same in countries whose low wages might threaten Swedish wages, as in Leamer and Lundborg (1997). This can be a blunt instrument, because knowledge of the global distribution of human and physical capital by itself cannot tell us whether Sweden is a partner or a competitor of China and other low-wage countries. It depends on how much of each productive resource is absorbed in nontraded goods, and it depends also on the technologies of production.

Another way to measure Swedish distinctiveness is to compare the products made in Sweden and the products made in China and other countries.

Are they the same or not? If they are the same, and if they are traded, that makes Sweden and China competitors.

As is often the case, the theory yields important insights, but there is a great gulf between the literal theory and the real world. In the theory, product mix differences can be determined merely by the presence or absence of a product in the mix originating in each country. In reality, data are collected at a high enough level of aggregation that almost every product category is present in almost every country. If the category is women's dresses, high-fashion gowns might be sewn in Los Angeles and Boston, while high-volume standardized dresses might be sewn in Guonddong.[4] Thus, to measure Swedish distinctiveness through its product mix, we will have to tolerate a somewhat casual link between the theory and the data.

We also will want to make use of export data, which are much more detailed than production or value added data. The problem with export data is that Chinese wages can come to Stockholm, because Swedish exporters compete in the same foreign markets as the Chinese, or because Swedish imports from China compete with Swedish production sold at home. A focus on exports ignores competition at home.

9.2.3   Export Correlations to the United States and the European Union

Correlations across products of Swedish exports to the United States and the European Union with the exports of other countries for 1987 and 1999 are illustrated in figure 9.1 and figure 9.2. These figures are sorted by similarity with Sweden in 1987, lowest to highest. At the right are the countries one suspects are the greatest competitors of Sweden. These countries on the right are offering these two large marketplaces about the same mix of products as Sweden offers. That means that for the 1987 EU market, Sweden's closest competitors were Finland, Germany, Canada, and the United States, and for the United States market, they were Germany, Canada, Mexico, and Japan. (Note that this comparison doesn't depend at all on total export values, only on the composition.) At the left in these figures are countries with export mixes unlike Sweden's. These are generally low-wage developing countries, such as China, Turkey, and Malaysia.

These 1987 correlations were good news for Sweden, as they suggest that Sweden had successfully isolated itself from the force of competition with the emerging low-wage exporters through a fortuitous choice of product mix, with Sweden concentrating on one set of exports and the low-wage developing world concentrating on another.

But figure 9.1 and figure 9.2 also reveal that things changed dramatically from 1987 to 1999, with sharply rising correlations between Swedish exports

4. If disaggregation were pursued far enough to create separate categories for high-fashion gowns and standardized dresses, we would need to deal with another problem: high-fashion gowns are not commodities sold in global markets, and global product price equalization could not be taken as a useful approximation.

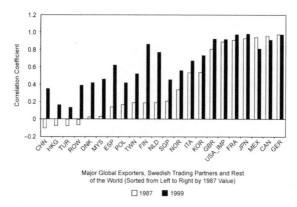

Fig. 9.1   Who competes with Sweden? Product mix correlation coefficient with Sweden, exports to the U.S. market, 1987 and 1999, three-digit ISIC

Note: Major global exporters, Swedish trading partners, and rest of the world (sorted from left to right by 1987 value).

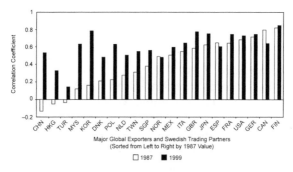

Fig. 9.2   Who competes with Sweden? Product mix correlation coefficient with Sweden, exports to the EU market, 1987 and 1999, three-digit ISIC

Note: Major global exporters and Swedish trading partners (sorted from left to right by 1987 value).

and exports of many of the low-wage developing countries in both the U.S. and EU markets. This is a very ominous development. We need to find out why these correlations have elevated so much. We also need to determine if these correlations are the correct measures of the problem.

9.2.4   A Measure of the Competition between Two Exporters

The increase over time in the correlation between the mix of Swedish exports and the mix of Chinese exports is suggestive of an increase in the intensity of competition. Another commonly used measure is the Finger-Kreinen export similarity index, to be discussed later. Neither of these measures depends on the level of exports coming from the hypothetical competitor, and neither answers a clear economic question based on a clear economic model. I suggest another measure that answers this question: which countries have the greatest impact on the prices that Sweden receives for its exports?

Expressed more precisely, the question is: what would be the impact on the value of Swedish exports if a competitor were to double the quantity of its exports while Sweden held fixed the quantity of its exports?

To answer this question, we need to commit to a model of competition, and we need to know the values of the models' most important parameters: the price elasticities. In principle, one might carry out an econometric exercise that estimated an elaborate model of demand, with products distinguished by place of production. Well, short of that lofty goal, I will assume that all products in a given disaggregated product category are perfectly substitutable, in which case it is the global supply that determines the Swedish price. Then, the impact on Swedish prices from a doubling of competitor exports depends on the size of the competitor. If, for example, the Chinese currently have a 1 percent market share, then a doubling of Chinese output would increase global output by a little less than 1 percent, driving down Swedish prices in that category by an amount that depends on the product price elasticity. For the numbers reported next, the price elasticities are all assumed to be equal to negative one, and the exposure of Swedish export prices to Chinese exports is simply equal to the weighted average Chinese market share, weighted by the importance of the product, measured by the Swedish export share.

Unlike the correlations discussed in the previous section, this measure properly allows for the economic size of a competitor. After all, if the competitor hardly exported anything, the competition for Sweden is small, even if the mixes of products are similar. But be alert, while I have given the proposed measure an explicit theoretical basis, that theoretical basis is entirely unlike the Heckscher-Ohlin model. In particular, no formal attempt is made to connect these measures with Swedish wages, though implicitly the mechanism is a terms-of-trade effect. Thus, our question is, which countries are large enough and similar enough to Sweden to affect the Swedish terms of trade?

In contrast, the Heckscher-Ohlin factor price equalization theory depends on the relative prices of labor-intensive products. The HO question is, which exporters of labor-intensive products are large enough to affect relative prices of labor-intensive products made in Sweden?

Notation

Measures of the intensity of competition between two exporters in third markets depend on the following data: x_j^c = export quantity by country c to destination/product market j; p_j = export price in destination/product market j, assumed to be the same for all exporters; T^c = total value of exports of country $c = \sum_j p_j x_j^c$; I_j^c = *importance* fraction of product j for country c = country c value share of export j = $p_j x_j^c/(\sum_j p_j x_j^c)$; and M_j^c = country c *market share* of export j = $p_j x_j^c/(\sum_c p_j x_j^c)$.

Note that the importance measures sum to one, $\sum_j I_j^c = 1$, while the market shares, which sum to the average market share multiplied by the number of products, depend on the size of the exporter, as well as the composition of exports.

Finger and Kreinin's Export Similarity Index

A commonly used measure of the similarity of exports of two countries (e.g., Sweden and China) to a third market is Finger and Kreinin's (1979) export similarity index, which is equal to the sum of the minimum of the importance measures:

$$\text{ESI(SWE, CHN)} = \sum_j \min(I_j^{\text{SWE}}, I_j^{\text{CHN}}).$$

Figure 9.3 illustrates the calculation based on importance distributions for Chinese and Swedish exports to a third market (e.g., the United States). The horizontal axis is a hypothetical measure of product sophistication, and it is assumed that the Chinese exports are concentrated at the lower end and the Swedish exports at the upper end. The overlap is the minimum value of the two importance numbers, and the ESI (export similarity index) is the area of the indicated overlap region.

This measure does have the feature that it is equal to zero if there is no overlap of products and is equal to one if the distributions are identical, but there are many other measures of the difference between two densities that have that feature. A very popular nonparametric measure is the Kolmogorov-Smirnov (KS) distance, which is the maximum difference between the two cumulative distributions. One minus the KS distance seems like an equally good measure, because it is also equal to one if the distributions are identical and is equal to zero if they do not overlap at all. (But the KS measure does require an ordering, like the skill intensity, because otherwise there is no way to compute the cumulative.)

What's the Question?

If the answer is the Finger and Kreinin export similarity index or the Kolmogorov-Smirnov statistic, it seems appropriate to ask, what is the question? I can't imagine what it might be.

One good question would be this: what would be the percentage reduction in the value of Sweden's total export if China were to double its exports of every product, assuming the elasticities in all markets were equal to negative one?

The following measure answers this question:

$$\text{Competition for Sweden's exports emanating from China} = \sum_j I_j^{\text{SWE}} M_j^{\text{CHN}}.$$

This is the inner product of the Swedish importance and the Chinese market share. Sweden faces intense competition from China if China has a

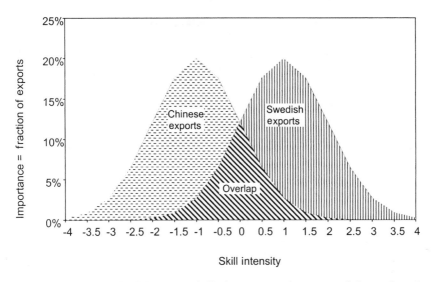

Fig. 9.3   Finger and Kreinin export similarity measure: A measure of the overlap of two distributions of exports sum of the minimum of the importance fractions

large market share of the exports that are most important for Sweden. Note that this is not a symmetric measure: the degree of competition for Sweden's exports from China is not the same as the degree of competition for China's exports from Sweden. Even if the composition of exports were exactly the same, the larger country competes for the smaller country's exports, but not the other way around.

The algebra needed to derive this measure is reported in the appendix.

Sweden and China Competing for the U.S. Market

Table 9.1 reports the competition measures applicable to exports to the United States for Sweden vis-à-vis the major exporters and regions of the world, excluding these major exporters. These are sorted by the change in the competition measures.

The measure of Chinese competition for Swedish exports to the United States rose from 0.5 percent in 1989 to 5.3 percent in 2004. Keep in mind that this is intended to estimate the effect on the value of Swedish exports to the United States if China were to double its exports and thereby drive down the prices of products for which the Chinese market share is considerable. By this measure, China hardly mattered in 1989 but became the number eight competitor by 2004.

Though Japan (12.7 percent) and Canada (12.5 percent) remained in 2004 the most important sources of competition for Swedish products in the U.S. marketplace, both had experienced sharp reductions in their competition intensities from lofty 1989 levels (27.8 percent and 19.4 percent). These reductions were offset by large gains for China, Korea, and Mexico.

Table 9.1   Who competes with Sweden in the U.S. market?

Region	1989 (%)	Rank	2004 (%)	Rank	Change (%)
China	0.5	15	5.3	8	4.8
Korea	2.1	11	5.8	7	3.7
Mexico	3.9	7	7.5	5	3.6
Europe	7.6	4	9.4	4	1.7
Great Britain	4.6	5	6.1	6	1.5
Germany	9.5	3	10.2	3	0.7
Middle East	0.7	13	1.1	14	0.4
East Asia	2.1	12	2.4	11	0.3
Central/Carribean	0.3	17	0.5	16	0.2
India	0.2	18	0.3	18	0.2
Africa	0.6	14	0.7	15	0.1
Not available	0.0	19	0.0	19	0.0
Pacific	0.5	16	0.4	17	−0.1
South America	2.6	8	2.4	10	−0.2
Italy	2.2	10	1.8	12	−0.5
France	4.2	6	3.6	9	−0.6
Taiwan	2.2	9	1.4	13	−0.8
Canada	19.4	2	12.5	2	−6.9
Japan	27.8	1	12.7	1	−15.1
Total	91.0		83.9		−7.1

Notes: Swedish competition is switching from Japan and Canada to China, Korea, and Mexico. Swedish importance times competitor market share; top ten Countries in 2004 and regions excluding these countries; sorted by change.

This raises some serious questions regarding the extent of competition for Swedish jobs. Are Swedish wages set in Guangdong, Seoul, and Monterrey? If not now, what about a decade from now?

We need to do a little detective work to find out what accounts for the rise in the competition between China and Sweden. Is it merely the rise in Chinese exports overall, or is there some significant change in the Chinese product mix—a more worrisome possibility? Product detail for computing the competition for Swedish exports to the United States coming from China is reported in table 9.2 at the two-digit Standard International Trade Classification (SITC) level of aggregation. The columns labeled "Swedish importance" are the Swedish shares of exports to the United States. The denominator in that fraction is total Swedish exports to the United States. For example, SITC 76, "telecommunications equipment, etc." in the first row of the table, comprised 1.7 percent of Swedish exports to the United States in 1989 and 8.7 percent in 2004.

The columns labeled "Chinese market share" are the Chinese fractions of U.S. imports. For example, 3.4 percent of U.S. imports of SITC 76 came from China in 1989 and 29.8 percent in 1976. The denominator in this fraction is the total U.S. imports in the product category.

Our measure of the intensity of Chinese competition for Swedish exports is the sum of the product of the Swedish importance multiplied by the Chinese market shares. If the Chinese market share were the same in every product, then this would be equal to the Chinese market share, because the Swedish importance measures sum to one. The competition measure will exceed or fall short of the Chinese market share, depending on whether the Chinese have large shares of markets that are important sources of Swedish export earnings.

The final columns in table 9.2 labeled "contribution to competition" report the Swedish importance multiplied by the Chinese market share, commodity by commodity. These numbers are summed to get to the overall competition indicator. The table is sorted by the change in this contribution, thus highlighting the sources of any change in competition for Swedish exports.

At the very bottom of the table is the overall Chinese market share, which rose from 2.5 percent in 1989 to 19.3 percent in 2004. From 1989 to 2004, the competition measure rose from 1.1 percent to 9.5 percent, in both cases about half the Chinese market share, suggesting that many Chinese exports are in products that are unimportant to Sweden. These are typically labor-intensive manufactures. For example, in 2004, Chinese goods comprised 72 percent of U.S. imports of SITC 83, "travel goods, handbags," and 69 percent of SITC 85, "footwear," for which Swedish exports are virtually nil. (Incidentally, the competition measure depends on the level of aggregation, and the difference between the measures in table 9.1 and table 9.2 come from the fact that the finest product detail is used in table 9.1.)

The products are sorted by their *increase in contribution* to Swedish-Chinese competition between 1989 and 2004. At the top of the list are not traditional labor-intensive products. These new sources of competition are telecommunications, manufactures of metal, electrical machinery, and road vehicles, a finding that parallels Schott's (2006) description of the increased sophistication of Chinese exports. This seems like a rather ominous development for the Swedish economy, as it suggests some serious erosion of the degree to which newness protects the Swedish economy from competition with China. It is an altogether good thing for Sweden if the Chinese drive down the prices of apparel, textiles, and footwear, because Sweden has virtually no exports of these items. That's only a terms-of-trade improvement for Sweden. But it is not such a good thing if electrical equipment becomes a commodity like T-shirts and jeans and if Swedish comparative advantage in other high-tech items likewise is eroded.

To explore this issue more carefully, we need to disaggregate the data to figure out where exactly the new competition resides. It is possible that at a lower level of disaggregation, what is important for Sweden has small Chinese market shares. Table 9.3 reports details for SITC 76, Sweden's biggest problem sector. The first panel has the three-digit detail. It is true that this disaggregation suggests somewhat less competition between China and Sweden, lowering the 2004 contribution to the measure from 2.59 percent to 2.12

Table 9.2   Chinese competition for Swedish exports to the United States, 1989 and 2004

SITC	Description	Swedish importance (%)			Chinese market share (%)			Contribution to competition (%)		
		1989	2004	Change	1989	2004	Change	1989	2004	Change
76	Telecommunications and sound recording and reproducing apparatus and equipment	1.7	**8.7**	7.0	3.4	29.8	26.4	**0.06**	**2.59**	2.53
69	Manufactures of metals, n.e.s.	**3.3**	4.1	0.8	3.7	27.2	23.5	**0.12**	**1.13**	1.00
77	Electrical machinery, apparatus and appliances, n.e.s., and electrical parts thereof (including nonelectrical counterparts of household type, n.e.s.)	**3.6**	**4.7**	1.1	1.1	15.0	13.9	**0.04**	**0.71**	0.67
78	Road vehicles (including air-cushion vehicles)	**43.5**	**21.7**	−21.7	0.0	3.0	3.0	0.02	**0.66**	0.64
74	General industrial machinery and equipment, n.e.s., and machine parts, n.e.s.	**7.5**	**7.3**	−0.2	1.2	9.5	8.2	**0.09**	**0.69**	0.60
89	Miscellaneous manufactured articles, n.e.s.	2.6	1.6	−0.9	11.5	**43.5**	32.0	**0.30**	**0.72**	0.42
75	Office machines and automatic data processing machines	1.7	1.1	−0.6	0.2	**38.2**	38.0	0.00	**0.42**	0.42
82	Furniture and parts thereof; bedding, mattresses, mattress supports, cushions, and similar stuffed furnishings	1.3	0.9	−0.4	1.2	**41.1**	39.9	0.02	0.37	0.36
98	Estimate of import items valued under $251 and of other low-valued items nonexempt from formal entry	0.0	2.5	2.5		10.5	10.5	0.00	0.26	0.26
87	Professional, scientific, and controlling instruments and apparatus, n.e.s.	1.8	3.6	1.8	1.1	6.6	5.5	0.02	0.24	0.22
72	Machinery specialized for particular industries	**3.3**	4.2	0.9	0.3	5.2	4.9	0.01	0.22	0.21
64	Paper, paperboard, and articles of paper pulp, paper, or paper board	3.3	1.0	−2.3	0.8	14.9	14.2	0.03	0.16	0.13
67	Iron and steel	0.6	2.2	1.6	4.2	6.6	2.4	0.03	0.15	0.12
66	Nonmetallic mineral manufactures, n.e.s.	0.6	0.8	0.2	2.7	17.9	15.1	0.02	0.14	0.12
71	Power-generating machinery and equipment	**6.9**	**4.5**	−2.4	0.5	3.3	2.8	**0.03**	0.15	0.11
63	Cork and wood manufactures other than furniture	0.1	0.5	0.4	2.2	21.1	18.9	0.00	0.10	0.10
59	Chemical materials and products, n.e.s.	0.2	1.2	1.0	0.8	7.6	6.8	0.00	0.09	0.09
81	Prefabricated buildings; sanitary, plumbing, heating, and lighting fixtures and fittings, n.e.s.	0.2	0.2	0.0	3.8	**58.8**	55.0	0.01	0.09	0.09
54	Medicinal and pharmaceutical products	1.2	**11.6**	10.4	1.3	0.8	−0.5	0.02	0.09	0.07

Code	Product									
65	Textile yarn, fabrics, made-up articles, n.e.s., and related products	0.2	0.3	0.1	**15.2**	28.0	12.8	0.02	0.08	0.05
68	Nonferrous metals	1.7	1.1	-0.6	0.3	4.4	4.1	0.01	0.05	0.04
62	Rubber manufactures, n.e.s.	0.5	0.3	-0.1	0.2	12.1	11.9	0.00	0.04	0.04
88	Photographic apparatus, equipment, and supplies and optical goods, n.e.s.; watches and clocks	0.5	0.2	-0.3	1.2	24.0	22.8	0.01	0.05	0.04
57	Plastics in primary forms	0.6	1.0	0.4	0.7	4.0	3.3	0.00	0.04	0.04
51	Organic chemicals	0.3	0.6	0.3	0.5	5.1	4.7	0.00	0.03	0.03
24	Cork and wood	0.2	1.2	1.0	0.0	2.3	2.3	0.00	0.03	0.03
52	Inorganic chemicals	0.2	0.4	0.2	4.1	8.8	4.7	0.01	0.03	0.02
73	Metalworking machinery	1.1	0.9	-0.2	1.0	3.6	2.6	0.01	0.03	0.02
61	Leather, leather manufactures, n.e.s., and dressed furskins	0.0	0.1	0.0	0.7	24.7	24.0	0.00	0.01	0.01
11	Beverages	2.7	3.3	0.6	0.4	0.7	0.3	0.01	0.02	0.01
55	Essential oils and resinoids and perfume materials; toilet, polishing, and cleansing preparations	0.0	0.2	0.2	1.5	4.9	3.4	0.00	0.01	0.01
85	Footwear	0.0	0.0	0.0	3.9	**69.1**	65.3	0.00	0.01	0.01
84	Articles of apparel and clothing accessories	0.3	0.2	-0.2	7.5	19.4	12.0	0.03	0.03	0.01
58	Plastics in nonprimary forms	0.1	0.2	0.1	0.1	5.2	5.1	0.00	0.01	0.01
33	Petroleum, petroleum products, and related materials	0.8	**4.3**	3.5	1.4	0.4	-1.0	0.01	0.02	0.01
93	Special transactions and commodities not classified according to kind	**4.2**	1.7	-2.5	0.7	2.1	1.4	0.03	0.04	0.01
83	Travel goods, handbags, and similar containers	0.0	0.0	0.0	**25.6**	**72.4**	46.8	0.00	0.01	0.00
4	Cereals and cereal preparations	0.0	0.2	0.2	0.3	1.3	1.0	0.00	0.00	0.00
53	Dyeing, tanning, and coloring materials	0.2	0.2	0.0	1.5	2.7	1.2	0.01	0.00	0.00
79	Transport equipment, n.e.s.	1.5	0.3	-1.2	0.4	2.2	1.9	0.01	0.01	0.00
9	Miscellaneous edible products and preparations	0.1	0.0	0.0	0.9	3.9	3.0	0.00	0.00	0.00
5	Vegetables and fruit	0.0	0.0	0.0	2.4	7.1	4.7	0.00	0.00	0.00
26	Textile fibers (other than wool tops and other combed wool) and their wastes (not manufactured into yarn or fabric)	0.0	0.0	0.0	0.0	7.4	7.3	0.00	0.00	0.00
27	Crude fertilizers (imports only), except those of division 56, and crude minerals (excluding coal, petroleum, and precious stones)	0.0	0.0	0.0	0.9	2.4	1.6	0.00	0.00	0.00

(continued)

Table 9.2 (continued)

SITC	Description	Swedish importance (%)			Chinese market share (%)			Contribution to competition (%)		
		1989	2004	Change	1989	2004	Change	1989	2004	Change
43	Animal or vegetable fats and oils processed; waxes and inedible mixtures or preparations of animal or vegetable fats or oils, n.e.s.	0.0	0.0	0.0	0.3	0.8	0.6	0.00	0.00	0.00
21	Hides, skins, and furskins, raw	0.0	0.1	0.1		0.1	0.1	0.00	0.00	0.00
34	Gas, natural and manufactured	0.0	0.0	0.0		0.1	0.1	0.00	0.00	0.00
41	Animal oils and fats	0.0	0.0	0.0		0.0	0.0	0.00	0.00	0.00
56	Fertilizers (exports include group 272; imports exclude group 272)	0.0	0.0	0.0		1.4	1.4	0.00	0.00	0.00
97	Gold, nonmonetary (excluding gold ores and concentrates)	0.0	0.0	0.0		0.2	0.2	0.00	0.00	0.00
0	Live animals, other than fish, crustaceans, molluscs, and aquatic invertebrates of division 03	0.0	0.0	0.0	0.1	0.8	0.8	0.00	0.00	0.00
23	Crude rubber (including synthetic and reclaimed)	0.0	0.0	0.0	0.5	1.1	0.6	0.00	0.00	0.00
1	Meat and meat preparations	0.0	0.0	0.0	**23.2**		−23.2	0.00	0.00	0.00
12	Tobacco and tobacco manufactures	0.0	0.0	0.0	0.1	0.0	−0.1	0.00	0.00	0.00
95	Coin, including gold coin; proof and presentation sets and current coin	0.0	0.0	0.0	**19.7**	3.3	−16.4	0.00	0.00	0.00
42	Fixed vegetable fats and oils: crude, refined, or fractionated	0.0	0.0	0.0	4.1	0.9	−3.2	0.00	0.00	0.00
6	Sugars, sugar preparations, and honey	0.1	0.0	−0.1	1.1	6.8	5.6	0.00	0.00	0.00
2	Dairy products and birds' eggs	0.1	0.0	−0.1	1.1	1.1	−1.1	0.00	0.00	0.00
3	Fish (not marine mammals), crustaceans, molluscs, and aquatic invertebrates, and preparations thereof	0.0	0.0	0.0	10.9	3.3	−7.6	0.00	0.00	0.00
7	Coffee, tea, cocoa, spices, and manufactures thereof	0.3	0.2	0.0	4.1	0.7	−3.4	0.01	0.00	−0.01
29	Crude animal and vegetable materials, n.e.s.	0.2	0.0	−0.2	**15.2**	30.6	15.4	0.03	0.00	−0.03
28	Metalliferous ores and metal scrap	0.4	0.1	−0.2	**18.3**	0.3	−18.0	**0.07**	0.00	−0.07
	Total	100	100		2.5	19.3		**1.08**	**9.54**	**8.46**

Notes: SITC = Standard International Trade Classification; n.e.s. = not elsewhere specified. Swedish importance = Swedish share of Swedish exports to the United States. Chinese market share = U.S. imports from China as share of total U.S. Imports. Contribution to competition = Importance times market share. Commodities ordered by change in contribution. Noteworthy numbers in bold.

Table 9.3   Chinese competition for Swedish exports to the United States, 1989 and 2004, three-digit and four-digit detail for SITC 76

SITC		Swedish importance (%)			China market share (%)			Contribution to competition (%)		
		1989	2004	Change	1989	2004	Change	1989	2004	Change
76	Telecommunications and sound recording and reproducing apparatus and equipment	1.7	8.7	7.0	3.4	29.8	26.4	0.06	2.59	2.53
761	TV receivers (including video monitors and projectors) whether or not incorporating radio-broadcast receivers or sound or video recording or reproducing apparatus	0.0	0.0	0.0	5.3	12.8	7.5	0.00	0.00	0.00
762	Radio-broadcast receivers, whether or not incorporating sound recording or reproducing apparatus or a clock	0.0	0.0	0.0	4.8	49.8	45.0	0.00	0.00	0.00
763	Sound recorders or reproducers; television image and sound recorders or reproducers	0.0	0.0	0.0	1.9	56.2	54.3	0.00	0.01	0.01
764	**Telecommunications equipment, n.e.s., and parts, n.e.s., and accessories of apparatus falling within telecommunications, etc.**	**1.7**	**8.7**	**7.0**	**4.1**	**24.4**	**20.4**	**0.07**	**2.12**	**2.05**
	764 total	1.7	8.7	7.0	4.1	24.4	20.4	0.07	2.12	2.05
7641	Electrical apparatus for line telephony or line telegraphy (including such apparatus for carrier-current line systems)	0.1	0.2	0.1	13.6	29.5	15.9	0.01	0.06	0.04
7642	Microphones and stands thereof; loudspeakers, headphones, earphones, and combined microphone/speaker sets; audio-frequency electric amplifiers, etc.	0.0	0.1	0.1	3.2	50.2	46.9	0.00	0.04	0.04
7643	**Transmission apparatus for radiotelephony, telegraphy, broadcasting, or television, whether or not including reception or sound recording apparatus, etc.**	**0.4**	**5.7**	**5.3**	**1.4**	**24.8**	**23.5**	**0.01**	**1.41**	**1.40**
7648	Telecommunications equipment, n.e.s.	0.1	0.2	0.1	3.0	9.5	6.6	0.00	0.02	0.01
7649	Parts and accessories suitable for use solely or principally with the apparatus of telecommunications and sound recording and reproducing equipment	1.1	2.5	1.5	1.6	16.1	14.5	0.02	0.41	0.39
	Total all Products, two-digit analysis	100.0	100.0	0.0	2.5	19.3	16.8	2.47	19.27	16.80

percent, all of which is from SITC 764. Next, this is disaggregated into the four-digit detail, revealing that it is SITC 7643, "transmission apparatus for radiotelephony," and SITC 7643, "parts for telecommunications and sound recording," that is the main source of this increase in competition.

Table 9.4 has the three-digit detail for two subsets of products: those that contributed most to the increase in competition from 1989 to 2004 and those that are important for Sweden for which the Chinese market shares are relatively small. Again, at the top of the list of contributors to increased competition is SITC 764, telecommunications equipment. Next comes SITC 775, "household electrical and nonelectrical equipment," then SITC 821, "furniture," then tools and then pharmaceutical products. While these last two products are not very important to Sweden, the increase in the Chinese market shares was great enough that these products contribute substantially to the increase in the measured intensity of Chinese competition for Swedish exports.

The most important sector for Sweden that faced little Chinese competition is SITC 781, "motor vehicles," which comprised 41.4 percent of Swedish exports in 1989 but only 20.2 percent in 2004. While China has hardly any exports to the United States in this category, plans are already in place to produce vehicles in China for export to the United States.

Parenthetically, one reason why the rise of Chinese exports is not as ominous as it sounds is that a significant fraction of Chinese export value originates in Japan and other high-wage countries, which ship intermediate products and ideas to China, where they are transformed into final goods for export. Nonetheless, some of the value added in Chinese exports surely originates in China, and the cost reductions from global production sharing with China create a cost disadvantage for Sweden if the same production sharing is not exploited also by Swedish manufacturers.

The changing nature of the global marketplace can be met by a clinging to the old industries or by a rapid adjustment away from the sectors in which low-wage competition is most problematic. Ideally, losses in jobs and production in the losing sectors would be offset by gains in jobs and production in the winning sectors. Sweden is not clinging to the past, but on the other hand, the winning sectors in manufacturing are few and far between. That fact of life puts greater emphasis on the transition from industrial to postindustrial work, which is discussed in the next section.

The bad news regarding Swedish employment is displayed in table 9.5, which reports the number of Swedish workers in two-digit International Standard Industrial Classification (ISIC) industries in 1980, 1990, 2000, and 2003. Industries are sorted by percentage job loss in this period, reported in the last column. That loss varies from a 69.2 percent loss in textiles (wearing apparel, footwear, and textiles) to a loss of 10 percent in gasoline. The only gain was 11.6 percent for motor vehicles. Theses changes in the mix of manufacturing jobs are symptomatic of the increased competition from

Table 9.4   Chinese competition for Swedish exports to the United States, 1989 and 2004, three-digit detail: Selected sectors

SITC 3		Swedish importance (%)		Chinese market share (%)		Contribution to competition (%)		
		1989	2004	1989	2004	1989	2004	Change
	Sectors for which the increase in competition was greatest							
1	764	Telecommunications equipment, n.e.s., and parts, n.e.s., and accessories of apparatus falling within telecommunications, etc.	1.7	8.7	4.1	24.4	0.07	2.12	2.05
2	775	Household-type electrical and nonelectrical equipment, n.e.s.	0.1	1.6	13.7	39.4	0.02	0.63	0.61
3	821	Furniture and parts thereof; bedding, mattresses, mattress supports, cushions, and similar stuffed furnishings	1.3	0.9	1.2	41.1	0.02	0.37	0.36
4	695	Tools for use in the hand or in machines	1.6	1.7	5.4	19.8	0.09	0.33	0.24
5	541	Medicinal and pharmaceutical products, other than medicaments (of group 542)	0.1	5.5	1.7	4.5	0.00	0.25	0.25
6	894	Baby carriages, toys, games and sporting goods	0.4	0.3	33.8	81.1	0.15	0.24	0.09
7	745	Nonelectrical machinery, tools, and mechanical apparatus, and parts thereof, n.e.s.	1.1	1.8	0.7	11.8	0.01	0.21	0.20
8	699	Manufactures of base metal, n.e.s.	1.1	0.7	2.1	24.5	0.02	0.18	0.16
9	893	Articles of plastics, n.e.s.	0.8	0.5	6.7	36.9	0.05	0.18	0.13
10	751	Office machines	0.2	0.4	1.2	41.4	0.00	0.18	0.18
11	874	Measuring, checking, analyzing, and controlling instruments and apparatus, n.e.s.	1.1	2.2	0.8	8.0	0.01	0.18	0.17
12	691	Metal structures and parts of iron, steel or aluminum, n.e.s.	0.1	1.5	0.2	9.8	0.00	0.15	0.15
13	752	Automatic data-processing machines and units thereof; magnetic or optical readers; machines transcribing coded media and processing such data, n.e.s.	0.6	0.3	0.2	41.6	0.00	0.14	0.14
14	743	Pumps (not for liquids), air or gas compressors and fans; ventilating hoods incorporating a fan; centrifuges; filtering apparatus, etc.; parts thereof	1.6	1.2	2.6	11.7	0.04	0.14	0.09
15	778	Electrical machinery and apparatus, n.e.s.	0.9	0.7	1.6	19.4	0.01	0.13	0.11
16	772	Electrical apparatus for switching or protecting electrical circuits or for making connections to or in electrical circuits (excluding telephone, etc.)	1.2	0.9	0.6	12.9	0.01	0.12	0.11
17	771	Electric power machinery (other than rotating electric plant of power-generating machinery) and parts thereof	1.0	0.3	1.3	33.8	0.01	0.11	0.10

(continued)

Table 9.4 (continued)

SITC 3		Swedish importance (%) 1989	Swedish importance (%) 2004	Chinese market share (%) 1989	Chinese market share (%) 2004	Contribution to competition (%) 1989	Contribution to competition (%) 2004	Contribution to competition (%) Change
18	759	Parts and accessories suitable for use solely or principally with office machines or automatic data-processing machines	1.0	0.3	0.1	31.4	0.00	0.10	0.10
19	744	Mechanical handling equipment and parts thereof, n.e.s.	1.5	1.3	1.5	7.2	0.02	0.10	0.07
20	728	Machinery and equipment specialized for particular industries and parts thereof, n.e.s.	1.0	1.3	0.2	6.7	0.00	0.09	0.09
		Important Swedish sectors facing little Chinese competition							
1	781	Motor cars and other motor vehicles principally designed for the transport of persons (not public transport), including station wagons and racing cars	41.4	20.2	0.0	0.2	0.00	0.04	0.04
2	542	Medicaments (including veterinary medicaments)	1.1	6.1	0.6	0.1	0.01	0.00	0.00
3	334	Petroleum oils and oils from bituminous minerals (other than crude), and products therefrom containing 70 percent (by weight) or more of these oils, n.e.s.	0.6	4.3	0.2	0.4	0.00	0.02	0.02
4	112	Alcoholic beverages	2.7	3.3	0.4	0.2	0.01	0.01	0.00
5	713	Internal combustion piston engines and parts thereof, n.e.s.	1.5	2.2	0.1	0.9	0.00	0.02	0.02
6	931	Special transactions and commodities not classified according to kind	4.2	1.7	0.7	2.1	0.03	0.04	0.01
7	723	Civil engineering and contractors' plant and equipment	1.2	1.6	0.4	2.3	0.00	0.04	0.03
8	714	Engines and motors, nonelectric (other than steam turbines, internal combustion piston engines, and power-generating machinery); parts thereof, n.e.s.	3.9	1.4	0.4	1.8	0.02	0.03	0.01
9	248	Wood, simply worked, and railway sleepers of wood	0.2	1.2	0.0	2.3	0.00	0.03	0.03
10	784	Parts and accessories for tractors, motor cars, and other motor vehicles, trucks, public transport vehicles and road motor vehicles, n.e.s.	2.0	1.2	0.1	4.0	0.00	0.05	0.05
11	872	Instruments and appliances, n.e.s., for medical, surgical, dental, or veterinary purposes	0.6	1.1	2.1	3.0	0.01	0.03	0.02
12	598	Miscellaneous chemical products, n.e.s.	0.1	1.0	0.6	4.4	0.00	0.05	0.04
13	575	Plastics in primary forms, n.e.s.	0.6	1.0	0.5	8.8	0.00	0.08	0.08
14	641	Paper and paperboard	3.1	1.0	0.1	4.0	0.00	0.04	0.04
		Grand total (including omitted sectors)	100.0	100.0	2.5	19.3	0.95	8.37	7.16

Table 9.5   **Swedish number of employees in two-digit ISIC manufacturing industries**

	Number of employees				Annualized rate of growth (%)				Total (%) 1980–2003
	1980	1990	2000	2003	1980s	1990s	2000s	All	
Total	968.3	885.9	745.7	713	−0.9	−1.7	−1.5	−1.3	−26.4
Textiles (17–19)	40.2	24.6	13.6	12.4	**−4.8**	**−5.8**	**−3.0**	**−5.0**	−69.2
Metals, basic (27)	67.7	45	31	33.2	**−4.0**	**−3.7**	2.3	**−3.1**	−51.0
Transportation: other (35)	39.9	26.2	20.1	19.7	**−4.1**	−2.6	−0.7	**−3.0**	−50.6
Mineral products (26)	30.5	26.7	17.5	18.5	−1.3	**−4.1**	1.9	−2.2	−39.3
Printing (22)	72.5	70.6	50.9	44.2	−0.3	**−3.2**	**−4.6**	−2.1	−39.0
Paper (21)	61.6	53.9	42.1	38.4	−1.3	−2.4	**−3.0**	−2.0	−37.7
Wood (20)	54	49.6	38.4	36.5	−0.8	−2.5	−1.7	−1.7	−32.4
Food processing (15–16)	82.8	79	62.2	62.8	−0.5	−2.4	0.3	−1.2	−24.2
Electrical (30–33)	103.5	91.6	96.8	79.9	−1.2	0.6	**−6.2**	−1.1	−22.8
Metal, fabricated (28)	95	93.7	80.4	73.9	−0.1	−1.5	−2.8	−1.1	−22.2
Not elsewhere classified (36–37)	65.4	61.4	54	52.1	−0.6	−1.3	−1.2	−1.0	−20.3
Rubber (25)	29.2	26.7	25.2	23.8	−0.9	−0.6	−1.9	−0.9	−18.5
Chemicals (24)	44.3	39.2	38.6	39.5	−1.2	−0.2	0.8	−0.5	−10.8
Machinery, n.e.c. (29)	110.7	116.3	96.5	99.3	0.5	−1.8	1.0	−0.5	−10.3
Gasoline (23)	3	3.2	2.8	2.7	0.6	−1.3	−1.2	−0.5	−10.0
Motor vehicles (34)	67.9	78.2	75.6	75.8	1.4	−0.3	0.1	0.5	11.6

Notes: Sweden suffered two periods of substantial declines in manufacturing employment: 1980 to 1983 and 1989 to 1993. These declines were pretty much across all sectors, though they were somewhat greater in labor-intensive sectors. Boldface numbers are those greater than 0.0 percent. Boldface numbers in shaded boxes are those less than −3.0 percent. Not elsewhere classified = "n.e.c."

low-wage suppliers of standardized products, to which a response helps to maintain the Swedish distinctiveness barrier. As will be discussed in the next section, the across-the-board losses are not so unusual, as many advanced developed countries are experiencing declines in manufacturing employment.

It is not just the jobs that are changing. It's also value added reported in table 9.6, which is sorted from losers (of which there are many) to winners (of which there are none). Here, we see more of the same.

All in all, the degree of competition between Swedish products and products made in low-wage emerging economies remains quite low, but storm clouds are gathering on the horizon, suggesting the need to take preventative measures to maintain the distinctiveness barrier that has protected Swedish workers from low-wage foreign competition. The proper antidote is increased emphasis on innovation in manufacturing and thus educational investments for the humans who do the innovating. But the decline in jobs in manufacturing and the stagnation overall in value added means that Sweden increasingly will have to look elsewhere for sustained economic growth.

Table 9.6   **Swedish value added in manufacturing (millions of constant U.S. dollars, 2003)**

	1970	1980	1990	2000	2002	Max	Year	Loss (%)
Communication (32)		2,083	1,997	2,803	383	4,089	1998	−91
Apparel (18)		584	277	119	112	584	1980	−81
Transportation: ships (351)		1,221	473	251	242	1,221	1980	−80
Computers (30)		1,019	588	253	267	1,269	1988	−79
Leather (19)		212	103	50	48	212	1980	−77
Textiles (17–19)	1,713	1,555	1,087	611	576	2,126	1975	−73
Gasoline (23)		328	772	553	283	942	1986	−70
Textiles (17–18)		1,343	984	560	528	1,343	1980	−61
Metals, nonferrous		737	748	421	391	899	1988	−57
Electrical (30–33)		5,319	5,738	6,144	3,886	8,291	1998	−53
Transportation: other (35)		2,557	2,005	1,208	1,246	2,557	1980	−51
Transportation: railroad (352, 359)		591	536	260	352	693	1992	−49
Wood (20)	2,229	3,871	3,982	2,209	2,161	4,160	1974	−48
Transportation: aircraft (353)		746	997	697	652	1,206	1992	−46
Metals, basic (27)		4,047	3,387	2,323	2,207	4,047	1980	−45
Metals, steel (271+)		3,310	2,639	1,902	1,816	3,310	1980	−45
Textiles (17)		759	707	441	416	759	1980	−45
Mineral products (26)	1,389	1,782	2,015	1,125	1,119	2,015	1990	−44
Chemicals: other (not 2423)		3,082	3,022	2,193	1,931	3,269	1988	−41
Paper (21)		4,784	5,722	4,830	4,120	6,697	1995	−38
Machinery and equipment (29–33)	6,302	12,335	13,986	12,457	10,094	16,290	1996	−38
21–22	5,010	8,110	9,273	8,231	7,102	10,766	1995	−34
Printing (22)		3,327	3,551	3,400	2,983	4,325	1996	−31
Metals (27–28)	5,753	8,385	8,533	6,694	6,164	8,938	1975	−31
Metals and equipment (27–35)	15,252	27,100	29,847	26,792	22,209	32,161	1996	−31
Food processing (15–16)	2,350	3,670	5,346	4,020	3,975	5,576	1996	−29
Motor vehicles (34)		3,823	5,322	6,433	4,705	6,433	2000	−27
Transport (34–35)	3,197	6,380	7,327	7,641	5,951	7,969	1988	−25
Instruments (33)		541	1,462	1,480	1,703	2,279	1998	−25
Machinery, n.e.c. (29)		7,017	8,249	6,313	6,208	8,249	1990	−25
Metal, fabricated (28)		4,338	5,146	4,371	3,957	5,146	1990	−23
Not elsewhere classified (36–37)	967	1,414	1,558	1,422	1,291	1,673	1996	−23
Rubber (25)		1,432	1,540	1,433	1,381	1,752	1996	−21
Electric, other (31)		1,675	1,691	1,608	1,533	1,810	1996	−15
23–25	2,939	5,664	6,915	7,198	7,441	7,626	1998	−2
Chemicals (24)		3,904	4,602	5,213	5,777	5,777	2002	0
Chemicals: pharmaceutical (2423)		822	1,580	3,019	3,846	3,846	2002	0
Total	31,848	53,166	60,022	51,609	45,875	61,182	1996	−25

9.3   The Difficult Transition to a Postindustrial Creative Economy

While the problem of competition with low-wage countries intensifies, there is a new problem emerging—Sweden and all other advanced developed countries are experiencing a difficult transition from industrial to postindustrial economies, symptomized by a declining fraction of GDP and employment in manufacturing production and a rising fraction of GDP and employment in creative/intellectual services. While manufacturing is reasonably compatible with a compressed income distribution and an aggressive welfare state, the efficient production of creative services is likely to produce much greater natural income inequality and greater dissonance with the goals of a welfare state. It's the difference between Detroit, where there are good jobs for many, and Hollywood, where there are great jobs for few.

The transition from industrial to postindustrial economy is likely to be more difficult than the transition from agrarian to industrial economy. The transition from agrarian to industrial society was driven fundamentally by a *pull* of manual workers off of the farms into *higher*-paying mechanical jobs on the factory floor and a *parallel elimination* of skilled craft jobs in artisan shops because of standardization and mechanization in manufacturing. Though entrepreneurial activities at the early stages of industrialization required great concentrations of capital, giving rise to the inequality that so bothered Karl Marx, by the second half of the twentieth century, manufacturing had proven its worth in generating good jobs for many and a comfortable degree of income equality.

The next transition from industrial to postindustrial economy is being driven fundamentally by a *push* of manual workers off of the factory floor into *lower*-paying service jobs in retail and hospitals and a parallel expansion of skilled creative craft jobs in the intellectual services, both traded and nontraded.

The word itself—manufacturing—tells us much about the transition from agrarian to industrial economies in the first part of the twentieth century. "Manu" in manufacturing is a reference to manual labor. Manufactured literally means "built by hand" (with the help of equipment, of course.) In a postindustrial age, manufacturing is giving rise to neurofacturing—made with the mind. In the industrial age, a mechanic was one who operated the equipment, producing reliably identical output, hour after hour. In the postindustrial age, mechanical is an epithet, referring to intellectual output that is the same as all the others—the last thing we want.

While innovations in equipment spurred by the electric motor have greatly increased productivity in manufacturing, most of the innovations of the industrial age have made very little encroachment on intellectual tasks, mundane or otherwise. An attorney, an architect, a teacher, and a clerk all did about the same work in 1970 as they did in 1800—pushing pencils and filing the work. But the microprocessor has changed the future of intellectual work, eliminating the mundane intellectual tasks and the filing. Think about an architect. In 1970, the time of a creative architect partly was consumed by the task of rendering the drawings. Some of this work could be done by assistants, but the communication costs were often so high that it made more sense to have the master do the drawings. The personal computer, however, has allowed the architect to render the drawings with great efficiency, thus freeing up time to do the creative tasks that the computer cannot ever perform. Doing economics is the same. I used to hire teams of research assistants and secretaries, but now I do all that work at the touch of a button or two on my computer keyboard.

The effect of the personal computer and Internet access has been to eliminate the mundane and to leave mostly the creative tasks. That puts a heavy emphasis on creativity and talent, which tends to create a highly unequal Hollywood-style income distribution.

9.3.1   The U.S. Transition from Industrial to Postindustrial Economy

For more than a century beginning in the mid-1800s, the U.S. economy created wealth by moving workers off of the family farm, where annual earnings were low, and onto the factory floor, where annual earnings were three times as high (see figure 9.4).

The transition from agrarian to industrial society reduced the fraction of the U.S. workforce on farms from 41 percent at the beginning of the twentieth century to 2.5 percent at the end (see figure 9.5). During the first seven decades of the twentieth century, job losses in agriculture were partly offset by job gains in manufacturing, as the fraction in manufacturing rose from 22 percent in 1900 to a peacetime peak of 31 percent in 1953.

1970 Marks the Beginning of the Postindustrial Age for the United States

The U.S. transition from agrarian to industrial society ended in 1970, with the workforce in agriculture down to 5 percent and the workforce in manufacturing hovering at 27 percent. Thence commenced the more difficult transition from industrial to postindustrial society, whose prominent symptom is a collapse in manufacturing jobs, from 27 percent in 1970 to a meager 11 percent after the recession of 2001.

The speed of this decline in manufacturing opportunities after 1970 from a 28 percent share to an 11 percent share was every bit as rapid as the speed in the decline of agricultural jobs in the first seven decades of the twentieth century.

9.3.2   This Transition Is Occurring for All
the Advanced Developed Countries

It is not only the United States that has experienced a sharp decline in manufacturing jobs. Figure 9.6 illustrates the declining fraction of manufacturing for all OECD countries. In the middle, you can see both the industri-

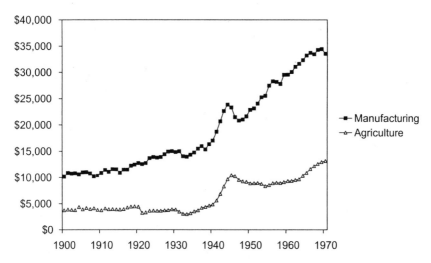

Fig. 9.4   Annual earnings in agriculture and manufacturing (Consumer Price Index 1999 U.S. dollars)

Source: BLS = Bureau of Labor Statistics; HSUS = Historical Statistics of the United States.

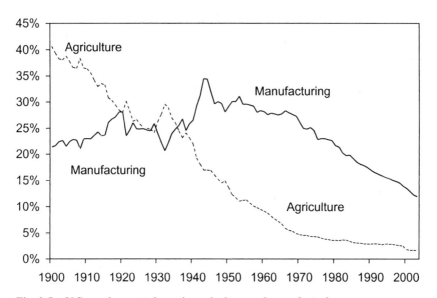

Fig. 9.5   U.S. employment shares in agriculture and manufacturing

alization period and the postindustrial period for Korea, with the fraction of the workforce in manufacturing peaking in 1990 at 28 percent of the workforce. The only other exception to the experience of sharply declining manufacturing jobs is the Czech Republic, which had a small increase in the share of manufacturing in the 1990s.

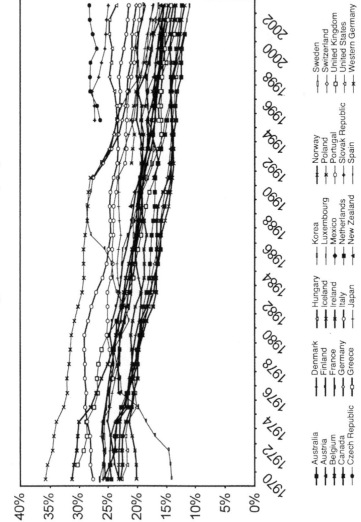

Fig. 9.6   Declining manufacturing shares of employment in OECD countries

Further information about the transitions experienced by these OECD countries is reported in table 9.7, which indicates the total number of workers from the OECD STructural ANalysis (STAN) database in 1970, 1980, 1990, 2000, and 2003, together with the employment shares in manufacturing, agriculture, mining, and the rest (services, including government). Countries are sorted by their manufacturing shares in 2000, from largest to smallest. The values that are in the top 20 percent are printed in bold.

This table indicates the rapid transition into a postindustrial economy for almost all of these OECD countries. The Korean data are particularly interesting, because this period encompasses both the period of industrialization, in which workers were moved off of the farm and onto the factory floor, and the beginning of the postindustrial period, in which a diminishing share of the workforce found jobs in manufacturing. The Korean agricultural share falls steadily in this period, from a peak of 47 percent in 1970 to a low of 9 percent in 2003. That 9 percent is still among the highest, suggesting that this trend is not likely to abate. Meanwhile, the Korean share of the workforce in manufacturing rose from 14 percent in 1970 to a peak of 28 percent in 1990 but has fallen dramatically in the 1990s to 20 percent.

Table 9.8 reports the current and the peak levels of employment in manufacturing since 1970 for the OECD countries in the STAN database. The penultimate column indicates the percent by which the latest available figure is less than the peak value, and the last column indicates the year in which the peak occurred. The countries are sorted by this last column, roughly the point at which this country begins the difficult transition into a postindustrial economy. By this measure, *Sweden was among the first countries to experience the end of the manufacturing age.* Employment in manufacturing in Sweden was the greatest at the very start of the time period covered. From that value of 1.04 million in 1970, manufacturing employment had fallen 32 percent by 2003. The long-term downward trend in manufacturing employment was punctuated by a very sharp decline in the crisis of the early 1990s, from which Swedish manufactures recovered only in the sense of not losing more workers (see figure 9.7). Meanwhile, value added in manufactures, illustrated in figure 9.8, has only the most modest upward trend, if any, and is punctuated by periodic recessions.

9.3.3   The Industrial Model and the Postindustrial Model

Figure 9.9 compares the growth in real per capita incomes for fourteen OCED countries in three decades for which the data are complete with the corresponding decline in agricultural share. Sure enough, we see the force of the old business model: those countries that most rapidly moved workers off of the farms are the ones that experienced the most rapid increase in per capita incomes. With agricultural shares very low in many OECD countries, most notably only 2 percent in Sweden, that industrialization process is mostly historical. Now, economic growth will come in the intellectual service sectors.

Table 9.7 Employment: OECD STAN database

	Total: Millions of employees					Manufacturing share (%)					Agricultural share (%)					Mining and quarrying share (%)					Government and services (%)				
	1970	1980	1990	2000	2003	1970	1980	1990	2000	2003	1970	1980	1990	2000	2003	1970	1980	1990	2000	2003	1970	1980	1990	2000	2003
Czech Republic				4.8	4.9				**27**	**28**				5	4				1	1				67	67
Slovak Republic				2.0	2.1				**26**	**25**				6	4				1	1				68	70
Hungary			3.8	3.8	3.9				**24**	**24**				7	5				0	0			69	69	71
Italy	19.9	21.4	22.6	**23.1**	24.3	**28**	**29**	**25**	22	21	21	13	7	5	4	0	0	0	0	0	52	57	68	73	74
Portugal		4.5	4.6	4.9	5.0		**25**	**24**	20	20		21	16	**10**	**10**		1	0	0	0		54	61	70	70
Korea	9.6	13.7	18.1	**21.1**	**22.1**	14	23	**28**	20	19	**47**	**31**	**16**	11	9	1	1	0	0	0	38	45	56	69	72
Finland	2.3	2.4	2.5	2.3	2.4	23	**25**	20	20	19	**21**	13	9	6	5	0	0	0	0	0	55	62	71	74	76
Japan	**54.4**	**58.7**	**64.3**	**66.6**	**65.1**	26	23	23	19	17	**20**	13	9	6	6	0	0	1	0	0	54	64	68	75	77
Spain		12.4	13.8	15.7	16.6		23	20	18	17		17	**11**	6	6		1	1	**2**	0		59	69	75	77
Poland				15.0					18					**26**					2					54	
Ireland	1.1	1.2	1.2	1.7	1.8	20	21	19	18	16	**27**	**18**	**15**	8	7	1	1	1	0	0	52	60	65	74	77
Sweden	3.9	4.3	4.6	4.3	4.3	26	23	19	17	16	7	5	3	3	2	0	0	0	0	0	66	72	77	80	81
Denmark	2.5	2.5	2.6	2.7	2.7	26	20	19	17	15	11	8	6	4	4	0	0	0	0	0	63	72	75	79	81
New Zealand			1.2	1.4	1.5			20	16	16			1	0	1			0	0	0			**79**	**83**	**83**
Austria		3.8	3.9	4.1	4.1		23	20	16	15		**20**	**17**	**13**	**13**				0	0		57	63	70	71
Belgium	3.8	3.8	3.9	4.1	4.1	**31**	24	20	16	15	6	4	3	2	2		1	0	0	0	63	72	77	82	**83**
France	21.1	22.2	22.9	**24.3**	**24.9**	25	24	19	16		14	9	6	4	4				0		61	68	75	80	
Iceland				0.2	0.2				15	14				8	7				0	0				76	79
Greece				3.9	4.0				15	14				**17**	**15**				0	1				67	70
Canada	8.4	11.1	13.4	15.2	16.0	23	19	16	14	13	6	5	4	3	3	**2**	**2**	1	1	1	69	75	79	81	**83**
United Kingdom	**26.5**	**27.1**	**29.0**	**29.4**			**25**	18	14			2	2	2			1	1	0			71	**79**	**84**	
The Netherlands	6.1	6.2	6.7	8.1	8.3	25	20	17	13	12	6	5	4	3	3	0	0	1	0	0	68	75	78	**83**	**84**
Norway	1.6	1.9	2.1	2.3	2.3	23	19	14	13	12	13	8	6	4	4	1	1	1	1	1	63	71	78	82	**83**
United States	**86.9**	**107.1**	**128.3**	**149.7**		23	19	15	13		4	3	3	2		1	1	1	0		73	76	82	**85**	
Luxembourg			0.2	0.3	0.3			19	12	11			3	2	1			0	0				78	**86**	**87**
Australia		6.3	7.8	9.1			20	15	12			7	6	5		**2**	1	1	1			72	78	82	
Germany				38.7	38.3				**21**	**20**				2	2				0	0				76	77
Western Germany	**26.6**	**27.4**	**30.3**			**36**	**31**	**28**			9	5	4			1	1	1			54	63	67		
Mexico																									
Switzerland																									

Note: Values in the top 20 percent in bold.

Table 9.8   **Employment in manufacturing: Millions of workers**

	Post-1970 Max	Latest values			Loss	Year max
		2001	2002	2003		
The Netherlands	1.53	1.08	1.06	1.03	−33	1970
Sweden	**1.04**	**0.75**	**0.73**	**0.71**	**−32**	**1970**
Belgium	1.17	0.66	0.63	0.61	−48	1970
Denmark	0.64	0.45	0.43	0.42	−34	1970
United Kingdom	7.88	4.08	3.88		−51	1971
Australia	1.38	1.10			−21	1973
Austria	0.88	0.66	0.65	0.64	−27	1973
France	5.64	3.85	3.79		−33	1974
Finland	0.58	0.46	0.45	0.44	−25	1974
Norway	0.39	0.29	0.29	0.27	−30	1974
Spain	2.98	2.93	2.92	2.86	−4	1978
United States	**21.53**	**18.07**			**−16**	**1979**
Italy	6.21	5.16	5.20	5.21	−16	1980
Portugal	1.14	1.01	0.99	0.98	−14	1981
Luxembourg	0.04	0.03	0.03	0.03	−12	1986
Canada	2.20	2.17	2.15	2.15	−2	1989
New Zealand	0.26	0.23	0.24	0.25	−4	1989
Germany	10.58	8.13	7.95	7.74	−27	1991
Korea	5.16	4.27	4.24	4.21	−18	1991
Japan	15.27	12.16	11.58	11.33	−26	1992
Hungary	1.05	0.96	0.96	0.93	−12	1992
Greece	0.63	0.60	0.58	0.57	−9	1996
Poland	3.13	2.64	2.56		−18	1997
Czech Republic	1.45	1.34	1.38	1.38	−5	1997
Slovak Republic	0.59	0.52	0.51	0.51	−13	1997
Iceland	0.02	0.02	0.02	0.02	−13	1997
Ireland	0.30	0.30	0.29	0.28	−6	2001

Note: Transition to a postindustrial society; sorted by year in which maximum occurred.

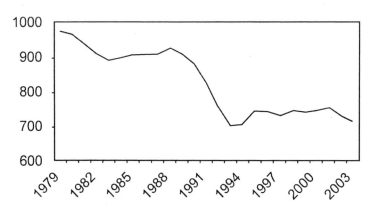

Fig. 9.7   **Swedish employment in manufactures (thousands)**

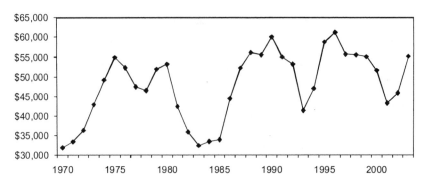

Fig. 9.8   Swedish value added in manufactures: Millions of U.S. dollars, 2003

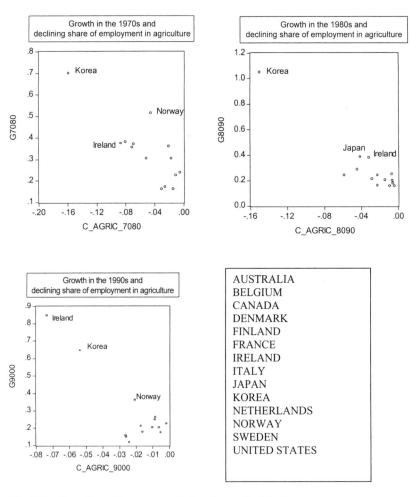

Fig. 9.9   Growth and the movement of workers off of the farm

Figure 9.10 displays the value added fractions of manufacturing and finance, insurance, and real estate (FIRE) over time for the United States. In 1987, 20 percent of U.S. GDP originated in manufacturing and 16 percent in FIRE. But the data trace out a large and ominous X, with FIRE crossing manufacturing in 1996, just when the Internet rush was beginning. Is that the essence of the new economy? We don't make anything anymore, but instead celebrate our genius in a gigantic parasitic bonFIRE?

Further details about the structure of U.S. earnings are reported in table 9.9, which reports the shares of earnings at the two-digit North American Industry Classification System (NAICS) level of aggregation. This new NAICS scheme was explicitly adopted to deal with the emerging knowledge work in the United States, and I have grouped the categories into manufacturing (including construction and transportation), distribution, services, government, and neurofacturing (information, finance, and professional and business services). Neurofacturing by this imperfect rendering now encompasses about 36 percent of earnings, while manufacturing is only 24 percent.

The Bureau of Economic Analysis discussion of 2007 first-quarter U.S. growth further illustrates the importance of financial activities in U.S. growth:

> Personal income in only five states (New York, Connecticut, New Jersey, Illinois, and Delaware) grew faster than the national average. Another four states matched the national growth rate and the rest of the states and the District of Columbia grew slower. This geographical concentration of personal income growth is attributable to the unusually strong contribution to earnings growth of the finance industry centered in New York (and to a lesser extent in Connecticut, New Jersey, and Illinois). The finance industry alone accounted for 38 percent of the nation's earnings growth in the first quarter of 2007 and earnings growth in these five states accounted for 36 percent of the nation's growth. Connecticut and New Jersey also benefited disproportionately because of their commuting flows into New York—personal income represents the income of a state's residents regardless of where it is earned. (U.S. Department of Commerce, Bureau of Economic Analysis 2007)

9.3.4   Postindustrial Earnings, Inequality, and Opportunity

While the shift out of manufacturing and into finance is clear in the data, what is not clear is the effect that the personal computer and the Internet are having on the market for intellectual services. A proper time series study of this hypothesis is beyond the scope of this chapter, but a look at the compensation in finance and manufacturing in the United States and in Sweden at one point in time sheds some light on the issues. The U.S. hourly and weekly earnings in 1999 to 2000 at the 10th, 50th, and 90th percentiles are reported in table 9.10 by gender and by skills (blue- and

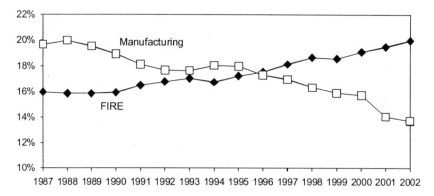

Fig. 9.10   Manufacturing and FIRE fraction of national income
Note: FIRE = finance, insurance, and real estate.

Table 9.9   **U.S. earnings shares, 2006 (%)**

U.S. 2006 national income without capital consumption adjustment	100
Manufacturing	**24.3**
Agriculture, forestry, fishing, and hunting	0.7
Mining	1.7
Utilities	1.6
Construction	5.3
Manufacturing	12.1
Transportation and warehousing	3.0
Distribution	**13.5**
Wholesale trade	6.1
Retail trade	7.3
Services	**14.5**
Other services, except government	2.4
Educational services, health care, and social assistance	8.4
Arts, entertainment, recreation, accommodation, and food services	3.6
Government	**11.7**
Neurofacturing	**35.5**
Information	3.7
Finance, insurance, real estate, rental, and leasing	18.0
Professional and business services	13.8
Rest of the world	**0.5**

white-collar occupations) and by sector (manufacturing, finance, and real estate). Weekly earnings are divided by hourly earnings to estimate apparent weekly hours.

This table and the corresponding figures are intended to help answer this question: what kind of earnings, inequality, and effort are characteristic of a postindustrial society? The table is sorted first by gender and then by the inequality measure: 90/10 ratio of weekly earnings.

Table 9.10   U.S. earnings and hours in real estate, manufacturing, and finance: Current Population Survey, 1999/2000

Sex	Industry	Occupation	n	Fraction (%)	Hourly earnings				Weekly earnings				Apparent hours = weekly earnings/hourly earnings			
					10	50	90	90/10	10	50	90	90/10	10	50	90	90/10
F	Real estate	Blue	2	0.0	8.7	10.3	12.0	1.4	346	413	481	1.39	40.0	40.0	40.0	1
F	Manufacturing	Blue	2,222	11.2	6.1	9.6	16.8	2.7	250	385	712	2.85	40.8	40.0	42.3	1.04
F	Finance	White	2,655	13.4	8.2	13.8	26.4	3.2	333	577	1,135	3.40	40.8	41.7	42.9	1.05
F	Finance	Blue	13	0.1	7.5	12.5	26.4	3.5	308	481	1,058	3.44	41.0	38.4	40.1	0.98
F	Manufacturing	White	2,172	11.0	8.7	15.1	28.8	3.3	346	625	1,250	3.61	40.0	41.4	43.3	1.08
F	Real estate	White	568	2.9	7.7	13.5	27.3	3.6	327	577	1,308	4.00	42.5	42.9	47.9	1.13
M	Real estate	Blue	110	0.6	7.4	14.1	23.8	3.2	300	564	962	3.21	40.5	40.0	40.4	1
M	Manufacturing	Blue	6,111	30.8	7.7	14.1	24.5	3.2	320	596	1,077	3.37	41.6	42.3	43.9	1.06
M	Manufacturing	White	3,701	18.7	11.5	23.1	43.3	3.8	500	1,019	1,981	3.96	43.3	44.2	45.8	1.06
M	Finance	Blue	26	0.1	6.9	15.3	28.8	4.2	288	712	1,154	4.00	42.0	46.6	40.0	0.95
M	Finance	White	1,730	8.7	11.5	24.0	57.7	5.0	495	1,058	2,692	5.44	42.9	44.0	46.7	1.09
M	Real estate	White	517	2.6	9.1	19.7	58.1	6.4	402	940	2,981	7.42	44.2	47.7	51.3	1.16
			19,827	100.0												

Notes: Occupation or industry of job last week and longest job last year were not the same; Usual hours < 35; Weeks worked < 26; wh < $5. A few service workers (e.g., janitors) were dropped. Integrated Public Use Microdata Series: white collar = occupation codes 3–389; blue collar = occupation codes 503–889.

First, consider the mix of jobs. (Keep in mind that to highlight the transition issues from industrial to postindustrial work, the jobs here are limited to those in three sectors: manufacturing, finance, and real estate.)

- The three largest job categories for both men and women are blue-collar jobs in manufacturing and white-collar jobs in manufacturing and finance. That's a pretty fair characterization of the job transition from industrial to postindustrial: from semiskilled manual work in manufacturing to highly skilled brain work in intellectual services.
- Men are greatly overrepresented in the blue-collar occupations in manufacturing. In contrast, there are almost as many white-collar as blue-collar women in manufacturing, and there are more white-collar women in finance than blue-collar women in manufacturing.

Possible implication: the transition from manufacturing to finance and real estate requires a more educated and more talented workforce. This may be more difficult for men than for women. After all, manufacturing starts with man.

Next, consider earnings. For this discussion, some figures are helpful. Figure 9.11 illustrates U.S. data on weekly earnings at the 10th and 90th percentiles for men and women. (The female blue-collar real estate sector is excluded, because the data includes only two observations.) Figure 9.12 illustrates the corresponding 90/10 ratios.

- One thing that stands out in these figures is the clear positive association between median pay and inequality. If the higher-paid white-collar occupations were a simple translation of the low-paid occupations, with each individual in the higher-paid occupation receiving a fixed multiple of the lower-paid job, then the median would change, but the 90/10 ratio would stay exactly the same. In fact, what happens is that the 90/10 ratio increases along with the median, making the 90/10 ratio higher for the white-collar jobs than the blue-collar jobs.
- In addition to the skill effect, there is also a gender effect: males have both higher earnings and greater inequality than females.
- The inequality of the white-collar jobs comes especially at the top of the distribution—the 50th percentiles are only moderately higher than the 10th percentile. This is particularly the case for males in white-collar jobs in finance and real estate.

Implication: the U.S. postindustrial economy has a lot of inequality at the top, especially for men.

Next, we can take a look at the relationship between hours per week and the hourly wage rate. Inside of manufacturing, there is a close association between hours worked, capital intensity, and hourly rates of pay. There is an economic reason for this, explained in Leamer (1999) and explored in

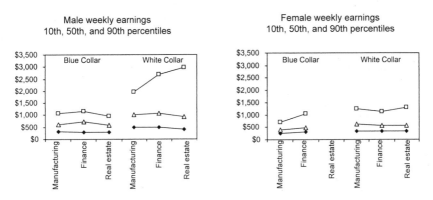

Fig. 9.11   **Earnings: 90/10 ratio of weekly earnings**

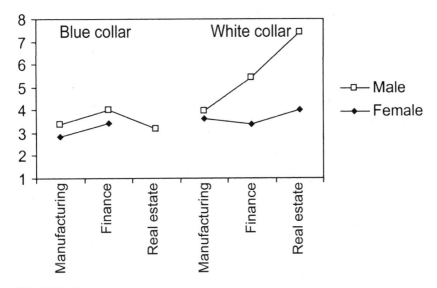

Fig. 9.12   **Inequality**

Leamer and Thornberg (2000). Expensive capital is efficiently deployed by spreading the fixed capital charges over the largest amount of labor input, which means operating the equipment at high speed for long hours during the day. Accordingly, the capital-intensive operations in manufacturing offer workers a special contract: a high hourly wage for hard work and long hours per day.

Figure 9.13 explores this idea for the data in table 9.10 by comparing the apparent hours worked per week with the average hourly earnings at the 10th, 50th, and 90th percentiles. The association between effort as measured by hours per week and wages for blue-collar workers is weak,

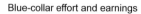

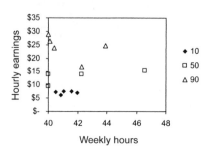
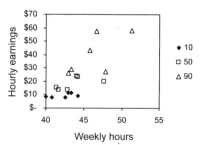

Fig. 9.13   Effort and pay

possibly because over this sample, these workers are operating about the same amount of capital. But for white-collar workers, there is a very clear tendency for higher hourly pay to come with higher weekly hours. The human capital that these knowledge workers acquired in school and on the job is very great, and it is economically inefficient to have that sit idle during short work weeks, long coffee breaks, and abundant vacation time. The U.S. economy responds efficiently to that reality with a reward system that puts a premium on hard work. You could call it inequality, but it is also opportunity. *Possible implication: the very expensive human capital operated by knowledge workers in the intellectual service sectors will earn its highest rate of return if operated for long hours over the lifetime. A country seeking to have high growth, therefore, will see that scarce human capital is allocated to those willing to work hard.*

Sweden

The corresponding Swedish earnings are reported in table 9.11. The earnings compression of the Swedish economy is evident in comparison of the 90/10 ratios with the U.S. ratios. For white-collar workers, these are illustrated in figure 9.14. (To make the next point, I would also need data on hours worked.) *Possibility: to get the highest return on its investment in human capital, Sweden needs more opportunity.*

9.4   Conclusions

Once, the United States entreated Europe (a plaque on the Statue of Liberty):

Give me your tired, your poor,
Your huddled masses yearning to breathe free,
The wretched refuse of your teeming shore.
Send these, the homeless, tempest-tost to me,
I lift my lamp beside the golden door!

Table 9.11   **Swedish earnings**

	Manufacturing ISIC 15–37				Financial activities ISIC 65–67				Real estate ISIC 70–74			
	D9	D5	D1	D9/D1	D9	D5	D1	D9/D1	D9	D5	D1	D9/D1
	Blue collar											
Male	2,919	2,437	2,065	1.41	n.a.	n.a.	n.a.	n.a.	2,869	2,276	1,855	1.55
Female	2,634	2,214	1,917	1.37	n.a.	n.a.	n.a.	n.a.	2,424	1,979	1,793	1.35
Total	2,882	2,399	2,028	1.42	n.a.	n.a.	n.a.	n.a.	2,721	2,127	1,830	1.49
	White collar											
Male	5,491	3,376	2,474	2.22	7,198	3,896	2,461	2.92	5,566	3,463	2,226	2.5
Female	4,329	2,746	2,152	2.01	4,440	2,869	2,177	2.04	4,242	2,696	1,942	2.18
Total	5,195	3,166	2,300	2.26	5,887	3,191	2,239	2.63	5,096	3,092	2,028	2.51
	Total											
Male	4,193	2,647	2,115	1.98	7,186	3,884	2,437	2.95	5,182	3,018	1,991	2.6
Female	3,636	2,412	1,979	1.84	4,428	2,857	2,140	2.07	3,983	2,474	1,830	2.18
Total	4,057	2,585	2,065	1.96	5,862	3,179	2,214	2.65	4,774	2,746	1,892	2.52

Note: n.a. = not applicable.

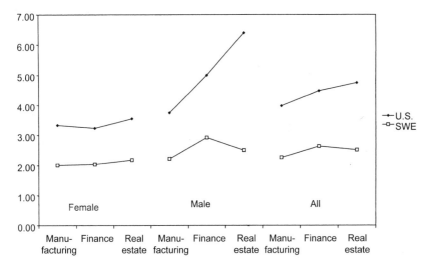

Fig. 9.14   U.S. and Sweden white-collar 90/10 ratios

Then, we needed manufacturing workers. Today, wealth is created in the postindustrial intellectual services. Now, our Statue of Liberty says to Sweden:

> *Give me your educated, your bright,*
> *Your hardworking youth yearning to breathe free,*
> *The sweet cream of your egalitarian consommé.*
> *Send these, the suppressed, becalmed to me,*
> *I lift my lamp beside the golden door!*

Appendix

Competition Measure

The algebra needed to derive the competition measure depends on the price elasticity,

$1/\gamma_j$ = price elasticity in destination/product market j.

If the demand function in destination/product market j (three exporters) is

$$p_j = \beta_j(x_{1j} + x_{2j} + x_{3j})^{-\gamma_j},$$

then the export revenue of country 1 is

$$R_1 = \sum_j x_{1j} p_j = \sum_j x_{1j} \beta_j(x_{1j} + x_{2j} + x_{3j})^{-\gamma_j}.$$

To compute the hypothetical increase in exports, note that the importance measure is the value of exports in the category divided by total exports T:

$$I_{2j} = \frac{x_{2j} p_j}{T_2}.$$

Holding prices fixed, an across-the-board expansion of exports increases T and increases each export item by a like amount:

$$\frac{dx_{2j}}{dT_2} = \frac{I_{2j}}{p_j}.$$

Given this increase in exports, the responsiveness of the revenue of country 1 to an increase in the exports of country 2 is:

$$\frac{dR_1}{dT_2} = -\sum_j x_{1j}\beta_j\gamma_j(x_{1j} + x_{2j} + x_{3j})^{-1-\gamma_j}\frac{dx_{2j}}{dT_2}$$

$$= -\sum_j R_{1j}\gamma_j(x_{1j} + x_{2j} + x_{3j})^{-1}\frac{I_{2j}}{p_j}$$

$$\frac{dR_1/R_1}{dT_2/T_2} = -\frac{\sum_j R_{1j}\gamma_j(x_{1j} + x_{2j} + x_{3j})^{-1}(I_{2j}/p_j)T_2}{\sum_j R_{1j}}$$

$$= -\frac{\sum_j R_{1j}\gamma_j(x_{1j} + x_{2j} + x_{3j})^{-1}x_{2j}}{\sum_j R_{1j}}$$

$$= -\sum_j I_{1j}\gamma_j\left(\frac{\sum_j I_{1j}\gamma_j M_{2j}}{\sum_j I_{1j}\gamma_j}\right)$$

= average elasticity of the exports of country 1 multiplied by the average market share of country 2.

Then, if all markets have the same elasticity, this becomes

$$\frac{dR_1/R_1}{dT_2/T_2} = -\gamma \sum_j I_{1j} M_{2j},$$

which finally reduces to $\sum_j I_{1j} M_{2j}$ when $\gamma = 1$.

References

Finger, J. M., and M. E. Kreinin. 1979. A measure of "export similarity" and its possible uses. *Economic Journal* 89 (356): 905–12.

Freeman, R. B., R. Topel, and B. Swedenborg, eds. 1997. *The welfare state in transition: Reforming the Swedish model.* Chicago: University of Chicago Press.

Leamer, E. E. 1999. Effort, wages and the international division of labor. *Journal of Political Economy* 107 (6): 1127–63.

Leamer, E. E., and P. Lundborg. 1997. A Heckscher-Ohlin view of Sweden competing in the global market. In *The welfare state in transition: Reforming the Swedish model,* ed. R. B. Freeman, R. Topel, and B. Swedenborg, 399–465. Chicago: University of Chicago Press.

Leamer, E. E., and C. Thornberg. 2000. Effort and wages: A new look at the inter-industry wage differentials. In *The impact of international trade on wages,* ed. R. Feenstra, 37–84. Chicago: University of Chicago Press.

Organization for Economic Cooperation and Development (OECD). 2005. *OECD economic surveys: Sweden.* Paris: OECD.

Schott, P. K. 2006. The relative sophistication of Chinese exports. NBER Working Paper no. 12173. Cambridge, MA: National Bureau of Economic Research, April.

U.S. Department of Commerce, Bureau of Economic Analysis. 2007. Available at: http://www.bea.gov/.

Contributors

Thomas Aronsson
Department of Economics
Umeå University
SE-901 87 Umeå, Sweden

Anders Björklund
Swedish Institute for Social Research
  (SOFI)
Stockholm University
SE-106 91 Stockholm, Sweden

Steven J. Davis
Booth School of Business
University of Chicago
5807 South Woodlawn Avenue
Chicago, IL 60637

Stefan Fölster
Confederation of Swedish Enterprise
  (Svenskt Näringsliv)
Storgatan 19
SE-114 82 Stockholm, Sweden

Anders Forslund
Institute for Labour Market Policy
  Evaluation (IFAU)
Department of Economics
Uppsala University
P.O. Box 513
SE-751 20 Uppsala, Sweden

Peter Fredriksson
Institute for Labour Market Policy
  Evaluation (IFAU)
Department of Economics
Uppsala University
P.O. Box 513
SE-751 20 Uppsala, Sweden

Richard B. Freeman
Department of Economics
Littauer Building
Harvard University
Cambridge, MA 02138

Magnus Henrekson
Research Institute of Industrial
  Economics
P.O. Box 55665
S-102 15 Stockholm, Sweden

Ann-Sofie Kolm
Department of Economics
Stockholm University
SE-106 91 Stockholm, Sweden

Alan Krueger
Department of Economics
Woodrow Wilson School
Princeton University
Princeton, NJ 08544

Edward P. Lazear
Graduate School of Business
Hoover Institution
Stanford University
Stanford, CA 94305

Edward E. Leamer
John E. Anderson Graduate School of
  Management
University of California, Los Angeles
P.O. Box 951481
Los Angeles, CA 90095

Lars Ljungqvist
Stockholm School of Economics
Sveavagen 65 (P.O. Box 6501)
SE-113 83 Stockholm, Sweden

Sam Peltzman
Booth School of Business
University of Chicago
5807 South Woodlawn Avenue
Chicago, IL 60637

Thomas J. Sargent
Department of Economics
New York University
19 West 4th Street, 6th Floor
New York, NY 10012

Birgitta Swedenborg
Center for Business and Policy Studies
  (SNS)
P.O. Box 5629
S-114 86 Stockholm, Sweden

Robert Topel
Graduate School of Business
University of Chicago
1101 East 58th Street
Chicago, IL 60637

James R. Walker
Department of Economics
University of Wisconsin-Madison
1180 Observatory Drive
Madison, WI 53706

Author Index

Aaberge, R., 25
Aarbu, K., 148n16
Ackum Agell, S., 174
Agell, J., 18, 138, 139, 243, 244, 244n15
Aguiar, M., 234
Ahn, N., 175n7
Albrecht, J., 72, 177, 216
Alesina, A., 138n12, 151n22, 153, 154
Alessie, R., 137n8
Alexandersson, G., 261n9
Andersson, D., 117, 117n25
Andrén, T., 63, 64
Aronsson, T., 84n3, 127, 134, 135n7, 138, 138n9, 150, 150n19
Autor, D., 99, 194, 213n13
Axelsson, R., 177

Bekken, J.-T., 256, 259
Bennmarker, H., 173
Bergdahl, P., 264
Bergemann, A., 65
Bergman, M., 260
Bergström, F., 261
Besley, T., 274n24
Björklund, A., 25, 26n2, 28, 174
Blanchard, O., 219
Blomquist, S., 134n6, 135, 138, 149, 149n17, 151
Blundell, R., 113, 113n4, 183
Boarini, R., 51
Brännlund, R., 150

Brock, W., 137, 137n8
Broda, C., 105é19
Brunello, G., 151n21
Burda, M. C., 194n7
Burdett, K., 259
Burgess, R., 274n24
Burkhauser, R., 32n8
Burtless, G., 84n3

Calmfors, L., 176n9, 178, 178n11, 180, 180n12, 180n13, 181
Campbell, J. Y., 194n5
Caner, A., 195n8
Card, D., 119n26, 182n14
Carling, K., 173, 175
Comin, D., 194n5
Crandall, R. W., 255

Dahlberg, M., 180
Damsgaard, N., 257
Datta Gupta, N., 63n2, 72
Davis, S., 138n12, 151n22, 194n5, 236, 236n8, 238, 242, 249n20
Del Boca, D., 71
Dew-Becker, I., 249, 249n20
Djerf, O., 242n13
Domeij, D., 72
Dormont, B., 175n7
Dougherty, C., 2n1
Duggan, M. G., 213n13
Durlauf, S., 137, 137n8

Edin, P.-A., 50, 72, 84n3, 85, 89, 96n10,
    96n11, 99, 119, 121, 139, 171, 180, 242
Edling, J., 209, 211, 213n13, 229
Eissa, N., 73, 73n5, 73n7
Ekberg, J., 60n1, 71
Eklöf, M., 134n6, 135
Ekman, E., 139
Ekström, E., 177
Elvander, N., 94, 242n13
Englund, P., 139, 244, 244n15
Enste, D. H., 237
Eriksson, R., 60n1, 71

Falkenhall, B., 259n7
Feldstein, M., 146, 147
Flood, L., 63, 64, 134n6, 135, 136
Fölster, S., 18, 253, 259, 261n9
Forslund, A., 7, 7n5, 160, 162, 169, 172,
    173n4, 174n6, 176, 176n9, 178, 178n11,
    179, 180, 180n12, 180n13, 181, 183, 218
Fougère, D., 175n7
Fredriksson, P., 96, 169, 171
Freeman, R. B., 3, 25, 26n2, 28, 59, 74, 114,
    233n6, 285
Friebel, G., 60n1, 71
Fröberg, D., 172, 218
Fuest, C., 150n19
Fukao, M., 241
Fullerton, D., 241

Garcia-Perez, J. I., 175n7
Garcia-Serrano, C., 175n7
Glaeser. E., 138n12, 151n22, 153, 154
Gordon, R., 152, 249, 249n20
Gottschalk, P., 194, 196, 207
Granqvist, L., 101n16
Green, R., 257
Grubb, D., 184n16
Gruber, J., 147, 148, 213n13
Gustavsson, M., 33, 49, 96n10

Hägglund, P., 175
Håkansson, C., 18, 226
Hallgren, A., 180
Ham, J., 175n7
Hanazaki, M., 241
Hansen, J., 63, 64, 134n6, 135, 136
Hansson, Å., 148
Harkman, A., 171, 174
Heckman, J. J., 195
Heiborn, M., 171

Hemström, M., 176n9, 178, 178n11, 180n13,
    181
Henrekson, M., 18, 138n12, 141, 151n22,
    226, 236, 236n8, 238, 242, 244, 249n20,
    262
Hibbs, D., 88, 99, 242
Holmes, T., 274n24
Holmlund, B., 11, 50, 94n8, 96n10, 119,
    149n18, 150, 173, 180, 182n14
Hoynes, H., 73n5, 73n7
Huber, B., 150n19
Hultén, S., 261
Hunt, J., 200n10
Hurst, E., 234

Jackman, R., 160, 180, 195, 195n9, 200n10,
    219
Jacobson, L. S., 194, 196, 207, 208
Jahoda, M., 218
Jakobsson, U., 244
Jäntti, M., 25
Jaumotte, F., 72
Jenkins, S., 175n7
Johansson, K., 180
Johansson, P., 171, 179, 180
Jonung, L., 244
Juhn, C., 102
Juster, T., 233n6

Kainelainen, A., 117, 117n25
Kambourov, G., 195
Kapteyn, A., 137n8
Katz, L., 99, 175n7, 182, 194
Kennerberg, L., 62
King, M. A., 241
Klein, P., 72
Kleven, H., 57
Kolm, A.-S., 73, 150, 180n12
Kolmodin, A., 259n7
Korpi, W., 18
Krueger, A., 119n26, 160, 162, 169, 173n4,
    174n6, 176, 178, 180
Krugman, P. R., 190

LaLonde, R. J., 194, 196, 207, 208
Lang, H., 180n12
Larsson, M., 60n1
Layard, R., 92, 160, 195, 195n9, 200n10, 219
Leamer, E. E., 285, 288, 292, 320, 321
Le Grand, C., 96n10
Leibman, J., 146

Leuven, E., 92
Levine, P. B., 182n14
Liebman, J., 73
Lindbeck, A., 3, 3n2, 5, 18, 84n2, 137, 142,
    146, 189, 192, 208, 213, 226
Lindblad, J., 60n1
Lindgren, B., 98f, 171
Lindquist, M. J., 50
Lindqvist, L., 172, 179, 218
Lindsay, T., 147
Ljunge, M., 148
Ljungqvist, L., 152, 153, 189, 191, 192,
    193, 198, 200, 201, 202n11, 205, 214,
    218n15, 219n16
Locking, H., 242
Lockwood, B., 150n20, 151n21
Lundborg, P., 99, 182n14, 242, 285, 288, 292
Lundin, D., 72
Lundvall, K., 256n4

Machin, S., 193
MaCurdy, T., 113, 113n4
Malmer, H., 244
Manning, A., 150n20, 193
Manovskii, I., 195
Manski, C., 137n8
Markowski, A., 180
Martin, J., 184n16, 200n10
McCall, J. J., 189, 191
McConnell, M. M., 194
McCormick, B., 171
McLure, C. E., 244
Mertens, A., 194n7
Meyer, B., 73, 175n7
Millard, S. P., 202n11
Moffitt, R., 175n7, 194, 196, 207
Mörk, E., 72
Mortensen, D., 143n10, 202n11
Murphy, K. M., 102
Myers, R. J., 200n10

Nahum, R.-A., 50
Nättorp, B., 171
Newey, W., 134n6, 135
Nickell, S., 92, 160, 195, 195n9, 200n10, 219
Niilola, K., 247n19
Nilsson, C., 171
Nordenmark, M., 218
Nordström Skans, O., 50, 96n10, 183
Norrman, E., 244
Nyberg, A., 63n2, 137

Nyberg, S., 142

Ockert, B., 72
Odlander, R., 256n4
Ohlsson, H., 18
Olovsson, C., 151, 151n22, 233n6
Oosterbeek, H., 92

Palda, F., 236n9
Palme, J., 18
Palme, M., 134, 146n13, 147, 153
Parisi, M., 151n21
Parrado, E., 195n8
Pasqua, S., 71
Peltzman, S., 253
Perez-Quiros, G., 194
Persson, M., 138, 141, 146, 243, 244
Philippon, T., 194
Pissarides, C., 180, 192n4
Poupore, J. G., 32n8
Prescott, E., 151, 151n22, 238n12
Prieto, A., 175n7
Pylkkänen, E., 63, 64, 70

Ragan, K., 148
Rea, S., 175n7
Regnéer, H., 101n16
Reinbrand, J., 117, 117n25
Rogerson, R., 138n12, 230n5, 231, 249n20
Romalis, J., 105n19
Ronsen, M., 71
Rosen, S., 57, 89, 245
Rosenbaum, D., 73
Rosenfeld, C., 195
Ruhm, C., 71, 194

Sacerdote, B., 138n12, 151n22, 153, 154
Sacklén, H., 136, 138, 243, 244
Saez, E., 147, 148
Sandström, M., 261
Sargent, T. J., 153, 189, 191, 192, 193, 198,
    200, 201, 214
Savouri, S., 180
Schettkat, R., 59, 74, 114, 233n6
Schmieding, H., 2n1
Schott, P. K., 299
Sclhneider, F., 237n10
Sehlin, H., 149, 149n17, 151
Selén, J., 149
Shavell, S., 219n16
Shaw, K., 195n9

Shelling, T., 142
Shorrocks, A., 33n10
Sianesi, B., 175
Sillamaa, M.-A., 148
Simonsen, M., 72
Sinfield, A., 214
Sjögren, T., 138n9, 150n19
Skedinger, P., 118f, 119, 171
Skogman Thoursie, P., 18
Slemrod, J., 136
Slök, T., 151n21
Smeeding, T., 35n11
Smith, N., 63n2, 70, 72
Södersten, J., 139, 244, 244n15
Söderström, M., 11, 101n16, 149n18
Solon, G., 25
Sonedda, D., 151n21
Sorensen, P. B., 57
Stafford, F. P., 233n6
Stenberg, A., 177
Stenlund, M., 262
Stock, J. H., 194
Storrie, D., 171
Strand, J., 236n9
Strandh, M., 218
Strauss, H., 51
Sullivan, D. G., 194, 196, 207, 208
Sundström, M., 71
Svallfors, S., 41
Svensson, I., 146n13, 147, 153
Swedenborg, B., 3, 285
Szulkin, R., 96n10

Tählin, M., 96n10
Thoresen, T., 148
Thornberg, C., 321
Topel, R., 3, 84n3, 85, 89, 92, 99, 102, 121,
    194, 242, 285
Tranaes, T., 151n21

Valtakari, M., 247n19
Vand, 216
Van den Berg, G. J., 65, 177
Van Ophe, H., 92
Veall, M., 148
Veiderpass, A., 259n7
Vejsiu, A., 173
Verner, M., 63n2, 72
Vroman, S., 72, 177, 216

Wadensjö, E., 180
Wahlberg, R., 63, 64, 134n6, 135, 136
Walker, J., 84n3, 127, 134, 135n7, 143n11
Wasmer, E., 88, 109
Watson, M. W., 194
Weibull, J., 137, 142
Weiss, L., 219n16
Westerlund, L., 60n1, 171
Westerlund, O., 177
Widerstedt, B., 171
Wikström, M., 150
Winston, C., 255
Wise, D. A., 213n13
Woittiez, I., 137n8
Wolff, E. N., 195n8

Subject Index

The letters f *and* t *following page numbers denote figures and tables, respectively.*

Active labor market policy (ALMP), 11–12, 17, 85–86; international cross-country evidence on, 180–81; introduction, 159–62; recent changes in Swedish, 181–83; since early 1990s in Sweden, 171–73; survey results of Swedish, 175–80; unemployment insurance and, 173–75
Anticompetitive regulations, 14
Attitudes, toward economic inequality, 39–45
Aviation, deregulation of, 257–58

Black market activity, 14, 237, 238
Business income, taxation on, 244–45
Business tax policy, 239–41

Centralized bargaining, 84, 85, 88–89, 94. *See also* Industrial agreement (IA)
Child care subsidies, 66; model of female work behavior and, 68–70; patterns of, and model of female work behavior, 72
China, 15–16; competition for Swedish exports to United States, 300–303t; rise of, as manufacturing powerhouse, 286; U.S. market and, 297–308
Competition, in Sweden, 289–308
Competition policies, 14, 255; in retail trade, 255–56

Confederation of Swedish Enterprise (SN) survey, 263–68

Daddy months, 78–79
Defined benefit pension systems, 11
Deregulation: assessment of overall effects of, 259–61; of aviation, 257–58; of electricity market, 256–57; of postal services, 258; of railways, 258; of taxi companies, 259; of telecommunications, 259

Earned income tax credit (EITC), 73, 245–47
Earnings: changes in distribution of, 27–2832; Swedish households at bottom of distribution of, 31–32
Economic incentives, women's labor force participation and, 135–36
Economic inequality. *See* Inequality, economic
Education, returns to, 99–102, 106–9; Sweden vs. United States, 107f
Electricity market, deregulation of, 256–57
Employment: of immigrants, by industry size, Sweden vs. United States, 115–17; in ISIC industries, 304–7, 307t; minimum wages and, 117–20; Swedish, in working-age population, 229; tax burdens and, 237–39

Employment differentials, 102; by skill groups, 105
Employment subsidies, effectiveness of, 179–80
Equality, 19; gender, 8–9; income, 7–8. *See also* Inequality
Exports, Swedish, 289; correlations to United States and EU, 293–94; U.S. market and, 297–308

Factor price equalization theorem, 289–90
Farm workers, decline in, 313, 316f
Female labor participation, 114; economic incentives and, 135–36; Sweden vs. United States, 58–59, 59t. *See also* Women; Women with children
Female work behavior, model of, 67–70, 76–79
Finger-Kreinen export similarity index, 294, 296, 297f
Free rider problem, 18

Gender. *See* Women
Global economy, 15

Heckscher-Ohlin (HO) model of international trade, 290–92
Hours worked, 229–32
Household substitutes, tax relief for, 67; model of female work behavior and, 69–70; patterns of, and model of female work behavior, 74
Household work, 14

Immigrants: employment of, by industry, Sweden vs. U.S., 115t, 117; skill content of Swedish, 109–14; test scores of, Sweden vs. United States, 111, 113t; wage distributions of, Sweden vs. United States, 109–11, 110f, 112f
Incentives, work, single women with children and, 63–64
Income-elastic services, government production of, 245
Income equalization, 7–8
Incomes. *See* Earnings
Industrial agreement (IA), 94–96, 242
Industrial structure, 13–14
Inequality, economic, 25–26; attitudes toward, 39–45; international perspective of, 33–39; long-run vs. transitory,

32–33; Sweden's position in competitiveness and, 48–50; in United States, 320, 321F
Inequality, wage, 98–99
Institutional developments (1990–2005), 241–45
Intellectual services sector, compensation for, 287–88
International migration, skill content of, 109–14
Internet, 287
In-work benefits, 66–67; model of female work behavior and, 69; patterns of, and model of female work behavior, 72–74

Knowledge economy, Sweden and, 50–53
Kolmogorov-Smirnov (KS) distance, 296

Labor force participation: of women with children, parental leave and, 64–67; women with children and, 59–61
Labor market, Swedish, features of, 83–87; in 1970s and early 1980s, 87–89
Labor supply: incentives and, 127–29; parental benefits and, 141–44; pensions and, 146–47; quantitative constraints and, 136; responsiveness of, taxation and transfer systems, 134–35; sickness insurance and, 140–41; social norms and, 137–38, 141–43; studies of, 11; tax avoidance and, 138–40; taxes on wages and, 150–51; trends in, 129–31
Labor unions, 83–84
Local economy, political economy and, 268–74
Local government monopolies, 261–62
Local government policies: private sector and, 263–83; 2001 to 2004 panel, 263–68
Local governments, 14–15
Local public policies, long-term growth and, 274–83
Longitudinal Individual Data (LINDA) panel survey, 96
Long-term growth, local public policies and, 274–83

Manufacturing: employment in, for OECD countries, 313, 314t, 315t; employment in, Sweden and, 315f; Swedish value added in, 316f

Marginal tax rates, 149–50
McCall search model, 189; for Sweden, 191–93
Minimum wages: by country, 118t; employment and, 117–20; type of industry and, 117–19, 118t. *See also* Wages
Monopolies. *See* Local government monopolies; Natural monopolies, deregulation of
Municipalities, 14

National Bureau of Economic Research, study of Swedish economy by, 3–7
Natural monopolies, deregulation of: aviation, 257–58; electricity, 256–57; postal services, 258; railways, 258; telecommunications, 259
Neurofacturing, 309
Notional defined contribution pension systems, 11

OECD countries, transition from industrial to postindustrial economy and, 310–13, 312f
Output growth, Swedish, 226, 228t

Parental benefits, labor supply and, 141–44
Parental leave, paid, 60; labor force participation of women with children and, 64–67; model of female work behavior and, 68; patterns of, and model of female work behavior, 70–72
Pension reform, 11, 144–45
Pensions, labor supply and, 146–47
Pension system, Swedish, 144–45
Personal computer (PC), 287
Personal outcomes, satisfaction with, 45–48
Political economy, local economy and, 268–74
Population characteristics, changes in, since early 1990s, 92–94
Postal services, deregulation of, 258
Postindustrial economy, transition to, 286–89; advanced developed countries and, 310–13, 312f; difficulty of, 309–10; model, 313–17; United States, 310, 311f
Poverty, 25–26
Price levels, 254–55
Product differences, role of, 290
Productivity growth, 254

Product mixes, 15–16; determining, 292; empirical measurement of, 292–93
Public-sector policy, 14

Quantitative constraints, labor supply and, 136

Railways, deregulation of, 258
Recession of 1991–1994, 26–27
Reforms, effects of recent, 245–48
Retail trade, competition in, 255–56

Schooling, returns to. *See* Education, returns to
Sickness absence, 11, 27
Sickness insurance, labor supply and, 140–41
Skill groups: employment by, 105; wages by, 102–5
SN. *See* Confederation of Swedish Enterprise (SN) survey
Social norms, labor supply and, 137–38, 141–43
Social Security tax rates, 247
Standard International Trade Classification (SITC), 298–304
Sweden: changes in distribution of earnings in, in 1990s, 27–28, 28f; changes in hours worked in, in 1990s, 28–29, 29t; competition in, 289–308; cumulative changes in employment and population of, 227, 229f; earnings in, 322, 323f; economic statistics for, 1–2; inequality in monthly earnings and hours worked in, 29–32, 30–31f; National Bureau of Economic Research study of, 3–7; political system of, 263; recession of 1991–1994 in, 26–27, 89–91; U.S. market and, 297–308, 298f
Swedish economic model, 1–2, 83–84
Swedish labor market: regional adjustments in, 169–71; since early 1990s, 162–69

Tax base determination, literature on, 147–49
Tax burdens, consumption and, 235–37
Tax factors, for types of Swedish workers, 242–44, 243f
Taxi companies, deregulation of, 259
Tax policies, 13–14, 18; business income and, 244–45; labor supply and, 134–35

Telecommunications, deregulation of, 259
Tenure rights, 248
Time-use surveys, 14, 232–34
Transfer systems, labor supply and, 134–35, 141–43

Underground economy, 14. *See also* Black market activity
Unemployment, European: basic search model for analyzing, 196–201; results search model, 201–8; salient facts about, 193–96
Unemployment, Swedish, 12–13, 229; analysis of, in mid-1990s, 191–93; introduction, 189–91; need for reforms and, 219–20; outcomes viewed through study's search model, 213–14; proposals for reducing, viewed through study's search model, 216–19; recent outcomes, 208–11; two views on, 211–13
Unemployment insurance, active labor market policy and, 173–75
Unions, work hours and, 153–54
United States, 41n15; attitudes toward economic inequality in, 39–45; hourly and weekly earnings in 1999 to 2000 by percentiles by gender and skills, 317–20, 317t; manufacturing and finance, insurance, and real estate (FIRE) fraction of national income, 317, 318f; shares of earnings in, 317, 318t; transition from industrial to postindustrial economy,

310, 311f; weekly earnings in, 320, 321f; workforce of, 99
United States market: China and, 297–308; competitors in, 298f; Sweden and, 297–308

Wage agreements, 94–97
Wage compression, 9–10, 85
Wage determination, introduction, 83–87
Wage differentials, changes in, 96–102
Wage policies, 105; less-skilled workers and, 114–20
Wages, by skill group, 102–5, 104f. *See also* Minimum wages
Welfare state, continuous transition of, 16–17
Women: labor supply of, 58–61; taxes and incentive to work for, 57–58; working time of, 61–63. *See also* Female labor participation
Women with children: labor supply of, 58–61; policies that affect participation of, 64–67; single, work incentives for, 63–64. *See also* Female labor participation
Work activity, effects of recent reforms and, 245–48
Working hours, 131–40; changes in distribution of, 28–29, 29t; cross-country comparison of, 151–53; market structure and, 153; unions and, 153–54; of women, economic incentives and, 135–36; women vs. men, 61–63